PSYCHOTHERAPY
AND AIDS

D0222273

PSYCHOTHERAPY
AND AIDS
The Human Dimension

Edited by

Lucy A. Wicks
Presbyterian Hospital
Columbia-Presbyterian Medical Center
New York, New York

Taylor & Francis
Publishers since 1798

USA	Publishing Office:	Taylor & Francis 1101 Vermont Avenue, NW, Suite 200 Washington, DC 20005-3521 Tel: (202) 289-2174 Fax: (202) 289-3665
	Distribution Center:	Taylor & Francis 1900 Frost Road, Suite 101 Bristol, PA 19007-1598 Tel: (215) 785-5800 Fax: (215) 785-5515
UK		Taylor & Francis Ltd. 1 Gunpowder Square London EC4A 3DE Tel: 171 583 0490 Fax: 171 583 0581

PSYCHOTHERAPY AND AIDS: The Human Dimension

Copyright © 1997 Taylor & Francis. All rights reserved. Printed in the United States of America. Except as permitted under the United States Copyright Act of 1976, no part of this publication may be reproduced or distributed in any form or by any means, or stored in a database or retrieval system, without prior written permission of the publisher.

1 2 3 4 5 6 7 8 9 0   E B E B   9 8 7

This book was set in Times Roman. The editors were Kathleen Baker, Catherine Simon, and Laura Haefner. Cover design by Michelle Fleitz.

A CIP catalog record for this book is available from the British Library.

∞ The paper in this publication meets the requirements of the ANSI Standard Z39.48-1984 (Permanence of Paper)

Library of Congress Cataloging-in-Publication Data

Psychotherapy and AIDS: the human dimension/edited by Lucy A.
  Wicks.
      p.   cm.
  Includes bibliographical references.

      1. AIDS (Disease)—Patients—Mental health.   2. Psychotherapy.
  I. Wicks, Lucy A.
  RC607.A26P797   1997
  616.97'9206—DC21
                                                                    97-1721
                                                                    CIP

ISBN 1-56032-617-4 (case)
ISBN 1-56032-618-2 (paper)

Contents

PART THREE: SPECIALIZED POPULATIONS
AND TREATMENT ISSUES

Contributors

Carlos Almeida, MD, is the Assistant Director of Psychiatric Emergency Services, Columbia University College of Physicians and Surgeons, as well as Clinical Supervisor at Columbia-Presbyterian Medical Center in New York. Additionally, while maintaining a private practice in New York, Dr. Almeida is a practicing psychiatrist at the HIV Mental Health Clinic at Columbia-Presbyterian Hospital.

Ivan C. Balan, PhD, is on staff at the HIV/AIDS Mental Health Clinic at Columbia-Presbyterian Medical Center in New York. He is also a research scientist at the HIV Center for Clinical and Behavioral Studies at the New York State Psychiatric Institute where his current work relates to the impact of ethnocultural variables on psychotherapy, HIV risk behavior, and adaptation to HIV/AIDS. Dr. Balan received his Master's in Psychology and Doctorate in Clinical Psychology from the California School of Professional Psychology in Fresno.

John Budin, MD, is director of Psychiatry for the HIV/AIDS Center Programs at St. Luke's/Roosevelt Hospital Center. Dr. Budin maintains an active private practice in New York City, is an associate attending in the Department of Psychiatry at the Hospital Center, and is an instructor of Clinical Psychiatry at the Columbia University College of Physicians and Surgeons. He received his Doctorate of Medicine from Tel Aviv University, Israel.

Linda Jaffe Caplan, PhD, is a clinical psychologist in private practice in New York City. She is currently completing her postdoctoral training in psychotherapy and psychoanalysis at the New York University Postdoctoral Program.

Maria R. Derevenco, PsyD, has been Supervising Psychologist for the HIV/AIDS Center Programs at the St. Luke's/Roosevelt Hospital Center since 1988. These programs provide comprehensive medical and psychiatric/psychological services to adults and to children and their families on an in-patient and out-patient basis. Dr. Derevenco is Assistant Clinical Professor of Medical Psychology (in Psychiatry) at the College of Physicians and Surgeons at Columbia University and Assistant Clinical Professor of Psychology at New York University, from which she received her doctorate. For the past five years she has directed a postdoctoral fellowship training program in Medical Psychology/AIDS at the St. Luke's/Roosevelt Hospital Center. She serves as a consultant to the Family Studies Project at the HIV Center for Clinical and Behavioral Studies at Columbia University and to the New York State Psychiatric Institute. Dr. Derevenco also maintains a private practice of psychoanalytic psychotherapy and neuro-psychological diagnosis in New York. She has written and presented papers on HIV/AIDS psychological/psychosocial, and neuropsycho-pharmacological topics.

George V. Gushue, PhD, is a member of the clinical staffs of the HIV/AIDS Mental Health Clinic and the Tavare Clinic of New York's Columbia-Presbyterian Medical Center. He is an adjunct assistant professor in the Department of Counseling and Clinical Psychology at Teachers College, Columbia University and is the co-director of an AIDS therapy group at Gay Men's Health Crisis, New York. Dr. Gushue's current research examines the influence of racial identity attitudes on social cognition. He has previously published on the impact of racial-cultural identity on family treatment, gender identity, and career values. Dr. Gushue received his PhD from Teachers College, Columbia University.

Clayton Guthrie, PsyM, is a clinician at the HIV/AIDS Mental Health Clinic at Columbia-Presbyterian Medical Center in New York and is the co-director of an AIDS therapy group at Gay Men's Health Crisis, New York. He received his Master's in Psychology from and is currently completing his PsyD at the Graduate School of Applied and Professional Psychology at Rutgers University.

Jennifer F. Havens, MD, is Assistant Professor of Clinical Psychiatry at the College of Physicians and Surgeons at Columbia University in New York. In 1991, Dr. Havens and her colleagues founded the Special Needs Clinic, one of the first comprehensive mental health programs serving children and families affected by the linked epidemics of HIV and substance abuse. She completed her residency in Adult Psychiatry at the Payne Whitney Clinic at New York Hospital/Cornell Medical Center, her fellowship in Child and Adolescent Psychiatry at Columbia-Presbyterian Medical Center, and a NIMH-funded research fellowship at the HIV Center for Clinical and Behavioral Studies at New York State Psychiatric Center.

Claude Ann Mellins, PhD, is a clinical and research psychologist at the HIV Center for Clinical and Behavioral Studies at the New York State Psychiatric Institute and Columbia University. She is also the co-founder and co-director of the Special Needs Clinic at Columbia-Presbyterian Medical Center, a mental health clinic for children and families affected by HIV disease and substance abuse, and the neurodevelopment supervisor at the Women and Children's Care Center at Presbyterian Hospital. She received her PhD from the University of Southern California and did her post-doctoral research training at the HIV Center. She also received an Aaron Diamond Foundation Fellowship and grant to study the impact of HIV disease on HIV-infected women and children. Since she joined the HIV Center in 1990, Dr. Mellins' research has focused on the psychosocial impact of HIV disease on women, children, and families, and on related psychotherapeutic interventions.

Robert H. Remien, PhD, is a clinical psychologist specializing in direct service to adults and couples living with HIV/AIDS. He chairs the New York State Psychological Association's Task Force on AIDS and works as an American Psychological Association Senior Faculty Trainer for psychologists working with AIDS. Dr. Remien is a research scientist at the HIV Center for Clinical and Behavioral Studies at the New York State Psychiatric Institute and an assistant professor of Clinical Psychology at the Columbia University College of Physicians and Surgeons. He coordinates volunteer activities at Body Positive and Gay Men's Health Crisis. His research and writings have focused on mental health and coping with HIV/AIDS, long-term survival, and challenges faced by couples of mixed HIV status. Dr. Remien received his PhD in Clinical Psychology from the Graduate Faculty of the New School for Social Research, New York.

Laura Epstein Rosen, PhD, is a clinical psychologist who received her doctoral degree from New York University. She is a supervising psychologist at the Special Needs Clinic at Columbia-Presbyterian Medical Center where she specializes in family therapy work with HIV-affected women and children. She has a private practice in New York City in which she works primarily with families and couples struggling with depression and chronic illness. Dr. Rosen is the author of the recently published book, *When Someone You Love Is Depressed*, a self-help book for the families and friends who are coping with a depressed loved one.

Sheila Ryan, MSW, is on staff at the Special Needs Clinic at Columbia-Presbyterian Medical Center where she specializes in pediatric and family AIDS work.

Johns Sahs, MD, is the Medical Director of Columbia-Presbyterian Medical Center's HIV/AIDS Mental Health Clinic, New York. He also directs the center's Adult Psychiatry Clinic, is the coordinator of Third Year Clinical Education of the Psychiatric Residency at New York State Psychiatric Institute, Columbia University, and is Assistant Professor of Clinical Psychiatry at the Columbia

University College of Physicians and Surgeons. Dr. Sahs has written, lectured, and conducted research on the mental health aspects of HIV and AIDS. He received his Doctorate of Medicine from Rush Medical College, Illinois.

Joan E. Storey, CSW, PhD, maintains a private practice and is a clinical social worker affiliated with Columbia-Presbyterian Medical Center's HIV/AIDS Mental Health Clinic, New York. Dr. Storey conducts research on psychotherapy with HIV/AIDS patients and leads staff support groups for health care professionals working with HIV/AIDS patients. She is a faculty member at Columbia University Psychiatry, Post-Graduate Medical Education. Dr. Storey received her Master of Social Work from and is currently completing her PhD at New York University's School of Social Work.

Foreword

While enemy bombs fell on London, Melanie Klein kept interpreting the dreams and free associations of the children brought to her for psychotherapy. Similarly, while AIDS ravages the bodies, lives, and social networks of their clients, committed psychotherapists and pharmacotherapists continue their methodic work in helping patients achieve more satisfying and fulfilling lives.

This book presents the diverse experiences of mental health practitioners working within the spectrum of HIV disease. Different treatment modalities and their appropriateness for various populations are discussed. The voices of men, women, children, couples, and families are heard through their therapists, speaking about distress and pain, but also about hope and wisdom.

Reading this book, one senses the profound impact that the HIV epidemic has had on the discourse of psychology and psychiatry. Old paradigms needed reformulation, traditional provider roles had to mutate and widen, and miracles had to be given space in the clinical consultation.

The field continues to change. New dilemmas appear. The 1996 International AIDS Conference substantially transformed our view of the disease. New drugs seem to offer hope that HIV may be not a terminal disease but a chronic one. A few scientists have dared to think of the possibility of a cure. This momentous change is translating into both hope and anxiety for parents—hope of living full-term lives, seeing children grow, and completing natural cycles and anxiety about career, old age, love, and retirement issues that had been made relative by the prospect of death and that now reemerge with poignant intensity. Yet, whether the medication will work in the long run is not known, and this ambiguity is more distressing to some patients than was their previous grim prognosis. The perils of inconsistent adherence to drug treatments and consequent resistance development are now being discussed in psychotherapy, as well as the ethical implications of transmitting resistant virus to another person. Psychotherapy of HIV-infected and -affected individuals is progressively becoming a specialty of its own.

The therapist's work transcends the microcosms of patients' needs. By documenting their observations and compiling their collective wisdom, mental health providers are underscoring the political ramifications of the disease. Psychological and psychiatric care are, like medical care in general, inalienable rights of the people. Yet our capitalistic society disregards this fact, leaving many individuals without minimal coverage and treating most people differentially when it comes to mental health needs. As providers, we are painfully aware of this situation. We cannot but voice our discontent and demand more responsible social policies from our government.

Alex Carballo-Dieguez, PhD

Preface

AIDS and its associated medical treatments can be an overwhelming experience. Although the majority of all patients diagnosed HIV positive develop ways to cope with their disease, it is never easy. Fear, anger, shame, and guilt are common emotional responses. People with chronic or terminal illnesses often have difficulty understanding their medical situation and do not know what they need to do to best care for themselves. The added stress of stigma experienced by AIDS patients can lead to even greater difficulties. Within couples, HIV status can create extreme stress. When one member is diagnosed as HIV positive, the other must deal with his or her own status while helping the partner adjust to the diagnosis. Often questions of who infected whom and what one did to become infected become divisive and enraging issues. If several members of a family are seropositive, then they must cope with feelings about infection and fears about illness in each other.

Medical practitioners and family members often urge people to seek mental health services to address their fears and get support. People come to treatment with many aims: to get help in coping with an HIV-positive diagnosis, to understand the disease, to resolve conflicts within themselves or their families, and to reduce their loneliness. Often they feel they simply need a place to talk. HIV-infected patients are also referred to psychotherapy for long-standing psychological and psychosocial issues that get in the way of their getting good medical treatment.

Some say that when one works psychologically with this population, HIV is merely another stressor and must be addressed accordingly. This is only partly true. Specific concerns relating to the virus—to the progression of the disease, to the medical care of chronically and severely ill people, as well as the fact of the stigma attached to these groups—must be considered within the treatment. Clinicians themselves are faced with heightened levels of stress and anxiety in their work. Patients with HIV disease are typically confronted with multiple medical and psychosocial stresses that will influence the psychotherapeutic relationship.

All psychological treatments seek to support changes in patients' lives; indeed, change is the aim of most therapy. Normally, therapy patients get better and move on with their lives. They get better jobs or better relationships or have more satisfying experiences. This is rewarding to both patient and clinician. The time line is often different in dealing with medically ill patients. In the treatment of HIV-affected patients, change is something that is sometimes feared. Patients worry about changes in their immune system and deterioration in their health. This can become confused with fears about psychological changes. As patients struggle to maintain their current level of physical functioning, they come to fear taking risks or trying out new ways of being. Often psychological improvement is lost as the patient's health deteriorates. Often patients who have been working to achieve greater psychological autonomy become more dependent physically. Although the psychological gains are not lost, the medical issues cloud psychological progress. Clinicians must find other ways to find satisfaction in their work that take into account these losses.

Although not necessarily the focus of treatment at all times, the patient's medical diagnosis is omnipresent in the treatment. It colors the experience of both the patient and the clinician in their work and progress. For example, a patient in the clinic recently reported a dream of being pregnant and being overjoyed at the prospect of the new birth, but she was also saddened by the fact that the child would be born HIV positive. After initial discussion about the patient's wish to bear children, we explored her sadness about how AIDS had affected every part of her life, especially her expectations about the future. She was aware of how she had changed greatly in therapy. In her words, she had been reborn. Nonetheless, she is still HIV positive. As the therapeutic process unfolds, therapists must also work with their own frustrations and anxieties induced by the patient's health status.

The psychosocial effects of the HIV disease cannot be understood without some knowledge of the disease itself and an understanding of medical and societal reactions to the disease. As a psychotherapist, one can only work with these issues through the process of working to understand the meaning each patient attributes to illness and treatment. This work is a dynamic process rooted in developing an understanding of the patient's character as well as understanding his or her personal and cultural history. Experience shows that when patients are helped to resolve conflicts and develop coping strategies, they can more effectively address the multiple social pressures they face. This requires specialized awareness of the needs of these patients struggling to cope with AIDS, both due to the progressive nature of their medical disease and due to the specialized needs of many of the subpopulations infected by AIDS.

Mental health practitioners must be prepared to address these many needs. Psychiatric services must be developed to meet the complex psychosocial and psychiatric needs of families and support networks of people struggling with AIDS. Clinicians must understand their own reactions to the multiple problems presented by this very social disease. It is important that therapists learn to work

with the many challenges these patients face psychologically. Too often, therapists and their patients blame HIV for every conflict in their lives. Clinicians
must deal with difficulties associated with future planning, employment concerns, decisions about pregnancy and child rearing, feelings of guilt and anger,
fantasies of fleeing, fear of abandonment, and fear of intimacy in the context of
potential loss. These issues must be understood as multiply determined, considering the patients' HIV illness and their personalities, as well as the conflicts
and concerns that preceded their diagnosis. How people cope with the disease is
a function of long-standing character styles.

The changes in patients' physical capabilities are evocative for therapists,
raising concerns about their own health and future, as well as issues of control,
frustration, and wishes to rescue within the treatment. Therapists must adjust
their expectations to the fluctuating needs of the patients—one week they might
be too ill to attend, the next week they might feel strong and vigorous and then
again become weak. It is of the greatest importance that clinicians explore and
understand their reactions to these issues to prevent their countertransference
from interfering with treatment. There must be a continuous process in which
therapists seek to understand the meaning of events in patients' lives, evaluating
the source of patients' behavior while simultaneously being aware of their own
countertransference.

In this book, we present information and clinical material to support psychologically informed treatment. The chapters in Part One of the book introduce
material pertinent to working with HIV-infected adults; those in Part Two define and explore issues in families and couples; and those in Part Three present
material relating to special needs groups. It is our belief that services must be
developed to meet patients' psychological needs, permitting them to move into
greater self-awareness and personal capability. Clinicians need to establish networks of professional supports—supervisors as well as specialists—to permit
them to develop and maintain good working alliances with their patients. Each
chapter proposes techniques and methods to address different concerns commonly encountered with this population in an attempt to broaden the discussion
of HIV and psychotherapy.

The HIV Mental Health Clinic at the Columbia-Presbyterian Medical Center is an outpatient program that provides specialized psychiatric evaluation and
intervention for people affected with HIV, their families, care partners, and
health care professionals. It began serving the public in September 1988. The
experience gained in the clinic has led to the development of a multidisciplinary
treatment model that integrates a continuum of services and therapeutic expectations. The clinic's experience highlights the advantages of a full-service specialized mental health center for these patients by both using case material and
outlining common themes in treatment. Material presented will be useful not
only to those working in medical centers but to clinicians working in private
practices or small group settings, as it provides needed information about specific treatment concerns. We hope to give clinicians clinical and diagnostic tools

to do this work. We also hope it will support clinicians in seeking expert advise on issues beyond their scope.

Each chapter presents a program, treatment issue, or treatment approach developed to address AIDS patients' psychological needs. It is our premise that AIDS patients' psychological needs can and must be directly addressed. The therapist's awareness that these patients require both psychoeducational supports and psychodynamic understanding is of the greatest importance in the treatment of individuals affected by HIV. Woven through the chapters are reminders of the need for clinicians to maintain their commitment to work with these patients psychologically by developing greater self-awareness and self-understanding. The creation of this book is, in fact, a direct consequence of this process. We have found that when each of us is involved in a range of projects, professional endeavors, and personally satisfying relationships, we are less likely to become lost in our patients' lives. For myself, both writing and talking with colleagues within an intellectual context supports my ability to maintain my professional identity and demeanor. The process of writing requires, in a way similar to supervision, that I step back and review what works best, what my goals are, and what I believe is essential in this work. It requires that I find a larger perspective rather than being lost in each patient's story. Each clinician needs support in understanding what best facilitates his or her own ability to care for him- or herself. As we each developed these chapters, we thought about our cases in new ways, deepening our awareness of each of our patients, understanding them within a wider context. Each of us experienced, along with the pain of writing, a sense of renewal in our work.

Lucy A. Wicks

Part One

Introducing the Issues: HIV Treatment Specialization

The diagnosis and treatment of psychiatric disorders require one to know and understand what is normal and expected in a given situation and to consider the etiology of symptoms and experience. Traditionally, symptoms with biological causes have been treated medically, whereas psychologically based symptoms have been treated within the psychiatric realm. A more comprehensive approach is to work within a bio-psychosocial model, considering the continual interaction among a patient's medical, psychological, and social experiences. Diagnosis and treatment require that clinicians tease apart which aspect of a patient's manifest mood disorder or cognitive impairment is a function of medical illness, psychological reaction, or cultural expression. Is a patient who presents with vegetative signs of depression truly depressed? Is his or her evident lack of motivation a result of central nervous system impairment, or experiences of loss? Is his or her sleep disorder related to mood, or a reaction to medicine or physical discomfort? Is he or she irritable because of a disruption in mood, or in reaction to pain and physical discomfort? Is he or she socially isolated because of fatigue, or fear of being discovered by a hostile community?

The authors of this section present general issues that will be useful in the diagnosis and treatment of HIV-infected patients. The intention of each chapter is to help inform readers about common AIDS-related symptoms and reactions in order to help them develop appropriate treatment plans. The material will be useful to both medical practitioners and general psychological clinicians as they work to optimize their treatment of patients with AIDS.

Chapter 1

HIV and Psychotherapy in an Urban Medical Center: An Introduction

Lucy A. Wicks

A MODEL FOR OUTPATIENT CARE: THE HIV MENTAL HEALTH CLINIC

The HIV Mental Health Clinic at the Columbia-Presbyterian Medical Center is a specialty outpatient psychiatry clinic established in 1988 to meet the needs of patients at all stages of HIV infection as well as those of their families, care partners, health care workers, and worried well persons. The clinic was designed to provide psychological support to patients in need of mental health intervention. From the outset, it has been clear that clinic staff need to be sensitive to a group of patients who have a wide range of psychological, medical, and social concerns. To do their work well, the staff must attend to their own needs as well as those of the patients. Without clear supervisory and personal supports, it is easy to get lost in this work; patients tell many very sad stories, some of which are personally evocative, and clinicians often need support. This chapter outlines the clinical and therapeutic issues found to be common concerns when working with HIV-infected patients. It also addresses some of the ways the clinical staff manages these issues.

The majority of all people diagnosed with HIV disease are able to adjust to the diagnosis and cope with treatment (Perry et al., 1993). Nonetheless, the psychological toll of chronic and terminal illness can be extreme for both patients and their caregivers. Predictably, confusion, misinformation, uncertainty about the future, fear of suffering, social stigma, concern for loved ones, and loss of capabilities lead to psychological distress, which can in turn lead to

3

deeper psychological dysfunction and social isolation (Cournos et al., 1991; Crandall & Coleman, 1992; Herek, 1990; O'Dowd, Natali, Orr, & McKegney, 1991; Taylor, 1986; Taylor & Aspinwall, 1990). As with any stressor, patients' response to their illness is a function of long-standing character and personality traits (Horowitz, 1986).

Clinical experience, along with a large body of research, has indicated that psychological treatment improves compliance with medical care, enhances quality of life, and improves measurable medical outcomes (Coates et al., 1987; Taylor, 1986; Winiarski, 1991). Though patients' medical reality may not be changed, their experience of that reality can be profoundly effected by increasing their understanding and reducing their isolation. As Kalichman (1995) noted, the perception of control develops from a sense of mastery that one can have over illness. Patients' health status can improve with an increased understanding of their situation. An improved sense of mastery can lead to increased compliance and a reduction in self-destructive behaviors. Within the context of psychotherapy, patients come to understand their experiences and develop more effective coping skills. Although they cannot undo their infection, they can come to understand, in a personally meaningful way, how to live with the illness. They can learn to identify what can change and what cannot, thus gaining a sense of agency in managing their illness and their perceptions of it.

An important facet of treatment is the therapist's ability to be neutral about the issues patients bring to treatment. The multiple pressures on these patients are extreme: medical questions, family dysfunction, socioeconomic distress, and substance abuse, to name a few. Not uncommonly, patients present a therapist with a long list of questions, social service needs, and requests for support. In most settings, health care workers have obligations to "do for" the patient; medical doctors prescribe and advocate for certain treatments, social service agencies produce entitlements and services, and community-based organizations provide advocacy and activism. As members of a psychiatry clinic that focuses on HIV care, the staff of the HIV Mental Health Clinic maintain a clear and consistent emphasis on being present for patients, supporting their understanding and resolution. Because therapy care is separate from patients' medical care or social service providers, patients feel free to talk about any aspect of their experience without concern for repercussions. Not uncommonly, patients are fearful of expressing their frustrations and emotional concerns to their medical doctors and can have difficulty questioning or disagreeing with their doctors for fear of alienating them. This can lead to complications and miscommunication between doctor and patients. By not taking a particular position concerning patients' medical care, their choices, or their social service needs, clinicians can effectively encourage patients to examine the psychological impact of both their illness and their medical care. Therapists' work is to facilitate patients' understanding as well as their ability to make effective choices. Comprehensive mental health care is provided at one site with one multidisciplinary clinical team that offers individual, group, family, and psychopharmacologic treatments.

Permanent staff provide continuity both over the course of the illness and through the multiple attempts of some patients to seek psychological treatment. Therapists maintain patients' psychological needs as central, permitting them to resolve conflicts and develop coping skills. Therapists work to facilitate and support the resolution of patients' psychological concerns, without assuming any concrete casework responsibility.

A component of the clinical treatment ethos is the importance of working within a multicultural framework (Davis, 1986). When the clinic opened in 1988, the client population was predominantly gay men and IV-drug–injecting men. As the epidemic has moved into the wider community, clinic demographics have evolved. Located in Washington Heights in Upper Manhattan, the clinic serves a diverse population: 40% African American, 38% Hispanic, and 22% White. Of the clinic's patients, 95% are HIV infected; men comprise slightly more than half of the patients (56%). Patients with all risk factors are equally represented (one third use injecting drugs, one third have had homosexual contact, and one third have had heterosexual contact). Approximately one half of all patients have dual diagnoses: a psychiatric diagnosis and a substance use diagnosis. Approximately one fourth of the women and one half of the men have symptomatic HIV illness or AIDS. The majority of uninfected patients are family members or care partners treated individually, within couples, or in family treatment.

Although each individual reacts to the illness as a function of his or her individual style, group membership has profound effects on the experience of being HIV positive. For instance, large support networks now exist for gay men in most urban areas. Extensive educational outreach and counseling exists in the gay community. Generally, men have awareness of the risk of unprotected sex, although they might discount it. If infected, gay men are aware of groups established to help them cope. Unlike gay men, women infected by their husbands often neither were aware of the risk of infection nor have found resources easily available in their community. They experience being infected as a betrayal and feel victimized. Often their issues revolve around the impact of HIV on their children as much as on themselves. Isolation is an enormous issue with women who fear for their reputations and think that only prostitutes get AIDS. Clinicians work to understand the patients' world view in order to understand their experience of the disease. While exploring the patients' thoughts and feelings about events, there is time for discussion of what the patient believes about AIDS, death, and dying. The work is to understand what patients believe their community's reaction will be. Clinicians view individual experiences within the context of family and culture of origin, as well as within the mainstream medical culture. Patients often need to understand what their community thinks about AIDS and how they treat AIDS patients to understand how to deal with their illness with their family and friends. Different communities stigmatize the illness in different ways. Seemingly irrational fears make sense when viewed within the context of a patient's beliefs, family, religion, and social world.

Another component built into the structure of the HIV Mental Health Clinic is an awareness of the needs of the clinic staff. Given the demands and stresses of the work, staff burnout is a concern that must be addressed (Brody, 1989; Vachon, 1987). The clinic has developed formal and informal supports for all the staff members to cope with job stress and reduce burnout. In doing so, staff turnover has effectively been limited and continuity in treatment for patients has been facilitated while maintaining high levels of personal satisfaction for the staff. Weekly supervision and staff meetings serve to address countertransferential conflicts and help clinicians cope with feelings of isolation, loss, anger, and hopelessness in themselves. Treatment planning and case management, as well as celebrating and grieving, are integrated into regular discussions. Peer supervision and support from other clinicians who also deal with these difficult treatment issues is an integral part of the clinic. Several times a year, there are clinic parties where staff members and their families get together for dinner and fun. Without this kind of support, clinicians can become overwhelmed and exhausted by the powerful demands of patients' needs and experiences.

PSYCHOLOGICAL AND THERAPEUTIC ISSUES FOR THE PATIENT: THE IMPACT OF HIV DISEASE ON PSYCHOTHERAPY

Death and dying, as reality and as metaphor, permeate the treatment of AIDS-infected patients. As with all treatments of terminally ill individuals, clinicians working with HIV-infected people must struggle to understand their involvement with people who they know will die. The social stigma of AIDS and the complexity of the illness and associated treatment regimes can complicate the struggle to work from a truly psychological perspective. Therapist and patient must be able to understand the value of clarifying and working through issues despite having no clear framework for the future. Helping patients understand that they have choices, even when the choices are limited by physical failure, is paramount. Clinicians must balance an awareness of the medical reality with an awareness of the patient's psychological needs. Specific psychological issues arise at different points in patients' medical illness—adjustments to the diagnosis, to multiple losses, to losses in functioning, to deterioration, and to the approach of death. The therapist and the patient must respond to these changes within the context of the treatment alliance, and their work must address the effect of these changes on their expectations in treatment. Therapists must also titrate their own level of involvement, making clinical decisions that take into account the patient's health and their own willingness to step beyond the boundaries of the psychotherapeutic session. For instance, how much of an advocate will the therapist be for patients with medical staff, how flexible can the therapist be in terms of rescheduling appointments, will the therapist visit patients when hospitalized, and will he or she attend memorial services when patients die? These questions are commonly resolved by the clinicians according to their own personal levels of comfort.

Psychotherapy with this patient population often reflects the progression of the HIV illness, developing in stages that address concerns only relevant at that point of the disease. The following sections identify a number of typical concerns that arise in the treatment of HIV-infected patients.

MEDICAL TREATMENT ISSUES AND CASE STUDIES: THE CRISIS OF DIAGNOSIS AND DISCLOSURE

The first stage of dealing consciously with one's HIV infection is at diagnosis. Although people have concerns about infection when involved in high-risk activities or during discussion with others who are infected, they can maintain a sense of immunity or invulnerability that is shattered when they know they are infected. Getting diagnosed is a complex process. First the person must decide to be tested, wait for the results of the test, and then adjust to the diagnosis. In and of itself the decision to be tested can be a major hurdle, even for those who are certain they are HIV positive. The test makes the disease real, and many fear that they will not be able to tolerate the knowledge that they are infected. Others think it is impossible for them to be HIV infected, having constructed elaborate psychological defenses against the possibility. To some patients, testing is irrelevant, as so many other issues take priority. Others cannot believe it when they test negative and compulsively have themselves retested. For people struggling with this decision, therapy revolves around clarifying their fears and addressing the reality of risks and the possible need for treatment.

The decision to be tested may come soon after the individual has taken risks, or it may come later in the course of illness, after hospitalization with an opportunistic infection. Soon after learning the results of an HIV test, often within minutes of becoming aware of their HIV status, patients must consider who they will tell of their situation and when. Many factors affect how someone who is newly diagnosed as HIV positive will respond, including preexisting psychological problems, perceived responsibility for having contracted the illness, fear of having infected others, fears about the future, and social context. Shame, about both personal behaviors and the societal stigma, permeate the HIV-infected patients' experience.

Psychological treatment must address both the actual changes in health and the patient's concerns and fantasies about these changes. Patients often experience the initial diagnosis as an immediate death sentence, without understanding what it actually means to them. Not uncommonly, patients become preoccupied with fantasies of suffering and death and lose their ability to enjoy their current good health. This is particularly true when patients have already experienced multiple losses of friends or family to AIDS. Loss is a common theme—the loss of others who have died, the loss of their image of themselves as healthy, and the loss of functioning and autonomy, to name a few. Treatment must address the changes that patients expect as well as those they actually experience. The goal of treatment is to help patients to understand their reactions to life changes related to the virus and how their expectations of what is to come color their experiences.

The case of Robert exemplifies several common themes. Robert, a 32-year-old Puerto Rican man, was referred to treatment by his infectious disease doctor, Dr. Z. Robert was notified that he tested HIV positive when his application for life insurance was denied. Although his health was good, he appeared to be in the later stages of infection as he had a very low T-cell count, a medical indicator that his immune system was beginning to fail. Dr. Z. was worried about Robert's seeming lack of concern about his health and the fact that he did not want anyone in his family, including his wife and children, to know about his diagnosis.

Robert initially presented for evaluation in the HIV clinic as a down-to-earth man who was experiencing feelings of hopelessness, shame, and anxiety. He had had no idea that he might be infected and had signed the testing consent of his life insurance form with little reflection. He was worried about being a good provider for his family and a role model for his two sons. Clinically, he appeared to be experiencing an adjustment reaction with mixed clinical features. He reported that since being diagnosed it had been as though his heart had frozen into a block of wood, and he had no feeling for life anymore. The only feelings he had were fear that someone would find out he had AIDS and pervasive guilt about all that he thought he had ruined. He was having difficulty concentrating and sleeping. The diagnosis was a severe blow to his self-image, and it was important to him that his therapist understood that he never used drugs and was not gay. He presented himself as a successful business man in his community and did not want anyone to know his diagnosis as he felt it would destroy him professionally and ruin his family.

Robert agreed to enter therapy to deal with his fears. After several meetings, he became overwhelmingly depressed. He became preoccupied with images of dying a lingering, painful death. Though he denied suicidal thoughts, Robert had begun to fantasize about dying accidently in a car crash. As he explored these fantasies, Robert became aware of how this would achieve three things: He would be punished for putting his family at risk, he would not suffer physically, and his family would not be ashamed of him. Robert became aware of how the profound sense of shame he felt was affecting his ability to think about his illness in an effective way. In a subsequent session, he acknowledged speedballing, injecting heroin and cocaine, when involved with the club scene. He had never become a heavy drug user and had stopped using when he met his wife and joined a church 12 years ago. At this time, he felt dirty and full of poison and considered leaving his home. He had hoped to leave the shameful feelings behind when he had joined the church and stopped using drugs. He soon decided to have a couples session to talk with his wife about the diagnosis and to encourage her to be tested. Robert began to move out of his wooden depression and deal more effectively with his situation. When he discovered that his wife and two of their four children were infected, Robert once again became overwhelmed with guilt. His wife, though very fearful, did not blame him. Instead, she sought to help him cope with his guilt, understanding his drug use as a childhood folly. They began family sessions to resolve issues about the disease and deal with the changes it would bring. It is not uncommon for therapists to be asked to help in disclosure issues. Further, it is not uncommon to be introduced to family members when patients are hospitalized or experiencing significant changes in health status. Consequently, clinicians must consider what level of involvement they deem appropriate.

Case Discussion

With this referral, Dr. Z. was most concerned that Robert tell his family about his HIV status so that they could be tested and treated if necessary. As Robert's psychologist, however, her first concern was to develop a treatment alliance with him. Treatment focused on the need for Robert to understand his reaction to the diagnosis and to understand what his diagnosis meant to him and how he could best help his family. It was very important that his psychologist not take the position that disclosure was the right or the moral thing to do. Robert had to come to his own decision. Although the clinician personally felt that Robert must notify his family, she was aware that this had to wait until Robert knew how to do so. In New York, confidentiality laws mandate that patients must sign consent for any level of HIV disclosure. There is no duty to inform; although medical doctors can inform someone who is at risk, they are not mandated to do so. The therapist had to work with Robert about his fears about disclosure while also working with her own reactions to the idea that he might have infected his wife and children. Both the American Psychological Association and the American Psychiatric Association (1992) maintain that the need to respect confidentiality must be maintained as a primary concern. This is both to protect the therapeutic alliance and to ensure that patients will not be dissuaded from testing, treatment, and counseling. Duty to warn applies only to intentional infection.

Treatment with Robert revolved around the blow he had experienced to the image of himself as a good husband, father, and provider for his family. Before this experience, he had taken great pride in his role and in his success as a salesman in a small neighborhood store. With his HIV-positive diagnosis, he was confronted with the consequence of his actions, which made him feel like a bad husband and father—one who, rather than keeping his family safe, had poisoned them. A key here, as with many patients' struggling with disclosure, was Robert's struggle to manage his shame about his infection. In treatment, he was able to understand how his diagnosis changed the way he thought about himself and made him hateful to himself. By talking this through, he was able to repair it and to get support from the therapist and then later from his wife to forgive him for his teenage behavior. As a family member, he learned to grieve for the losses he felt and became able to support his wife and children in a new way.

Clinical Implications

This case highlights the need for therapists to receive support with counter-transference: worries about the patient's family's safety, feelings of responsibility for them, and anger that the patient might endanger them or not take care of them.

These are common reactions in working with situations such as this. As a member of a specialized clinic, the therapist was able to turn to the group for clarification and support. Case discussion clarified the fact that Robert was no longer putting his wife at risk as he was avoiding sex. Although this is not an optimal solution, it served to protect her. Although there was still concern that the family get tested, it was clear with Robert's treatment that it would not be long before he would include his wife. Other cases can be more difficult, such as when patients do not commit to protecting those with whom they are intimate or to discontinue sharing drug paraphernalia. It is rarely useful to try to force patients to disclose their status against their will as they will conceal contacts or stop treatment prematurely. Rather, treatment is most successful when disclosure is made a goal of treatment. Regular supervision is essential to maintain a commitment to the therapeutic alliance and treatment process with these patients.

THE STAGES OF DISEASE PROGRESSION

At this time, AIDS is a disease with a somewhat predictable course and little hope for cure. Medically, the disease is understood in terms of stages: HIV negative, HIV positive with a negative response, HIV positive and asymptomatic, HIV positive and asymptomatic but with a T-cell below 200 indicating significant immune suppression, and then stages of increasingly debilitating illness. Each transition into a new stage requires significant adjustment. Often the course of psychological treatment is affected by the course of the disease, with patients requiring different levels of supportive therapy or interpretive work depending on the psychological nearness of the disease. Often, each transition brings about psychological regression and repetition of previous emotional upheaval. At the same time, changes in health status put pragmatic strains on treatment. Therapists must anticipate the course of the disease and establish plans for the continuation of treatment if patients are unable to attend sessions or are hospitalized.

> John, a 32-year-old gay White man, is an example of a patient whose treatment revolved around his relationship to the disease and its progression. He initially came into treatment because of feelings of anxiety. He had been diagnosed 3 years earlier when his ex-lover became ill. His ex-lover died soon after. At that time, John reported becoming immobilized with fear, depression, and hopelessness. He stayed home from work for a month, avoiding all friends and family. His medical doctor prescribed Xanax and Prozac, which John said helped get him back to work. Since then he had maintained his professional life as his central activity, socializing minimally with old friends. He sought psychotherapy because he had just been told his T-cells had dropped below 200 and he had just started on AIDS-related medication. He was once again feeling panicked and hopeless and was trying to ward off the total collapse he had felt when he was first diagnosed. He felt terribly ashamed of his situation and had recurrent fantasies and nightmares of being bedridden with a wasting disease and needing others to care for and clean him.
>
> John sought to use therapy to explore his reactions to the changes in his health.

After several sessions, he became aware of how his fear of losing his autonomy and the ability to care for himself had always been present, even before his diagnosis. He had difficulty understanding why his feelings of shame were so much stronger than his fears. As he worked to understand this, he came to connect his reactions to his upbringing, which had centered on being successful, and to his feelings about his own sexuality. His family valued being athletic and active, and they were very rejecting of John's "sissy" side. John was frightened of being seen as weak, needy, and dependent, things that his family had scorned. He became aware of how his internalized homophobia controlled much of his reaction. He wanted to show his dad that he was a "man" and the only way he could do that was by being successful. He feared not working because then he would feel useless and pathetic. After a year-long treatment, John felt more secure with his situation. He became more able to tolerate his own needs for support and to reach out to others. At this point, treatment stopped as John felt secure with the network of friends he was developing.

John reentered treatment a year and a half later when he developed mycobacterium intracellulare, a serious opportunistic infection that, though temporarily containable, is not curable. John was experiencing shame, panic, and feelings of helplessness once again. In treatment he was able to address this as a repetition of the prior changes and to move quickly into addressing the grief and fear he felt at the loss of his health and his ability to work. During this time, John focused on feelings of sadness about all that he would not be able to do. Like many young men and women forced into disability, he was acutely aware of having to let go and reorient his life in a meaningful way. He became more involved with his church's senior outreach program, visiting homebound elders. He enjoyed listening to their stories and helping them, with an awareness that he hoped others would visit him when he needed it. John again left treatment, understanding that for him community had become central instead of his career. The therapist predicted that each transition he faced would evoke similar reactions and worked to help John understand ways to prepare himself without becoming preoccupied with fears about transitions. Many cases in the clinic have a similar course, with patients returning when transitions cause them to once more feel overwhelmed with fear, depression, or anxiety.

Clinical Implications

It has been found that this multiple admission policy also serves a large group of patients who have difficulty entering treatment because of character problems, substance abuse, or severe interpersonal dysfunction. Given the cyclic nature of crises induced by changes in medical status, patients who have developed uneasy truces with their fears often return multiple times to treatment. These patients commonly come at times of crisis, and when things calm down they stop attending. Patients with substance abuse problems fall in and out of treatment depending on their degree of abstinence and the stress they are experiencing. The two states often go hand in hand. In a traditional setting, these patients would soon lose the right to be admitted for treatment. Over time, with multiple attempts, therapists make alliances with individuals who would otherwise be unavailable for treatment and help them to begin a process of change.

THE PRESSURE OF MEDICAL TREATMENT

Difficulty in adhering to medical regimes that produce adverse psychological and physical effects is an ongoing treatment issue with this population. Patients who are often poorly equipped to do so are regularly faced with very difficult medical treatment decisions and complex medical regimes. Many of the clinic's patients lack the educational, intellectual, and emotional strengths needed for truly informed consent. Treatment must include support for information gathering and problem solving without becoming overly identified with case management. HIV patients often want therapists to take care of them by explaining treatments and giving advice about what is the best plan. It is important for therapists to tread carefully here, maintaining their independence from the medical establishment through a neutral stance while supporting patients' effective decision making. The therapist must work with the patient to understand the meaning of the patient's medical experiences and to help the patient to make important decisions regarding medical treatment.

A working understanding of HIV-related medical information assists therapists to facilitate coping in patients whose illness is progressing; however, clinicians must not lose sight of the need to understand this material in terms of its meaning within the psychotherapeutic setting. The ability to differentiate depression from dementia, from medication side effects, and from substance abuse is a significant diagnostic challenge that is essential for good treatment. It is not uncommon for a combination of these problems to be present (see chapter 3 for a more extensive discussion of this issue). For the clinician, good working relationships with neurologists, neuropsychologists, and medical practitioners facilitate diagnostic evaluations, treatment, and tracking. The HIV Mental Health Clinic offers this support through ongoing liaisons with other services in the medical center. Clinic staff members participate in weekly rounds, AIDS Task Force activities, and cross-discipline rounds. Because of this networking, therapists are exposed to a broad spectrum of AIDS-related information and have a format to form professional relationships with experts in all fields.

One of the most common reasons medical clinicians refer patients to the clinic is noncompliance with medical treatment. In this field, clinicians must work with patients to understand why they are noncompliant. At times their noncompliance is the result of becoming overwhelmed by the sheer number of appointments combined with complicated medical protocols. One patient who was referred to deal with resistance to her medication reported that she was required to take 86 pills a day at 13 different times and had appointments at eight clinics that week—a feat she was unable to master. When the therapist suggested that her problems with compliance related to the complexity of the medical regime rather than to her own weaknesses, she was deeply relieved. When she reported this back to her medical doctor, he worked to coordinate her care, combining and reducing the medications and clinic appointments. In other cases, patients have conflicted histories with the sociomedical system because of a history of psychiatric or substance abuse. Some patients simply do not understand what is being recommended, and others do not trust their doctors and prefer other methods of healing. Clinicians must work with patients to understand whether their difficulty in complying with medical plans results from their fears, and thereby must be understood as acting out, or if it relates to difficulties resulting from the disease. For instance, patients' ill health, number of appointments, or understanding of the care they are receiving may decrease their ability to comply with medical treatment.

Mary was a 27-year-old African American woman who was referred for psychotherapy for noncompliance with her medical treatment. She had been diagnosed a year earlier, when her husband became ill. At that time, the two of them were active cocaine users, supporting their habits through prostitution and petty drug sales. Since being diagnosed, Mary had entered a detox program and was generally abstinent. Her doctor, Dr. B., referred Mary for treatment because she rarely took her medication as prescribed, failed to get her blood drawn for testing, and often missed appointments. Dr. B. felt angry and frustrated, as she liked Mary and it seemed that Mary was intentionally harming herself. When Mary came to the evaluation appointment, she appeared to be confused, depressed, and angry. She was unclear about why her doctor had referred her for therapy as she was very involved with her 12-step program, Narcotics Anonymous, and felt she did not need a psychologist. When told that it was the therapist's understanding that she was having difficulty coping with medical treatment, she became agitated and angry at Dr. B. for treating her like a child. She was upset because she very much respected and idealized Dr. B. and valued their relationship as one of the most important in her life. Mary denied any difficulty with her treatment and appeared committed to following through with her medical care.

Mary's therapist raised the apparent mismatch between her intention and her behavior over the next three sessions, and several issues emerged. First, Mary had a phobia about needles and blood. She was clear that she had never used heroin for this reason. When confronted with a needle, she experienced catastrophic anxiety, fearing that all her blood would be stolen. She called herself crazy for this and had not told Dr. B. because she thought it was too embarrassing. She felt driven to avoid situations that would expose her to needles. In a session with the therapist, it was clear that blood tests were a trigger for relapse into cocaine use that needed to be addressed. She wanted to be able to have her blood tested and so became involved in using behavioral therapy specifically aimed at reducing the anxiety through systematic desensitization. She was soon able to control her fears and began to cope with her appointments more successfully. Second, during the evaluation it was revealed that Mary was unable to read. When asked to complete a consent form for information from previous treatments, she was unable to do so. She was very ashamed of this and had actively concealed her illiteracy from Dr. B. A goal for Mary became to overcome her shame and to work with the medical social worker to develop appointment reminders and then to enter into an adult literacy program. Mary was also referred for a learning evaluation. Finally, Mary was afraid to ask Dr. B. questions. Although Mary appeared vague and confused about her medical condition, it was clear that she had many questions about the medication she was being prescribed. She felt that she should not ask Dr. B. questions because it would be insulting as questions would imply that she did not trust her.

As Mary began to express these conflicts, her appearance changed; she was revealed as a woman with a strong survival instinct, a lot of common sense, and a good sense of humor. Within a few sessions, Mary began to feel more comfortable asking questions of the therapist—someone whom she identified as a professional—and in turn, she felt more comfortable asking Dr. B. questions. Her idealized relationship with Dr. B. had made it more difficult for her to get the treatment she needed, as in her desire to have Dr. B. respect her equally she had concealed important information. In treatment she began to shift, seeking to understand the underlying conflicts that she had been acting out through her lack of compliance. In particular, Mary explored the pattern of avoidance that she followed as a result of her feelings of shame and fear. She became clearer about how often she felt that people would hurt her when she did not understand something. In her life, it had always been important for her to protect herself, especially when she was using drugs. Treatment focused on moving this dynamic into one that served her better in the medical establishment: being an advocate for herself by being honest with doctors and asking questions when she needed to.

Clinical Implications

Interpersonal conflicts or misunderstandings with medical doctors can be extremely disruptive to treatment. Often patients have limited abilities to confront or question authorities in appropriate ways and have severely conflicted interpersonal relationships. The emotionally laden material regarding health status makes communication even more difficult. When patients fail to follow medical recommendations, physicians often have strong personal reactions. Often doctors feel rejected and become angry. Dr. B., a highly committed infectious disease specialist, felt this way. She had taken a liking to Mary and felt that Mary's noncompliance was a personal rejection. Patients routinely request support in helping their doctors understand their difficulty with medical treatment. As a therapist, it is important to work with patients to understand why it is so difficult for them to express themselves, aiming to empower patients to be active in their own treatment rather than having the therapist assume responsibility. Too often patients seem to have been trained by other health care providers to hand over responsibility and understanding, thus reinforcing their helplessness. Clinicians must understand the meaning patients give medical protocols and work to support the patients' abilities to cope with their treatment rather than merely react out of fear. When Mary was able to talk through her fears, she was able to explain this to Dr. B, who then could let go of her own feelings.

On occasion, however, it becomes the clinician's responsibility to act as liaison for patients with the medical establishment. Conflicts resulting from cultural misunderstanding, racism, sexism, homophobia, classism, and prejudice against substance abusers can complicate professional relationships. Clinicians must work with patients to understand the source of problems they are experiencing. Clinicians must also understand their own expectations of medical treatment and their fantasies about the health care of HIV-infected patients.

PAIN MANAGEMENT

One of the greatest fears of AIDS patients and their families is of the suffering they expect to go through in their illness. In fact, pain is a reality to many patients, as a consequence of the illness or as a factor in medical treatments. When asked what they fear most about their illness, most patients report fear of pain (Melzack, 1973). Often patients, clinicians, friends, and families have difficulty recognizing and respecting the impact of pain on patients' lives. Patients do not want to be seen as complainers or weak, yet they are angered by the lack of compassion or support from those around them. Seemingly untreatable pain makes patients and doctors alike feel overwhelmed and helpless and can lead to complications in treatment and outcome. The anticipation of untreatable pain is equally disabling. Social, psychological, and biochemical factors come to bear in each patient's experience of pain (Wall, 1978). Depression and anxiety are related to the pain experience, both neurochemically and psychosocially, and must be addressed (Adams, 1996; Breznitz & Folkman, 1993).

An important issue to understand in dealing with pain is that pain means different things to different people. From the patient's point of view, the pain is the problem. To the medical practitioner, pain is only a symptom or a by-product of the disorder (Taylor, 1986). Pain, such as severe stomach cramps, can indicate illness in need of diagnosis and treatment. In this way, pain is an essential component of a process leading to diagnosis and good treatment. Often, however, pain, such as neuropathy in the feet, can be a consequence of viral action on the nervous system that is without medical solution and unresponsive to pain medications. In this case, patients are expected to live with chronic pain, and under circumstances such as this, teaching pain and stress management techniques can be crucial. Biofeedback and relaxation techniques are other valuable tools that can provide people with the means by which to modulate their pain experiences.

Acute pain is experienced differently than chronic pain; many patients cope better with one than with the other. Pain is a subjective feeling, one without clear external measure. Two people with the same injury will express significantly different experiences of pain. The same injury can elicit different experiences in different situations. There is no way to quantify pain, nor is there a good predictor as to pain's intensity or impact on the individual. To further complicate the situation, many people involved with patients in pain have little awareness, understanding, or empathy. This difficulty results from various sources. At times pain sufferers are viewed as complainers or attention seekers, even as drug seeking. The denial of another's pain also grows from the helplessness people feel when someone they love is suffering.

In the outpatient setting, clinicians can offer significant support to patients suffering with acute or chronic pain. Each patient seeking support with pain must have a complete pain workup with clinicians specializing in pain management. Often pain can be alleviated through appropriate medication, diet, and exercises. Not uncommonly, patients experience pain unnecessarily as a result of medical practitioners who discount their patients' pain or are fearful of offering medication because of issues of addiction or psychological complications. Clinicians can educate patients about these issues and work with them to develop appropriate plans. At times simply acknowledging the disabling effect of pain begins a movement toward more effective coping strategies. Psychotherapists can also help patients understand how to cope more effectively with their medical and social situations and reduce the extra stress that many patients experience as a result of anticipatory anxiety. A component of a pain evaluation seeks to understand the interaction of psychological and biological influences on the experience of pain. Adams (1996) noted that, among other things, pain can represent aggression, be a means of controlling behavior, be representative of guilt and atonement, or be the somatization of emotional concerns. Anxiety about pain can lead to stress that increases pain.

> Tom, a 36-year-old Black man, was referred to treatment by his physician Dr. Y. because he had grown increasingly irritable and angry since beginning treatment at the Infectious Disease Clinic the previous year. When asked why he thought he was more irritable, Tom expressed concern that he had changed so much over the last year. He thought he must have something wrong with his brain because of the virus. He reported that he used to be very calm, liked people, and enjoyed life a lot. Now, he often felt tense and angry and did not like being around people. He was upset that he often snapped at his family and had no patience for delays. Dr. Y. discounted an organic cause for the change in mental status, having done a full neurological workup that revealed no significant changes in Tom's brain.
>
> Tom hypothesized that what he was experiencing was related to the fact that he had stopped working. His health had deteriorated, and for a brief time he had been bedbound. Now, although he felt better, his days were filled with waiting for appointments in medical clinics. He felt that his difficulty related specifically to anxiety and fear. He wanted to use therapy to work through his anger, and he felt that his problems were related to the difficulty he had in expressing his feelings to his family. Tom was an ideal psychotherapy client with an adjustment reaction.
>
> As Tom discussed his experiences, he noted, in passing, that he had cryptosporidiosis in his intestine, a parasitic disease that often leads to severe cramping and chronic diarrhea. When asked about this he reported that 6 months ago he had been bedbound because of the cramps but that now, with treatment, the pain was much better. In completing a pain inventory, it became clear that a plausible explanation for his change in mood was pain. He reported regular abdominal cramps, headaches on a daily basis, and a severe burning sensation in both feet due to neuropathy.
>
> In considering the effects of pain on his life, he acknowledged how limited the pain made him feel. He refused pain medication because he was worried about

becoming addicted. In talking about his experience of pain, a pattern of denial emerged. Tom did not want to acknowledge the pain because he felt he should be able to handle it. He reported that he often worried about his health and linked his headaches to the times when he was worried that the stomach cramps would return. He reported getting very tense when his stomach began to rumble, and this made his stomach cramps worse. He became preoccupied with trying to avoid getting sick and often had difficulty sleeping. Also, he worried about the pain in his feet, fearing that it would worsen and prevent him from walking. Tom was afraid that his parents and friends would worry or be upset, so he avoided telling them about his pain. He did not want to be seen as a complainer.

In our sessions, Tom began to understand how his anxiety and his need to protect others were creating part of the pain he experienced by making him tense and preventing him from getting to sleep. Treatment focused on using pain management techniques, which included relaxation, distraction, and stress management techniques. As he became adept with these techniques, he felt less dominated by pain and his mood brightened considerably.

Clinical Implications

Tom was having difficulty adjusting to AIDS. Although all his complaints were accurate, they were fueled by an underlying pain syndrome that made everything much more difficult to deal with. Because he was so articulate about his psychological pain, clinicians were unaware of the degree of physical discomfort he was experiencing. This is not an uncommon phenomenon and practitioners must be alert to diagnose it. The opposite is also common—the patient who complains so much that no one believes him or her anymore or discounts the complaints because they are so out of proportion with what the practitioner thinks the patient should be experiencing. A third and very common issue is dealing with pain experienced by people with a history of substance abuse. Many patients' realistic concerns are ignored because practitioners believe the pain complaints are only "drug-seeking" behaviors. Clinicians must remember that pain is a subjective thing that cannot be quantified or predicted for each individual, and they must work with patients individually to understand their experience. Within the context of psychotherapy there is the time to tease apart pain and secondary gain from that pain. By understanding the patient's psychological process often the meaning of complaints of pain becomes clearer. Experience working with this population shows that pain and stress management have become an integral part of treatment in clinic work, improving the quality of patients' lives.

DEATH AND DYING

Death and dying, especially fear of suffering while dying, are topics of significance in the treatment of all terminally ill patients. Clinicians must confront their own beliefs and fears about the process of dying and about death itself.

Working closely with those preoccupied with death reminds people about their own vulnerability. Clinicians' difficulty facing their own mortality can lead to denial and may cause the therapist to be deaf to latent death content or may, conversely, cause them to be overly sympathetic and intrusive with patients. Clinicians' own fears about loss can be evoked as they become close to patients with AIDS.

AIDS patients' feelings about dying are often complicated by feelings of guilt and anger about contracting the disease, difficulty coping with multiple losses of friends and family, concerns about societal stigma and prejudice, and personal experiences of the deterioration and suffering of loved ones. Issues relating to the patient's experience of loss pervades treatment and directly affect the patient's concerns about the dying process. Key to the treatment is a thorough exploration of the patient's experiences of loss: the loss of functioning, the loss of self-image, the loss of his or her role as a healthy and productive member of society, the loss of health, and the loss of others who have died. The clinician must also struggle with experiences of loss; as patients decline, therapists must adapt their expectations, and when patients die clinicians must cope with their own grief (Perry, Fishman, Jacobsberg, & Frances, 1992).

It is important for therapists to explore what death means to each patient. Understanding patients' beliefs and fantasies about what will happen when they die often plays a central role in the treatment of AIDS patients. Cultural and religious beliefs need to be explored even when patients deny any current religious affiliation. At times patients become despondent because they fear a punitive God; others find renewed spirituality and hope through their beliefs. It is important to work with patients to understand how their childhood beliefs color their adult experiences. Although this is an obvious conclusion relating to the therapeutic process, it becomes one of the central concerns in coping with AIDS.

Two otherwise similar cases highlight this issue.

Helena and Joyce were two African-American women who were referred to treatment by their infectious disease doctor to resolve their feelings of depression and self-hatred. Both were preoccupied with dying, and both had contracted the AIDS virus through drug use. Each had several children and had infected the youngest while pregnant. The respective treatments of these two patients were very different because of their differing beliefs about the future. Helena was a devout Baptist who had been raised into a strict community of believers. She had been reborn into a new spiritual relationship with her church when she had stopped using drugs several years before being diagnosed. In her view, AIDS was a divine punishment for her sins, and she deserved to suffer. She was terrified of dying as she believed that she deserved eternal punishment. She felt hopeless about the possibility of any other consequence. Helena's treatment focused on developing self-acceptance and understanding and the ability to reach out to her minister. As she was more able to cope with her feelings, she talked with him about ways to seek salvation. It required her to face the deep fear that he would reject her as had happened so many other times in her life.

Joyce came from a different perspective. Her family's religious beliefs were more liberal, and her community did not directly link AIDS with sin. In fact, her family was concerned about her drug use and was angry that she continued to associate with people using drugs. Joyce viewed death as a release, a time when she would no longer have to struggle. Joyce's fatalism was revealed to be a defense against her fear that she would not succeed. In her childhood, she had always been the slow one in school, and although her brothers were academically gifted and worked to attain scholarships, she did not enjoy school and dropped out. In treatment, she began to understand that she had not gotten the support she had wanted and so she had given up—partially because she was angry at her family and partially because she agreed with her family that she was no good. She struggled with how to get her family to respect her and her children.

Clinical Implications

The self-hatred experienced by both patients was intensified by their anguish regarding their children's futures. Women with HIV infection often have the additional stress of having to contend with their role as primary caregiver to their children. HIV-infected women list concerns related to caring for their children and for their children's future as a primary stressor (Hackl, Kalichman, & Somlai, 1995). Although this is not unique to the HIV-infected population, it becomes a special consideration because of the stigma and shame associated with the illness. This process becomes even more stressful when the mother has children who have been infected and become ill. As with many women struggling with AIDS, Helena and Joyce were most concerned about their children. Death meant they could not care for their children, would not see them grow up, and would expose them to pain and grief through their deaths. Clinicians must help such women understand how to help their children cope with illness and loss. These women must address complex bureaucracies to ensure that the children will get the medical and social supports they need and to ensure plans for the children's future. At the same time, they wrestle with the guilt of having infected their children and the fears of having to leave them. Helena used treatment to cope with her fears about death and to resolve anger at herself for her behavior. Joyce's work centered on repairing family ties to make good permanency plans for her children.

SUICIDE

An active debate about suicide is currently raging in American society. Do circumstances exist in which suicide is an acceptable response? Or is suicide unacceptable under all circumstances? When, if ever, is suicide an acceptable response to life events? This discussion contrasting the ideas of rational and irrational suicide is an important issue in work with HIV-infected patients. For example, rational suicide is often viewed as a positive coping mechanism; the patient—in face of catastrophic anxiety about future suffering—may plan to take all of his or her medication in the face of a debilitating untreatable illness. Under such circumstances, patients may seek to die with dignity, which others generally find understandable and acceptable. However, irrational suicide is generally rejected as a legitimate coping device; rather, it is seen as an emotionally reactive gesture that is devoid of value. A patient, for example, may be so frightened of dying that he or she tries to kill him- or herself to escape this fear. In these cases, popular wisdom holds that with psychiatric and psychological treatment these patients can once again enjoy life. They should, therefore, be protected from their impulses and supported in the resolution of their psychological conflicts.

Clinicians working with HIV-infected patients must address patients', as well as their own, thoughts and feelings about suicide. In an informal survey of the staff working in the clinic, therapists reported that suicide was a topic discussed in every treatment. Each patient reports suicidal thoughts at some time in treatment: as an active concern, as passing thoughts, or as plans for the future when they get sick. Suicidal ideation and suicidal behavior is more common with HIV-infected people than in the general population (Zamperetti et al., 1990). O'Dowd (1993) noted that there is an increased risk of suicide in both substance abusers and gay men when depression is present, a common scenario in the HIV-infected population. The idea of suicide evokes a strong response that must be understood and addressed by both the clinician and the patient. In advance of the emergence of the topic in the therapy, the clinician should explore his or her personal feelings and beliefs regarding rational suicide and doctor-assisted suicide or euthanasia. Suicidal ideation can serve a variety of psychological functions for the patient. It should be handled differently when based on pathological fears and fantasies than when the ideation serves to bestow a sense of control for a patient who feels helpless in the face of the unpredictable yet relentless progression of HIV infection.

> Mirium, a 35-year-old Dominican woman, came to treatment at her family's request. They were concerned because she was depressed and talking about wanting to die. She had been tested for HIV when she entered a drug treatment program 2 years earlier, but refused to get the results. Instead, she left the program and continued to use drugs. She had been fearful of discovering her diagnosis and fled into her addiction to avoid facing it. When she came to the first evaluation session, she had been abstinent for a month, after having been diagnosed with tuberculosis. Her family had established a guardian schedule to make sure she was never alone, hoping to prevent a drug relapse or suicide attempt. At the time of the initial evaluation interview, Mirium was in fact profoundly depressed. She reported sleeping more than 12 hours a night and still feeling tired. Every night she had terrible nightmares about friends who had died coming to get her. When she was awake, she felt hopeless and depressed about her illness, interpreting every ache as the first sign of a terrible disease. She said that she often thought of killing herself because everything was so bad for her. Mirium acknowledged she had a plan to kill herself with an overdose of street drugs as soon as she could escape her family's vigilance.

Mirium reported that she was frightened to do this and agreed that she told the therapist about it to get some help. At this time it was decided that it was best for her to enter the hospital.

Mirium entered the hospital's inpatient Mentally Ill Chemical Abuser Unit—a program especially developed to address the combined issues of substance abuse and psychiatric illness—for the next 3½ weeks. During that time, she kept in touch with her outpatient therapist, double checking her inpatient doctor's plans for her. She started taking antidepressant medication, and her depression began to remit. During her hospitalization Mirium was again tested and diagnosed HIV positive. When told, she again became very depressed, and adjusting to the diagnosis became a focus of treatment. Mirium returned to outpatient treatment when she was discharged. She became affiliated with local Alcohol Anonymous groups and aimed to attend 90 meetings in 90 days. She felt fully committed to her recovery. In therapy sessions, Mirium began to work through some of her fears and feelings of loss that had originally driven her to do drugs. In the hospital she had already begun to understand how drugs had served her as a way to feel in control—of herself, of her feelings, and of her relationships. Soon, suicide once again became an issue, one that she feared talking about as she did not want to be hospitalized again. The topic was unveiled first in a dream that concluded in her search for a gun with which to kill herself. She acknowledged having thoughts once more of ending her life, but she felt it was different. Now when she fantasized about dying, it was related to her HIV diagnosis—what would happen when she was very ill and in agony. She imagined that when she was unable to care for herself she would take an overdose to end the dying process. Here her imagery was not reactively suicidal; she was seeking control over her fears about the future. As Mirium discussed this difference, her fear lessened. She decided to write a living will and to complete a health care proxy requesting that no extraordinary measures be taken if she were severely and permanently debilitated. She also scheduled meetings with her family and her doctors to explain her wishes. Having done this, she felt at peace and stopped being so anxious about her health. Deciding that she could die when it was good to do so gave her more freedom to enjoy life in the present.

Clinical Implications

As with death, suicide is a topic that will emerge often in a treatment and serve many purposes. Suicidal thoughts are prevalent in treatment with AIDS patients and these thoughts must be addressed by clinicians. If a therapist is too fearful of a patient's expressions of suicidal material and becomes overly cautious, the treatment will suffer. While any discussion of suicide must be taken seriously, too strong a reaction from the therapist often limits the treatment and prevents the patient from understanding important material. When patients are fearful of their thoughts of committing suicide, the clinician can normalize their experiences, identifying what the process means. As they become aware of the function of the thought—and can differentiate "dangerous plans" from "future fantasies"—they can experience a feeling of mastery and security.

BEREAVEMENT

Bereavement is a topic closely linked to the issue of death and presents similar psychotherapeutic concerns. Many HIV-positive people have experienced the deaths of partners and friends from AIDS. It has been noted that AIDS is a disease of friends and families, owing to the sources of transmission (Gupta, Anderson, & May, 1989). Infection suggests relationships with other infected people, either through sexual contact or through interactions based on sharing of needles. Studies have indicated that, depending on risk groups, between 25% to 52% of HIV-infected people have close friends or relatives who have died from AIDS (Martin, 1988; Perry et al., 1992). Kessler et al. (1991) noted that men who are HIV infected suffer the greatest number of AIDS-related losses (Kessler et al., 1991). Health care providers are aware of the stress of multiple bereavements for these patients and for providers themselves. A significant contributor to health care provider burnout is the multiple-loss syndrome (Gordon, Ulrich, Feeley, & Pollack, 1993). Work with this population means facing these losses while helping patients cope with their reactions. Clinicians must work with patients to manage their grief, understanding how their feelings about the losses affect their experience of themselves and their medical situation. Patients who have been care partners for others who have died express stronger feelings of hopelessness and vulnerability. They have seen firsthand what they believe to be their future. Often they have horrible memories, and they often have difficulty appreciating their current health status. Martin (1988), in evaluating a cohort of gay men, found that demoralization, problematic sleep patterns, affective disturbance, intrusive thoughts, and illicit and prescription drug use predictably increased in proportion to the number of AIDS-related deaths the men experienced.

> Marilyn was one such patient. She sought treatment following the death of her brother. Her stepfather had died of AIDS 4 years ago and her husband had died 3 years ago. She reported feeling relieved when her husband died because he had been ill for a year, and she had been overwhelmed trying to care for him. She was also aware of a great deal of anger toward her husband. She felt that her husband had knowingly infected her with HIV during unprotected sex because he wanted her to have a baby. She believed that he had infected her brother by sharing drug paraphernalia with him. During the 2½ years after her husband's death, Marilyn felt that she dealt well with her reaction to her infection and she was enjoying her life. Then her brother became ill and died after a 2-week stay in the hospital. He had apparently developed a bacterial meningitis that did not respond to treatment. Since his death 3 months earlier, Marilyn had been grief stricken, unable to care for her children or her home. She was completely reliant on her mother for the simplest things and felt nothing was worth living for anymore. She remained in bed, ate little, and had stopped bathing unless her mother pushed to do so. Her medical doctor, Dr. K., had prescribed an antidepressant and sleeping medication, both of which had no effect.

During the evaluation and the first several weeks of therapy, Marilyn moved between tearful memories of her brother and feelings of rage toward her husband. Slowly, over time, she began to calm down. She reported that her mother had forbidden her to talk of any of the three deaths and that for months before her brother's illness these things had been dominating her thoughts. Marilyn came to see that she had allowed her mother's stalwart denial to trap her inside her own head. She could get no support from others because no one could know what had happened. Treatment began with releasing the feelings while also working out ways for Marilyn to get support. She became aware that her brother's death was so sudden that she had had no time to prepare herself, and as a result, she felt defenseless against the loss. She also talked about how vulnerable she felt physically from having seen so much death. She was unable to imagine a hopeful fantasy for her own future.

Marilyn joined a women's group in addition to her individual treatment, seeking to hear others' stories and to feel less isolated. She found, however, that she could not talk in the group. She found that not only had she internalized her mother's prohibition about exposure but that she was terrified the other women would die. In her thinking, these women were in an HIV group and were therefore sure to die. Marilyn had to struggle to become involved; understanding how the many losses she had already experienced made her want to hide and never be close to others again. Marilyn was astonished when the group sponsored a memorial service for a member who died. Not only was the event inconceivable within her family, but through her attendance she experienced a sense of closure and caring that had previously been unavailable to her. She still felt the sadness and loss, but it did not feel meaningless. She felt hopeful because she felt that these women would not forget her when she died.

Clinical Implications

Clinicians also have to cope with their personal experiences of bereavement. Therapy is an intimate treatment form, with each person in the room forming attachments. When patients become ill and die, therapists who have been involved with them feel the loss. Therapists must decide if they wish to meet with patients in the hospital and if they will attend memorial services. Often these activities can help one deal with the losses. Health care professionals must develop ways to care for themselves when they have losses. In the clinic, staff members take time to talk during staff meetings about patients who die, reviewing the treatment but, more important, talking about how the patient affected them. This marking of the relationship helps with the transition and sharing in this way fits into the support network. Successes are celebrated with parties when staff members complete a project or a degree. Time is made for holidays, and staff are responsible for taking vacations, ensuring that their lives outside of the clinic are fulfilling and satisfying. They hold each other in times of sadness. Regular supervision helps to ground experiences and regular vacations support getting the rest needed to heal.

RISKY BEHAVIOR AND ACTING OUT

All treatment with HIV-involved patients must take place within the context of psychological concerns predating or independent of HIV illness. In this work, the clinician works with the patient to understand both the meaning and the process of illness. In psychotherapy treatment, acting out has been identified as a defense against experiencing feelings or conflicts. By engaging in these behaviors, patients avoid the negative psychological experience. Acting out for HIV-positive patients causes added stress for the therapist owing to the severe consequences for the patient and for those with whom they interact. Ongoing substance abuse or risky sexual behavior are the two areas that, in addition to suicidal expressions, can be the most provocative in working with this population. Acting out is common in any client group that includes substance use and severe personality disorder diagnoses. With HIV added to the equation, the risks involved in the behavior are often grave. Medical practitioners and psychotherapists cannot help having a strong response to this patient population, which can affect their work (Weinberg, Conover, Samsa, & Greenberg, 1992). Noncompliance with treatment, including relapses to drug use or promiscuity, must be handled as ongoing treatment issues and not as behavior to be punished. It is imperative that the therapist seek support with these powerful countertransferential issues.

HIV-infected substance abusers are a doubly stigmatized group of patients. These patients require specialized expertise from a psychological treatment that integrates substance abuse treatment with an understanding of the unique stressors faced by people within this group. The medically ill chemical-abusing patient with HIV infection is triply diagnosed and faces phenomenal stressors with extremely limited resources for coping and maintaining emotional stability. At the clinic, therapists work within a harm reduction model, seeking to engage patients in a treatment that addresses high-risk behaviors as a symptom of the severe stresses they experience. Patients work to identify triggers—in the environment, in their relationships, or in their thoughts and emotions—and to develop strategies for handling the situations as they arise. Therapists encourage the development of supportive relationships through participation in 12-step programs and group therapy. The progressive nature of the HIV illness is particularly difficult for this group to cope with as it provides a series of continually evolving stresses.

> Toby was an HIV-infected man with a 15-year history of both intravenous drug use and hospitalization for paranoid psychosis. His history was cyclic. Toby would experience a trauma or threat, then use drugs to calm down. The drug use would escalate, and then he would stop using his psychiatric medication, feeling that it gave him too many side effects. Each hospitalization followed serious drug binges. While hospitalized, Toby would become stabilized psychiatrically soon after the drugs cleared his system and he was on his psychiatric medication again, and he would be quickly discharged. When Toby came to our clinic he was aware of this

cycle but felt unable to stop it. He also refused to enter a long-term substance abuse facility, fearing that he would never be released.

Initially, Toby came to treatment irregularly, often missing appointments around the time that he had medical appointments, a behavior that had led to the termination of his case in several other clinics. Over time his attitude to treatment changed, and it became clear that he had developed a strong attachment to the clinic and to his therapist. He began to drop by the clinic on unscheduled visits prior to appointments with his medical doctor to plan how to handle things. The clinician dealing with Toby maintained as flexible a schedule as she could, permitting him to enter the alliance on his own terms. He was hospitalized once during the first year of therapy and she visited him on the ward, maintaining their relationship. Additionally, she remained nonjudgmental about his drug use, pointing out the obvious costs without rejecting him. Drug abstinence was the goal, not the requirement, of treatment. To engage in this treatment the therapist needed to work through her own countertransference about dangers of his drug use (i.e., sharing needles) as well as about his resistance to engaging in consistent treatment. Toby began to use her as a support to fight his fears and relied less on drug abuse to sedate them.

Pharmacologic treatment of severe anxiety and chronic pain is complicated in work with recovering addicts. Clinicians must acknowledge that addicts experience pain that should be treated. Because these patients are often drug seeking, medication issues are complicated for the clinician and can lead to the undermedicating of real pain. Addicts in recovery who are denied appropriate pain medication are often more likely to relapse to drug use in an effort to cope with their pain. Therapists working with this group will often be required to be involved in liaison work with the patient's primary care doctor and psychiatrist to understand the application of pharmacologic and analgesia treatments. In addition, teaching patients pain and stress management techniques can be invaluable.

Many patients come seeking help in coping with sexual issues. Sexual conflicts—whether acting out or physical dysfunction—can also be stressful to cope with for both patients and clinicians. Sexual acting out is evocative in any psychotherapy treatment; however, when the patient is HIV infected the stress produced by the patient's behavior can be severe. Again, this behavior must be understood as a symptom of a deeper conflict, in a way similar to substance abuse, to be addressed and resolved. HIV-infected patients come to treatment with complaints about changes in sexual desire, function, or pleasure. Patients have reported in sessions being told by other health care providers not to worry about sexual dysfunction because sex is too dangerous to their partners. Clinicians must be aware of their own fears and fantasies about the sexuality of HIV-infected individuals. Clinicians need to understand and be comfortable with safer sex information and education.

Organic causes of sexual dysfunction related to HIV infection must be ruled out medically; however, the role psychological factors play in sexuality cannot be underestimated. These patients often feel contaminated and dangerous. Many associate sex so closely with disease that healthy expression of sexual desire is inconceivable to them. Patients' inability to stop engaging is high-risk sexual behaviors is another cause of anxiety. Risky sexual activity can be an extremely evocative and provocative treatment issue for clinicians. When a patient reveals continued unsafe sexual practices, the clinician must consider the purpose of the communication within treatment, as well as the meaning of the acts.

> Jason was referred to treatment by his infectious-disease doctor, Dr. P., to address issues of noncompliance with medical treatment and to stop high-risk sexual behaviors. Jason was refusing to take most medications because he believed they contributed to impotence. Dr. P. reported that this was not an identified side effect and was considering not working with Jason because he would not change his sexual behaviors. Jason, on the other hand, was angry at Dr. P. for telling him in an offhand way that he should curtail his sexual behavior because of the risk of infecting others. The first several sessions were difficult, because Jason was a very expressive and emotional man who often became overwhelmed with feelings of anger and abandonment. It was clear that his relationship with his doctor was very negative, in part due to his doctor's refusal to discuss his impotency and in part to Jason's difficulty with anger.
>
> As treatment unfolded, Jason became aware of his own discomfort about sexuality and his fears that he was poisonous. He reported that he would go cruising in the park several times a week and have multiple sexual partners. These outings were followed by intense feelings of guilt and self-hatred, both for the behavior, which he felt was dirty, and for the threat he posed to his partners. Jason thought he acted this way to prove he was not impotent, but he was never reassured no matter how many times he performed. As he spoke of this pattern, identifying the compulsive nature of his sexual behavior, Jason began to identify his feeling of longing for a deeper relationship that blended with intense fears about what a relationship would be like. At one session he jokingly noted that Dr. P. was his only long-term relationship—and "look how awful it is." Soon afterward Jason changed his physician, feeling that he did not have to have a doctor who was homophobic. His new doctor ordered a impotency workup, which was negative. The results were very reassuring to Jason, who returned to therapy the next day saying his goals in treatment were changing and he wanted to use his time dealing with the fact that he was sexually compulsive. Although fears about medical treatment continued to emerge from time to time, issues of intimacy and sexuality continued to form the core of Jason's treatment. His acting out lessened and he began to explore relationships that are more meaningful to him.

Clinical Implications

In both cases reviewed in this section the clinicians were challenged by patients who were endangering themselves and others by their behavior. Key to each treatment was the therapists' accepting the patients where they were, understanding that the risky behaviors were symptoms of a self-destructive dynamic that needed to be understood and worked with. In each case the clinician worked first at building the treatment alliance, accepting the behaviors. This did not mean ignoring the risk; however, it did require that the risk be discussed with the patient. At times both clinicians became frustrated and angry about the behaviors, but they worked within supervision to contain their own reactions. By creating an open environment for exploration, each therapist permitted the patients to begin to work through and change their behaviors. Simply telling a patient to stop a dangerous behavior rarely works. Instead, clinicians must work with patients to help them understand the function of their behavior and to develop a more satisfying repertoire of activities.

CONCLUSION

The role of psychological treatment in HIV-positive patients can be of significant benefit when clinicians can maintain their commitment to the value of the treatment alliance. Psychotherapy often provides the only opportunity that HIV-positive patients have to discuss their feelings and reactions to their experiences. Contrary to other interventions—medical or casework services, for example—it provides an opportunity for patients to become collaborators in their treatment, offering a sense of control and empowerment. This treatment can help them understand their illness within the context of their life and to maintain perspective as to issues as they arise. Further, it can offer support throughout the course of the disease. Given the progressive nature of the disease, this is of particular importance. An undeniable aspect to the process is patients' expectations about their future and their belief that they know how they will die. The dying process, death, and bereavement will—implicitly or explicitly—be a topic throughout treatment to be worked with and understood within the context of the patients' current life events. When making the commitment to treat these patients, therapists must consider how these changes will affect the treatment and the treatment relationship.

Addressing the needs of these patients means meeting them where they are psychologically and working to facilitate their ability to cope with their experience rather than reacting out of fear, shame, and anger. It requires understanding the barriers HIV-infected people experience and helping them address the prejudice they encounter. Clinicians must understand their own feelings and reactions to the medical concerns of HIV-infected patients and work to resolve their own prejudices about these patients. Clinicians, like patients, must develop supportive networks and cope with material evoked in the process of treatment.

Medically, an improved sense of self-mastery can lead to better medical outcomes through increased compliance and a reduction in self-destructive behaviors. As patients come to understand their experiences and develop more effective coping skills, the quality of their lives improves. Although they cannot undo their infection, they can come to understand, in a personally meaningful way, how to live with the illness.

REFERENCES

Adams, D. B. (1996). Psychopharmacologic management of patients with chronic residual pain. *Psychotherapy Bulletin, 31*, 13–20.
American Psychiatric Association. (1992). AIDS policy: Guidelines for outpatient psychiatric services. *American Journal of Psychiatry, 149*, 721.
Breznitz, S., & Folkman, A. (1993). Psychosocial effects of HIV infection. In Leo Goldberger & Schlomo Breznitz (Eds.), *A handbook of stress* (2nd ed.). New York, NY: The Free Press.
Brody, C. M. (1989). Jenny: Treatment of a client who is HIV seropositive. *Psychotherapy in Private Practice, 7*, 95–101.
Coates, T. J., Stall, R., Mandel, J. S., Boccellari, A., Sorensen, J. L., Morales, E. F., Morin, S. F., Wiley, T. A., & McKusick, L. (1987). AIDS: A psychosocial research agenda. *Annals of Behavioral Medicine, 9*, 21–28.
Cournos, F., Empfield, M., Horwarh, E., McKinnon, K., Meyer, I., Phil, M., Schrage, H., Currie, C., & Agosin, D. (1991). HIV seroprevalence among patients admitted to two psychiatric hospitals. *American Journal of Psychiatry, 148*, 1225–1230.
Crandall, S.C., & Coleman, R. (1992). AIDS-related stigmatization and the disruption of social relationships. *Journal of Social and Personal Relationships, 9*, 163–177.
Davis, K. (1986). Medicine in the melting pot. *Geriatrics, 7*, 32–37.
Gordon, J. H., Ulrich, C., Feeley, M., & Pollack, S. (1993). Staff distress among hemophilia nurses. *AIDS Care, 5*, 359–367.
Gupta, S., Anderson, R., & May, R. (1989). Networks of sexual contacts: Implications for the pattern of spread of HIV. *AIDS, 3*, 807–817.
Hackl, K., Kalichman, S.C., & Somlai, A. (1995, February). *Women with HIV/AIDS: The dual challenges of patient and primary caregiver.* Paper presented at the conference on HIV Infection in Women, Washington, DC.
Herek, G. M. (1990). Illness, stigma, and AIDS. In P. T. Costa, Jr., & G. R. VandenBos (Eds.), *Psychological aspects of serious illness: Chronic conditions, fatal diseases, and clinical care* (pp. 105–149). Washington, DC: American Psychological Association.
Horowitz, M. J. (1986). *Stress response syndromes* (2nd ed.). Northvale, NJ: Jason Aronson.
Kalichman, S. C. (1995). *Understanding AIDS: Guide for mental health professionals.* Washington, DC: American Psychological Association.
Kessler, R. C., Foster, C., Joseph, J., Ostrow, D., Wortman, C., Phair, J., & Chmiel, J. (1991). Stressful life events and symptom onset in HIV infection. *American Journal of Psychiatry, 148*, 733–738.
Martin, J. L. (1988). Psychological consequences of AIDS-related bereavement among gay men. *Journal of Consulting and Clinical Psychology, 56*, 856–862.
Melzack, R. (1973). *The puzzle of pain.* New York: Basic Books.
O'Dowd, M. A. (1993). Suicidal behaviors and AIDS. *HIV/AIDS & Mental Hygiene, 3*, 1–4.
O'Dowd, M. A., Natali, C., Orr, D., & McKegney, F. P. (1991). Characteristics of patient attending an HIV-related psychiatric clinic. *Hospital and Community Psychiatry, 42*, 615–619.
Perry, S., Fishman, B., Jacobsberg, L., & Frances, A. (1992). Relationships over 1 year between lymphocyte subsets and psychosocial variables among adults with infection by human immunodeficiency virus. *Archives of General Psychiatry, 49*, 396–401.
Perry, S., Jacobsberg, L., Card, C. A., Ashman, T., Frances, A., & Fishman, B. (1993). Severity of psychiatric symptoms after HIV testing. *American Journal of Psychiatry, 150*, 775–779.
Taylor, S. E. (1986). *Health psychology.* New York: Random House.
Taylor, S. E., & Aspinwall, L. (1990). Psychosocial aspects of chronic illness. In G. M. Herek, S. M. Levy, S. Maddi, S. Taylor, & D. Wertlieb (Eds.), *Psychological aspects of chronic illness: Chronic conditions, fatal diseases, and clinical care* (pp. 7–60). Washington, DC: American Psychological Association.

Vachon, M. L. S. (1987). *Occupational stress in the care of the critically ill, the dying and the bereaved.* Washington, DC: Hemisphere.

Wall, P. D. (1978). The gate control theory of pain mechanisms: A reexamination and restatement. *Brain, 101,* 1.

Weinberg, M., Conover, C. J., Samsa, G. P., & Greenberg, S. M. (1992). Physicians' attitudes and practices regarding treatment of HIV-infected patients. *Southern Medical Journal, 85,* 683–686.

Winiarski, M. G. (1991). *AIDS-related psychotherapy.* New York: Pergamon Press.

Zamperetti, M., Goldwurm, G. F., Abbate, E., Gris, T., Muratori, S., & Vigo, B. (1990, June). *Attempted suicide and HIV infection: Epidemiological aspects in a psychiatric ward* (Abstract No. S.B. 387). Paper presented at the sixth International Conference on AIDS.

Chapter 2

General Principles of HIV Psychopharmacology

Carlos Almeida and John Sahs

Psychopharmacologic treatment can be crucial to the well-being of a person living with HIV or AIDS. As other chapters in this book demonstrate, individuals infected with HIV suffer psychologically, and the clinician must work aggressively to relieve these patients' mental symptoms. Although symptom relief may not be the primary goal of a particular talking therapy, the importance of this focus is clear for some patients, for example, a young woman who recently learned she is HIV positive and whose anxiety is preventing her from making even a first medical appointment to determine her health status or a man who is on eight different HIV-related medications every day and who is becoming lethargic, dysphoric, and isolative. In both of these instances, the quality, and perhaps length, of these patients' lives can be enhanced by effective psychopharmacologic interventions that address their debilitating symptoms.

This chapter discusses the special issues pertaining to psychiatric treatment for patients infected with HIV. First, the authors describe some of the general considerations involved in assessment and referral as well as some factors regarding prescribing for this population as a whole. The various clinical situations in which psychopharmacologic assistance is critical—including depression, anxiety, psychosis, dementia, and delirium—are then presented in more detail.

GENERAL CONSIDERATIONS

Recommending a psychiatric consultation invariably requires much thought and discussion—by the referring clinician, the patient, and the psychiatrist. This

31

dialogue is even more necessary when the patient is HIV positive. Not only must the clinician evaluate the symptoms in the usual manner to determine whether a psychological approach should be attempted first, but he or she must also decide whether the clinical picture may require evaluation for a physical (organic) cause that needs rapid intervention. The single most important element of a patient's history when considering organicity is the time course: Did the mental symptoms begin after a change in medical status or medications, did they begin simultaneously with new physical symptoms like fever, or are these problems unrelated temporally? Any uncertainty of this sort should trigger a psychiatrist's involvement. A psychiatrist is best suited to address the complex issues involved in evaluating these patients. Although the patient may prefer not to see one more doctor, the issues of AIDS psychopharmacotherapy are always complex, and the patient's primary medical caregiver may not be equipped to address these concerns adequately.

Even absent the concern that a patient's mental symptoms are caused by a treatable central nervous system (CNS) disease, a skilled psychiatrist's expertise in detangling the physiological and psychological issues to determine diagnosis and treatment plan is crucial and usually not feasible for the harried primary care provider. In addition, successful psychopharmacologic treatment for HIV-positive patients requires heightened scrutiny of adverse effects and extensive experience with a variety of psychotropic options. A young gay man with AIDS who was quite depressed had been treated with a standard antidepressant regimen (fluoxetine [Prozac] 20 mg) by his infectious disease physician without success; he was referred for consultation, and his symptoms fit a pattern that the HIV psychiatrist recognized and that was relieved by combining two different antidepressants at lower than usual doses (fluoxetine 10 mg and desipramine 50 mg) to minimize the side effects he was experiencing and achieve a good clinical outcome. This patient was treated medically by a sophisticated and caring doctor; nonetheless, ascertaining which of this patient's difficulties were related to his recent bereavement, which were related to adverse medication effects, and which were caused by a primary psychiatric disorder and then devising a successful strategy required time and experience that the psychiatrist was able to provide.

Effective psychopharmacologic therapy also requires that nonpsychiatric mental health providers address patients' resistances: Not only may patients dislike seeing another physician, they may also abhor taking yet another medication. Active confrontation of these resistances must be integral in the ongoing psychotherapy of these patients, who can be at great risk of noncompliance to their medication regimens even after they have agreed to them. It is useful for therapists to periodically question clients directly about the psychotropic medication and to listen for any indication that compliance is an issue. Therapists should not take the position of "policing" patients' adherence to prescriptions, but therapists are in the ideal position to explore patients' behavior and to help patients to understand their choices.

FOR THE PSYCHIATRIST

Psychiatric assessment and treatment decisions for patients infected with HIV are difficult. As mentioned, ruling out treatable CNS causes of the mental symptoms is vital. To accomplish this task, one must consider medical indicators, in addition to examining the course of illness: The likelihood of serious CNS opportunistic infections rises considerably when a patient's CD4 lymphocyte count is below approximately 100 per µl, but such infections can occur earlier in the illness as well. A threshold for viral load (viral DNA, polymerase chain reaction) has not been established, but high levels can safely be considered an indicator of poorer health and increased likelihood of CNS infections. In addition to constitutional signs like fevers, neurological symptoms must be vigorously sought out; organic mental syndromes related to HIV itself can cause changes in mood, personality, and cognitive and motor functions. In general, where a patient fits on the spectrum from early asymptomatic HIV infection to full-blown AIDS helps determine how one treats that patient psychiatrically. Early in HIV infection, diagnosis and treatment decisions are more similar to those for uninfected individuals; as the illness progresses, the considerations discussed in this chapter become increasingly important.

In addition to diagnosing CNS involvement that requires further medical evaluation, psychiatrists must use all of their diagnostic acumen. Learning patients' mental histories before they were infected with HIV can be extremely helpful; often this requires speaking with other clinicians or family members to define the often confusing time course of symptoms and other changes in patients' status. The gay man mentioned above who benefited from the combination of fluoxetine and desipramine had an elaborate history to unravel. He was quite despondent and hopeless and described himself as never happy; his lover of 4 years had died 4 months before the consultation, after being debilitated for nearly a year. The patient had been told that his CD4 count had dropped below 200 per µl, so he had begun zidovudine (AZT) treatment several weeks before; shortly thereafter, his internist had added the fluoxetine. The psychiatrist was able to determine that the patient had not been chronically depressed; his sister had clearly noted a change in his mood beginning shortly before the lover's death and escalating since beginning the AZT, and a rapid decline to the hopeless state in which the patient presented had accompanied the Prozac prescription, which had caused serious nausea and anxiety. Clearly, obtaining an exhaustive and precise history was essential, as was devising a treatment that the patient could tolerate. With the proper psychopharmacologic treatment, the patient's condition improved significantly.

Compliance for a patient already on many medications can be enhanced not only by the therapist's interventions but also by extensive discussion with the patient by the psychiatrist regarding concerns about taking another medication and about side effects and drug interactions, as well as by choosing the simplest effective regimen (once per day dosing, for example). A woman with asymptomatic

HIV infection, but with mixed anxiety and depressive symptoms as she contemplated the future for her two young children, had been prescribed paroxetine (Paxil) by a psychiatrist. This medication frequently causes no side effects, so there was little discussion of the potential consequences; the patient, however, experienced serious sedation and spent several days panicked, convinced that HIV had begun its progressive destruction of her faculties. This treatment caused the patient distress rather than relief because there was inadequate conversation about the medication.

Finally, because HIV-infected patients are more susceptible to side effects from psychotropics, even early in HIV infection, it is necessary to begin treatment with lower dosages and to increase dosages more slowly than in the general population. Rationale for this strategy comes from the clear evidence that HIV invades the CNS within days of infection (Davis et al., 1992; Levy et al., 1985), which may explain the exquisite sensitivity these patients have to psychiatric medications. In addition, because patients who have progressed along the spectrum of HIV illness are likely to be on several medications to slow the progress of the virus and as prophylaxis against specific opportunistic infections, concerns about drug interactions must always be considered seriously. Experience proves that these problems can be avoided by following the low-dose, slow-titration guidelines. Questions frequently arise regarding the liver enzyme system known as cytochrome P450, as this group of enzymes is important in the metabolism of commonly prescribed psychiatric medications (including the serotonin agents like Prozac) as well as many of the drugs regularly prescribed to fight HIV (especially the protease inhibitors like ritonavir). If a patient is taking more than one medication that is metabolized by these enzymes, the serum level of either could be elevated at a typical dose; whether this will happen, and which drug will accumulate, is unpredictable. Because the occurrence of this phenomenon is theoretical and unforeseeable, it is not generally advisable to change medication strategies initially. Instead, if a patient is on a dose of a psychotropic that is helpful and a potentially interactive HIV medication is then added, the patient should be monitored carefully for excess side effects from either medicine, and if these occur, the dose of the psychiatric drug should be reduced. If the patient is still unable to tolerate the full dose of HIV medication, then it is time to consider changing to a different psychotropic that does not depend on the cytochrome P450 system.

DEPRESSION

Dysphoria, or depressed mood, is an affective state common to all humans and seen often in people with HIV. This section distinguishes states of dysphoria from major depression and culminates in a discussion of various treatment modalities.

A major depressive episode, as defined by the *Diagnostic and Statistical Manual of Mental Disorders* (4th ed., or *DSM–IV;* American Psychiatric Association, 1994), consists of a constellation of symptoms, including depressed mood; anhedonia, or a loss of the ability to experience pleasure; weight change; insomnia or hypersomnia; psychomotor agitation or retardation; fatigue, or loss of energy; feelings of worthlessness or guilt; decreased ability to think or concentrate; recurrent thoughts of death; or suicidal ideation. To make a diagnosis of major depression, the patient must have at least five of the aforementioned symptoms present for at least 2 weeks, with depressed mood, anhedonia, or both. Also, these symptoms must represent a change from the individual's previous level of functioning and must cause clinically significant distress.

Although one must always consider the presence of a major depressive episode, other conditions may also produce depressed mood. Adjustment disorder with depressed mood is commonly seen during periods of uncertainty, or transition, in HIV-positive patients: converting to seropositive status, becoming symptomatic, receiving the first AIDS-defining diagnosis, and being hospitalized for the first time. Also, loss of loved ones may produce a state of bereavement that mimics a major depressive episode. Further, dementia or advanced systemic medical illness can produce apathy, fatigue, and anergia similar to that seen in major depression. Other causes of mood change must also be considered, including substance abuse and adverse effects of medications used in the treatment of HIV. Some frequently implicated agents include alcohol, cocaine, marijuana, co-trimoxazole, interferon, isoniazid (INH), steroids, vinblastine, vincristine, and AZT.

Suicidal Ideation

Suicidal ideation should always be taken seriously, especially given that the individual may be facing a chronic and potentially life-threatening condition. It is important to note that an open discussion does not increase the risk of suicide; in fact, there may be a psychotherapeutic benefit in sharing the burden of hopelessness with a skilled and caring therapist. The clinician should maintain a neutral, nonjudgmental, and empathic stance to best assist in this evaluation. In assessing suicidal ideation, one must consider the individual's support systems, coping mechanisms (including past history of suicide gestures or attempts), psychiatric diagnoses, and underlying medical status. Depression, substance use, organic syndromes (such as dementia and delirium), and personality disorders are diagnoses associated with the greatest risk of suicide (Alfonso & Cohen, 1992; Rundell, Kyle, & Brown, 1992). Pivotal in the evaluation of suicidal risk is an assessment of the patient's hopelessness and the acuity or chronicity of the despair (Schneider et al., 1991). In addition, the stage of a patient's illness is an important factor to consider. Suicidal ideation and attempts may be more common early in the illness, as compared with later stages, once the diagnosis of AIDS has been made (McKegney & O'Dowd, 1994). This observation may relate to patients' anxieties and uncertainties about the disease being more overwhelming than what they actually face when confronted with the illness.

Epidemiologic investigation of major depression has revealed a prevalence of 8%–33% of ambulatory patients with HIV who are referred for psychiatric consultation and 5%–15% of patients who are hospitalized for medical conditions (Buhrich & Cooper, 1987; Dilley et al., 1985; Hintz et al., 1990; O'Dowd, Biderman, & McKegney, 1993). One must be cautious not to generalize these data, as most studies have had a selection bias toward educated, middle-class White men and few have included adequate representation of women, minorities, and injection drug users. Studies estimating the suicide rate in the HIV population are quite varied, with the increased suicide risk ranging from 7.4 to 36 times the risk for suicide in the general population (Cote, Biggar, & Donnenberg, 1992; Marzuk et al., 1988). The basis for the wide variance in suicide risk may relate to the timing of the studies; in earlier years, the disease was more stigmatized and life expectancy and availability of effective treatment were less, making the diagnosis more devastating. In addition, the comparison groups in these studies vary. Also, because the individuals affected by the HIV epidemic typically belong to population subgroups (gay men and drug users) whose suicide risk is greater than average even without HIV involvement (Atkinson et al., 1988; Gala et al., 1989; Roy, 1995) and because the risk of suicide is increased in any group diagnosed with chronic, debilitating, or life-threatening illnesses (McKenzie & Popkin, 1987; Whitlock, 1986), attributing the excess suicide rate specifically to HIV is dubious.

Although depression and suicidal ideation are common in this patient population, the diagnosis of major depression is the exception, not the norm. Therefore, the clinician should err on the side of overconsultation for possible medication therapy as treatment in this patient group is generally safe and effective and may greatly enhance the quality of these patients' lives.

Psychopharmacologic Therapies

The selective serotonin reuptake inhibitors include agents such as fluoxetine (Prozac), sertraline (Zoloft), and paroxitene (Paxil); these are often the "first-line" agents used for the treatment of a major depressive episode given their ease of administration (often single day dosing), relatively mild side effect profile, and general safety in those who are medically ill and in overdose. Primary side effects include, but are not limited to, headaches, nausea, diarrhea, tremor, decreased libido, and "activation," which may lead to anxiety and insomnia. Studies on HIV-positive, depressed individuals have shown a range in efficacy of 57% (paroxitene, across spectrum of illness) to 83% (fluoxetine) and 88% (paroxitene, early stages of disease; Rabkin, Rabkin, & Wagner, 1993; Worth et al., 1994).

Tricyclic antidepressants (TCAs), previously the mainstay in the treatment of depression, have been replaced by the newer agents, largely because of the TCAs' less desirable side effect profile. In general, use of tricyclics as the primary treatment of a major depressive episode are reserved for individuals early in the course of their illness and without significant cognitive impairment. The most common side effects are anticholinergic, causing dry mouth, constipation, and potential worsening of organic syndromes such as dementia and delirium; antihistaminergic, causing sedation; and antiadrenergic, causing postural, or orthostatic, hypotension, which may lead to dizziness and falls (Fernandez & Levy, 1991). This last concern is especially relevant to those medically ill with advanced HIV disease, given the possible coexistence of dehydration and autonomic neuropathy that may make unsteady gait more likely and the use of these agents quite hazardous.

Agents such as nortriptyline (Pamelor), desipramine (Norpramine), and imipramine (Tofranil) are examples of TCAs that are generally well tolerated and effective. Trazodone (Desyrel), although not a tricyclic medication, is often used as a primary treatment agent for depression and as an adjuvant for individuals with insomnia (Fernandez & Levy, 1994). Trazodone is a useful choice because it is a sedating compound with limited anticholinergic and cardiotoxic properties.

Psychostimulants have proven effective treatments for major depression in HIV-positive patients; commonly used agents are methylphenidate (Ritalin), dextroamphetamine (Dexedrine), and pemoline (Cylert). Stimulants are especially useful in patients who are medically ill, cognitively impaired, or unable to tolerate conventional antidepressants (White, Christensen, & Singer, 1995). In particular, those patients who show a predominance of apathy, anergy, fatigue, or anorexia may benefit from stimulant therapy. An advantage to these agents is their relatively short half-life and rapid onset of action; responses are often seen within several days. Insomnia is a common side effect, and therefore the latest dose should be at midday. These are controlled substances and should be prescribed judiciously with a special awareness of the potential for abuse, particularly by patients with a prior history of psychoactive substance abuse.

Although there is little literature on the use of electro-convulsive therapy as a treatment modality for the HIV-positive patient, there are several case reports of effective use in some patients (Schaerf et al., 1989). One must be cautious in recommending this form of treatment for those patients with baseline cognitive impairment as this is often exacerbated during the course of therapy.

Roberto was a 38-year-old homosexual man who was referred by his psychologist for psychiatric consultation to evaluate the need for antidepressant medication. He was a partner in his law firm, living alone with few significant interpersonal relationships. Roberto had sought psychotherapy approximately 1 month after testing HIV positive to help him deal with the reaction to his diagnosis. He initially reported feeling down, having frequent bouts of tears and some difficulty sleeping; he periodically considered life not worth living and contemplated an overdose, but adamantly denied any intention to act on these thoughts.

As psychotherapy progressed, the patient noticed some resolution of his symptoms; he reported feeling a little better, with decreased tearfulness and resolution of his suicidal ideation. Although he remained functional at work and consistently attended his therapy appointments, he had persistent insomnia, and he reported feeling less energetic and more withdrawn with a diminished interest in his usual hobbies. His friends reported him as not being his usual self.

Roberto had no prior psychiatric history, and he was medically healthy, without problems besides the positive HIV antibody test. His CD4 count was above 800 per μl.

Roberto was diagnosed with a major depressive episode; although his initial symptoms had diminished, making the first impression adjustment disorder, the persistence of some of his depressive symptoms made the proper diagnosis major depression. Although his dysphoria was quite understandable as a reaction to the HIV diagnosis, his persistent decrement in personal function was a prominent feature of his presentation on consult.

Antidepressant medication was recommended, and Roberto requested a trial of Prozac because several of his friends had had a good response to it. He was started on 20 mg of Prozac each morning; after the first dose, he reported loose bowel movements, but this effect resolved after several days. He also reported increased anxiety and often felt jittery; his insomnia worsened as well.

At the recommendation of the psychiatrist, Prozac was stopped after the second week of treatment. Roberto was started on nortriptyline (Pamelor), chosen because of its sedative properties and its relatively mild anticholinergic effects. After medical clearance by his internist (including a normal electrocardiogram), he began taking 50 mg of Pamelor at bedtime; the dosage was then increased to 125 mg per day. He immediately noticed improved sleep, and after several weeks noticed improvement in his mood and increased interest in going out with friends and participating in his hobbies. The TCA was helpful in returning Roberto to his previous level of functioning.

Roberto's history provides a useful example of a typical pharmacologic treatment of major depression in a person infected by HIV. As mentioned earlier, few factors distinguish Roberto's case from that of someone who is not infected with HIV because his diagnosis and treatment were determined when he was still medically asymptomatic. As individuals become sicker, greater attention would need to be paid, for instance, to issues of side effects and drug interactions. A patient with full-blown AIDS might not tolerate these standard doses of medication, and the psychiatrist would be prudent to begin the Prozac at, for example, 10, or even 5, mg per day. In summary, the presence of depressive symptoms in the HIV population is extremely high. Clinicians must be cautious, though, to carefully assess the severity of these symptoms rather than to see sadness as an expected and common response to the many losses an HIV diagnosis routinely brings. If the patient is significantly impaired by the depression, consultation with a psychiatrist must be sought as these patients' suffering can be relieved safely and effectively.

ANXIETY

In modern culture, anxiety about HIV is virtually ubiquitous, and understandable, based on the potential threat to life and well-being if one is infected. This does not mean, however, that all people suffer from anxiety about AIDS. Anxiety disorders in the HIV population are quite varied, ranging from short-term adjustment disorders precipitated by health events to more debilitating states such as panic disorder, posttraumatic stress disorder, or obsessive–compulsive disorder. Symptoms of anxiety may include excessive worry, fear, and preoccupation with the stressor or generalized anxiety without a clear conscious precipitant. Accompanying these symptoms may be a cadre of physical symptoms such as tremor, diaphoresis, palpitations, dyspnea, nausea, and diarrhea.

There is a significant patient population, described as the "worried well," who suffer from anxiety about AIDS, although medical evidence does not support their concern. These patients suffer from intense preoccupation with somatic concerns or worries about seroconversion, despite medical evidence and reassurance to the contrary. These symptoms may represent a type of phobia, or they may be a manifestation of an underlying obsessive–compulsive disorder, major depression, delusional disorder, or factitious disorder (Miller, Acton, & Hedge, 1988).

In the evaluation of anxiety states, it is important to rule out nonpsychiatric causes of the anxiety, ranging from medical conditions to medications themselves. Early manifestations of cognitive decline (as seen in AIDS dementia complex) may result in a defensive anxiety; pulmonary disorders may result in hypoxia and resultant anxiety; pentamidine, used in the prophylaxis of *Pneumocystis carinii* pneumonia (PCP) may induce hypoglycemia and therefore mimic anxiety states. Other medications often implicated in anxiety include acyclovir, gancyclovir, INH, vincristine, and AZT.

Pharmacologic management of anxiety is usually limited to the conventional agents: benzodiazepines and antidepressants. Benzodiazepines are indicated for the short-term treatment of anxiety following an acute event. The best agents are intermediate acting ones with few active metabolites, for example, alprazolam (Xanax) and lorazepam (Ativan). One should always be cautious of the potential for abuse and dependence with these medications, especially in cognitively impaired persons who may forget having taken medication and therefore "pill pop"; also of concern are individuals who have prior histories of substance abuse disorders. Psychiatrists have often chosen benzodiazepines more readily for their HIV patients than for medically well patients; the favorable side effect profile, lack of drug interactions, and short half-lives make these drugs ideal for someone who is seriously ill.

Antidepressants such as fluoxetine (Prozac), sertraline (Zoloft), and paroxetine (Paxil), used in low doses, are often quite effective in treating anxiety and helping patients feel more relaxed and calmer. It is unclear whether in these instances the manifest anxiety is a symptom of an underlying depressive or obsessive–compulsive disorder. Trazodone (Deseryl) has also been shown to be effective in the treatment of anxiety on the basis of its sedative properties; it is often used in lower, divided doses of from 25 to 200 mg/day. Tricyclics can be used similarly with good results.

Lisa was a 23-year-old secretary who sought psychiatric consultation at the recommendation of her primary physician. Approximately 18 months earlier, she had learned that a former boyfriend had been diagnosed HIV positive; although she generally practiced safe sex, there had been occasions of unprotected intercourse with this man. She had been sexually abstinent subsequent to this relationship's ending.

On learning about her former lover, Lisa had had a physical examination and HIV antibody test, both of which were negative. Although she was initially reassured, she presented to her physician 1 month later, concerned about a "lesion" on her leg. She was convinced the blemish was Kaposi's sarcoma, despite assurance by her physician that it was a bruise. She returned several times over the next 6 months with persistent fears that she had AIDS; a repeat HIV test (also negative) reassured her only temporarily.

During the psychiatric consultation, she appeared quite anxious while discussing her fear about developing AIDS, which she recognized was not rational. There was no evidence of psychotic symptoms, overt neurovegetative symptoms of depression, or symptoms of panic disorder. Her primary concern was the persistent, generalized fear of having an HIV infection that had just not been diagnosed yet. These preoccupations interfered with her functioning in many respects: She was inattentive at work, took longer to complete tasks, would not even respond to dating invitations, and incessantly thought about her health.

Lisa was diagnosed with obsessive–compulsive disorder owing to her specific intrusive fear of having AIDS, making her an extreme case of the worried well. Lisa was begun on 10 mg of Prozac per day and tolerated the medication well, without side effects. After 3 weeks on Prozac, she noted a marked diminution in her level of anxiety and had few ruminations about HIV.

As with depression, anxiety is an exceedingly common symptom in those affected by HIV. The case example above describes the successful treatment of an entity mental health practitioners see frequently. HIV-positive patients may also suffer from debilitating anxiety related to concerns about their health and future. Usually, a brief period of psychotherapy should be attempted to relieve this symptom before deciding that medication would be helpful. However, the burden of anxiety can tax a patient's ability to function, and due consideration must be given to the option of psychopharmacologic treatment. As with depression, impairment in life functions directly caused by the emotional symptom must be the primary criterion in deciding whether to provide relief with medications. However, a dangerous stance toward anxiety with HIV-positive patients must be avoided: Clinicians sometimes fear anxiety of any severity is harmful for these individuals because there could be damage to the immune system. These fears are wholly unfounded on the basis of the literature available (Gorman & Kertzner, 1990; Sahs et al., 1994). Moreover, to encourage, even implicitly, a patient's belief that his or her every mood can enhance or diminish his or her health can be extremely detrimental, especially since HIV's progressive destruction is essentially guaranteed. Therefore, a balanced approach that explores a patient's fears about the unpredictable and uncontrollable nature of illness while monitoring for pathological anxiety states is the optimal procedure.

PSYCHOSIS AND MANIA

More than any other clinical syndrome, psychosis in an HIV-positive patient, particularly in someone with no previous history of delusions or hallucinations, must be considered organic until proven otherwise. Cryptococcal meningitis and dementia are examples of physiologic insults that can manifest as psychosis in patients with AIDS. Other common causes to consider for a new-onset psychotic disorder are cocaine or other substance abuse, major depression or mania with psychotic features, and reactive psychosis (currently known as psychotic disorder not otherwise specified, in *DSM–IV* nomenclature). Even with these many possible diagnoses for psychotic symptoms, the high likelihood of CNS pathology manifesting as psychosis makes a neurological evaluation virtually mandatory. Unfortunately, though, after completing a medical evaluation, the diagnosis is often HIV encephalopathy, and the symptoms remain. In addition to encouraging patients and the primary care doctor to pursue aggressive antiviral treatments that can help somewhat, the psychiatrist must treat the residual psychosis regardless of its cause. This treatment can be limited by side effects. HIV-positive patients are exquisitely susceptible to extrapyramidal symptoms, which include the typical Parkinsonian stiffness as well as the distressing motor restlessness known as akathesia, making high potency agents like haloperidol (Haldol) problematic; anticholinergic effects can worsen candidiases by drying mucous membranes or can exacerbate cognitive difficulties by affecting the CNS, making low potency drugs like chlorpromazine (Thorazine) troublesome. Limited data (Singh & Catalan, 1994) and our experience have suggested that low-dose risperidone (less than 3 mg per day) can be an effective solution, but if traditional antipsychotics are chosen, the low-dose, slow-titration warnings must be followed assiduously.

Although psychosis is notorious for being the harbinger of acute CNS disorders like cryptococcal meningitis, the most common clinical scenario for psychosis in HIV is in patients with a moderate to severe dementia. Treating the psychotic symptoms (typically paranoid delusions) of demented patients is difficult, whether in elderly persons or in AIDS patients. A young man with AIDS had become demented rapidly, progressing from full-time employment at the post office to being disoriented, delusional, and agitated. He was off all antiviral treatments because of severe anemia, and he had a normal medical evaluation. His paranoia focused on the belief that his home attendant was poisoning him. The psychosis remitted on 1 mg of risperidone per day. His therapy then centered on providing supports in his environment and ultimately enrolling him in a day treatment program for AIDS patients where he did quite well.

Mania occurs in AIDS patients far more frequently than in the general population (Lyketsos et al., 1993). The pathogenesis of this finding is unclear, but in general the syndrome occurs late in the course of illness (after AIDS diagnosis, with CD4 less than 100 per μl, usually associated with cognitive decline or dementia) for patients without a personal or family history of mood disorder. In those patients with a bipolar diathesis, though, expression of the hidden syndrome seems to be triggered by HIV infection itself, unrelated to stage of illness. Furthermore, specific HIV medications like AZT and ddI and some opportunistic infections like cryptococcosis have been associated with manic episodes. As with psychosis, the clinician must consider other etiologies such as drug and alcohol abuse as well HIV-related causes. Once a treatable source such as an acute CNS infection has been ruled out, treatment must proceed, whether the patient is merely HIV positive and has a history of hypomania (for instance) or whether the patient has a CD4 count of 12 per μl, is on multiple antivirals, and is demented. No reliable studies have determined a preferable treatment strategy for mood stabilization in patients with AIDS. Some psychiatrists oppose lithium because of its renal toxicity in patients whose kidneys are already compromised by their immune disease; others oppose anticonvulsants because of the risk of hematologic toxicities in patients with debilitated bone marrow responsiveness. The wise course is to weigh these concerns along with the side effect profile of a medication and determine the best choice for a given patient; mania in these patients is then quite treatable, and effective prophylaxis can also be successful.

> Gloria, a 42-year-old Black woman, had known she was HIV positive for 3 years when she developed manic psychosis. Gloria had been addicted to heroin and then cocaine for much of her adult life and had always expected an early death. She learned she was HIV positive during a hospitalization for PCP, and her fatalistic attitude changed: She stopped using drugs, she became a counselor in a 12-step program, she attended medical appointments and was taking AZT, and she began seeking custody of one of her children in foster care. She was doing well until her physician detected an increase in the marker for cytomegalovirus (CMV) in her blood. Gloria became frightened of losing her vision, and the anxiety led her to seek psychotherapy in the clinic. Three months later, her doctor noted that Gloria's CD4 count had dropped, and he added ddI to the AZT. One month later, Gloria was diagnosed with CMV retinitis, and she began suffering symptoms of mania almost simultaneously: She was sleeping fewer than 4 hours per night, she had a steep resurgence in her craving for illicit drugs, she had several episodes of irrational and irresponsible behavior with money and sex, and when she came to therapy sessions, she was late, disorganized, pressured, and nearly delusional.
>
> Gloria's therapist referred her for psychiatric consultation. At this point, Gloria was taking the following medications: AZT, ddI, oral gancyclovir, acyclovir, trimethoprim-sulfamethoxazole (Bactrim), and vitamins. She had no family or personal history of mania. Her cognitive exam was essentially normal; she had had a normal head computed tomography (CT) scan 1 month earlier when she was diagnosed with the retinitis. Was Gloria's mania secondary to medications? Was it related to an undiagnosed brain infection? Were the symptoms a defense against the profound loss and depression she faced in contemplating blindness? Was this syndrome a manifestation of HIV's progression in her brain?

Because Gloria was at risk for serious infections given the level of her immunosuppression, we considered scheduling further diagnostic tests. After consultation with Gloria's primary care physician and a neurologist, a lumbar puncture was postponed until after a trial wherein her antiviral regimen was changed by her infectious disease physician. (She had no fever and no focal neurological signs of a brain lesion to warrant urgent tests.) The ddI was discontinued, and Gloria's symptoms began to wane. Two weeks later, she was able to discuss her mental state with insight and resumed her work in psychotherapy with renewed vigor as she realistically faced the short time she probably had to achieve her goals.

As this case illustrates, the medications prescribed to fight HIV and its sequelae can have significant psychiatric effects. Discontinuing the offending agent, the nucleoside analog ddI in this example, caused the manic symptoms to remit. Luckily, there are other antiretroviral treatment options, so this medication could be safely changed to another without substantially jeopardizing the patient's health. In many instances, the psychiatric side effects must be balanced against the benefits from a medication that has no alternative; often the treatment team and patient instead choose to manage the psychiatric symptom while maintaining the medication that is causing it. In addition, some patients may experience the onset of a mental syndrome that is conclusively linked to the introduction of a new medication and then have the symptoms persist even after cessation of the medication. One hypothesis regarding this phenomenon, for mania in particular, is that the physiologic state that induced the symptom actually unmasked an underlying propensity for mania. These patients are best treated with mood stabilizers as though the mania had occurred independent of any medications.

When psychosis or mania appears in a previously stable individual with HIV, physiological causes must be pursued with diligence. Active consultation with the patient's medical provider is essential to determine the appropriate work-up. Once treatable neurologic and systemic pathology have been ruled out, the treatment should proceed cautiously to minimize the adverse effects commonly encountered with the powerful psychotropic agents used to treat these syndromes.

DEMENTIA AND DELIRIUM

AIDS dementia complex (ADC) is a clinical syndrome comprised of behavioral, motor and cognitive changes. Formerly called AIDS dementia, ADC has many synonyms, including HIV-1 associated dementia, HIV/AIDS encephalopathy, or dementia due to HIV disorder (according to the *DSM–IV*; American Psychiatric Association, 1994; Navia, Jordan, & Price, 1986; Wallack, Bialer, & Prenzlauer, 1995). An additional syndrome, HIV-1–associated minor cognitive/motor disorder, is recognized earlier in the course of HIV infection and usually causes minimal clinical impairment. This syndrome occurs in about 67% of all patients with HIV, and in 10% of patients, it is the initial AIDS-defining illness (Fauci & Lane, 1994).

Patients may present with a wide array of clinical signs and symptoms: (a) behavioral, with early changes including apathy, withdrawal, fatigue, and "depression" and late changes including blank stare, disinhibition, organic psychosis, and agitation, (b) cognitive, with early changes including memory loss (names, historical details, appointments), decreased concentration (losing track of conversation or reading), mental slowing (being less verbal, not as quick) and late changes including distractibility, confusion, and disorientation; and (c) motoric, with early changes including tremor, loss of coordination (especially hand–eye and visuospatial), and impaired handwriting and later changes including weakness, especially in the legs, pyramidal symptoms and generalized slowing (Worley & Price, 1992).

Staging of dementia is complicated, and no one set of criteria has been chosen as superior. In general, an emphasis on the individual's ability to per-

Table 1   Clinical Staging of the AIDS Dementia Complex

Stage	Description
Stage 0 (normal)	Normal mental and motor function.
Stage 0.5 (equivocal/subclinical)	Absent, minimal, or equivocal symptoms without impairment of work or capacity to perform activities of daily living (ADL). Mild signs (snout response, slowed ocular or extremity movements) may be present. Gait and strength are normal.
Stage 1 (mild)	Able to perform all but the more demanding aspects of work or ADL but with unequivocal evidence (signs or symptoms that may include performance on neuropsychological testing) of functional intellectual or motor impairment. Can walk without assistance.
Stage 2 (moderate)	Able to perform basic activities of self-care but cannot work or maintain the more demanding aspects of daily life. Ambulatory, but may require a single prop.
Stage 3 (severe)	Major intellectual incapacity (cannot follow news or personal events, cannot sustain complex conversation, considerable slowing of all output) or motor disability (cannot walk unassisted, usually with slowing and clumsiness of arms as well).
Stage 4 (end stage)	Nearly vegetative. Intellectual and social comprehension and output are at a rudimentary level. Nearly or absolutely mute. Paraparetic or paraplegic with urinary and fecal incontinence.

Note. From "AIDS and Related Disorders" by A. Fauci and H. Lane, in *Harrison's Principles of Internal Medicine* (Vol. 2, 13th ed.), by Iffelbacher, Braunwald, et al. (Eds.), 1994, p. 1590. Copyright 1994 by McGraw Hill. Adapted with permission.

form useful daily functions is probably most useful clinically. See Table 1 for a summary of some rating schema currently in use.

The diagnosis of ADC is one of exclusion and is assisted by CT scan or magnetic resonance imaging, which often reveal cerebral atrophy. Specific treatment is equivocal; AZT in high doses may be of benefit in slowing the progression and, in some cases, in reversing prior decline (Gray et al., 1994). The principles of psychopharmacologic management are similar to those that are described for the delirious patient.

Delirium is an acute CNS process with an underlying medical etiology, as opposed to a functional or primary psychiatric disorder. The possible causes are varied, as listed in Table 2, including CNS infections, metabolic abnormalities, and drug intoxication (including both psychoactive and other prescribed substances). Delirium is quite common in hospitalized patients with advanced systemic disease. Key features in delirium include acute or subacute onset of symptoms, a waxing and waning of the patient's sensorium characterized by

Table 2   Potential Causes of Altered Mental States

Alcohol or drug withdrawal
  Alcohol
  Opiates
  Sedative hypnotics
Disorders of fluid, electrolyte, and acid–base balance
  Water intoxification, dehydration, hypernatremia, hypokalemia, hypocalcemia,
    hypercalcemia, alkalosis, and acidosis
  Endocrine disorders
Hypoglycemia
Infections
  Systemic: Bacteremia, septicemia, subacute bacterial endocarditis, pneumonia,
    Pneumocystis carinii pneumonia, cryptococcal pneumonia, herpes zoster,
    disseminated *Mycobacterium avium intracellularae*, disseminated candidiasis
  Intracranial: Cryptococcal meningitis, HIV encephalitis, tuberculous meningitis,
    toxoplasmosis
Epilepsy
Head trauma
Space-occupying lesions of brain: Central nervous system lymphoma,
    toxoplasmosis, cytomegalovirus infection, abscesses
Blood: Anemia
Intoxication
  Drugs: Antibiotics, anticonvulsants, sedative hypnotics, opiates, phencyclidine,
    antineoplastic drugs, anticholinergic agents, cocaine
  Alcohol
Metabolic encephalopathies
  Hypoxia
  Hepatic, renal, pulmonary, pancreatic insufficiency

Note. From "Management of Neuropsychiatric Disorders in HIV-Spectrum Patients" by J. Dilley, in *The Medical Management of AIDS*, by M. Sande and P. Volberding (Eds.), 1992, p. 224. Copyright 1992 by W. B. Saunders. Adapted with permission.

disorientation, visual or tactile hallucinations, and inattention or decreased concentration. There is no specific treatment for delirium, other than to address the underlying medical condition.

Psychiatrists are frequently called to assist in behavioral management and to help clarify the diagnosis. Neuroleptics and benzodiazepines are used to assist in agitation; use of either class of drugs warrants caution. Often the best course is to avoid all psychotropic drugs, which may further cloud the sensorium. When necessary, neuroleptics are often the treatment of choice for the agitated, delirious patient; one must, however, be wary of their anticholinergic properties, which can exacerbate cognitive deficits and extrapyramidal side effects like Parkinsonism, making the patient more susceptible to falls. Therefore, low doses of high potency agents (e.g., haloperidol, or Haldol) are commonly preferred. Alternatively, benzodiazepines may be used for the management of behavioral disturbances; low doses of short-acting agents with limited active metabolites (e.g., lorazepam) are favored. Benzodiazepines carry the risk of paradoxical disinhibition wherein an already agitated patient becomes more agitated, rather than calmed, by the tranquilizer; this possibility must be considered in a patient who is difficult to manage.

> Chris was a 50-year-old man who had contracted HIV several years before the consultation, presumably from an infected blood transfusion during a surgical procedure. He had had numerous medical complications over the years, including PCP, CMV colitis, and CNS toxoplasmosis. An accountant in earlier years, Chris was now on permanent medical disability. He was referred for psychiatric consultation by his internist for evaluation of depression. His symptoms included depressed mood, apathy, fatigue, anorexia, decreased concentration, and anhedonia. His internist had started him on amitriptyline several weeks earlier, and he was taking 150 mg at bedtime when first seen. His CD4 count was 60 per μl, and he was on several anti-HIV medications that had not changed for more than 1 year.
>
> Chris was quite frail, with psychomotor retardation. He complained of depression and fatigue. In addition, his wife stated that after taking his Elavil each night, he appeared confused; he frequently had conversations in which he did not make sense and engaged in purposeless behaviors. She had also noted that 6 to 8 months before the depression, he was becoming increasingly forgetful, misplacing objects and forgetting well-known names, dates, and telephone numbers.
>
> Diagnostically, several syndromes were considered, including HIV dementia, pseudodementia (the cognitive deficits that can accompany a primary major depression), delirium, or organic mood disorder due to AZT or another of his medications.
>
> As per the clinical history, it was apparent that this patient's nocturnal disorientation was temporally associated with the Elavil and was likely a delirium secondary to this medication and its anticholinergic effects. The Elavil was discontinued, and after a week these episodes had completely resolved. His depressive symptoms remained, however.
>
> Another consideration was that Chris had a mood disorder induced by one of his medications, like AZT; however, the history indicated that the depressive symptoms developed unrelated to any change in his medication regimen. Further-

more, the patient's internist felt there was little flexibility in changing any of these medications in the HIV treatment of this medically fragile man.

After careful consultation with the internist, we recommended that Chris begin a trial of the psychostimulant methylphenidate. He started taking 5 mg of Ritalin each morning and gradually increased the dose to 10 mg at both breakfast and lunch. His depressive symptoms resolved, and he had more energy and interest in interactions and activities.

His poor concentration and memory persisted, however. Soon he was also noted to be clumsy and unsteady when ambulating. A repeat head CT scan and lumbar puncture were normal. He was diagnosed with HIV-associated dementia in addition to the treated major depressive disorder.

This case illustrates the complex nature of diagnosing depression and detecting delirium in those who are seriously medically ill. As mentioned, cognitive decline can be detected in a majority of patients early in HIV infection; these changes are minimal and usually only discernible with thorough neuropsychological testing. Later in the course of HIV illness, clinically significant losses of motor and cognitive function can accumulate, leading to the diagnosis of dementia when the impairment becomes severe (Fauci & Lane, 1994). Delirium is a crucial diagnosis to eliminate when evaluating any new symptom in a seriously ill patient on a variety of medications. As illustrated above, this task can be difficult, but the rewards can be substantial.

OTHER SPECIAL TOPICS

Substance Abuse

Substance abuse is a particularly important issue when treating the HIV-infected population with psychiatric medications. The percentage of HIV patients who present for psychiatric services who have a psychoactive substance use disorder—past or current—varies from 40% to 50% (O'Dowd et al., 1993; Sahs & Storey, 1994). Clearly, the psychiatrist must ascertain substance use issues carefully to adequately diagnose or treat any patient, and more so with a patient with HIV. The already complex task of constructing a careful time line to assess psychiatric symptoms becomes more difficult when, in addition to medical events and psychosocial stressors, one must include intermittent substance use. The reluctance of patients in recovery from substance dependence to taking mind-altering medications is another intricate problem that requires collaborative solutions among everyone involved; substance abuse counselors, 12-step sponsors, family members, medical providers, therapists, psychiatrists, and patients themselves must be educated regarding the necessity, efficacy, and safety of the prescribed treatment. The psychiatrist must be wary of a reluctance to deem a substance user's symptoms as warranting medical intervention as well as of the difficulty—or ease—of prescribing potentially addictive medications like benzodiazepines. This decision can be perilous regardless of a specific psychiatrist's tendencies: If the doctor is too strict in limiting availability of this useful treatment, he or she may burden a patient with unnecessary side effects by choosing medications that are not addictive when addiction is not the primary concern for a patient who is gravely ill; however, if another doctor freely gives benzodiazepines to any patient with HIV ("they're dying, why not give some comfort?") without adequate attention to the risk for dependence, he or she might overlook the options for long-term solutions that are less risky.

A flexible treatment stance is pivotal in the successful treatment of the HIV-infected person with a history of substance abuse. Traditional concepts such as requiring a patient to be substance free for 6 months before diagnosing or treating a mood disorder may be untenable in this population, who have a shortened life expectancy. In addition, the risk for relapse to chemical abuse is extremely high when one considers the staggering stressful events these patients face due to their illness, prognosis, and family rejection and fears of contagion. Therefore, minor "slips" in recovery should be handled contextually, with the clinician working with the patient to minimize the severity of the relapse and to understand, and find ways to cope with, the stressors in the patient's life.

Pain Management

Pain management is a common concern for HIV-positive patients. The role of the mental health team varies from facilitating patients' communications with medical providers to offering cognitive–behavioral interventions for the pain symptoms to prescribing pain medications directly to providing liaison to the medical team to educate them on adequate pain relief strategies. Studies have indicated that pain is extremely common in HIV infection (Worth & Halman, 1996), so mental health clinicians must at least provide a safe environment for patients to express this and receive support and acknowledgment.

Often, nonpsychiatrist physicians prescribe antidepressant or anxiolytic medications as adjuvant analgesics. Most commonly, low-dose tricyclics are used to relieve the painful lower extremity neuropathy associated with HIV infection. Therapists and psychiatrists must remember to inquire about these medications specifically to assess the impact they have on the patient's well-being, as well as to ensure that any decisions regarding medications prescribed for emotional symptoms account for the psychotropic and adverse effects of the pain medications. This example highlights the importance of the mental health clinician's obtaining a complete and accurate inventory of all ongoing treatments, including prescription and nonprescription drugs, homeopathic and herbal remedies, and physical and spiritual therapies.

Sexual Dysfunction

Sexual dysfunction is another very frequent complaint for this population. Although the psychological causes are obvious and numerous (risk of infectivity, fear about sexuality), the physiologic etiologies are as prevalent: Opportunistic infections as well as a variety of HIV-related and psychiatric medications can cause changes in libido or sexual responsiveness. Complaints of change in sexual functioning must be taken seriously and addressed, ideally through both psychotherapy to address the potential psychological issues and a simultaneous medical evaluation to address the physiological issues. Evidence has indicated that seriously ill men with complaints of mild depressive symptoms, anergia, and decreased libido may have low or low-normal serum testosterone. Replacement therapy with intramuscular testosterone can benefit these men mentally as well as physically by enhancing the appetite and lean muscle mass (Rabkin, Rabkin, & Wagner, 1995). The evaluation of desire dysfunctions or impotence in men should include at least a simple and inexpensive assay of serum testosterone to help direct treatment.

CONCLUSION

Psychopharmacologic intervention for HIV-affected individuals is a crucial treatment modality for this population who are at risk of significant psychological morbidity. The burden that HIV infection imposes (owing to the seriousness of the diagnosis as well as the stigma associated with it) is often just another of many serious risks for psychiatric difficulties that the patients who are most affected by the epidemic already face. The minority, gay male, and drug-using groups most affected have higher rates of psychopathology even without HIV. When the stress of HIV infection as well as the effect of the virus directly on the CNS are added to the already vulnerable mix that is typical of these patients' psyches, the need for active intervention becomes paramount. For all these same reasons, diagnosis is extremely complicated when evaluating this population. Thorough assessment, though, usually can yield sufficient clarity to allow treatment to proceed. The hopeful note is that the wide range of treatment options provides effective, low-risk therapies that can truly enhance these patients' lives.

REFERENCES

Alfonso, C., & Cohen, M. (1992). HIV dementia and suicide. *General Hospital Psychiatry, 16,* 45–46.

American Psychiatric Association. (1994). *Diagnostic and statistical manual of mental disorders* (4th ed.). Washington, DC: Author.

Atkinson, H., Grant, I., Kennedy, C., et al. (1988). Prevalence of psychiatric disorders among men infected with human immunodeficiency virus. *Archives of General Psychiatry, 45,* 859–864.

Buhrich, N., & Cooper, D. A. (1987). Requests for psychiatric consultation concerning 22 patients with AIDS and ARC. *Australia and New Zealand Journal of Psychiatry, 21,* 346–353.

Cote, T., Biggar, R., & Donnenberg, A. (1992). Risk of suicide among persons with AIDS: A national assessment. *JAMA: Journal of the American Medical Association, 268,* 2066–2068.

Davis, L. E., Huelle, B. L., Miller, V. E., et al. (1992). Early viral brain invasion in iatrogenic human immunodeficiency virus infection. *Neurology, 42,* 1736–1739.

Dilley, J. (1992). Management of neuropsychiatric disorders in HIV-spectrum patients. In M. Sande & P. Volberding (Eds.), *The medical management of AIDS* (3rd ed., pp. 218–233). Philadelphia: W. B. Saunders.

Dilley, J. W., Ochitill, H. N., Perl, M., et al. (1985). Findings in psychiatric consultations with patients with AIDS. *American Journal of Psychiatry, 142,* 82–86.

Fauci, A., & Lane, H. (1994). HIV disease: AIDS and related disorders. In K. J. Iffelbacher, E. Braunwald, et al. (Eds.), *Harrison's principles of internal medicine* (Vol. 2, 13th ed., pp. 1566–1618). New York: McGraw-Hill.

Fernandez, F., & Levy, J. (1991). Psychopharmacotherapy of psychiatric syndromes in asymptomatic and symptomatic HIV infection. *Psychiatric Medicine, 9,* 377–394.

Fernandez, F., & Levy, J. (1994). Psychopharmacology in HIV spectrum disorders. *Psychiatric Clinics of North America, 17,* 135–148.

Gala, C., Martini, S., Pergami, A., et al. (1989). Psychiatric history among homosexuals and drug-addicts infected with human immunodeficiency virus [abstract]. *Fifth International Conference on AIDS,* 387.

Gorman, J. M., & Kertzner, R. (1990). Psychoneuroimmunology and HIV infection. *Journal of Neuropsychiatry, 2,* 241–252.

Gray, F., Belec, L., Keohane, C., et al. (1994). Zidovudine therapy and HIV encephalitis: A 10 year neuropathological survey. *AIDS, 8,* 489–493.

Hintz, S., Kuck, J., Peterkin, J., et al. (1990). Depression in the context of HIV infection: Implications for treatment. *Journal of Clinical Psychiatry, 51,* 497–501.

Levy, J. A., Shimbakuro, J., Hollander, H., et al. (1985). Isolation of AIDS associated retroviruses from cerebrospinal fluid and brain of patients with neurological symptoms. *Lancet 2,* 586–588.

Lyketsos, C., Hanson, A., Fishman, M., et al. (1993). Manic syndrome early and late in the course of HIV. *American Journal of Psychiatry, 150,* 326–327.

Marzuk, P., Tierney, H., Tardiff, K., et al. (1988). Increased risk of suicidality in persons with AIDS. *JAMA: Journal of the American Medical Association, 259,* 1333–1337.

McKegney, F., & O'Dowd, M. (1994). HIV dementia and suicide. *General Hospital Psychiatry, 16,* 45–46.

McKenzie, T. B., & Popkin, M. K. (1987). Suicide in the medical patient. *International Journal of Psychiatric Medicine, 17,* 1–22.

Miller, D., Acton, T., & Hedge, E. (1988). The worried well: Their identification and management. *Journal of the Royal College of Physicians, London, 22,* 158–165.

Navia, B. A., Jordan, B. D., & Price, R. W. (1986). The AIDS dementia complex. *Annals of Neurology, 19,* 517–524.

O'Dowd, M.A., Biderman, D. J., & McKegney, F. P. (1993). Incidence of suicidality in AIDS and HIV+ patients attending a psychiatry outpatient program. *Psychosomatics, 34,* 33–40.

Rabkin, J. G., Rabkin, R., & Wagner, G. (1993). Effect of fluoxetine on mood and immune status in depressed patients with HIV illness. *Journal of Clinical Psychiatry, 55,* 92–97.

Rabkin, J. G. , Rabkin, R., & Wagner, G. (1995). Testosterone replacement in HIV illness. *General Hospital Psychiatry, 17,* 37–42.

Roy, A. (1995). Suicide. In H. Kaplan & B. Sadock (Eds.), *Comprehensive textbook of psychiatry VI* (Vol. 2, pp. 1739–1752). Baltimore: Williams & Wilkins.

Rundell, J., Kyle, K., & Brown, G. (1992). Risk factors for suicide attempts in a human immunodeficiency virus screening program. *Psychosomatics, 33,* 24–27.

Sahs, J. A., Goetz, R., & Reddy, M. (1994). Psychological distress and natural killer cells in gay men with and without HIV infection. *American Journal of Psychiatry, 151,* 1479–1484.

Sahs, J. A., & Storey, J. E. (1994, November). *An HIV mental health clinic.* Presented at Arden House Annual Scientific Conference, Department of Psychiatry, College of Physicians & Surgeons of Columbia University, New York.

Schaerf, F., Miller, R., Lipsey, J., et al. (1989). ECT for major depression in four patients infected with HIV. *American Journal of Psychiatry, 146,* 782–784.

Schneider, S. G., Shelley, E. T., Kemeny, M. E., et al. (1991). AIDS-related factors predictive of suicidal ideation of low and high intent among gay and bisexual men. *Suicide and Life-Threatening Behavior, 21,* 313–328.

Singh, A., & Catalan, J. (1994). Risperidone in HIV related manic psychotics [letter]. *Lancet, 344,* 1029–1030.

Wallack, J., Bialer, P., & Prenzlauer, S. (1995). Psychiatric aspects of HIV infection and AIDS. In A. Stoudemire & B. Fogel (Eds.), *Medical-psychiatric practice* (Vol. 3). Washington, DC: American Psychiatric Press.

White, J., Christensen, J., & Singer, C (1995). Methylphenidate in the treatment of neurobehavioral slowing associated with cancer and cancer treatment. *Journal of Neuropsychiatry and Clinical Neuroscience, 7,* 347–349.

Whitlock, F. A. (1986). Suicide and physical illness. In R. Baltimore (Ed.), *Suicide.* New York: Williams & Wilkins.

Worley, J., & Price, R. (1992). Management of neurologic complication of HIV-1 infection and AIDS. In M. Sande & P. Volberding (Eds.), *The medical management of AIDS.* Philadelphia: W. B. Saunders.

Worth, J., & Halman, M. (1996). HIV disease/AIDS. In J. Rundell & J. Wise (Eds.), *Textbook of consultation-liaison psychiatry* (1st ed.). Washington, DC: American Psychiatric Press.

Worth, J. L., Halman, M. H., & Hamburg, N. M. (1994, May). Clinical efficacy of paroxetine in HIV/AIDS patients. In *New research program and abstracts: American Psychiatric Association 150th Annual Meeting.* Washington, DC: American Psychiatric Association.

Chapter 3

Understanding Neuropsychiatric and Psychological Symptoms in the Context of HIV Illness

John Budin

In the early years of the HIV pandemic, patients were noted to present with a wide variety of neuropsychiatric symptoms. There were reports that patients with HIV infection evidenced mood disturbances, impairments in cognition, and alterations in behavior (Levy & Bredesen, 1988; Levy, Rosenbloom, & Perett, 1986; Snider et al., 1983). There seemed to be many possible underlying and interrelated causes for these symptoms, including medical illness, neurological disease, psychiatric disorders, and psychological distress. Mental health assessments of these patients were difficult because the symptoms could be attributed to many different, yet interdependent, etiologies.

Today, clinicians continue to be confused about the cause of the HIV-related "mental health" symptoms seen in their patients and are also uncertain about how the complex interactions between medical, neurological, psychiatric, and psychological factors affect symptom expression. The purpose of this chapter is to provide an understanding of how these factors affect the expression of the mental health–related symptoms seen in HIV illness. On the basis of this understanding, basic principles useful in guiding the mental health assessment of patients with HIV are offered.

UNDERSTANDING THE NEUROLOGICAL SUBSTRATE UNDERLYING HIV-RELATED CENTRAL NERVOUS SYSTEM DISEASE

History

In the early 1980s, it was becoming evident that the central nervous system (CNS) was susceptible to a host of opportunistic infections and malignancies (Perry & Jacobsen, 1986; Pitlik et al., 1983). Though the mechanism of this CNS invasion was unclear, the number of case reports indicating such involvement continued to increase. Over time, there began to appear reports, though, of patients without any such demonstrable CNS pathology who nonetheless evidenced neuropsychiatric symptoms such as cognitive impairment or disturbance in mood or behavior (Navia, Jordan, & Price, 1986; Petito, 1988). At first, there was supposition that these symptoms were the result of overwhelming medical or systemic illness, clinical depression, or delirium. As time went on, patients with these symptoms, without any evident neurological disease, were reported with increasing frequency, and it was postulated that HIV itself was somehow responsible for the clinical symptoms seen (Ho, Pomerantz, & Kaplan, 1987; Price, Brew, & Sidtis, 1988).

Pathology and Pathogenesis

It is now known that HIV can enter the CNS early in the course of infection. HIV has been cultured from the cerebrospinal fluid (CSF) of patients early on (McArthur et al., 1989; Sonnerborg et al., 1988) and the presence of antibodies to HIV (Elovaara et al., 1989), elevated proteins (Levy & Bredesen, 1988), immunoglobulins (Andersson, Bergstrom, & Bloomstrand, 1988), and increased white blood cells (Chalmers, Aprill, & Shepard, 1990) in the CSF early in the course of HIV illness speaks to invasion soon after seroconversion. A small subset of patients develop an acute HIV-induced meningitis around the time of seroconversion, with symptoms of headache, meningeal signs, and alterations in mental status (Cooper et al., 1985) further supporting the theory that HIV can enter the CNS at an early stage.

Some viruses (e.g., polio and herpes simplex) can enter the CNS by directly crossing the protective barrier separating the bloodstream and the brain space (called the *blood–brain barrier*). HIV seems to gain access to the CNS by a different mechanism. It is thought that HIV "hides" in certain cells in the peripheral bloodstream (monocytes and macrophages), perhaps in a proviral form, and that these infected cells, in turn, cross the blood–brain barrier and enter the CNS to become productively infected cells. This "Trojan Horse" theory has gained popularity as the most likely mechanism of brain invasion by HIV (Haase, 1986; Resnick, Berger, & Shapshank, 1988).

Histopathological reports have described the typical patterns of HIV-related brain disease. These reports have documented the presence of multinucleated giant cells, microglial nodules throughout the gray and white brain matter, perivascular infiltration of monocytes and macrophages, diffuse myelin pallor with astrocytosis, neocortical neuronal dropout, vacuolation, and gliosis (Budka, 1991; Everall, Luthert, & Lantos, 1991; Glass, Wesselingh, Selnes, & McArthur, 1993; Sharer, 1992). Nerve cells (neurons) that are infected with HIV have not been consistently reported. This microscopic picture is suggestive of an inflammatory process. Because HIV itself does not appear to infect neurons directly, it is hypothesized that an indirect mechanism is responsible for the damage seen. It has been suggested by Tyor, Wesselingh, Griffin, McArthur, and Griffin (1995) that once HIV gains entry into the CNS, the resultant infection initiates an inflammatory response, causing an influx of additional monocytes into the CNS, activation of these monocytes, and, perhaps, further damage to an already "leaky" blood–brain barrier. Tyor et al. speculated that as T-cells (CD4 lymphocytes) normally function to inhibit monocyte and macrophage activation, their loss with advancing HIV disease allows an unopposed monocyte and macrophage activation to occur. It is thought that compounds elaborated by the activated macrophages (tumor necrosis factor, quinolinic acid, neopterin, gp120, nitric acid, and others) are toxic to neurons and other brain cells necessary for neural transmission (Heyes et al., 1991; Kimes, London, Szabo, Raymon, & Tabakoff, 1991; Merrill & Chen, 1991). The presence of HIV in the brain, therefore, seems to initiate a cascade of inflammatory and immunological events that ultimately lead to neuronal damage. How additional factors such as HIV strain diversity might be involved in initiating or maintaining this destructive process has yet to be clarified (Power & Johnson, 1995).

Involved Structures and Functions

Whatever the pathogenetic mechanism of damage, it does appear that HIV has a predilection for subcortical brain regions. The most often cited subcortical areas involved are the deep white matter, the basal ganglia (corpus striatum, globus pallidus), the thalamus, the ventral midbrain, and the dentate nuclei (Dal Pan et al., 1992; Levy, Rosenbloom, & Perett, 1986; Post et al., 1988). The cortex is not entirely spared, though. Cerebral atrophy, with enlargement of the ventricles and widened sulci, is a common finding in computerized tomography (CT) or magnetic resonance imaging (MRI) scans in patients who have clinical evidence of HIV-related brain disease, confirming that brain parenchyma is lost (Gelman & Guinto, 1992; McArthur, 1994). Besides atrophy, other frequent findings on MRI scanning have included scattered foci of high signal intensity with, at times, more confluence in the centrum semiovale–periventricular areas and isolated lesions of unclear significance (Grafe, Press, & Berthoty, 1990; Navia et al., 1986). Quantitative MRI analysis suggests that overall cerebral atrophy and atrophy in the region of the caudate nucleus and in gray matter structures occurs (Dal Pan et al., 1992). Single photon emission CT scans have confirmed (Masdeu et al., 1991) that multifocal or diffuse areas in both the cortex (frontal, parietal, and temporal lobes) and the basal ganglia are hypoperfused (blood perfusion is thought to be correlated with cerebral metabolism and, therefore, neuronal function). Positron emission tomography scans, which provide estimates of cerebral metabolism and regional blood flow, have also confirmed that subcortical (basal ganglia and thalamus) and prefrontal regions are affected in patients with HIV disease (Van Gorp, Mandelkern, & Gee, 1992).

It is generally accepted that subcortical brain regions are crucial in the initiation and regulation of many primal human functions. These basic and essential functions are subserved by a complex network of neurons, part of which has been designated the limbic system. There is general agreement that aggregates of neurons in the hypothalamus, the amygdala, the hippocampal formation, the septal nuclei, the cingulate region, the reticular activating system, the orbital frontal lobes, and various thalamic and cerebellar nuclei comprise the limbic system (Adams & Victor, 1981). Although the reader is referred elsewhere for a more complete description of this neuroanatomy and neurofunction (Joseph, 1992), it is sufficient here to note that these regions, in consort with higher cortical centers, are involved in controlling or modulating many aspects of emotion, motivation, arousal, sexual and social behavior, attention, memory, and learning. It is this basic and primitive neurological substrate that appears to be damaged by HIV, causing dysregulation of some of the most fundamental of human functions.

Despite the radiographic and histological evidence of damage to areas within the CNS by HIV, there can be a striking lack of correlation between these findings and the presence and severity of the clinical symptoms seen. Some patients who seem relatively asymptomatic have marked radiographic or histopathological evidence of CNS damage, and others who have fairly benign CT or MRI results, or who have little evidence of CNS disease on histological examination, can, at times, be profoundly symptomatic (Glass et al., 1993; Price, Sidtis, & Rosenblum, 1988). These discrepancies raise questions, of course, about the relationship between the symptoms seen and the disease process measured, and much remains to be understood about this lack of correlation.

SYMPTOMS

The original descriptions of HIV-related CNS disease spoke of a triad of symptoms consisting of alterations in cognition, behavior, and motor abilities (Navia et al., 1986; Price & Brew, 1988). Though there is great variation in the neuropsychiatric symptoms seen, this original description still stands as a good framework for understanding HIV brain disease. There is no implication that patients will necessarily have evident clinical symptoms from all three categories during the course of their HIV illness. The common cognitive, mood–behavioral, and

Table 1   Symptoms of HIV-Related Central Nervous System Disease

Cognitive	Behavioral/mood	Motor
Mental slowing	Apathy/depression	Incoordination
Impaired attention or concentration	Social or occupational Impaired motivation/drive	Slowed movements Tremors
Deficits in memory	Impaired emotional control	Weakness, especially
Deficits in learning	(lability/disinhibition)	of lower extremities
Deficits in abstraction/ reasoning	Loss of desire or interest Personality change	Unsteady gait or inability to ambulate
Deficits in visuospatial or visuoconstructional abilities	Inappropriate behavior Agitation Mutism	Incontinence of urine/ stool Frontal release signs
Mental confusion		
Disorientation		

Note. From "The AIDS Dementia Complex: I. Clinical Features" by B. A. Navia, B. D. Jordan, and R. W. Price, 1986, *Annals of Neurology, 19,* p. 519. Copyright 1986 by Little, Brown and Company. Adapted with permission.

motor symptoms, modified from the original description, are described below (Table 1).

Cognitive Symptoms

Patients typically complain that they feel mentally slowed, that they have difficulties with their memory, attention, and concentration. They describe, for example, that they cannot think as quickly. It takes them longer, they feel, to process information and to express themselves. Many have been told by others (relatives, friends, partners, employers) that they do not seem as sharp as they once were, and patients are often aware of this themselves. Memory deficits are evident as an impaired ability to learn new information and to recall previously stored information. Patients typically find, for example, that they forget their appointments or to take their medication and often attribute these symptoms to stress. One patient of mine reported that at work he found it increasingly difficult to remember the daily to-do list that his boss gave him verbally each morning. Attention and concentration deficits are evident in many ways. Patients feel that it requires more effort to stay tuned in to a conversation, for example, to watch TV, or to read. They feel somewhat more distractible and more easily shifted off their mental course. Other deficits in abstract reasoning, visuoconstructional abilities, and visuospatial abilities can occur, although higher cortical functions tend to be preserved until late in the course of illness. Cognitive symptoms can progress to produce severe impairment. Gross slowing of mental processes and delayed verbal responses can present as near or complete mutism. Marked confusion and profound memory impairment with disorientation can occur. Distractibility and impaired attention can prevent patients from learning or retaining any new information. At times, patients can become locked in their present mental state with no remembered history, where each experience seems new without any prior anchoring frame of reference. They repeatedly ask the same questions in an attempt to reorient themselves in a world that no longer makes sense to them. Given that patients may also be concurrently experiencing worsened medical illness, it is not hard to understand how overwhelming and frightening this can be.

Mood-Behavioral Symptoms

Early on, patients are noted to be somewhat withdrawn from their usual work-, social, and school-related activities. They often report a lack of desire, drive, or motivation to engage in their usual activities and may appear disinterested and apathetic. This altered motivation and drive can have profound consequences for patients. One patient began to receive negative evaluation reports from his supervisor as the early signs of HIV-related brain involvement became more evident at work. He was criticized for not having the "killer instinct" that he had always displayed, for acting as if he did not care. Another patient's life partner called to complain that he was sure that his partner needed an antidepressant because he was withdrawn, disengaged and "didn't seem to care about anything anymore. . . . He has this vacant stare, it's like he's no longer there." Emotional responsiveness, flexibility, and control can also be impaired. Many patients report that they feel more easily irritated by things and that their frustration tolerance is low. They find it more difficult to control their temper, and some become increasingly aggressive. Family, friends, and the patients themselves can be bewildered and frightened by these mood swings. In fact, as CNS disease advances, many patients can articulate an awareness that they are losing control of their behavior and emotions. A large yet gentle man whom I saw in twice weekly psychotherapy became aware that for the first time in his life he was making people around him uncomfortable and frightened because of his emotional lability. Unfortunately, this dysregulation and dyscontrol of behavior, emotion, and mood is a cardinal feature of HIV-related brain disease. With worsened CNS disease, patients can have a degree of disinhibition leading to aggressive outbursts or inappropriate behavior. At times there may be a hardening of personality traits, changes in personality, or the presence of psychotic symptoms. A young woman with AIDS and no previous psychiatric history was referred to me for evaluation of insomnia and reported that she was hearing voices at night and believed that poison gas was being vented into her apartment. She had profound cognitive impairment with deficits in memory, attention, and concentration, all consistent with the symptoms seen in HIV CNS disease.

Motor Symptoms

At first, there may be subtle signs of motor incoordination. Patients retrospectively report that they have been more clumsy than usual, either tripping as they walk or dropping things. One young male patient of mine joked that as he became more clumsy, he had learned to use only dishes given to him by his ex-lover because he has dropped and broken so many. Noticeable changes in handwriting can occur early on, with patients reporting that they do not have the steadiness and control they once had. A graphic artist seen in consultation was dismayed to find out that the cause of his deteriorated drawing abilities was early HIV brain disease. Tremors, especially of the upper extremities and hands, and weakness, especially of the lower extremities, are not uncommon. Some patients notice over time that it is increasingly difficult, for example, to rise from a seated position, as this requires strength they no longer have in the proximal muscles of their legs. Unsteady gait can lead to increased likelihood of falls. A former alcoholic patient of mine repeatedly tried to reassure his family that he had not started to drink again, given that he had become unsteady on his feet and had fallen twice at home. Most often seen in late-stage AIDS, severe neurological involvement can occur. Frontal lobe release signs, gross ataxia, inability to walk, incontinence of urine and stool, and pyramidal tract signs like hypertonia, spasticity, and hyperreflexia can be seen.

A 44-year-old African American man with AIDS came for consultation at the insistence of his mother. He reported that he was doing OK and had "no problems with anything, I'm just feeling tired." Questions about mood, cognitive, and behavioral symptoms were met with denials. His mother, with whom he lived, reported that over the past 6 to 8 months she had noted increasing forgetfulness and confusion. She reported that he was no longer able to remember what medications he was taking or his medical appointments. She said that he would stop mid-sentence, seemingly forgetting what he was saying, and at other times couldn't find the words. He would spend long periods sitting, staring without communicating with her unless she initiated conversation. She found that he had lost his desire to do the things he once enjoyed (e.g., playing with his nephews). When she would try to explain things to him, she said, "It's like he's just not there. I can't get through." It was particularly worrisome to her that he did not seem to care about what was happening to him and acted as if everything was OK. His past medical history was notable for cytomegalovirus retinitis, two previous episodes of bacterial pneumonia, and *mycobacterium avium intracellularae* complex. He was on multiple HIV-related medications. His mother denied that he had any prior psychiatric history, but acknowledged that he had a history of injection drug use and had maintained his abstinence for the past 3 years. He presented as a fatigued and cachectic man. His mental status exam was notable for slowed mentation and movements, an apathetic and vacant stare, mildly dysphoric mood, somewhat confused and disorganized thought processes, the absence of psychotic symptoms, and impairments in short-term memory, attention, concentration, and word-finding abilities. A brain CT scan showed moderate cerebral atrophy without evidence of space-occupying lesions, and a lumbar puncture (spinal tap) was notable only for elevated protein. He was started on zidovudine (AZT), which was increased to 900 mg per day, and methylphenidate (Ritalin), which was eventually increased to 10 mg in the morning and 5 mg in the early afternoon. He responded to these medications with improved energy and interest and a lessening of his dysphoria, but his cognitive impairment continued without change. The patient and his mother were provided with information about the cause of his symptoms and were given recommendations about practical tips to help aid memory and other cognitive impairments.

This case illustrates many of the typical symptoms seen in HIV-related CNS disease. Patients themselves can be apathetic and, hence, unaware of their impairments, so obtaining history from other sources is essential. The mood, behavioral, and cognitive symptoms coupled with the results of the diagnostic tests in this example are classic for the brain disease caused by HIV. Although high-dose antiretroviral medication like zidovudine can be helpful in halting progression of brain damage or reversing some of the deficits seen, this did not occur in this patient. The psychostimulants, like methylphenidate, can help alleviate both the mood and cognitive symptoms seen.

A 28-year-old Caucasian woman was referred by her psychotherapist for an evaluation of her depressive symptoms and for recommendation of antidepressant medication. She was an accountant and reported feeling down and uninterested in her usual activities. Her most recent performance evaluation at work prompted her therapist to refer her for the medication consultation. This work evaluation described her as unmotivated, no longer committed to the work, not high powered (as she had once been), and scattered. She herself reported being "less interested in work, and in everything else, too." Her boyfriend of 3 years had become increasingly frustrated with her because she did not want to socialize with friends, was withdrawn from him, and was uninterested in sex. She reported interrupted sleep, but no other vegetative signs of depression. Of note were her complaints of feeling more easily irritated and more distractible and that it seemed to require more energy than usual just to get through the day. She denied any difficulties with her memory, but did feel that it was harder to sustain her attention during activities like reading and watching TV. She had known her HIV status for 4 years, having become infected from sexual contact with a former boyfriend, and had had one episode of *Pneumocystis carinii* pneumonia approximately 1 year earlier. Her mental status exam was notable for speech of normal rate, dysphoric mood with constricted affect, organized thought processes, and the absence of psychotic symptoms. There were deficits in speeded tasks and attention, but her memory functions were intact. An MRI revealed mild cortical atrophy, and lumbar puncture was normal. Her usual dosage of zidovudine was increased to 1,000 mg per day, and she was started on 10 mg of fluoxetine (Prozac), which was increased to 20 mg per day after 2 weeks. She responded with improved mood and libido and a normalized sleep pattern. She continued, though, to be unmotivated, somewhat apathetic, and withdrawn and to evidence the cognitive impairments noted above.

This case illustrates an HIV-related CNS process that presents primarily with mood and behavioral symptoms that mimic a clinical depression. The patient's response to antidepressant medication does not necessarily imply that she suffered from a major depressive episode or other clinical depression, as mood disorders of other organic origins (e.g., poststroke depression, post–head-injury mood disorders) can also respond to such medication. Given her altered motivation and drive, her inattention and distractibility, the more likely cause of her mood symptoms was HIV-related brain disease.

EARLY HIV-RELATED CNS DISEASE

There has been much debate about whether the above-noted cognitive, mood, and behavioral symptoms can occur before the onset of other symptoms of systemic illness and, if so, how often this happens. Though there is histopathological and gross pathological evidence that HIV can cause damage to the CNS early on before other medical symptoms are apparent, the studies that have attempted to quantify the prevalence of such neuropsychiatric impairment have yielded conflicting results. The Multicenter AIDS Cohort Study (McArthur et al., 1989) and some other large studies (Franzblau et al., 1991; McAllister et al., 1992) failed to demonstrate prevalent cognitive impairment in HIV-positive patients who did not have medical symptoms (weight loss, fatigue, diarrhea, night sweats). Other studies have demonstrated higher rates of neuropsychological test abnormalities in patients who have no demonstrable HIV-related medical symptoms (Grant et al., 1987; Janssen et al., 1988). The most commonly noted impairments in such asymptomatic patients were in the areas of speeded cognitive tasks, attention, and the ability to learn new information. There are many factors that have led to these discrepancies in reported rates, including small sample size, selection bias in patient and control populations, the widely varying test batteries used to measure neuropsychological impairment, and the way the data were analyzed. Despite the conflicting results in these reports, there does seem to be a growing body of evidence suggesting that mild neuropsychological impairment can be seen in some medically asymptomatic or mildly symptomatic patients. What renders such patients more susceptible to these early effects of HIV-related brain damage remains unclear. It does not seem, though, that such early neuropsychological disease is a necessary prerequisite for more severe impairment later on, nor is there clarity that such early disease is necessarily progressive. In fact, there are reports that in many cases, early CNS-related symptoms can remain stable for significant periods of time (Saykin et al., 1991; Selnes et al., 1990). Most have agreed, though, that with advancing systemic disease and the presence of medical symptoms, neuropsychiatric impairment is more likely to be evident.

In addition to the effects of HIV itself on the CNS, there are many other potential neurological and medical causes for neuropsychiatric symptoms in persons with HIV illness. The immmunosuppression that results from HIV disease renders the CNS susceptible to invasion by infectious agents (viral, bacterial, protozoal, and fungal) and malignancies. Metabolic impairments, reactions to medications or illicit substances, and other CNS insults (head trauma, cerebrovascular events) can also cause disturbances in mood, behavior, and cognition or other alterations in mental status. Although it is not the purpose of this chapter to enumerate these causes and the reader is referred elsewhere for more extensive descriptions (Markowitz & Perry, 1990; McArthur, 1994), it is important to be aware that many diverse etiologies can cause neuropsychiatric symptoms in people with HIV.

PROPOSED NOMENCLATURE

Over the past decade, there have not only been questions about the pathogenetic mechanism underlying HIV-related brain disease and the natural history of the disease process(es) itself, but questions, as well, over how best to classify the impairments that are seen. Over the years, different terms (subacute encephalitis, HIV or AIDS encephalopathy, HIV dementia, and AIDS dementia complex) have been used to describe what might, or might not, have been the same disease process. In 1991, the American Academy of Neurology (AAN) AIDS Task Force proposed nomenclature for the CNS disorders caused by HIV. Though other classification systems have been proposed (Atkinson & Grant, 1994), the AAN diagnostic criteria seem most clinically relevant and useful. *HIV-1–associated cognitive/motor complex* is the term used to define the spectrum of CNS disorders due to HIV. Beneath this umbrella term are delineated the severe manifestations, termed *HIV-1–associated dementia complex,* or HDC (brain disease; Table 2), and *HIV-1–associated myelopathy* (spinal cord disease) and the mild manifestations, termed *HIV-1–associated minor cognitive/motor disorder*

Table 2   Diagnostic Criteria for HIV-1-Associated Dementia Complex

1. Acquired abnormality in at least two of the following cognitive abilities (present for at least 1 month): attention/concentration, speed of processing of information, abstraction/reasoning, visuospatial skills, memory/learning, and speech/language.
    Cognitive dysfunction causes impairment of work or of activities of daily living.
2. At least one of the following:
    a. Acquired abnormality in motor function or performance verified by clinical examination, neuropsychological tests, or both.
    b. Decline in motivation or emotional control or change in social behavior, characterized by change in personality with apathy, inertia, irritability, emotional lability, or new onset impairment of judgment, characterized by socially inappropriate behavior or disinhibition.
3. Absence of clouding of consciousness during a period long enough to establish the presence of No. 1.
4. Evidence of another etiology, including active central nervous system infection or malignancy, psychiatric disorders, active substance use or substance withdrawal must be sought and, if present, is not the cause of the cognitive, motor, or behavioral symptoms.

Note. From "Nomenclature and Research Case Definitions for Neurologic Manifestations of Human Immunodeficiency Virus—Type 1 (HIV-1) Infection" by American Academy of Neurology AIDS Task Force, 1991, *Neurology, 41,* p. 780. Copyright 1991 by Little, Brown and Company. Adapted with permission.

Table 3   Diagnostic Criteria for HIV-1–Associated Minor Cognitive/ Motor Disorder

1. Cognitive–motor–behavioral abnormalities (must have each of the following):
   a. At least two of the following acquired symptoms, present for at least 1 month: impaired attention or concentration, mental slowing, impaired memory, slowed movements, incoordination, personality change, or irritability or emotional lability.
   b. Acquired cognitive–motor abnormality verified by clinical neurological examination or neuropsychological testing.
2. Disturbance from cognitive–motor–behavioral abnormalities causes mild impairment of work or activities of daily living.
3. Does not meet criteria for HIV-1–associated dementia complex or HIV-1–associated myelopathy.
4. No evidence of another etiology, including active central nervous system opportunistic infection or malignancy, or severe systemic illness. The above features should not be attributed solely to the effects of active substance usage or withdrawal, or psychiatric disorders.

Note. From "Nomenclature and Research Case Definitions for Neurologic Manifestations of Human Immunodeficiency Virus–Type 1 (HIV-1) Infection" by American Academy of Neurology AIDS Task Force, 1991, *Neurology, 41*, p. 781. Copyright 1991 by Little, Brown and Company. Adapted with permission.

(Table 3). It is primarily the degree of impairment in activities of daily living that distinguishes HDC and HIV-1–associated minor cognitive/motor disorder. What had been called AIDS dementia complex, AIDS-related dementia, HIV encephalopathy, and subacute encephalitis is now termed HDC. If a patient has evidence of cognitive, motor, and behavioral impairment of sufficient severity, then the diagnosis would be HDC. A diagnosis of HDC warrants a diagnosis of AIDS. Although cognitive impairment is, by definition, the cardinal and essential feature of HDC, there are patients who have behavioral symptoms without motor disease and vice versa. Within the HDC diagnostic category, therefore, it is possible to subcategorize patients by the major symptoms present, either motor (if patients have only cognitive and motor involvement) or behavioral (if patients have only cognitive and behavioral impairment). It is also possible to signify the level of cognitive dysfunction in HDC as mild, moderate, or severe and to qualify the diagnoses of HDC and HIV-1–associated minor cognitive/ motor disorder as *possible* or *probable*, depending on the certainty of the etiology. (Note that the criteria shown in Tables 2 and 3 list the criteria satisfying the *probable* designation. The *possible* designation would imply that another potential etiology is present and that the cause of the symptoms is, therefore, unclear or that there has been an incomplete clinical evaluation.) Whether HIV-1–associated minor cognitive/motor disorder is a necessary prerequisite for HDC, and whether the two forms are, in fact, the same disease process, is unclear.

It should be noted that the criteria used by the American Psychiatric Association's *Diagnostic and Statistical Manual of Mental Disorders* (4th ed., or *DSM–IV;* American Psychiatric Association, 1994) for a diagnosis of dementia due to

HIV are different than those proposed above by the AAN AIDS Task Force (1991). The *DSM–IV* continues to rely on memory impairment as the necessary and cardinal feature of all dementias, including dementia due to HIV. There also tends to be a focus on impairment of higher cortical functions, as evidenced by aphasia, apraxia, agnosia, or all of these. These criteria are more appropriate for dementias that primarily affect the cortex, like Alzheimer's disease, in contrast to the predominantly subcortical dementing process seen in HIV illness. Because the AAN criteria give weight to these subcortical symptoms, they are more clinically relevant and useful.

UNDERSTANDING THE PSYCHIATRIC AND PSYCHOLOGICAL SUBSTRATES

HIV-Related Psychiatric and Psychological Morbidity

As with HIV-related CNS disease, there are conflicting reports in the literature about the prevalence of psychiatric morbidity in HIV disease. Early studies, which relied on self-assessment rating scales, reported very high rates of symptomatic depression and anxiety in patients with HIV disease (Dilley, Ochitill, Perl, & Volberding, 1985; Perry & Jacobsen, 1986). One early report (Tross, Hirsch, Rabkin, Berry, & Holland, 1987), for example, documented that 56% of patients with AIDS, 78% of patients with AIDS-related complex, and 39% of HIV-positive patients who were medically asymptomatic met the *Diagnostic and Statistical Manual of Mental Disorders* (3rd ed.; American Psychiatric Association, 1980) diagnostic criteria for adjustment disorder with anxiety, depression, or both. These high rates of diagnosable psychiatric disorders were not found in other, more recent studies (Atkinson et al., 1988; Ostrow et al., 1989; Williams, Rabkin, Remien, Gorman, & Ehrhardt, 1991). Rundell, Paolucci, Beatty, and Boswell (1988), for example, reported that although clinical depression is the most frequently observed psychiatric disorder in patients with HIV disease, the rates range from 4% to 14% in gay men and non–substance-using women. Some studies (Rabkin, Remien, Katoff, & Williams, 1993) have reported rates of current major depression for patients with HIV to be in the range of rates seen in other chronic medical diseases (5%–8%), which are twice the rate as in a non–medically ill population. Lipsitz et al. (1994) reported elevated rates of current depressive disorders (26%) in both HIV-positive and HIV-negative IV drug users. Although there was an association between seropositivity and depression in these IV-drug-using men, it was more the history of drug use than HIV serostatus itself that was felt to correlate with the presence of a mood disorder. Lipsitz et al. noted higher rates of diagnosable depression in seropositive men as compared with seropositive women. In this study, women reported higher levels of stress and scored higher on measures of symptomatic anxiety and depression rather than having diagnosable anxiety or depressive disorders. A number of reports have suggested that anxiety of several months duration is common during HIV illness (Atkinson et al., 1988; Atkinson, Patterson, & Summers, 1991). Although there are reports that correlate HIV serostatus with the presence of personality disorders (Brooner, Greenfield, Schmidt, & Bigelow, 1993; Perkins et al., 1993), other studies have not supported this association, finding no differences in the prevalence of personality disorders between HIV-positive and HIV-negative persons (Johnson, Williams, Rabkin, Goetz, & Remien, 1995). In this latter study, up to one third of seropositive patients who had a personality disorder also had a concurrent Axis I disorder.

Because the rates of depressive disorders and some anxiety disorders among HIV-positive gay men have not been reported to be notably different from those of HIV-negative gay men (Williams et al., 1991; Perry, Jacobsberg, & Fishman, 1990) but are elevated in comparison to those of heterosexual men, the higher rates of depression and some anxiety disorders seen in HIV-positive gay men may be more related to their previous histories of such disorders than to HIV per se. Because this may be true for others with HIV as well (substance users), the implication is that many depressive and anxiety disorders, in the context of HIV illness, are not so much "caused" by HIV as they are expressions of reactivated disorders that existed before seroconversion.

A 26-year-old African American, HIV-positive woman, with a 2-year-old seropositive son, was referred for evaluation of depression. She reported feeling anxious and having constant ruminative worrying, crying episodes, and initial and terminal insomnia. Despite her initial denials, she eventually reported feelings of hopelessness, worthlessness, and guilt and admitted having passive suicidal thoughts. She was concerned that her son would be removed from her care if she was found to be "crazy" and, therefore, initially resented the psychiatric evaluation. (Her son had been removed from her custody for a 6-month period after a former boyfriend was charged with physically abusing the child.) She reported no cognitive impairments or psychotic symptoms. Her psychiatric history dated back to age 18 when she had the first of three psychiatric hospitalizations for depressive episodes with accompanying suicidal ideations. In all cases, her hospitalizations were brief, and she was treated with antidepressant medications with excellent response but continued the medications in each case for only a few months. She described a long and traumatic history of sexual abuse by her stepfather, which she identified as the cause of her subsequent depressions and psychiatric hospitalizations. There was no history of substance use. She reported that both her mother and sister took some medication for depression. She had no HIV-related medical complications, and her most recent CD4 count was about 500. Her mental status was notable for mild psychomotor agitation, anxious and dysphoric mood, tearfulness, passive suicidal thoughts, the absence of psychotic symptoms, and an intact cognition. She responded well to sinequan (doxepin), which was eventually increased to 150 mg at night, with resolution of all vegetative signs of depression. Given her history of recurrent depressive episodes, it was suggested that she might benefit from continuing on the medication for a longer period of time than she had in the past to lessen the likelihood of a future exacerbation. She was also referred for psychotherapy and to an HIV-positive women's group.

This case demonstrates that depressive episodes during the course of HIV illness may be due to an exacerbation of a preexisting mood disorder. The current symptom presentation in the case above was not much different from prior episodes, and the family history of depression strengthens the belief that her symptoms were the result of a recurrent clinical depression.

HIV-Related Distress

The assumption that patients who are seriously medically ill and who may be facing pain, disability, and death are destined to suffer from depressive and anxiety disorders of such severity to satisfy diagnostic criteria does not seem to be the case. As noted above, the majority of patients with HIV disease do not suffer from such disorders and those who do are more likely than not to have had such disorders before their seroconversion. It must be noted, though, that although psychiatric disorders that meet diagnostic criteria may not be as prevalent as one might suspect, anxiety and depressive symptoms and subjective distress are commonplace during HIV illness. One early report (Chuang, Devins, Hunsley, & Gill, 1989) noted elevated levels of distress in HIV-positive persons and correlated this distress with disease stage. Patients with AIDS-related complex and those HIV-positive patients without medical symptoms showed significantly greater levels of depressive symptoms, mood disturbance, and trait anxiety than did patients with AIDS, although the latter also showed elevated rates of distress compared with controls. HIV-positive patients with personality disorders exhibited higher levels of distress than either seronegative persons or those who did not have personality disorders (Johnson et al., 1995; Perkins, Davidson, Leserman, Liao, & Evans, 1993).

That there is prevalent distress in all stages of HIV disease is no surprise to clinicians who work in the field. Isolation from friends, family, and partners; discrimination; multiple losses; disability from work; altered body image; and fears of debilitation are just some of the issues HIV-positive persons can face. It is important to acknowledge that distress may be of such severity and may be so unrelenting in some patients that even if strict diagnostic criteria for depression and anxiety are not met, quality of life may be affected as if they were. Therefore, the prevalence of diagnosable psychiatric syndromes must be interpreted with caution for it does not speak to all the psychological morbidity seen in HIV disease. Feeling bereft and filled with the heartache of many losses is an experience that many patients with HIV have. Even though these feeling states may not be clinically definable and quantifiable as diagnostic criteria, they nonetheless can color a patient's life in profound ways. A patient had difficulty putting into words just how he felt after a friend, whom he reported he was not close to, died from AIDS. "It's not that I knew him so well, and I don't really feel so sad, but there is an ache that won't go away, that's been with me every day since he died." Another patient reported that she was not overly anxious or sad, and although she had no difficulty taking care of herself or her 4-year-old HIV-positive daughter, she lived with the fear that her daughter would one day become ill and die, or, worse, that she herself would become ill and not be able to take care of her daughter. She described it this way: "It's a worry that never goes away, no matter how well we're doing. If I could have just one day without this feeling."

In addition to the neurological impairment, psychiatric disorders, and psychological distress that accompany HIV illness, the medical complications of the disease itself produce symptoms that can be mistaken for symptoms of mental illness or distress. Fatigue, malaise, low energy level, altered appetite with weight loss, impaired sleep, and decreased libido are just a few of the HIV-related medical symptoms that overlap with psychiatric symptoms. Because there are reports that have suggested that psychological distress is more prevalent in patients with medical symptoms (Lipsitz et al., 1994), the co-occurrence of these symptoms complicates the picture further. It can be confusing to both the patient and the clinician to have an array of symptoms that could be attributed to both the psyche and the soma. Some patients prefer to believe that such symptoms are of psychiatric origin because they are frightened to think that their presence may imply advancing medical disease. Others may tend to attribute such symptoms to medical disease because the possibility of psychiatric morbidity is unacceptable to them.

> A 31-year-old Caucasian gay man with AIDS presented on referral from his internist with symptoms of low energy level, fatigue, depressive mood, and decreased libido. He had been diagnosed with Kaposi's sarcoma 6 months earlier, which upset him primarily because this meant he had an AIDS-defining illness. Because he had become increasingly uninterested in sex, there was discord in his relationship with his partner of 10 years. He said that he was constantly fatigued, had little energy, and was depressed about this as it restricted his activities. He wanted an antidepressant that would restore his "sagging spirit and energy." He had no other vegetative symptoms, no complaints of cognitive impairment, and no previous psychiatric or substance usage history. It was suggested that he have his testosterone levels checked, and it was found that they were subnormal. His internist prescribed twice monthly injections to replace his deficient testosterone, and within 4 to 6 weeks, he reported resolution of all his "psychiatric" symptoms.

This case illustrates only one of the many HIV-related medical conditions that can present with psychiatric symptoms. The presence of more advanced HIV disease, the absence of any psychiatric or substance use history, and the symptom constellation in this case suggested a more active search for an underlying medical cause.

Any understanding of HIV-related mental health symptoms is only complete by acknowledging the familial, community, cultural, and gender-related context in which the symptoms are expressed. These important areas are addressed in other chapters of this book.

Summary

HIV-related CNS disease can produce marked impairments in mood, cognition, and behavior that can mimic psychiatric illness; there are many other neurological and medical etiologies that can cause symptoms that appear psychiatric in origin. Psychiatric disorders that meet diagnostic criteria are far from inevitable during the course of HIV illness, but when they do occur, their presence may indicate a reactivation of a disorder present before seroconversion. Psychological distress in the course of HIV disease can cause profound morbidity, and the medical symptoms of HIV infection can overlap with symptoms of neuropsychiatric or psychological origin. It is knowledge of these symptom etiologies and of the factors that affect their expression that allows for a thoughtful mental health assessment of people with HIV. The basic mental health assessment and treatment principles for patients with HIV illness are included here.

PRINCIPLES OF MENTAL HEALTH ASSESSMENT AND TREATMENT IN HIV ILLNESS

1   Mental health assessment in HIV illness can be complex as medical, neurological, psychiatric, psychological, and other (social, cultural, gender-related) issues may be involved.

2   It is not the symptoms per se, but understanding the symptoms in their context, that helps to clarify their etiology.

3   Knowledge of the particular aspects of the history and mental status to highlight allows for the elucidation of information most critical for a mental health assessment.

4   First, clarify whether HIV-associated cognitive/motor complex or other neurological or medical causes may underlie the symptoms seen.

5   Divest oneself of the myth that mood and anxiety disorders are "normal" and to be expected in people with HIV.

6   Because many episodes of anxiety, depression, and substance use in the course of HIV illness will be reactivations of disorders that were present before seroconversion, there may be treatment implications for such recurrent disorders.

7   Symptoms of distress that may not satisfy the criteria for a psychiatric diagnosis may nonetheless cause profound morbidity and may warrant treatment.

8   Knowledge of the pertinent familial, cultural, gender-related, and community issues allows one to more fully understand the context in which the symptoms are expressed.

9   Psychopharmacological and psychotherapeutic treatments are effective and underused in persons with HIV illness.

10   There are times when, despite efforts, it is not possible to clarify the etiology of the evident symptoms, so treatments may need to be initiated on the basis of the most likely (though unproven) cause.

Because any particular symptom or symptom cluster in the context of HIV illness might be attributable to a wide array of etiologies and because all symptoms are altered in their expression by gender-related, cultural, familial, and personality issues, it is essential to remember that it is not the symptoms per se but an awareness of the symptoms in their context that will help to clarify their etiology. For example, insomnia might be a manifestation of a depressive, anxiety, or psychotic disorder; the result of distress; a reaction to medication or substance use; the effect of medical disease (pain, frequent urination, diarrhea); or the result of HIV-related CNS disease itself. It is possible to understand symptoms only within the context in which they arise. In the example above, if the insomnia is one of many vegetative symptoms in a relatively medically well, HIV-positive person with a prior history of depression who is not on any medications likely to cause sleep disturbance and who has intact cognition, then it would seem likely that the insomnia is a symptom of a recurrent major depressive disorder. In the context of a patient with advanced AIDS complaining of pain, being treated with multiple medications, and evidencing apathy, slowed mentation, memory and attention deficits, one would need to consider that the sleep disturbance might be due to HDC or somatic disease (pain) or caused by a prescribed medication. Insomnia in a medically well HIV-positive mother who reports anxious, ruminative worrying about the health of her ill child without other symptoms of anxiety, depression, or cognitive impairment might be attributable to distress, even in the absence of a diagnosable psychiatric illness. Of course, the pharmacological and nonpharmacological treatment implications are quite different in the above scenarios. A hypnotic agent (like a short-acting benzodiazepine) and psychological support might be helpful in the latter case; an antidepressant would seem indicated in the first; controlling pain, adjusting medications that may be interfering with sleep, and the addition of a low-dose neuroleptic like haloperidal (Haldol) or thioridazine (Mellaril) at bedtime might be helpful in the medically ill patient with HIV dementia. As the above example illustrates, a thoughtful understanding of the context helps to clarify the cause of symptoms seen in HIV illness.

UNDERSTANDING THE MENTAL HEALTH HISTORY AND MENTAL STATUS EXAMINATION IN HIV ILLNESS

Aspects of the Mental Health History to Highlight

The following questions help to highlight pertinent aspects of the history and thereby help to define the symptom context. This targeted history is not meant to replace the necessity for a thorough mental health history, but rather to complement it.

What Are the Current Psychiatric, Psychological, and Medical Symptoms? The following symptoms warrant particular attention in a mental health assessment of people with HIV: sleep or appetite disturbance; altered libido; anergia; fatigue; anhedonia; feelings of guilt or hopelessness; suicidal thoughts; the cognitive, behavioral, and motor symptoms listed in Table 1; and any current medical symptoms (pain, weakness or fatigue, anorexia, weight loss, night sweats, diarrhea, fevers, headaches). It is important to be specific about each symptom present to help clarify the context. For example, because altered libido in an HIV-positive man can be a symptom of depression or distress, a side effect of medications, or due to low testosterone levels, questions aimed at distinguishing between these etiologies would be helpful. Highlighting the symptoms listed above allows one to begin to ascertain whether there might be evidence of neurological or neuropsychiatric illness or other psychiatric morbidity and to determine the degree to which medical or somatic symptoms are present.

What Has Been the History of These Symptoms? It is helpful to know when the symptoms first started; whether they have been of insidious or abrupt onset; whether they have been static in nature, progressive, or fluctuating in course; and whether there was an identifiable trigger. Though there is much variation, some syndromes and illnesses tend to have a discrete onset (major depressive episodes, untoward reactions to medications), others can be more insidious and progressive in nature (HDC), and some typically fluctuate in their course (delirium). An identified stressor before symptom development could clarify the etiology. It should be pointed out that although the course of symptoms may be suggestive of certain etiologies, clinical presentations can vary to such great degrees that the course of symptoms alone cannot be defining. For example, HDC can have abrupt onset, and depressive disease can be slowly progressive for years.

What Is the Extent of Immunosuppressive and HIV-Related (Medical) Disease? It is important to have some sense of the degree of immunosuppression and the medical course of HIV illness. Because patients can remain asymptomatic for many years without evidence of clinically relevant immunosuppression, the length of time since seroconversion is not necessarily helpful in determining a patient's degree of medical illness. It is helpful to know whether there have been any HIV-related medical complications ranging from the mild (thrush, weight loss, night sweats) to the more severe (opportunistic infections, malignancies) and, also, to know the most recent CD4 count or viral load (a measure of HIV activity). This information is useful because certain symptoms and conditions are more likely to be present at different disease stages. For example, in a more medically well (CD4 count 600) patient with cognitive impairment (attention, concentration difficulties) and dysphoria, a diagnosis of depression (rather than HDC) might be likely, whereas the same symptom picture in a patient with multiple HIV-related medical complications and a CD4 count of 50 might suggest that other diagnoses, like HDC or other CNS pathology, would need to be considered.

What Medications Are Currently Prescribed? It is important to know all the medications being taken as so many have side effects or actions that mimic psychiatric symptoms. Medications used in HIV illness, including psychotropics, can have intended actions and unwanted side effects that can make diagnostic assessments difficult. It is not reasonable or necessary to know all the medications, their side effects, and their interactions with each other. Indeed, in many cases there have not been controlled trials assessing drug–drug interactions for the many medications that persons with HIV take. What is useful is to know is when medications might be a factor so that appropriate consultation can be obtained.

Is There a History of Psychiatric Illness Before Seroconversion? It is essential to know whether there was a history of psychiatric illness before seroconversion. Specifically, histories of depressive disease, anxiety disorders, chronic mental illness, and personality disorders must be elicited. Because depressive and anxiety disorders may be reactivations of previously existing disorders, there are treatment implications (both psychotropic and psychotherapeutic) for these "recurrent" illnesses. Specifically, there may be a need for longer term maintenance medication to prevent further reactivations in the future. Similarly, the psychotherapeutic work should be done with the knowledge that the patient has an illness that might act as if it were a recurrent disorder. There may, therefore, be implications regarding identification of triggers and strategies for long-term maintenance. Also, patients with personality disorders and HIV may be at higher risk for the development of Axis I pathology. For such patients with triple diagnoses, issues surrounding maintenance and prevention of symptom exacerbation might be relevant. The reader is referred elsewhere for the unique treatment issues in HIV-positive patients who have severe and persistent mental illness (Cournos, Horwath, Guido, McKinnon, & Hopkins, 1994; Meyer, Empfield, Engel, & Cournos, 1995).

Is There a History of Substance Use? Like some psychiatric illnesses, some substance use disorders present before seroconversion may be reactivated in the course of HIV disease, with treatment implications similar to those noted above. Intoxication and withdrawal syndromes and the psychiatric, psychological, and neurological effect of chronic substance use may need to be addressed in the assessment of a substance-using HIV-positive patient. Substance use can cause cognitive impairment and even sophisticated diagnostic procedures (single photon emission CT scans) and neuropsychological testing may not be helpful in differentiating the deficits due to HIV from those due to substance use (Holman et al., 1992). It may be particularly difficult, therefore, to clarify the etiology of cognitive deficits in the HIV-positive substance-using patient. There are times when, despite efforts, it is not possible to know the etiology of the symptoms, and treatment may need to be initiated to treat the most likely (though unproven) cause.

What Are the Stresses and Level of Distress Present?   Recent losses, grief and bereavement, worries, and stresses that patients have concerning finances, relationships, or family matters are all essential to elicit. It is clear that distress can cause notable psychiatric morbidity, even if the symptoms do not fit diagnostic criteria. Anxious ruminative worrying, for example, that is not in the context of a diagnosable anxiety or depressive disorder may warrant anxiolytic medication; bereavement, without an accompanying clinical picture of depression, might well require psychotherapeutic interventions, as might stresses within a family affected by HIV.

What Is the Current Perceived Support System?   It would be helpful to know the quality of the patient's relationships with spouse or partner, friends, and family and the quality of the current support system. It is also important to know whether the patient is engaged in psychotherapy or other treatments. Perceived support in patients with HIV is correlated with lower levels of distress and greater hopefulness. Lack of a meaningful support structure might have many psychotherapeutic treatment implications.

Is There a Family History of Psychiatric Illness?   A family history of mental illness might suggest a predisposition to the development and expression of symptomatic disease during the course of HIV infection. Mood symptoms in an HIV-positive patient with a family history of depressive disease, for example, might suggest that an inherited illness is manifesting itself. There may be implications both for the choice of the psychopharmacological agents used and for the need for family therapeutic interventions. Because response to psychotropic medications can tend to be similar in biological families, clarification of the medication history of such family members might prove useful.

Are There Pertinent Gender-Related, Cultural, Community, and Family Issues?   Other chapters in this book will help to highlight the important aspects of gender-related, cultural, community, and family issues that have an impact on people with HIV.

Aspects of the Mental Status Examination to Highlight

Although it is beyond the scope of this chapter to describe the neuropsychological assessment tools that are most appropriate for the evaluation of patients with HIV disease, it is useful to know that the National Institute of Mental Health (NIMH) Workshop on Neuropsychological Assessment Approaches has proposed an extended neuropsychological battery to evaluate patients with HIV illness (Butters et al., 1990). (There is also a brief version suggested if it is not possible to complete the more lengthy recommended battery.) On the basis of the nature of HIV-related CNS disease, the NIMH battery recommends assessment of the following domains: (a) indicators of premorbid intelligence,

(b) attention, (c) speed of processing, (d) memory, (e) abstraction, (f) language, (g) visuoperception, (h) constructional abilities, (i) motor abilities, and (j) psychiatric assessment. There is an acknowledgment that although the proposed battery addresses many areas of cognitive functioning, "specific emphasis has been placed on divided and sustained attention as well as speed of processing and retrieval from working and long-term memory" (Butters et al., 1990, p. 965). Brief screening tools like the Mini-Mental State Exam (Forstein & Folstein, 1975) have been criticized for being insensitive to the nature of the subcortical pathology seen in HIV disease. Other screening tools like the HIV Dementia Scale (Power et al., 1995) and the Mental Alteration Test (Jones, Teng, Folstein, & Harrison, 1993), although limited in usefulness by their brevity, do assess the areas likely to be impaired in HIV-related CNS disease. It has been suggested that these screens are most useful when subsequent scores are compared with a known baseline score, giving a very cursory and gross sense of cognitive changes over time. These brief screens may also indicate when further neuropsychiatric assessment is indicated. A thorough mental status exam with highlights as noted above is most likely to provide the information needed for a diagnostic assessment.

Although there remains much yet to be learned about the neuropsychiatric and psychological ramifications of HIV, there is much that is already known. This chapter summarizes information on many of the important mental health aspects of HIV illness, including sections on HIV-related central nervous system pathology, pathogenesis, neuroanatomy, and symptom expression; HIV-related psychiatric and psychological morbidity; HIV-related distress; the principles of mental health assessment and treatment in HIV illness; and highlighted aspects of the mental health history and mental status examination. Although all clinicians working with those who are infected or affected by HIV would benefit from a sound understanding of these issues, mental health clinicians in particular have a unique opportunity to assess the interplay of psyche and soma and to use this knowledge to the benefit of their patients. HIV illness can bring with it a host of medical and mental health complications that can be extraordinarily burdensome for patients. Misconceptions, myths, and misunderstandings about these issues make living with HIV needlessly more difficult. It is, therefore, our challenge to educate ourselves in ways that enhance our understanding so that a more true and human face can be put on this very human story.

REFERENCES

Adams, R. D., & Victor, M. (1981). The limbic lobes and the neurology of emotion. In R. Adams & M. Victor (Eds.), *Principles of neurology* (pp. 350–361). New York: McGraw-Hill.

American Academy of Neurology AIDS Task Force. (1991). Nomenclature and research case definitions for neurologic manifestations of human immunodeficiency virus-type 1 (HIV-1) infection. *Neurology, 41*, 778–785.

American Psychiatric Association. (1980). *Diagnostic and statistical manual of mental disorders* (3rd ed.). Washington, DC: Author.

American Psychiatric Association. (1994). *Diagnostic and statistical manual of mental disorders* (4th ed.). Washington, DC: Author.

Andersson, M. A., Bergstrom, T. B., & Bloomstrand, C. (1988). Increasing intrathecal lymphocytosis and immunoglobulin G production in neurologically asymptomatic HIV infection. *Journal of Neuroimmunology, 19,* 291–304.

Atkinson, J. H., & Grant, I. (1994). Natural history of neuropsychiatric manifestations of HIV disease. In L. Zegans & T. Coates (Eds.), *The psychiatric clinics of North America: Psychiatric manifestations of HIV disease* (pp. 17–34). Philadelphia: W. B. Saunders.

Atkinson, J., Grant, I., Kennedy, C., Richman, D. D., Spector, S. A., & McCutchan, A. (1988). Prevalence of psychiatric disorders among men infected with human immunodeficiency virus: A controlled study. *Archives of General Psychiatry, 45,* 859–864.

Atkinson, J., Patterson, T. L., & Summers, J. (1991, June). *Two year follow-up of psychiatric disorders among men infected with human immunodeficiency virus.* Paper presented at the VII International Conference on AIDS, Florence, Italy.

Brooner, R. K., Greenfield, L., Schmidt, C. W., & Bigelow, G. E. (1993). Antisocial personality disorder and HIV infection among intravenous drug abusers. *American Journal of Psychiatry, 150,* 53–58.

Budka, H. (1991). Neuropathology of human immunodeficiency virus infection. *Brain Pathology, 1,* 163–175.

Butters, N., Grant, I., Haxby, J., Judd, L., Martin, A., McClelland, J., Pequegnat, W., Schacter, D., & Stover, E. (1990). Assessment of AIDS-related cognitive changes: Recommendations of the NIMH workshop on neuropsychological assessment approaches. *Journal of Clinical and Experimental Neuropsychology, 12,* 963–978.

Chalmers, A. C., Aprill, B. S., & Shepard, H. (1990). Cerebrospinal fluid and human immunodeficiency virus. *Archives of Internal Medicine, 150,* 1538–1540.

Chuang, H. T., Devins, G. M., Hunsley, J., & Gill, M. J. (1989). Psychosocial distress and well-being among gay and bisexual men with human immunodeficiency virus infection. *American Journal of Psychiatry, 146,* 876–880.

Cooper, D. A., Gold, J., Maclean, P., Donovan, B., Finlayson, R., Barnes, T. G., Michelmore, H. M., Brooke, P., & Penny, R. (1985). Acute AIDS retrovirus infection: Definition of a clinical illness associated with seroconversion. *Lancet, 1,* 537–540.

Cournos, F., Horwath, E., Guido, J. R., McKinnon, K., & Hopkins, N. (1994). HIV-1 infection at two public psychiatric hospitals in New York City. *AIDS Care, 6,* 443–452.

Dal Pan, G. J., McArthur, J. H., Aylward, E., Selnes, O. A., Nance-Sproson, T. E., Kumar, A. J., Melllits, E. D., & McArthur, J. C. (1992). Patterns of cerebral atrophy in HIV-1-infected individuals: Results of a quantitative MRI analysis. *Neurology, 42,* 2125–2130.

Dilley, J. W., Ochitill, H. N., Perl, M., & Volberding, P. (1985). Findings in psychiatric consultations with patients with acquired immune deficiency syndrome. *American Journal of Psychiatry, 142,* 82–86.

Elovaara, I., Iivanainen, M., & Poutiainen, E. (1989). CSF and serum beta-2-microglobulin in HIV infection related to neurological dysfunction. *Acta Neurologia Scandanavia, 79,* 81–87.

Everall, I. P., Luthert, P. J., & Lantos, P. L. (1991). Neuronal loss in the frontal cortex in HIV infection. *Lancet, 337,* 1119–1121.

Forstein, M. F., & Folstein, S. E. (1975). "Mini-Mental State": A practical method for grading the cognitive state of patients for the clinician. *Journal of Psychiatric Research, 12,* 184–198.

Franzblau, A., Letz, R., Hershman, D., Mason, P., Wallace, J. I., & Bekesi, J. G. (1991). Quantitative neurologic and neurobehavioral testing of persons infected with human immunodeficiency virus type 1. *Archives of Neurology, 48,* 263–268.

Gelman, B. B., & Guinto, F. C. (1992). Morphometry, histopathology, and tomography of cerebral atrophy in the acquired immunodeficiency syndrome. *Annals of Neurology, 32,* 31–40.

Glass, J. D., Wesselingh, S. L., Selnes, O. A., & McArthur, J. C. (1993). Clinical-neuropathologic correlation in HIV-associated dementia. *Neurology, 43,* 2230–2237.

Grafe, M. R., Press, G. A., & Berthoty, D. P. (1990). Abnormalities in the brain in AIDS patients: Correlation of postmortem MR findings with neuropathology. *American Journal of Neuroradiology, 11,* 905–911.

Grant, I. H., Atkinson, J. H., Hesselink, J. R., Kennedy, C. J., Richman, D. D., Spector, S. A., & McCutchan, J. A. (1987). Evidence for early central nervous system involvement in the acquired immunodeficiency syndrome (AIDS) and other human immunodeficiency virus (HIV) infections: Studies with neuropsychologic testing and magnetic resonance imaging. *Annals of Internal Medicine, 107,* 828–836.

Haase, A. T. (1986). Pathogenesis of lentivirus infections. *Nature, 322,* 130–136.

Heyes, M., Brew, B. J., Martin, A., Price, R. W., Salazar, A. M., Sidtis, J. J., Yergey, J. A., Mouradian, M. M., Sadler, A. E., Keilp, J., Rubinow, D., & Markey, S. P. (1991). Quinolinic acid in cerebrospinal fluid and serum in HIV-1 infection: Relationship to clinical and neurological status. *Annals of Neurology, 29,* 202–208.

Ho, D. D., Pomerantz, R. J., & Kaplan, J. C. (1987). Pathogenesis of infection with human immunodeficiency virus. *New England Journal of Medicine, 317,* 278–286.

Holman, B. L., Garada, B., Johnson, K. A., Mendelson, J., Hallgring, E., Teoh, S. K., Worth, J., & Navia, B. (1992). A comparison of brain perfusion SPECT in cocaine abuse and AIDS dementia complex. *Journal of Nuclear Medicine, 33,* 1312–1315.

Janssen, R. S., Saykin, A. J., Kaplan, J. E., Spira, T. J., Pinsky, P. F., Sprehn, G. C., Hoffman, J. C., Mayer, W. B., & Schonberger, L. B. (1988). Neurological complications of human immunodeficiency virus infection in patients with lymphadenopathy syndrome. *Annals of Neurology, 23,* 49–55.

Johnson, J. G., Williams, J. B., Rabkin, J. G., Goetz, R. R., & Remien, R. H. (1995). Axis I psychiatric symptoms associated with HIV infection and personality disorder. *American Journal of Psychiatry, 152,* 551–554.

Jones, B. N., Teng, E. L., Folstein, M. F., & Harrison, K. S. (1993). A new bedside test of cognition for patients with HIV infection. *Annals of Internal Medicine, 119,* 1001–1004.

Joseph, R. (1992). The limbic system: Emotion, laterality and unconscious mind. *Psychoanalytic Review, 79*(3), 405–456.

Kimes, A. S., London, E. D., Szabo, G., Raymon, L., & Tabakoff, B. (1991). Reduction of cerebral glucose utilization by the HIV envelope glycoprotein Gp-120. *Experimental Neurology, 112,* 224–228.

Levy, J. A., & Bredesen, D. E. (1988). Central nervous system dysfunction in acquired immunodeficiency syndrome. *Journal of Acquired Immunodeficiency Syndrome, 1,* 41–64.

Levy, R. M., Rosenbloom, S., & Perett, L. V. (1986). Neuroradiologic findings in AIDS: A review of 200 cases. *American Journal of Roentgenology, 147,* 977–983.

Lipsitz, J. D., Williams, J. B., Rabkin, J. G., Remien, R. H., Bradbury, M., el Sadr, W., Goetz, R., Sorrell, S., & Gorman, J. M. (1994). Psychopathology in male and female intravenous drug users with and without HIV infection. *American Journal of Psychiatry, 151,* 1662–1668.

Markowitz, J., & Perry, S. (1990). AIDS: A medical overview for psychiatrists. In A. Tasman, S. Goldfinger, & C. Kaufman (Eds.), *American Psychiatric Press review of psychiatry* (pp. 574–592). Washington, DC: American Psychiatric Press.

Masdeu, J. C., Yudd, A., Van Heertum, R. L., Grundman, M., Hriso, E., O'Connell, R. A., Luck, D., Camli, U., & King, L. N. (1991). Single-photon emission computed tomography in human immunodeficiency virus encephalopathy: A preliminary report. *Journal of Nuclear Medicine, 32,* 1471–1475.

McAllister, R. H., Herns, M. V., Harrison, M. J. G., Newman, S. P., Connolly, S., Fowler, C. J., Fell, M., Durrance, P., Manji, H., Kendall, B. E., & Valentine, A. R. (1992). Neurological and neuropsychological performance in HIV seropositive men without symptoms. *Journal of Neurology, Neurosurgery, and Psychiatry, 55,* 143–148.

McArthur, J. C. (1994). Neurological and neuropathological manifestations of HIV infection. In

I. Grant & A. Martin (Eds.), *Neuropsychology of HIV infection* (pp. 56–106). Oxford, England: Oxford University Press.

McArthur, J. C., Cohen, B. A., Selnes, O. A., Kumar, A. J., Cooper, K., McArthur, J. H., Soucy, G., Cornblath, D. R., Chmiel, J. S., Wang, M. C., Starkey, D. L., Ginzburg, H., Ostrow, D., Johnson, R. T., Phair, J. P., & Polk, B. F. (1989). Low prevalence of neurological and neuropsychological abnormalities in otherwise healthy HIV-1-infected individuals: Results of the Multicenter AIDS Cohort Study. *Annals of Neurology, 26*, 601–611.

Merrill, J. E., & Chen, I. S. (1991). HIV-1, macrophages, glial cells, and cytokines in AIDS nervous system disease. *The FASEB Journal, 5*, 2391–2397.

Meyer, I., Empfield, M., Engel, D., & Cournos, F. (1995). Characteristics of HIV-positive clinically mentally ill patients. *Psychiatric Quarterly, 66*, 201–207.

Navia, B. A., Jordan, B. D., & Price, R. W. (1986). The AIDS dementia complex: I. clinical features. *Annals of Neurology, 19*, 517–524.

Ostrow, D. G., Monjan, A., Joseph, J., VanRaden, M., Fox, R., Kingsley, L., Dudley, J., & Phair, J. (1989). HIV-related symptoms and psychological functioning in a cohort of homosexual men. *American Journal of Psychiatry, 146*, 737–742.

Perkins, D. O., Davidson, E. J., Leserman, J., Liao, D., & Evans, D. L. (1993). Personality disorder in patients infected with HIV: A controlled study with implications for clinical care. *American Journal of Psychiatry, 150*, 309–315.

Perry, S., Jacobsberg, L. B., & Fishman, B. (1990). Psychiatric diagnosis before serologic testing for the human immunodeficiency virus. *American Journal of Psychiatry, 147*, 89–93.

Perry, S. W., & Jacobsen, P. (1986). Neuropsychiatric manifestations of AIDS-spectrum disorders. *Hospital & Community Psychiatry, 37*, 135–142.

Petito, C. K. (1988). Review of central nervous system pathology in human immunodeficiency virus infection. *Annals of Neurology, 23*(Suppl.), S54–S57.

Pitlik, S. D., Fainstein, V., Bolivar, R., Guarda, L., Rios, A., Mansell, P. A., & Gyorkey, F. (1983). Spectrum of central nervous system complications in homosexual men with acquired immune deficiency syndrome [letter]. *Journal of Infectious Diseases, 148*, 771–772.

Post, M. J., Tate, L. G., Quencer, R. M., Hensley, G. T., Berger, J. R., Sheremata, W. A., & Maul, G. (1988). CT, MR, and pathology in HIV encephalitis and meningitis. *American Journal of Roentgenology, 151*, 373–380.

Power, C., & Johnson, R. T. (1995). HIV-1 associated dementia: Clinical features and pathogenesis. *Canadian Journal of Neurological Sciences, 22*(2), 92–100.

Power, C., Selnes, O. A., Grim, J. A., & McArthur, J. C. (1995). HIV dementia scale: A rapid screening test. *Journal of Acquired Immune Deficiency Syndromes and Human Retrovirology, 8*, 273–278.

Price, R. W., & Brew, B. W. (1988). The AIDS dementia complex. *Journal of Infectious Disease, 158*, 1079–83.

Price, R. W., Brew, B., & Sidtis, J. (1988). The brain and AIDS: Central nervous system HIV-1 infection and AIDS dementia complex. *Science, 239*, 586–591.

Price, R. W., Sidtis, J., & Rosenblum, M. (1988). AIDS dementia complex: Some current questions. *Annals of Neurology, 23*(Suppl.), S27–S33.

Rabkin, J. R., Remien, R. H., Katoff, L., & Williams, J. B. (1993). Resilience in adversity among long-term survivors of AIDS. *Hospital and Community Psychiatry, 44*, 162–167.

Resnick, L., Berger, J. R., & Shapshank, P. (1988). Early penetration of the blood-brain barrier by HIV. *Neurology, 38*, 9–14.

Rundell, J. R., Paolucci, S. L., Beatty, D. C., & Boswell, R. N. (1988). Psychiatric illness at all stages of human immunodeficiency virus infection [letter]. *American Journal of Psychiatry, 145*, 652–653.

Saykin, A. J., Janssen, R. S., Sprehn, G. C., Kaplan, J. E., Spira, T. J., & O'Conner, B. (1991). Longitudinal evaluation of neuropsychological function in homosexual men with HIV infection: 18-month follow-up. *Journal of Neuropsychiatry, 3*, 286–298.

Selnes, O. A., Miller, E., McArthur, J. C., Gordon, B., Munoz, A., Sheridan, K., Fox, R., & Saah,

A. J. (1990). HIV-1 infection: No evidence of cognitive decline during the asymptomatic stages. *Neurology, 40*, 204–208.

Sharer, L. R. (1992). Pathology of HIV-1 infection of the central nervous system. A review. *Journal of Neuropathology and Experimental Neurology, 51*, 3–11.

Snider, W. D., Simpson, D. M., Nielson, S., Gold, J. M., Metroka, C. E., & Posner, J. B. (1983). Neurological complications of acquired immune deficiency syndrome: Analysis of 50 patients. *Annals of Neurology, 14*, 403–418.

Sonnerborg, A. B., Ehrnst, A. C., Bergdahl, S. K., Pehrson, P. O., Skoldenberg, B. R., & Strannegard, O. O. (1988). HIV isolation from cerebrospinal fluid in relation to immunological deficiency and neurological symptoms. *AIDS, 2*, 89–93.

Tross, S., Hirsch, D., Rabkin, B., Berry, C., & Holland, J. C. (1987). Determinants of psychiatric disorder in AIDS spectrum patients. In *Abstracts, III International Conference on AIDS*. Washington, DC: U.S. Department of Health and Human Services and the World Health Organization.

Tyor, W. R., Wesselingh, S. L., Griffin, J. W., McArthur, J. C., & Griffin, D. E. (1995). Unifying hypothesis for the pathogenesis of HIV-associated dementia complex, vacuolar myelopathy, and sensory neuropathy. *Journal of Acquired Immune Deficiency Syndromes and Human Retrovirology, 9*, 379–388.

Van Gorp, W. G., Mandelkern, M., & Gee, M. (1992). Cerebral metabolic dysfunction in AIDS: Findings in a sample with and without dementia. *Journal of Neuropsychiatric Clinical Neuroscience, 4*, 280–287.

Williams, J. B., Rabkin, J. G., Remien, R. H., Gorman, J. M., & Ehrhardt, A. E. (1991). Multidisciplinary baseline assessment of homosexual men with and without human immunodeficiency virus infection. *Archives of General Psychiatry, 48*, 124–130.

Chapter 4

Support Groups and Psychotherapy Groups for HIV: Toward an Integrated Model

Clayton Guthrie

People living with HIV and AIDS often confront feelings of shame and isolation and find themselves unable to share their experiences with friends and family members for fear of being rejected. Even before contracting the virus, many groups who are at greatest risk for infection have been ostracized from mainstream society. Stigmatization, resulting from such factors as the often unfounded fear of HIV infection and the more general discomfort with illness of any kind, contributes to the isolation experienced by people with HIV. After others learn of their seropositive status, no relationship can ever be the same. Family members may grow distant or turn their backs altogether. Lovers may prove unable to contend with the stresses of the situation and end the relationship. Sometimes, stigma plays itself out in subtle and unexpected ways. A person may learn of a friend's positive HIV status and begin to treat him or her as special. Such patronizing can actually intensify the feeling of stigmatization (Kalichman, 1995).

Therapeutic groups, which run the gamut from peer support groups to traditional psychotherapy groups, are the most common psychotherapeutic treatments for persons living with HIV and AIDS (Field & Shore, 1992). For one thing,

I would like to thank the following people for their help in preparing this chapter: Boaz Dalit, PsyD; David Deitcher; David Panzer, PsyD; John Sahs, MD; Ariel Shidlo, PhD; Jim Singlar, CSW; Joan E. Storey, CSW; Mark Thomas, PhD; and Lucy A. Wicks, PhD.

groups are a cost-effective means of treatment for clinics and other community-based organizations that often find themselves with ever-increasing client loads and ever-diminishing budgets. Moreover, the unique interpersonal consequences of living with the virus make psychotherapeutic support groups of particular use to this population.

Both support groups and traditional process-oriented psychotherapy groups contain elements that are beneficial to the unique dilemmas confronting persons living with HIV. Leading groups for HIV-positive individuals requires that leaders maintain a flexible attitude. Rigid commitment to any one modality may be inappropriate. Clinicians running these groups may need to give up strict adherence to any particular modality and adopt an integrated treatment model that will best serve this population.

GROUP THERAPY AND HIV: THERAPEUTIC BENEFITS

Group therapy offers certain unique opportunities that are different from those present in individual psychotherapies. Many of the therapeutic factors involved in the group process have been laid out by Yalom (1995). These therapeutic factors operate in all group therapies, whether they are process-oriented psychotherapy groups or support groups. These factors, which are interdependent, offer specific curative benefits for people living with HIV and AIDS.

Therapy groups allow members to interact with others who have had difficulties similar to their own and who have made psychological improvements since entering therapy. Learning of one's HIV status may feel like a death sentence. Attending group sessions with others who have found ways to cope with the devastating effects of the virus enables members to find hope for themselves. This is especially useful for people who have only recently received their diagnosis. Coming to group sessions and interacting with long-term survivors who are thriving can serve an inspirational function. In fact, this is one of the most compelling arguments for forming groups composed of individuals at different stages of the disease continuum. Peer-support groups, such as Alcoholics Anonymous, have always placed great emphasis on the curative benefits of the instillation of hope.

Reggie, who was newly diagnosed with HIV, entered into group therapy with reservations about joining a group in which there would be members at more advanced stages of the illness continuum. During his third session, Reggie spoke of how seeing others cope with their opportunistic infections gave him hope that he would be able to manage his own health concerns.

For persons with HIV, a psychotherapeutic support group can be life preserving (Field & Shore, 1992). Many persons living with HIV enter into group therapy feeling isolated and alone (Getzel & Mahony, 1990; Silven & Caldarola, 1989). Many of them do not know other people who are HIV positive and, as a result, feel alone in confronting their problems. Joining a group helps these individuals experience a much-needed sense of connectedness. Through interaction with others who are in the same boat, they can begin to develop a sense of acceptance about their infection.

A sense of belonging can also help members combat the powerful stigmatization that accompanies an HIV-positive diagnosis. Group members can share their experiences with others who are experiencing the same detrimental effects of stigmatization. Together, they can learn the sources of stigma, both in the outside world and within themselves. Ideally, as this process enables members to see themselves as proactive and empowered, they will begin to reconstruct a greater sense of self-esteem. To expect people with HIV to be able to locate these sources of stigma on their own is like expecting patients who have been physically or sexually abused to sort out the source of their abuse (Cadwell, 1994).

Groups can provide a wide range of information to persons with HIV. This information, which is provided by group leaders and other members, includes information concerning specific medical treatments, financial entitlements, and other services. For newly diagnosed group members, it is especially useful to hear how others have navigated the health care and social services systems or how they have handled the difficult task of revealing their HIV status to others. Besides offering explicit information about the members' illness and life situation, HIV groups can also assist members in examining their misconceptions and self-defeating responses to the virus (Yalom, 1995).

Steven was the "medical expert" in his therapy group for HIV-positive individuals. Whenever members had questions about a new treatment protocol, Steven was usually equipped with the latest information about the pros and cons of the treatment. In fact, his knowledge was always more comprehensive and up to date than the group leaders'.

Supportive comments, suggestions, or insights may be more readily accepted when they come from other members of a group rather than from the leader. Offering such altruistic comments can help members feel their importance to others and their impact on them. Many people with HIV come into a group feeling worthless. Acts of altruism can relieve alienation, self-doubt, and fear (Field & Shore, 1992). For members who are more comfortable in the role of caregiver, giving advice or support to others can provide them with a reason for living. It also allows them to rise above their own worries and shift the focus to others.

Most people entering groups have unsatisfactory family histories (Yalom, 1995). Within the group, interactions occur in which these maladaptive familial interactions are repeated. Leaders may be seen as parents, other members as siblings. The dynamics of an HIV-positive group allow members an opportunity to relive these familial conflicts correctly, just as they do in any other group.

Rosa came into group convinced that other members would not talk to her or take any interest in what she had to say. After a few weeks, it came out that Rosa's parents did not communicate with each other and would often ignore her when she tried to speak to them. After overcoming her initial shyness, Rosa was surprised to discover that group members listened attentively to what she had to say and often sought out her advice.

Social learning occurs in all group situations. Groups allow members the opportunity to improve their social skills, making them better able to respond to others in an empathic rather than a judgmental manner and helping them to develop conflict resolution skills. The stigmatization that accompanies a positive diagnosis leaves many group members feeling emotionally injured. On entering the group, members are often socially withdrawn and doubt their self-worth. Supportive and nonjudgmental interaction with other HIV-positive group members can help rectify this situation. Members will then potentially be able to apply the techniques they learn in the group situation to other social interactions.

Groups provide a good opportunity for members to model themselves on behaviors they observe in others. This can be extremely beneficial in groups for HIV-positive individuals. Most of these groups are composed of members who are at varying points on the continuum of HIV illness, which allows newly diagnosed members the opportunity to observe how others who have been living with the virus for a longer time physically care for themselves and cope emotionally with the virus and its effects. For example, newly diagnosed members who are still drinking heavily or taking recreational drugs may alter this potentially harmful behavior after hearing other members discuss how sobriety helped their state of mind and allowed them to achieve a more profound self-acceptance.

Juan, a new member in a gay men's group, spoke about a new romantic interest in his life. Juan was afraid that he would be rejected if he revealed his HIV status to this man. He was seriously considering ending the relationship to avoid a possible rejection. Others in the group offered advice on how they had dealt with similar situations, but Juan appeared unconvinced. During the next meeting, Juan told the group that he had taken their advice and revealed his status to this man. To his surprise, the man told Juan that he was also HIV positive and had been wondering how to break the news to him.

The open expression of emotion is vital to group process. Groups allow members to express feelings in new and different ways in order to relieve interpersonal tension and set the stage for interpersonal learning. Catharsis alone is not sufficient for change to occur, but it is a vital part of the process. People with HIV come to group with a wealth of intense emotions such as shame, anger, pain, and guilt. Many of them feel guilty about burdening their healthy friends and family and are more comfortable sharing negative feelings with the group (Rabkin, Remien, & Wilson, 1994).

Yalom (1995) believed that major therapeutic changes occur as a result of dynamic group interactions as they take place in the here and now. Through self-observation and feedback from others, individuals in a psychotherapy group are able to learn about their own interpersonal transactions. In this way, an HIV-positive therapy group functions as a social microcosm of each member's universe. The hope is that each member will then apply what he or she learns in the group to his or her everyday life, affecting other relationships and leading to a greater understanding of his or her own role within these interpersonal relationships. The group also provides the opportunity to risk new behaviors that will ultimately lead to a decrease in maladaptive behavior and social anxiety and to an increase in self-esteem.

The creation of a sense of acceptance, support, and affiliation is crucial for any successful group. Acceptance by others and of oneself are interdependent. Not only does self-acceptance often depend on the acceptance of others, but, according to Yalom (1995), acceptance of others is possible only after one accepts oneself. Stigmatized individuals in a group of other stigmatized individuals may experience a sense of nonjudgmental acceptance for the first time in their lives.

Because of the unpredictable course of AIDS, it is crucial that cohesiveness be established as quickly as possible (Beckett & Rutan, 1990). As group cohesiveness is often threatened by inconsistent membership and the death of individual group members, this poses a special challenge for the leader (Rutan & Stone, 1993). However, the fact that the members are all facing the same syndrome with the same unpredictable course may actually foster cohesion at a faster rate than in other groups.

There comes a time when all men and women must face the fact that no matter how close they get to others, they face life and death alone. For individuals confronting a syndrome whose course is so unpredictable, this realization becomes even more marked. By observing others who courageously are dealing with the inequitable insults of this life-threatening syndrome, group members often gain the strength necessary to prepare for the difficult challenges ahead. Only by accepting the prospects of an abbreviated life can individuals gain some sense of control over their destiny (Getzel & Mahony, 1990). Many seemingly ordinary discussions of everyday subjects that come up in groups are actually related to the profound existential issues of separation, loss, and death.

THERAPY GROUPS FOR OTHER ILLNESSES

The first known therapy group was set up in 1907 by Pratt in order to treat patients at an advanced stage of tuberculosis (Anthony, 1971). In more recent years, group treatment has been found to be effective in the treatment of other chronic illnesses, such as cancer (Spiegel & Glafkides, 1983; Tunnell, 1994). Spiegel and Yalom (1978) pointed out several potent factors involved in the group treatment of dying cancer patients that are not available in individual therapy, including universality, instillation of hope, group cohesiveness, and altruism. Just as they can for people with HIV, these groups allow patients with other chronic diseases to focus on living in an attempt to demystify and diminish the terror associated with the process of dying.

However, there are aspects of living with HIV that make it different from other chronic illnesses. Once a person receives a full AIDS diagnosis, the course of the illness is often unpredictable. The fact that HIV is identified with specific high-risk behaviors means that an HIV-positive diagnosis carries a stigma not associated with other illnesses, such as cancer. Also unique is the fact that an increasing number of young people are contracting the virus and facing physical deterioration and social losses that are not typically encountered until one is much older (Kalichman, 1995). Finally, cancer doctors can sometimes offer their patients hope of a curative intervention. Although HIV-related illnesses and symptoms can be treated, and lives extended, there are currently no curative interventions for the virus itself (Kalichman, 1995).

PSYCHOTHERAPY GROUPS

In the literature, more than 25 different models of group intervention have been identified, including psychotherapeutic growth groups, task groups, social action groups, and support groups (Land & Harangody, 1990). When starting a group for HIV-positive persons, leaders need to be clear about which of these models will be of the greatest use to their population. The question is not, "Does group treatment help?" but rather, "What type of group treatment is most beneficial for persons living with HIV?" Admittedly, it is difficult to differentiate between psychotherapy and support groups. As one clinician put it,

> You can't have one without the other. I don't believe you can have a therapy group without there being some element of support. And there has to be safety in the group for people to be able to confront each other. (Thomas, personal communication, May 16, 1996)

To answer the question of which type of group is most beneficial, it is necessary to examine support groups and psychotherapy groups as distinct entities; this requires distinguishing between the two as they are currently practiced. This examination includes a discussion of the goals and benefits of each modality as currently applied to people with HIV and the perceived role of the group leader in each.

Much of the interpersonal learning that takes place in a process-oriented psychotherapy group is the result of the here-and-now interactions that take place between members. In discussing the curative benefits of psychotherapy groups, Yalom (1995) placed a greater emphasis on the "corrective" emotional experiences that occur through such interactions and less emphasis on the results of traditional psychoanalytic techniques, such as transference and insight.

Yalom's (1995) interpersonal group psychotherapy is not the only model available to clinicians running HIV-positive groups. Variants of psychotherapeutic groups run the full spectrum of foci and dynamics. Foulkes's (1965) model of group analysis, for example, perceives group work as taking place in both the here and now and the there and then, continually shifting back and forth between the two. This model, which uses the classical Gestalt conception of figure and ground, also focuses on transference in all its varied forms: between members and leader, between members and other members, and between members and the group as a whole. Other psychotherapy groups draw on the intrapsychic approach of Wolf and Schwartz (1962). These groups, which focus very little on the here and now, attempt to conduct individual psychoanalysis in a group setting.

Benefits

Psychotherapy groups allow members to live out their relationships with others in front of professional facilitators who can help guide the process. Tunnell (1994) felt that despite the potential difficulties involved with HIV (stigma, threat of an early death, the unpredictable course of illness), the unique interpersonal experience of group psychotherapy provides the most effective form of treatment for people living with HIV. To illustrate this point, Tunnell used the example of projective identification. Feelings of shame and self-hatred are common among those infected with HIV. A member harboring such feelings may project them onto other members. This is likely to lead other members to distance that individual, thereby confirming the person's belief that she or he is unworthy. It is important for the group leader to detect this interaction, identify it, question or challenge it, and rally other members to support her or him in interrupting the process of projective identification.

Goals

As in all psychotherapy groups, groups for HIV-positive individuals can advance feelings of personal efficacy; increase understanding of maladaptive patterns; teach individuals to communicate more clearly about needs, fears, and conflicts; and thereby improve quality of life (Zegans, Gerhard, & Coates, 1994). Group psychotherapy can help individuals to adjust to life with a serious illness, but can also promote healing solutions of deeper, more conflictual issues about living with HIV. Although group members are often more comfortable avoiding these difficult, painful issues, for their own psychological well-being they should be encouraged to confront them. If members fail to address these issues they are likely to become dissatisfied with the group, and as a result, the group may dissolve (Tunnell, 1994). The goal of such groups is to assist members in living their remaining days in as conflict free and authentic a manner as possible (Beckett & Rutan, 1990).

Role of Group Leader

One of the major differentiations between a support group and a psychotherapy group is the function of the leader. The leader's role in an HIV-positive group psychotherapy is similar to any other: He or she must listen to the process of each meeting, deduce from that what the important unconscious feelings and conflicts might be, and assess how each member is contributing to the group process. Through this process, "the leader can offer insight to the members about their personal understanding of and responses to the common dilemma" (Beckett & Rutan, 1990, p. 26).

Tunnell (1991) offered an excellent example of how a leader of an HIV-positive psychotherapy group can make use of this process. As others in the group become ill, each member will respond differently. Some will attempt to get closer to the ailing member, supporting them even more; others will react by distancing themselves. The leader can observe this intrapsychic process as it is played out interpersonally. This will serve two purposes: It will allow the leader and the members to learn about each individual's intrapsychic process and it will strengthen group cohesion by "normalizing" members' ambivalent feelings toward illness, death, and loss (Tunnell, 1991).

A variation of this came up in an HIV-positive gay men's group the author currently co-leads. One member had just returned from a brief vacation where he had scattered his dead lover's ashes. His moving retelling of this incident led each member to begin discussing wishes for his or her own funeral. Some wanted the decisions left entirely to their families, and others had left stipulations in their wills that their families would have no say in the planning of the funeral. By asking what was behind their decisions, a wealth of information was revealed regarding unresolved issues each member was experiencing with his family.

A psychotherapy group leader must be careful not to take on too prominent a role in supporting members, but must help them to help each other. The leader must also assist in finding solutions to problems while avoiding extreme reactions, making sure that members neither become so preoccupied with death and dying that they become disengaged from others nor engage in magical, wishful thinking that denies the reality of their diagnosis (Getzel & Mahony, 1990). Irregular attendance, which is common in HIV-positive psychotherapies, may cause members to depend on the leader more than they do on other members. The challenge for the leader is to resist conducting multiple individual therapies (Tunnell, 1991).

Leaders must also listen actively for issues of stigma and encourage members to focus on them, as well as on existential issues such as untimely death and the unpredictable onset of illness. In a support group, these particular issues might be ignored or minimized (Tunnell, 1994).

Unlike other psychotherapy groups in which the leader may explore each member's long-standing characterological issues, Tunnell (1991) has advised leaders of HIV-positive psychotherapy groups to resist this for two reasons. Erratic attendance already makes this work extremely difficult. Also, exploring long-standing characterological issues is secondary to the here-and-now experience of supporting one another in group.

SUPPORT GROUPS

Support is a necessary part of any therapy group. Without it, members will not feel it is safe to open up and share personal information. Most support groups are formed around a common condition, crisis, symptom, or experience (Gitterman, 1989; Lieberman, 1990). Some support groups, such as those based on the 12-step model, are run by peers who themselves fit into the category that group membership is composed of. Other support groups, such as those for cancer patients, are more often run by trained professionals (Spiegel & Glafkides, 1983; Spiegel & Yalom, 1978).

Community-based AIDS organizations, such as Gay Men's Health Crisis (GMHC) in New York City, operate groups according to the support model. The majority of GMHC clients come into the organization asking for groups that stress support. Mark Thomas, clinical supervisor of group services at GMHC, defined a support group as a place that is set up to be as safe and comfortable as it can possibly be, so people who have concerns about their own mortality can feel they can talk about these subjects without worrying about how other people are going to hear them (Thomas, personal communication, May 16, 1996).

Another clinician describes support groups as "places where people with HIV can go for compassion, understanding, some information, and some way of holding themselves together" (Wicks, personal communication, May 15, 1996).

Benefits

Spiegel and Glafkides (1983) conducted a study comparing women with breast cancer who were in a support group with other women who received no group therapy treatment. The women in the treatment group improved on a variety of measures, whereas those in the control group experienced considerable psychological deterioration. Spiegel and Glafkides described their support groups as having a high degree of cohesion, with relatively little confrontation and little here-and-now interpersonal exploration. The leaders made few observations about ongoing interpersonal dynamics among group members. The focus was almost exclusively on content rather than the process (Spiegel & Glafkides, 1983).

Support groups have been found to be of therapeutic use to patients who are in emotional distress associated with an illness or physical condition, patients who are socially stigmatized, and patients who have difficulties negotiating transitions of their life cycle (Lieberman, 1990). All three of these conditions apply to persons with HIV. In addition to stress and stigmatization, the gravity and potential for precipitous decline associated with HIV requires these people to negotiate life cycle transitions at an accelerated rate. Many younger patients with HIV must navigate their way through stages of the life cycle that many of their peers will not face for decades. The supportive group provides individuals with the opportunity to "detoxify" the dying process by modeling the effective coping strategies of others (Spiegel & Glafkides, 1983).

Support groups can also serve as a social linkage system in which members can form meaningful, socially sustaining relationships. According to Katoff and Ince (1988), groups offer members the opportunity to "deal directly with social, emotional, and behavioral consequences of AIDS, to foster a network of mutual support and problem solving, and to observe role models among other persons who are coping with the stress associated with the disease" (p. 10). As a result of this intervention, social isolation and withdrawal decrease. This is essential for HIV-positive individuals, who may grow isolated after testing.

Many support groups also have an educational component, imparting information from leader to member and from member to member. This can play a crucial role in reducing illness-related fears and anxiety (Kalichman, 1995). Support groups are often offered in connection with other services, such as crisis services, entitlement advocacy, and referral.

Goals

Interaction with others who are also HIV positive can be empowering for members of support groups. In addition to providing information, such interaction can provide acceptance, offer hope, increase social support, decrease isolation, and enhance the quality of living with the virus (Gitterman, 1989). These groups also allow members an opportunity to work through feelings of dependency and loss of control that arise as other members die.

Role of Leader

Although the literature offers numerous views, there is a lack of consensus on what the leader's role in a support group should be. Most writers have agreed that they help the members to assist each other in an attempt to solve their common and individual difficulties (Gitterman, 1989; Land & Harangody, 1990). However, support group leaders must also be prepared at times to intervene in crisis situations, engage in direct problem solving, and assist in case management, as well as help members recognize feelings and gain insight into situations (Land & Harangody, 1990).

Addressing the various tasks of a support group leader, Gitterman (1989) spoke of helping members develop a sense of commonality and integration, inviting them to build on each other's contributions to the group, encouraging "cooperative mutual support norms," encouraging collective action, structuring collective decision making, actively pursuing individual members in an attempt to get them to participate, and clarifying members' role responsibilities and tasks. This final task differs from the role of psychotherapy group leaders, who often try to keep such things as role responsibilities less defined and more fluid.

PEER-LED SUPPORT GROUPS

Peer-led support groups, and other forms of self-help groups, have traditionally emerged when society is not meeting a need or when certain populations are not receiving necessary services (Lieberman, 1990). In the early years of the AIDS epidemic, health care providers, including mental health professionals, were slow to rally to the needs of persons with AIDS and HIV. As a result, community-based and other grassroots organizations arose to fill the gaps in services. Many of these organizations began offering support groups led by HIV-positive peers. Today, some community-based organizations continue to offer support groups led by peer facilitators rather than by professionally trained leaders (Rabkin et al., 1994).

When the leader and the other group members share the same condition, a psychological parity develops between the helper and those being helped. This reduction in psychological distance between members and leader promotes the development of identification and trust, which in turn leads to therapeutic change (Lieberman, 1990). Peer-led support groups for HIV-positive individuals have also been found to be effective in eliminating or reducing potentially harmful behaviors, providing role models for behavioral change, providing immediate positive reinforcement, and allowing members to share and develop information and techniques that are necessary if behavioral change is to occur (Magura, Shapiro, Grossman, & Lipton, 1989).

However, complications can arise when a support group is led by a peer facilitator. One clinician who has supervised peer-support group leaders has described difficulties that arose as a result of the facilitators' lack of training:

> When a clinician is trained as a psychotherapist, they learn to keep a therapeutic distance. Peer leaders who end up being called on to be therapists are not equipped to handle difficult situations that arise, and end up taking people home or completely losing any kind of separation. They end up feeling stressed out and guilty because people are suffering and they can't help them. Training helps us understand the limits of what we can do, and to understand our countertransference, what buttons are likely to be pushed. (Wicks, personal communication, May 15, 1996)

Members come into support groups with intriguing psychological issues. Unless the peer leader has a clear set of guidelines to follow (such as those used in 12-step programs), they may find it hard to resist delving into these deeper psychological issues in an attempt to understand them. A professionally trained support group leader may often be better able to maintain the structure of the group and recognize when it is more appropriate to refer a member out for individual psychotherapy.

GMHC maintains that all of their support groups are led by professionally trained clinicians:

> Often, people have certain expectations entering a group, like wanting a leader who is HIV positive. Once they are in the group they find out those things are less

important than they thought. In the context of the group, it doesn't come into play as much. I feel more comfortable having clinicians running groups because things can erupt that a clinician might be better trained for or be seen by group members as better trained for, which can have an impact on how the group develops. Group members feel safer with clinicians in the room. (Thomas, personal communication, May 16, 1996)

One clinician who has worked with peer counselors reported,

A group is a powerful, complex event, which requires skills to navigate. A group has to be kept safe. It takes time to learn to do that. One of the leader's jobs is to help members express anger in a safe way. I don't think peers can handle that. . . . Peers have trouble recognizing when they are burnt out. (Dalit, personal communication, May 17, 1996)

SIMILARITIES BETWEEN SUPPORT GROUPS AND PSYCHOTHERAPY GROUPS

Individuals in both support and psychotherapy groups feel they share elements of real or perceived commonalities with their fellow members. In an HIV-positive group, such feelings are intensified. These perceived similarities create a high level of cohesiveness that can also lead to greater acceptance. The establishment of a supportive atmosphere enables members to take the necessary risks that can lead to personal growth. These characteristics are the product neither of group ideology nor of leadership style, but are intrinsic conditions of all small groups (Lieberman, 1990).

Yalom (1995) pointed out that the therapeutic factors that exist in support groups are almost identical to those in psychotherapy groups: altruism, cohesion, universality, imitative behavior, instillation of hope, and catharsis. The sole distinction Yalom observed concerns interpersonal learning, which he saw as playing a far more important role in psychotherapy groups. Gitterman (1989), however, believed that as they function to point out maladaptive patterns, challenge group resistances, and pull for group conflict, support groups also focus on the here and now, which is an essential part of interpersonal learning theory.

Finally, it is often asserted that psychotherapy groups are distinct from support groups inasmuch as the former is the province of professionals and the latter of laymen (Lieberman, 1977). As an ever-greater number of trained professionals facilitate support groups, this distinction has become harder to maintain.

DIFFERENCES BETWEEN SUPPORT GROUPS AND PSYCHOTHERAPY GROUPS

Cadwell (1994) made a distinction between the function of psychotherapy and support groups for patients with HIV. He found that psychotherapy groups provide members with the opportunity to identify the personal suffering caused by social stigmatization, to examine internalized stigmatization, to feel the re-direction and support offered in the group, and to experience a catharsis of their pain and shame. Cadwell saw these activities as powerful antidotes to the shame and isolation experienced by most persons with HIV. Although he also believed support groups to be a useful resource in the struggle against stigmatization, he saw their benefits stemming from the establishment of a consistent focus on support issues, while avoiding any deeper therapy. To maintain the needed sense of safety, it is crucial that support group leaders resist engagement in these deeper issues (Cadwell, 1994).

Others have pointed out the structural and technical differences between the leaders of support and psychotherapy groups (Lieberman, 1977; Yalom, 1995). Leaders of psychotherapy groups are more likely to attempt to maintain psychological distance between themselves and the group members. In support groups, especially those conducted by peer leaders, the assumption is that re-ducing psychological distance promotes identification and trust and therefore leads to therapeutic change (Yalom, 1995).

For Lieberman (1990), the difference between psychotherapy and support groups lies in what transactions are thought to be most important. Although this will vary depending on the leader's ideology, psychotherapy groups operate under the assumption that change occurs through the exploration and reworking of relationships within the group. Support groups and self-help groups tend to deemphasize the importance of dynamic interaction between members as the impetus for change. The group functions as a supportive environment that allows new behaviors to develop outside the group (Lieberman, 1990).

Spiegel and Yalom (1978) found support groups to be the most beneficial form of treatment when working with dying patients. They felt that support groups are able to provide a kind of concrete guidance and support that is not common in psychotherapy groups. Others found that for persons with HIV and AIDS, a support group is preferable because of the unpredictable nature of the syndrome and the multiple demands of an HIV diagnosis (Land & Harangody, 1990). Furthermore, these authors believed that in support groups, members will be able to avoid confrontational transactions that are likely to increase already high levels of stress and anxiety. The implication is that psychotherapy groups cannot avoid such confrontations. Indeed, it is often through such confronta-tions that insights are gained.

There can also be a danger in being too supportive in the group context. By rushing in to save or protect a member in need, the leader risks sending the message that the group cannot bear what is being said. Believing that such avoidance is in the best interest of the group, the leader may actually be project-ing her or his own anxieties about loss, pain, and death and in so doing may ultimately leave members to face these issues alone. It is often easier to offer advice or solutions to problems, but just as often it can be more therapeutic to inquire into members' feelings and in that way buttress their particular experi-ence (Tunnell, 1991).

TOWARD AN INTEGRATED MODEL

Both support groups and psychotherapy groups offer therapeutic benefits to people with HIV. A recent study compared the effects of social support groups and cognitive behavioral groups with a control group that received no treatment (Kelly et al., 1993). This study found cognitive–behavioral groups less effective than social support groups in treating depressed HIV-positive patients. The term *social support group* is somewhat misleading. According to the Kelly et al. description, it appears that these social support groups consisted of elements from both support and psychotherapy group models. The cognitive–behavioral groups used behavioral skills strategies to reduce maladaptive anxiety and depression. Although both kinds of treatment groups showed more reduction in emotional distress than did the control group, the social support group produced favorable changes on more dimensions of adjustment for a greater number of participants. These changes included decreases in depression, anxiety, somatization, and hostility and a reduction in substance abuse. The Kelly et al. study pointed out the similar curative factors present in both support and psychotherapy group models.

Rigid commitment to any single therapeutic model may prove inappropriate when treating persons with HIV and AIDS. Because of the constant changes in their emotional, immunological, and cognitive states, a balance is desirable between therapeutic support, collaborative psychological examination, reality testing, and the development of new cognitive behavioral repertoires (Zegans et al., 1994). A clinician leading a therapy group for HIV-positive patients must be prepared to move back and forth between support and psychotherapy.

A blending of therapeutic support and psychological examination has often occurred in an HIV-positive therapy group that the author is currently co-leading. His co-leader's training and experience is primarily with support groups. In addition to the HIV-positive therapy group, the co-leader has led numerous support groups at an outpatient substance abuse treatment facility. The author's own experience leading groups has been with process-oriented psychotherapy groups, using the here-and-now techniques of interpersonal learning theory. The blending of these two styles has been a benefit to the group, as well as a learning experience for the co-leader and the author.

There are times when members in this group will engage in lengthy discussions about treatment protocols. The co-leader and the author both recognize the need for these discussions. During intakes, new members almost unanimously express their frustration at not having a forum to discuss medications and other treatment protocols. Members of the group will often say things like, "My doctor recommended a new protease inhibitor. I'm scared that altering my protocol might have a negative effect. Have any of the rest of you had experience with this drug?" In these instances, members need a supportive atmosphere in which to discuss these medications and the potential effects they will have on their lives.

There are also times when discussions of treatment protocols serve a defensive function. In one recent session, the author announced that William, a group member who had been in the hospital for several weeks, had just been admitted to a nursing home. After a brief discussion of how William had given up the fight to live, the group made an abrupt segue into a discussion of a new medication that was currently in the news. After a few minutes of this, the author pointed out that perhaps it was easier to speak about the hope attached to a new medication than to talk about what was happening with William. After a notable silence, the members began discussing the fears aroused by hearing the news about William and their need to believe that if they do not give up the fight, they may escape a similar fate.

There have also been times when the author and his co-leader have explored one member's interaction with another by asking what was behind a particular comment or question. Such interventions have often led to rich material related to the member's fear of dying or internalized stigmatization, which a more immediately supportive intervention may not have drawn out. Similarly, by questioning members about the dynamics within their families of origin, the author and his co-leader gain insight into how each member approaches difficult issues, such as disclosing their HIV status to potential sexual partners.

Because of the painful countertransferential feelings involved in working with persons with HIV, it is beneficial for group leaders to work in pairs. This allows them the opportunity to discuss their own fears and anxieties, their grief and sense of hopelessness, away from the group. By working with a co-leader, one can, it is hoped, find the proper balance of engagement and detachment that is necessary if one is to sustain the difficult job of working with this population. If one of the leaders is more support oriented and the other more psychodynamic, so much the better.

Field and Shore (1992) have developed a multimodal group therapy that responds to HIV-positive patients by combining elements of support and dynamic psychotherapy through education, information exchange, and psychodynamic insight. They have found the support group model helpful for discussing the more practical concerns of physical illness, whereas psychotherapeutic techniques allow members to explore motivation and relationships, as well as reactions to the syndrome and its outcome. The leaders attempt to help members understand their behavior in light of early patterns shaped by family relationships.

Tunnell (1991) also found that a supportive group psychotherapy is the treatment of choice for this population. Such groups can provide members with the support they need while also providing the necessary forum for addressing the critical psychological issues that result from testing HIV positive. Tunnell pointed out the importance of group members' addressing these critical issues, as well as other problems that arise as members avoid feelings of anger, grief, and bereavement.

Levine, Bystritsky, Baron, and Jones (1991) have developed a supportive psychoeducational psychotherapy group for the treatment of HIV-positive patients with major depression. According to this 20-session model, each meeting has a specific goal, known to leaders but not members, toward which the group work is directed. Having this structure allows leaders to achieve important developmental tasks, but the agenda for each session is essentially determined by the group members (Levine et al., 1991). Among goals for this hybrid model are offering accurate information about HIV infection and treatment, providing a supportive atmosphere for members to discuss the impact of HIV, addressing members' fears and concerns, helping members cope with the effect of HIV on loved ones, helping members integrate hope with grief, developing cognitive tools to cope with anxiety and depression, and facilitating the process of grieving.

One clinician who has led therapy groups for HIV-positive gay men and HIV-positive substance abusers uses what he calls a psychodynamic approach to support. He spoke of times in the gay men's group when members would bring up the topic of forming new romantic relationships:

> When they talk about relationships there is usually a discussion of negotiation because of their sero-status, so there's a feeling of support. But also what goes on within themselves with regard to their status: How do they want to reveal their status? When do they think they should? Even more advanced members, who are peer counselors themselves, sometimes surprise me by saying, "I don't want to tell my sexual partners." There's a dichotomy in these men. That's when the psychodynamic approach comes in. I ask them, "What's the difference? What's going on?" At the same time, I support them in their efforts to form relationships. (Singlar, personal communication, May 9, 1996)

Another clinician who has led numerous stress management groups for HIV-positive patients spoke of these groups as primarily supportive, dealing with dynamics only when they impede group progress:

> One member in the group who has low T-cells but is healthy was discussing the death of another member. She was feeling that she didn't want to be around other people who are dying and are leaving her behind. That got touched on a little bit, but she denied any negative feelings. All the material she presented after that clearly indicated that those feelings were there. But her denial was serving a function, so I did not interpret it. (Storey, personal communication, May 8, 1996)

If leaders are to adopt an integrated supportive–psychotherapeutic model, how are they to decide when to pursue psychodynamic material and when to ignore such material and adopt a more supportive stance? Very little has been written on this subject, and group leaders are often left to base this decision on instinct. One possibility is to make this decision on the basis of what is being discussed and how. For instance, there are times when defenses arising from discussions of death and dying should be explored and other times when support is more urgently needed.

Spector and Conklin (1987) have suggested that, to a great extent, the decision of whether a particular issue should be worked through should be dependent on the members. Leaders should not necessarily direct members to pursue issues that leaders may feel they should have a greater interest in. At most, the leaders should question the members about why certain subjects are discussed at length while others are ignored.

One clinician feels the choice of psychotherapy versus support should depend on the member's health status. At later stages of the illness, as members deal with medical problems, housing, and status disclosure, the group should be more supportive, more psychoeducational. At earlier stages of the illness, a more psychotherapeutic approach may be called for (Dalit, personal communication, May 17, 1996).

Others believe that the choice of treatment modality should be based on individual group members' psychological level of functioning, much the same as the decision would be made in individual therapy. One clinician compared two separate therapy groups he has led for HIV-positive gay men. One group, in which members were higher functioning, was conducted in a psychotherapeutic manner, with the focus on process, interpersonal relationships, and insight. In contrast, he conducted the second group in a more supportive manner "because the patients are not equipped psychologically to tackle more difficult issues or process interventions" (Sahs, personal communication, May 1, 1996). He continued,

> The first therapy group frequently dealt with death and dying. I was surprised how much. And it was not because of the members' stage of illness. Death and dying is not discussed in the second group in a meaningful way. It is joked about, not discussed, or briefly mentioned. The topics are not explored in a psychological manner . . . for two reasons: One, we see these patients as less capable of tolerating that level of discussion, and, two, because of the group members' interpersonal impairments it has taken much longer to develop the cohesiveness which would create a safe environment for that depth of discussion.

The decision of whether to be more support oriented or psychotherapy oriented may depend on a combination of factors: the material being discussed, the members' health status, the members' psychological level of functioning, and the theoretical leanings of the group leaders. It is impossible to know in advance how best to handle any given situation. However, before starting such a group, it is important for clinicians to consider how they will deal with certain situations as they arise. This includes deciding when and if it is appropriate to reveal one's own HIV status.

SELF-DISCLOSURE OF GROUP LEADER'S HIV SEROSTATUS

Whether a leader of an HIV-positive group should disclose his or her own HIV status to the group is a sensitive issue that raises many difficult questions. Are there times when it is appropriate and others when it is not? Is this issue similar to other areas of self-disclosure, such as marital status and sexual orientation, or does the issue of HIV make it unique? Will it be more helpful for a leader who is HIV positive to disclose to the group, more harmful for a leader who is HIV negative, or the reverse?

One might well assume that leaders of peer support groups are HIV positive. However, "in peer support groups, the assumption is that the leader is positive, but that is not always true. I think that is a problem. The patients are coming into the group assuming a relationship" (Wicks, personal communication, May 15, 1996). On learning that the leader of a peer-support group is HIV negative, members are likely to feel deceived. This could have adverse effects on the safety and cohesiveness of the group.

Several leaders of HIV-positive therapy groups have noted that most members assume that a professional who would lead such a group must be HIV negative. Perhaps members need to believe that the leader will remain healthy, a constant presence who will not vanish from the group. With the ever-present threat of other members getting sick or dying, it would be reassuring for members to know that the leader will not need taking care of in the same way.

Some clinicians feel it is inappropriate for group leaders to disclose their status:

> In both groups I led I was asked overt and covert questions about my HIV status. My feeling is that this discussion is not helpful. If the patients know you are not positive it gives them reason to think you can't understand them, which is reality based. If you are positive, it creates anxiety about the stability of the caregiver. (Sahs, personal communication, May 1, 1996)

> I'm not sure the clients need to know my HIV status. . . . They are here to be concerned about themselves and each other, not us. I would hesitate to self-disclose because I wouldn't want to interfere with that. If I were positive and disclosed, I would be closer to being a member, not a leader. That would interfere with the transference. (Singlar, personal communication, May 9, 1996)

> The danger is that the leader will then become more a part of the group, more a member than a facilitator. Down the road this results in a loss for the group. Initially, it feels good for everybody, but the role of facilitator is missing. (Thomas, personal communication, May 16, 1996)

When considering whether or not to disclose HIV status, a group leader must consider several points: How is the leader's self-disclosure going to be helpful to the group? What is the leader's motivation for wanting to self-disclose? If a group leader who is HIV positive reveals her or his status in order to feel closer to the group, the revelation may be of greater benefit to the leader than to the members. When asked directly what their status is, group leaders must consider the timing of the question. If it arises at a later stage of the group, the question may have to do with anger that members feel toward the leader. In such a case, it may be more appropriate to explore this anger than to answer the question directly.

Like other requests for personal information, the request to know the leader's HIV status is a clinical issue:

> It depends on the composition of the group, what they have been talking about, and how they are talking about it. . . . In my current group it came up as "No one understands what we're going through. Our doctors don't understand what it is like." This happened in a session after a lot of absences, with few patients present. The context was, the patients felt overwhelmed and alone. They come to group to feel like there are other people there like them. Since those other people aren't coming, what did it feel like to be there with just the leaders? Do they have the same feelings about us not understanding?. . . I think it's important to validate the feelings they were having of feeling alone and not understood. In other situations, it would not have served a therapeutic purpose to tell them we were negative. . . . It depends on where they are in the treatment, what material is being presented, and the person's way of looking at the world. (Storey, personal communication, May 8, 1996)

CONCLUSION

The unique psychological, social, and medical stressors that HIV-positive individuals face make psychotherapeutic support groups of particular use to this population. These groups, which run the gamut from peer support to traditional psychotherapy groups, are the most common psychotherapeutic treatments for persons living with HIV and AIDS (Field & Shore, 1992). As both psychotherapy and support groups offer therapeutic benefits to people with HIV, rigid commitment to either modality may prove inappropriate. It is recommended that a clinician running a group for HIV-positive individuals adopt an integrated treatment model that draws on the strengths of both psychotherapeutic and supportive group models. The decision of whether to be more support oriented or psychotherapy oriented in any given moment may be based on several factors, including the particular issues being discussed, individual members' psychological level of functioning, and members' health status.

REFERENCES

Anthony, E. J. (1971). The history of group psychotherapy. In H. Kaplan & B. Sadock (Eds.), *Comprehensive group psychotherapy* (pp. 4–31). Baltimore: Williams & Wilkins.

Beckett, A., & Rutan, J. S. (1990). Treating persons with ARC and AIDS in group psychotherapy. *International Journal of Group Psychotherapy, 40,* 19–29.

Cadwell, S. A. (1994). Twice removed: The stigma suffered by gay men with AIDS. In S. A. Cadwell, R. A. Burnham, & M. Forstein (Eds.), *Therapists on the front line: Psychotherapy with gay men in the age of AIDS* (pp. 3–24). Washington, DC: American Psychiatric Press.

Field, H. L., & Shore, M. (1992). Living and dying with AIDS: Report of a three-year psychotherapy group. *Group, 16*, 156–164.

Foulkes, S. H. (1965). *Therapeutic group analysis*. New York: International Universities Press.

Getzel, G. S., & Mahony, K. F. (1990). Confronting human finitude: Group work with people with AIDS. *Journal of Gay and Lesbian Psychotherapy, 1*, 105–119.

Gitterman, A. (1989). Building mutual support in groups. *Social Work with Groups, 12*, 5–21.

Kalichman, S. C. (1995). *Understanding AIDS: A guide for mental health professionals*. Washington, DC: American Psychological Association.

Katoff, L., & Ince, S. (1988). *Supporting people with AIDS: The GMHC model*. (Available from Gay Men's Health Crisis, 129 W. 20th St., New York, NY, 10011.)

Kelly, J. A., Murphy, D. A., Bahr, G. R., Kalichman, S. C., Morgan, M. G., Stevenson, L. Y., Koob, J. J., Brasfield, T. L., & Bernstein, B. M. (1993). Outcome of cognitive-behavioral and support group brief therapies for depressed, HIV-infected persons. *American Journal of Psychiatry, 150*, 1679–1686.

Land, H., & Harangody, G. (1990). A support group for partners of persons with AIDS. *Families in Society: The Journal of Contemporary Human Services, 7*, 222–230.

Levine, S. H., Bystritsky, A., Baron, D., & Jones, L. D. (1991). Group psychotherapy for HIV-seropositive patients with major depression. *American Journal of Psychotherapy, 3*, 413–423.

Lieberman, M. A. (1977). Problems in integrating traditional group therapies with new group forms. *International Journal of Group Psychotherapy, 27*, 19–32.

Lieberman, M. A. (1990). A group therapist perspective on self-help groups. In M. Seligman & L. E. Marshak (Eds.), *Group psychotherapy: Interventions with special populations* (pp. 1–17). Boston: Allyn & Bacon.

Magura, S., Shapiro, J. L., Grossman, J. I., & Lipton, D. S. (1989). Education/support groups for AIDS prevention with at-risk clients. *Social Casework, 70*, 10–20.

Rabkin, J., Remien, R., & Wilson, C. (1994). *Good doctors, good patients: Partners in HIV treatment*. New York: NCM.

Rutan, J. S., & Stone, W. (1993). *Psychodynamic group psychotherapy* (2nd ed.). New York: Guilford Press.

Silven, D., & Caldarola, T. J. (1989). The HIV-positive client. In J. W. Dilley, C. Pies, & M. Helquist (Eds.), *Face to face: A guide to AIDS counselling* (pp. 15–25). San Francisco: The AIDS Health Project.

Spector, I. C., & Conklin, R. (1987). Brief reports: AIDS group psychotherapy. *International Journal of Group Psychotherapy, 37*, 434–439.

Spiegel, D., & Glafkides, M. C. (1983). Effects of group confrontation with death and dying. *American Journal of Group Psychotherapy, 33*, 433–447.

Spiegel, D., & Yalom, I. D. (1978). A support group for dying patients. *International Journal of Group Psychotherapy, 28*, 233–245.

Tunnell, G. (1991). Complications in group psychotherapy with AIDS patients. *International Journal of Group Psychotherapy, 41*, 481–498.

Tunnell, G. (1994). Special issues in group psychotherapy for gay men with AIDS. In S. A. Cadwell, R. A. Burnham, & M. Forstein (Eds.), *Therapists on the front line: Psychotherapy with gay men in the age of AIDS* (pp. 237–254). Washington, DC: American Psychiatric Press.

Wolf, A., & Schwartz, E. K. (1962). *Psychoanalysis in groups*. New York: Grune & Stratton.

Yalom, I. D. (1995). *The theory and practice of group psychotherapy* (4th ed.). New York: Basic Books.

Zegans, L. S., Gerhard, A. L., & Coates, T. J. (1994). Psychotherapies for the person with HIV disease. *Psychiatric Clinics of North America, 17*, 149–162.

Part Two

Family, Children, and Couples: Exploring Therapy for Home Life

AIDS is a social disease. Spreading the disease requires intimate forms of contact with others. AIDS infects and affects social systems: the couple, the family, the peer group. Since the development of the disease, clinicians have become attuned to the existence of the multiple loss syndrome that complicates bereavement and resolution. Issues of overinvolvement or complete social isolation are common with this population. Talks about loss of all friends or descriptions of the deaths of multiple family members have become an integral part of treatment. Further, clinicians must address the impact of the disease on the ability of a couple or family to sustain a supportive and meaningful relationship. This section explores treatment issues within the context of couples, family, and group treatment, each working to design and understand family interventions that will promote the development of the system and individuals. The emphasis is to give clinicians and patients tools to cope more effectively with the transitions they face with those they love.

Chapter 5

Mental Health Treatment of Children and Families Affected by HIV/AIDS

Jennifer F. Havens, Claude Ann Mellins, and Sheila Ryan

As rates of HIV infection and AIDS rise steadily in women of child-bearing age (Centers for Disease Control, 1995), HIV/AIDS has evolved into a disease of families with children (Levine, 1990). To date, there have been 71,818 reported cases of AIDS in women in the United States, the vast majority of those in women between 20 and 40 years of age (Centers for Disease Control, 1995). The devastating effects of adult HIV infection are reflected in the increasing numbers of children, adolescents, and young adults who are losing parents to AIDS. In 1992, Levine and Michaels projected that between 72,000 and 125,000 children and adolescents will lose their mothers to AIDS by the year 2000, with 35,000 of these young people living in New York City (Michaels & Levine, 1992). Updated projections, which reflect the dramatic increase in AIDS among women of child-bearing age between 1991 and 1994, are that 50,000 children and adolescents in New York City will lose their mothers to AIDS by the year 2001 (Michaels & The Orphan Project, 1996).

In the United States, HIV infection in the heterosexual population is closely linked to drug use. Injecting drug use is the risk factor for HIV infection in 47% of AIDS cases in women; heterosexual contact with a drug-using man accounts for a significant percentage of the remaining cases (Centers for Disease Control,

This chapter was supported in part by Grant 5UDSSM51688-02 from the Substance Abuse and Mental Health Services Administration, HIV/AIDS Mental Health Services Demonstration Program. Parts of this chapter are based on "Mental Health Issues in HIV-Affected Women and Children," by J. Havens, C. Mellins, and D. Pilowski, *International Review of Psychiatry*, Vol. 8, No.2/3, 1996, pp. 217–225, Carfax Publishing Company, Oxfordshire, United Kingdom.

1995). Recently, crack cocaine use has been identified as a risk factor for HIV infection, independent of injecting drug use. Rates of HIV seropositivity in noninjecting female crack users in New York City are estimated at 30% (Edlin et al., 1994). In addition to confronting HIV infection in the parental generation, many of these families must also face HIV infection in one or more of their children. To date, there have been 6,948 reported cases of AIDS in children in the United States, more than 80% of these due to vertical transmission from an HIV-infected mother (Centers for Disease Control, 1995). Recent findings on the efficacy of AZT in reducing the rate of transmission of HIV from mother to infant have indicated a mechanism for minimizing the number of congenitally infected children (Connor et al., 1994). However, there is evidence that the women at highest risk for HIV infection (e.g., drug-using women) may be those most unlikely to access this important treatment advance (Wiznia et al., 1996).

Clearly, AIDS in women and children represents a confluence of two major epidemics plaguing American cities, HIV infection and drug addiction. The devastating losses due to AIDS occur most commonly in families already at tremendous psychosocial risk associated with familial substance abuse. Progressive HIV infection often represents the final stress on an already overburdened family system.

Mental health interventions designed to meet the complex psychosocial and psychiatric needs of these families are essential. Often, families present in crisis and need to be stabilized before they can begin to manage the overwhelming effects of HIV infection. Stigmatized and isolated adults often need mental health treatment in order to address one of the most difficult issues of all, planning for the placement of children after parental death. Children and adolescents need therapeutic relationships with continuity through parental illness, death, and placement to help them manage the devastating effects of these losses and maintain hope for their future. The family-based approach, which conceptualizes HIV illness within a series of stages, each with unique effects on the functioning and integrity of both the entire family and its individual members, holds particular promise for mental health treatment. In this treatment approach, the mental health needs of the family and its members are addressed in an integrated fashion, with the overall goal of meeting the needs of individual family members as well as supporting the functioning of the family.

MENTAL HEALTH NEEDS OF FAMILIES AFFECTED BY SUBSTANCE ABUSE AND HIV/AIDS

As a significant majority of the cases of AIDS in women and heterosexual men are linked to drug use, detailed understanding of the mental health issues in families affected by substance abuse is essential for clinicians working with this population. For the purpose of clarity, the mental health needs of families related to substance abuse and HIV/AIDS are presented separately, although they most typically present in an overlapping fashion.

Mental Health Needs Related to Substance Abuse

Women and Substance Abuse   Women with substance use disorders have high rates of psychiatric comorbidity, in particular depressive and anxiety disorders as well as childhood histories of attention deficit hyperactivity disorder (Blume, 1992; Carroll & Rounsaville, 1993; Haller, Knisely, Dawson, & Schnoll, 1993; Regier et al., 1990; Rounsaville, Weissman, Kleber, & Wilber, 1982). The presence of these psychiatric disorders in women has implications for their children, as there is ample evidence for the familial transmission of these disorders (Biederman et al., 1990; Downey & Coyne, 1990; Weissman et al., 1984). In addition, adult substance users have high rates of intellectual deficits and specific learning disorders, impairing academic and vocational functioning (Haller et al., 1993; Deren & Randell, 1990). Substance abuse complicates both the diagnosis and the treatment of comorbid psychiatric and cognitive disorders, often trapping women in a spiral of escalating drug use.

In addition, several studies have reported high rates of posttraumatic stress disorder in female substance abusers (Cottler, Compton, & Mager, 1992; Fullilove et al., 1991; Mellins, 1995). Life histories of severe trauma, especially those that include childhood sexual abuse, are associated with women's substance abuse (Fullilove et al., 1991; Hagan, 1988; Miller, Downs, Gondoli, & Keil, 1987; Zierler et al., 1991). These realities also have important implications for female substance abusers with children, as a history of parental victimization increases the risk of victimization in subsequent generations (Kaufman & Zigler, 1989; Rutter, 1989).

Children and Parental Substance Abuse   Children born to drug-addicted parents are potentially exposed to the negative effects of parental drug use both during the prenatal period and after birth. Several studies have described the developmental and behavioral problems of prenatally drug-exposed infants and children, including poor state organization; great sensorineural reactivity; impaired representational play; language, motor, and social skills delays; hyperactivity; and autistic features (Coles, Platzman, Smith, James, & Falek, 1993; Davis et al., 1992; Griffith, Azuma, & Chasnoff, 1994; Rodning, Beckwith, & Howard, 1989; Wilens, Biederman, Kiely, Bredin, & Spencer, 1995). Methodological problems in much of the research on prenatally drug-exposed children limit definitive conclusions regarding the link between specific drug exposures and behavioral or cognitive outcomes (Hutchings, 1993; Gonzalez & Campbell, 1994; Singer, Farkas, & Kliegman, 1992). However, it is clear that maternal drug use during pregnancy with its associated problems—such as inadequate prenatal care, premature birth, low birth weight, and the potential for inheriting parental psychiatric disorder—increases children's risk for developmental, cognitive, and psychiatric disorders.

There is also a potential for mental health problems associated with living with a severely drug-addicted parent. Children living in these families are at increased risk for neglect, abuse, exposure to domestic violence, and disruption of attachments (Singer et al., 1992). There is strong evidence that maternal characteristics associated with drug use (such as low self-esteem, social isolation, poor health, and insecurity about mothering capacity) place children at risk for impairments in attachment, especially when they occur during critical periods of development (Kelley, 1992; Rodning et al., 1989). Both impaired attachment and exposure to abuse, neglect, and violence increase the risk for psychiatric disorders and psychological distress in children (Cicchetti & Carlson, 1989; Green, 1993; Kelley, 1992; McLeer, Callagan, Delmina, & Wallen, 1994; Pelcovitz et al., 1994; Wildin, Williamson, & Wilson, 1991).

Thus, HIV illness commonly strikes families already struggling with the overwhelming problems associated with substance abuse, including impaired parenting capacities, high rates of psychiatric disorder in both children and adults (often undiagnosed and untreated), and multigenerational histories of victimization and trauma. The mental health issues related to substance abuse can greatly complicate a family's capacity to cope with the stresses of HIV illness. Frequently, problems associated with substance abuse dictate the mental health interventions as much as, if not more than, those related to HIV illness.

Mental Health Needs Related to HIV

HIV-Infected Women   The limited research on HIV-infected women has suggested that they are at high risk for psychiatric disorder and psychological distress. More specifically, studies have found high rates of affective disorders, most commonly major depression, as well as high rates of posttraumatic stress disorder (Franke, Jager, Thomann, & Beyer, 1992; Mellers et al., 1994; Mellins, 1995). Several factors may account for high rates of psychiatric disorders and psychological distress in HIV-infected women. As noted above, many HIV-infected women have histories of substance abuse, with high rates of comorbid psychiatric disorder (Mellers et al., 1994; Pergami et al., 1993). Second, many HIV-infected women are single mothers who must often cope with the stress of raising children who themselves may be HIV infected. Finally, HIV-infected women tend to be from ethnic minority populations who are socioeconomically disadvantaged and who have often experienced multiple traumatic life events (Mellins, 1995).

HIV-Infected Parents and Their Children   Although there has been little research on the specific mental health needs of HIV-affected families, it is clear that the issues associated with HIV infection are particularly complex for parents and their children. One useful model developed in the Special Needs Clinic, a family-based mental health service for HIV-affected children and families, organizes HIV illness into specific predictable stages, taking into account the dynamic course of HIV illness. These stages include the diagnosis of HIV infection, illness progression, late-stage illness, death, and, where relevant, family reconfiguration. Each stage presents particular challenges to family functioning and adaptation. What follows is an outline of the specific issues the authors have encountered in each of these stages, based on their treatment of more than 300 HIV-affected families.

HIV Diagnosis   A diagnosis of HIV infection presents a series of challenges to any individual, including anxiety about one's health status and adaptation to a foreshortened future. For parents with children, these issues are compounded by concerns about their capacity to provide for their children in the future. Women diagnosed during pregnancy must face concerns about potential transmission to their babies and decisions regarding continuation of pregnancy and antiretroviral treatment during pregnancy.

Many HIV-infected women are socially isolated and have experienced discrimination as a result of their substance abuse and poverty before their diagnosis. This baseline isolation can impede access to social and mental health supports as well as health care. In addition, guilt and shame about behaviors associated with the acquisition of HIV can impede effective communication about their HIV diagnosis, further isolating women from social supports. For women struggling with drug addiction, the stress of an HIV diagnosis can lead to relapse while in remission or to escalation of use among active users.

Progression of HIV Illness   As the medical sequelae of HIV illness increase, so does the pressure to communicate with family members about illness and the need to plan for children's future. Quite commonly, parents with advancing HIV illness have difficulty communicating effectively with their children about their illness. Andrews, Williams, and Neil (1993) found that only 33% of HIV seropositive mothers had disclosed their serostatus to children under age 16, whereas 67% had disclosed to those over age 16. Similarly, Mellins and Ehrhardt (1995) found, in a study of 40 HIV-infected mothers, that the majority had not told their children of their HIV status, particularly when children were younger than 12 years. Although this lack of disclosure to children is often perceived as protective by adults, it can serve to increase the anxiety of children experiencing ongoing physical and mental deterioration in their parents.

An important element in working with families regarding HIV disclosure is an assessment of the family's capacity to manage communication about HIV in an open and supportive way. In some families, such an assessment can be done directly, through open discussion of the parents' feelings about disclosing their serostatus to family members before disclosure. In those families resistant to or uncomfortable with such discussions, one can assess communication style with regard to other affectively loaded issues (such as non–AIDS-related family deaths, parental substance use, or other family events), providing clinicians with a sense of the parents' communication capacities. Those parents with significant communication problems will often benefit from help in framing their communications to children in ways that address the cognitive level and emotional needs of their children. Disclosing a diagnosis without addressing these issues (e.g., the child's understanding of the meaning of the information, including prognosis, fear of loss of the parent, and concerns for future security) can result in increased anxiety and emotional distress.

Disclosure to extended family members and children and adolescents in substance-use–affected families tends to be particularly complex, as its brings into direct light the risk behaviors associated with the acquisition of the virus. Feelings of guilt and shame about drug addiction and associated behaviors on the parents' part as well as an escalation of preexisting feelings of anger and abandonment on the children's part can greatly complicate open communication. In addition, the presence of active substance use or untreated psychiatric disorders (especially depressive disorders) can impede parents' capacity to communicate effectively with family members.

A particularly challenging task families face with HIV progression involves planning for the placement of children following parental death, commonly known as *permanency planning*. Communication about HIV illness and permanency planning tend to be closely intertwined, with difficulties in one area being reflected in the other. At the very least, effective planning requires the disclosure of HIV serostatus to the individuals selected to assume the children's care. In the authors' clinical experience, family-based permanency planning that actively involves the children, particularly teenagers, is much more likely to have a successful outcome than that which ignores or excludes the affected young people. As is the case for HIV disclosure, effective permanency planning can be undermined by active substance abuse, untreated psychiatric disorder, and family dynamics related to a parent's substance abuse.

Late-Stage HIV Illness   In the final phase of HIV illness, loss of parental functioning becomes paramount. Families with minimal social support can find themselves in crisis in this phase of the illness. The care of younger children may be left to older adolescents or young adult family members who are themselves facing the impending loss of a parent. Children whose parents develop AIDS-related dementia experience the changes in their parents' mental status, often without a clear understanding of the etiology or implications of these changes. In cases where parents develop AIDS-related psychiatric disorders (such as mania or psychosis), their disinhibited or disorganized behavior can be dangerous to children in their care.

Optimally, families affected by AIDS have begun the communication and permanency planning process before the final stage of parental HIV illness, and other adults are available to provide care and support for affected children. However, some parents—particularly those struggling unsuccessfully with mental illness, substance abuse, or both—present to medical care settings in end-stage AIDS without having addressed these issues. In the authors' experience, these are usually the most disorganized families with the highest burden of psychiatric and substance abuse disorder. In these families, special attention to the mental health needs of the children and adolescents is essential. Both the lack of family preparation and factors associated with that lack of preparation signal an increased risk for mental health problems in these children.

Bereavement and Family Reconfiguration   With parental death, grieving children and adolescents move into reconfigured families, most commonly into extended families also mourning the loss of the loved one. The social and concrete service supports available to the families by virtue of the parent's AIDS diagnosis generally diminish or disappear following the parent's death. Typically, children and adolescents orphaned by AIDS are moving from one situation of poverty to another, with the responsibility for the care of these children falling on financially limited families. In those cases where children and adolescents move into nonrelative foster care, they must make the difficult adaptation to new family members and often very different family lifestyles. Conversely, reconfigured families must assume the care of children who often have substantial emotional and behavioral disorders that may or may not be diagnosed and treated.

Specific issues complicating bereavement in the children of drug-abusing parents include their struggles with complex feelings about their parents, such as anger over abandonment or neglect, internalization of responsibility for parental inadequacies, or both. In several adolescent cases the authors have treated, the presence of ambivalent feelings in the child is reflected in pathological identification with the deceased parent, including the active assumption of parental risk behaviors (drug use, sexual promiscuity) following parental death.

HIV-Infected Children   Congenitally infected children living with their biological families share the complex set of familial issues described above. However, there are unique mental health issues for children confronting their own HIV illness. These include the specific effects of HIV progression on development and cognition and the psychological issues of adaption to a chronic, terminal illness.

The majority of research on HIV-infected children has focused on the neurodevelopmental effects of HIV infection. In general, there have been consistent findings of significant neurological, developmental, and cognitive deficits (Brouwers, Belman, & Epstein, 1991; Diamond et al., 1987; Epstein, Sharer, & Goudsmit, 1988; Mellins, Levinson, Zawadzki, Kairam, & Weston, 1994; Swayles et al., 1989). Two relatively distinct neurodevelopmental patterns have been described: progressive encephalopathy and static encephalopathy (Brouwers et al, 1991; Epstein et al., 1988). Progressive encephalopathy, corresponding with the AIDS dementia complex in adults, is characterized by the loss of developmental milestones in young children and by declining IQ scores. In older children, there are increasing difficulties with language, attention, concentration, and memory. This neurodevelopmental outcome is a direct consequence of HIV infection of the central nervous system and is associated with poor prognosis. Static encephalopathy, characterized by nonprogressive deficits in cognitive, motor, or language function, is not directly attributable to HIV and is associated with prenatal drug exposure, prematurity, and low birth weight (Epstein et al., 1988, Levenson & Mellins, 1992; Mellins, Levenson, Zawadzki, Kairam, & Weston, 1994).

There has been little research on emotional and behavioral disorders in HIV-infected children. Clinical reports have suggested that they are at high risk for anxiety, depression, guilt, and low self-esteem (Speigal & Mayers, 1991; Weiner & Septimus, 1991). In one of the few studies focusing on psychiatric disorder in HIV-infected children, Havens et al. (1994) found high rates of attention deficit hyperactivity disorder (21%) and oppositional defiant disorder (17%). However, these rates were no different than those in a matched control group of children from similar backgrounds (children living in foster care who had been born to women who had used drugs during pregnancy). Features associated with prenatal drug exposure, such as prematurity, low birth weight, and heritable parental psychiatric disorder, appear to be more potent predictors of psychiatric disorders in children than is HIV infection itself (Havens, Whitaker, Feldman, & Ehrhardt, 1994; Mellins et al., 1994).

In general, age, developmental level, or both dictate a child's capacity to understand the meaning of HIV illness. Preschoolers and children under the age of 6 or 7 cannot grasp the concept of chronic illness, so the strain and anxiety of knowing their diagnosis falls on their caregivers (Weiner & Septimus, 1991). Family members generally do not inform these young children of their HIV infection. For older children, who have a developing capacity to understand and contain information about HIV infection, several issues emerge. These include learning about one's diagnosis (either through family disclosure or individual deduction); coping with secrecy, stigma, and potential rejection by peers; coping with chronic illness; and anxiety about the future (Boyd-Franklin, Steiner, & Boland, 1995; Mellins & Ehrhardt, 1994; Weiner & Septimus, 1991). For adolescents, the normal developmental challenges of this stage, including puberty, sexuality, and the desire to fit in or be normal are seriously complicated by HIV disease. The detrimental effects of HIV on growth and pubertal development pose significant challenges for the growing number of congenitally infected young people living into their teen years.

As is the case for adults, the mental health issues for infected children change over the course of the disease. Many HIV-infected children remain relatively symptom free for long periods of time. They may not know their diagnosis, and their lives may be relatively unaffected by HIV. However, with disease progression, HIV-infected children must confront the physical and mental decline associated with AIDS. As they approach late-stage illness, they and their families must confront the terminal nature of the disease. Often, families are overwhelmed at this time and have difficulty communicating with the child about issues related to prognosis and death. Sensitive interventions by clinicians who have an ongoing relationship with the child and his or her family provide a setting for the child to express the inevitable anxieties and fears about separation from family members and dying. It also allows the child, if old enough, to communicate his or her wishes about medical treatment.

In children with HIV central nervous system involvement, recognition of dementia-related behavioral sequelae and accurate differential diagnosis is important for several reasons. The authors' have found in their clinical experience that parents and medical staff can misinterpret a child's increasing fatigue, decreased interest in and resistance to regular activities, and regressive behavior as volitional oppositional behavior or as depressive disorder. This can result in efforts to encourage the child to alter his or her behavior when in actuality the behavior is a sequelae of the disease process and not within the child's control. In several cases, the authors have found stimulants, such as methylphenidate, to be helpful to children struggling with the fatigue and attentional deficits associated with late-stage AIDS with cognitive involvement, both in raising children's energy level and in improving their quality of life. Finally, progressive brain involvement in children is an important prognostic sign, generally accompanied by severe immunocompromise and signaling the end stage of the disease. This is an important time to shift gears in work with children and their families to help them prepare for the final phase of the child's life.

MENTAL HEALTH SERVICES REQUIRED BY HIV-AFFECTED CHILDREN AND FAMILIES

As has been detailed, in many cases HIV/AIDS occurs in family environments already affected by complex psychosocial problems. Mental health practitioners working with these families must maintain a high index of suspicion for underlying mental illness and awareness of psychosocial stressors that can undermine a family's ability to manage the overwhelming stresses of progressive HIV infection. In addition to the routine psychotherapeutic skills, mental health clinicians working with these children and families need to have (a) an understanding of the natural history of HIV infection in both children and adults, including the potential nervous system effects of illness progression; (b) an understanding of psychiatric comorbidity in drug-using adults and drug-affected children and adolescents; (c) an empathic understanding of the effects of substance abuse on family structure and functioning; (d) a capacity to provide continuity of psychotherapeutic treatment to children and new guardians following parental death, with specific expertise in the management of bereavement complicated by ambivalence; and (e) experience with the social and psychotherapeutic issues associated with family-based permanency planning and disclosure and management of transition to new caretakers.

The following specific mental health services are necessary for the treatment of these children and families:

- psychiatric evaluation of children and adults
- individual psychotherapy for children and adults, with expertise in therapeutic issues associated with illness, death, bereavement, substance abuse, and family disruption
- family, group, and couples therapy
- psychopharmacological treatment of children and adults
- developmental, cognitive, and language evaluations with recommendations for educational placement
- permanency planning, with expertise in facilitating planning with entire families
- crisis intervention, including facilitation of psychiatric hospitalization when indicated and management of families with sudden parental incapacity
- outreach services, including home, school, and hospital visits
- access to substance abuse services, particularly those focused on women and dual diagnosis
- case management, including a working knowledge of the public assistance, foster care, and child welfare systems involved in permanency planning

ISSUES IN MENTAL HEALTH SERVICE DELIVERY

Coordinated Multidisciplinary Care

The multidisciplinary team approach provides the most optimal treatment strategy for meeting the complex needs of these families. Case sharing and access to the full range of services has further utility in reducing clinician isolation and preventing staff burnout. Access to all services in one site increases convenience for families and maximizes treatment compliance. Minimizing the need for multiple appointments (e.g., treatment of multiple family members, for psychotherapy with one clinician and psychopharmacology with another) is essential for families who also have to balance multiple medical appointments.

Flexibility in Treatment Approach

Flexibility in scheduling and nonjudgmental attitudes about missed appointments are also essential. Appreciation of the complexity and difficulty of patients' lives is readily communicated to patients and increases their motivation to undertake the difficult work involved in managing the effects of HIV on the family. A willingness on the part of mental health clinicians to address concrete service needs as they arise is essential; families in financial or housing crisis cannot be expected to attend to psychotherapeutic tasks until these crises are resolved. Ability to switch treatment modality as dictated by changes in individual or family needs is important (e.g., switching from an individual treatment approach to family interventions around times of family crisis). Finally, linguistic and cultural competence of clinical staff provides the foundation for effective treatment.

Concerted Case Finding and Intensive Patient Engagement

Given the overwhelming psychosocial stressors typically experienced by HIV-affected families, the traditional outpatient mental health service delivery model that depends on referral and independent patient follow-up is inadequate. Focused case finding and concerted outreach is often necessary to identify and successfully engage these overwhelmed families in mental health treatment. In the authors' clinical experience, it is usually the families most in need of these services who are the most difficult to engage. The authors have found that engagement of families can take up to several months, with repeated efforts to not only make contact but also to establish trust with patients.

CONCLUSION

Optimal assessment and treatment of HIV-affected families is based on an understanding of their complex backgrounds and the ongoing demands on families made by HIV illness. High-risk backgrounds related to substance abuse predominate, with the associated problems of psychiatric comorbidity in adults and potential heritable psychiatric disorder in children and teenagers, as well as frequent multigenerational patterns of trauma, abuse, and neglect. In this context, overwhelmed families must struggle with the relentless progression of HIV illness with the inevitable demands for the management of loss, family disruption, and reconfiguration.

Even in these difficult circumstances, there are opportunities for therapeutic work. HIV/AIDS brings an often marginalized population of children and families into the medical care system. In the context of HIV illness, clinicians can begin to address the long-standing problems in these families. With flexible and comprehensive treatment approaches, mental health clinicians can play an important role in supporting family structure and maintaining hope. The therapeutic work with affected children and teenagers, particularly when done in the context of their families, can begin the delicate work of addressing old wounds that are impairing coping with HIV illness. The recognition and treatment of multigenerational mental illness and learning disabilities can provide enormous relief to parents and grandparents and potentially divert the generation of children from the fate that befell their parents.

REFERENCES

Andrews, S., Williams, A. B., & Neil, K. (1993). The mother child relationship in the HIV-1 positive family. *Image*, 25, 193–198.
Biederman, J., Faraone, S. V., Keenan, K., Knee, D., & Tsuang, M. T. (1990). Family-genetic and psychosocial risk factors in DSM-III attention deficit disorder. *Journal of the American Academy of Child and Adolescent Psychiatry, 29*, 526–533.
Blume, S. (1992). Alcohol and other drug problems in women. In J. H. Lowinson, P. Ruiz, & R. B. Millman (Eds.), *Substance abuse: A comprehensive textbook.*. Baltimore: Williams & Wilkins.

Boyd-Franklin, N., Steiner, G. L., & Boland, M. G. (Eds.). (1995). *Children, families, and HIV/ AIDS.* New York: Guilford Press.

Brouwers, P., Belman, A. L., & Epstein, L. G. (1991). Central nervous system involvement: Manifestations and evaluation. In P. Pizzo & C. Wilfert (Eds.), *Pediatric AIDS: The challenge of HIV infection in infants, children and adolescents* (pp. 318–335). Baltimore: Williams & Wilkins.

Carroll, K. M., & Rounsaville, B. J. (1993). History and significance of childhood attention deficit disorder in treatment-seeking cocaine abusers. *Comprehensive Psychiatry, 34,* 75–82.

Centers for Disease Control and Prevention. (1995). *HIV/AIDS Surveillance Update, 7,* 2.

Cicchetti, D., & Carlson, V. (Eds.). (1989). *Child maltreatment: Theory and research on the causes and consequences of child abuse and neglect.* Cambridge, England: Cambridge University Press.

Coles, C., Platzman, K., Smith, I. E., James, M. E., & Falek, A. (1993). Effects of cocaine and alcohol use in pregnancy on neonatal growth and neurobehavioral status. *Neurotoxicity and Teratology, 15,* 289.

Connor, E. M., Spreling, R. S., Gelber, R., et al. (1994). Reduction of maternal-infant transmission of human immunodeficiency virus type 1 with zidovudine treatment. *New England Journal of Medicine, 331,* 1173–1180.

Cottler, L. B., Compton, W. M., & Mager, D. (1992). Posttraumatic stress disorder among substance users from the general population. *American Journal of Psychiatry, 149,* 664–670.

Davis, E., Fennoy, I., Laraque, D., Kanem, N., Brown, G., & Mitchell, J. (1992). Autism and developmental abnormalities in children with perinatal cocaine exposure. *Journal of the National Medical Association, 84,* 315–319.

Deren, S., & Randell, J. (1990). The vocational rehabilitation of substance abusers. *Journal of Applied Rehabilitation Counseling, 21,* 4–6.

Diamond, G. W., Kaufman, J., Belman, A. L., Cohen, L., Kohen, H. J., & Rubenstein, A. (1987). Characterization of cognitive functioning in a subgroup of children with congenital HIV infection. *Archives of Clinical Neuropsychology, 23,* 245–256.

Downey, G., & Coyne, J. C. (1990). Children of depressed parents: An integrative review. *Psychological Bulletin, 108,* 50–76.

Edlin, B., Irwin, K., Faruque, S., et al. (1994). Intersecting epidemics—crack cocaine use and HIV infection among inner-city young adults. *New England Journal of Medicine, 331,* 1422–1427.

Epstein, L. G., Sharer, L. R., & Goudsmit, J. (1988). Neurological and neuropathological features of human immunodeficiency virus infection in children. *Annals Neurology, 23*(Suppl.), S19–S23.

Franke, G. H., Jager, H., Thomann, B., & Beyer, B. (1992). Assessment and evaluation of psychological distress in HIV-infected women. *Psychology and Health, 6,* 287–312.

Fullilove, M. T., Fullilove, R. E., Kennedy, G., & Smith, M. (1991, June). *Trauma, crack and HIV risk* (Abstract No. POD-5477). Presented at the VIIIth International Conference on AIDS, Amsterdam, The Netherlands.

Gonzalez, N. M., & Campbell, M. (1994). Cocaine babies: Does prenatal drug exposure to cocaine affect development? *Journal of the American Academy of Child and Adolescent Psychiatry, 33,* 16–19.

Green, A. (1993). Child sexual abuse: Immediate and long-term effects and intervention. *Journal of the American Academy of Child and Adolescent Psychiatry, 32,* 890–902.

Griffith, D. R., Azuma, S., & Chasnoff, I. (1994). Three-year outcome of children exposed prenatally to drugs. *Journal of the American Academy of Child and Adolescent Psychiatry, 33,* 20–27.

Hagan, T. (1988). A retrospective search for the etiology of drug abuse: A background comparison of a drug-addicted population of women and a control group of non-addicted women. *NIDA Research Monograph, 81,* 254–261.

Haller, D. L., Knisely, J. S., Dawson, K. S., & Schnoll, S. H. (1993). Perinatal substance abusers:

Psychological and social characteristics. *Journal of Nervous and Mental Disease, 181,* 509–513.

Havens, J., Whitaker, A., Feldman, J., & Ehrhardt, A. (1994). Psychiatric morbidity in school-age children with congenital HIV-infection: A pilot study. *Journal of Developmental and Behavioral Pediatrics, 15,* S18–S25.

Hutchings, D. (1993). The puzzle of cocaine's effects following maternal use during pregnancy. Are there reconcilable differences? *Neurotoxicology and Teratology, 15,* 281–286.

Kaufman, J., & Zigler, E. (1989). The intergenerational transmission of child abuse. In D. Cicchetti & V. Carlson (Eds.), *Child maltreatment* (pp. 129–152). Cambridge, England: Cambridge University Press.

Kelley, S. (1992). Parenting stress and child maltreatment in drug-exposed children. *Child Abuse and Neglect, 16,* 312–328.

Levenson, Jr., R. L., & Mellins, C. A. (1992). Pediatric HIV disease: What psychologists need to know. *Professional Psychology: Research and Practice, 23,* 410–415.

Levine, C. (1990). AIDS and the changing concept of the family. *The Milbank Quarterly, 68,* 33–58.

McLeer, S., Callaghan, M., Delmina, H., & Wallen, J. (1994). Psychiatric disorders in sexually abused children. *Journal of the American Academy of Child and Adolescent Psychiatry, 33,* 313–319.

Mellers, J. D. C., Marchand-Gonad, N., King, M., & Laupa, V. (1994). Mental health of women with HIV infection: A study in Paris and London. *European Psychiatry, 9,* 241–248

Mellins, C. A. (1995, February). *Stress and psychosocial function in HIV-infected mothers and their children.* Paper presented at the HIV Infection in Women: Setting a New Agenda Conference, Washington, DC.

Mellins, C. A., & Ehrhardt, A. A. (1994). Families affected by pediatric AIDS: Sources of stress and coping. *Journal of Developmental and Behavioral Pediatrics, 15*(Suppl.), S54–S60.

Mellins, C. A., & Ehrhardt, A. A. (1995, February). *Stress, social support and psychosocial functioning in HIV-infected mothers and children.* Paper presented at the HIV Infection and Women: Setting A New Agenda Conference, Washington, DC.

Mellins, C. A., Levenson, R. L., Zawadzki, R., Kairam, R., & Weston, M. (1994). Effects of pediatric HIV infection and prenatal drug exposure on mental and psychomotor development. *Journal of Pediatric Psychology, 19,* 617–628.

Michaels, D., & Levine, C. (1992). Estimates of the number of motherless youth orphaned by AIDS in the United States. *Journal of the American Medical Association, 268,* 3456–3461.

Michaels, D., and The Orphan Project. (1996, June). *Families in crisis: Report of the Working Committee on HIV, Children and Families.* New York: Federation of Protestant Welfare Agencies.

Miller, B. A., Downs, W. R, Gondoli, D. M., & Keil, A. (1987). The role of childhood sexual abuse in the development of alcoholism in women. *Violence and Victims, 2,* 157–172.

Pelcovitz, D., Kaplan, S., Goldenberg, B., Mandel, F., Lehane, J., & Guarrera, J. (1994). Post-traumatic stress disorder in physically abused adolescents. *Journal of the American Academy of Child and Adolescent Psychiatry, 33,* 305–312.

Pergami, A., Gala, C., Burgess, A., Durbano, F., et al. (1993). The psychosocial impact of HIV infection in women. *Journal of Psychosomatic Research, 37,* 687–696.

Regier, D. A., Farmer, M., Rae, D. S., Locke, B. Z., Keith, S. J., Judd, L. S., & Goodwin, F. K. (1990). Comorbidity of mental disorders with alcohol and other drugs of abuse. *Journal of the American Medical Association, 264,* 2511–2518.

Rodning, C., Beckwith, L., & Howard, J. (1989). Characteristics of attachment organization and play organization in prenatally drug-exposed toddlers. *Development and Psychopathology, 1,* 277–289.

Rounsaville, B. J., Weissman, M. M., Kleber, H. D., & Wilber, C. H. (1982). Heterogeneity of psychiatric diagnosis in treated opiate addicts. *Archives of General Psychiatry, 39,* 161–166.

Rutter, M. (1989). Intergenerational continuities and discontinuities in serious parenting difficulties. In D. Cicchetti & V. Carlson (Eds.), *Child maltreatment* (pp. 317–348). Cambridge, England: Cambridge University Press.

Singer, L., Farkas, K., & Kliegman, R. (1992). Childhood medical and behavioral consequences of maternal cocaine use. *Journal of Pediatric Psychology, 17,* 389–406.

Speigal, L., & Mayers, A. (1991). Psychosocial aspects of AIDS in children and adolescents. *Pediatric Clinics of North America, 38,* 153–167.

Swayles, T. P., Scorr, G. B., & Cohen, D. S. (1989, June 4). *Neurocognitive functioning among infants exposed perinatally to HIV* (abstract). Paper presented at the Fifth International Conference on AIDS, Montreal, Canada.

Update: AIDS among women—United States. (1994). *Journal of the American Medical Association, 273,* 767–768.

Weiner, L., & Septimus, A. (1991). Psychosocial consideration and support for the child and family. In P. A. Pizzo & C. M. Wilfert (Eds.), *Pediatric AIDS: The challenge of HIV infection in infants, children and adolescents* (pp. 577–594). Baltimore: Williams & Wilkins.

Weissman, M. M., Gershon, E. S., Kidd, K. K., et al. (1984). Psychiatric disorders in the relatives of probands with affective disorders. *Archives of General Psychiatry, 41,* 13–21.

Wildin, S. R., Williamson, W. D., & Wilson, G. S. (1991). Children of battered women: Developmental and learning profiles. *Pediatric Clinics of Philadelphia, 30,* 299–304.

Wilens, T. M., Biederman, J., Kiely, K., Bredin, E., & Spencer, T. J. (1995). Pilot study of behavioral and emotional disturbance in the high risk children of parents with opioid dependence. *Journal of the American Academy of Child and Adolescent Psychiatry, 34*(6), 779–785.

Wiznia, A. A, Crane, M., Lambert, G., Sansary, J., Harris, A., & Solomon, L. (1996). Zidovudine use to reduce perinatal HIV type 1 transmission in an urban medical center. *JAMA: Journal of the American Medical Association, 275*(19), 1504–1507.

Zierler, S., Feingold, L., Laufer, D., Velentgas, P., Kantrowitz-Gordon, I., & Mayer, K. (1991). Adult survivors of childhood sexual abuse and subsequent risk of HIV infection. *American Journal of Public Health, 81,* 572–575.

Chapter 6

Family Therapy with HIV/AIDS-Affected Families

**Laura Epstein Rosen, Claude Ann Mellins,
Sheila Ryan, and Jennifer F. Havens**

In this second decade of the AIDS epidemic, HIV/AIDS is increasingly recognized as a disease of the family. Not only does HIV have an impact on the infected individual, but it also affects all those who interact with him or her on a regular basis and who offer social support and tangible care (Boyd-Franklin, Steiner, & Boland, 1995; Mellins & Ehrhardt, 1994). The impact of the disease on the mental health of HIV-infected individuals has received increasing attention as medical advances result in prolonged life spans. However, limited attention has been focused on the mental health of family members (Havens, Mellins, & Pilowski, 1996). Recent studies have found that family members can experience significant psychosocial stressors related to HIV, such as family disruption, caregiver burden, increased economic hardship, and illness and death of a family member (Bor, 1990; Mellins & Ehrhardt, 1994; Reidy, Taggart, & Asselin, 1991). Furthermore, uninfected children with HIV-infected parents are at risk for academic problems and behavioral difficulties (Draimin, 1993; Havens, Mellins, Ryan, & Locker, 1995). Clinical reports have suggested a complex interplay between HIV/AIDS, individual mental health, and family functioning (Boyd-Franklin et al., 1995). For example, the family is affected by a

This chapter was supported in part by an HIV/AIDS Mental Health Services Demonstration Program grant from the Substance Abuse and Mental Health Services Administration. The authors would also like to extend their appreciation to the parents and children in the Special Needs Clinic for teaching them so much about their own strengths and coping abilities, as well as their capacity to benefit from family systems interventions.

diagnosis of HIV in one of its members, and the infected individual is, in turn, affected by his or her family's response to their illness. Clearly, how the family reacts to HIV/AIDS and supports the infected individual depends on numerous factors, including general family functioning and relationships before HIV.

In spite of the recognition of an interpersonal context to HIV, particularly the importance of family, psychotherapeutic interventions have primarily been focused on the HIV-infected individual. There are surprisingly few studies and clinical reports on family systems approaches to psychotherapy with this population. Two exceptions are the work of Boyd-Franklin, Steiner, and Boland (1995) and Walker (1991), which clearly emphasizes the importance of family systems approaches in meeting the needs of HIV-infected individuals and HIV-affected family members.

The Special Needs Clinic at Presbyterian Hospital was founded in 1991 to address the needs of women, children, and families affected by HIV disease and substance use. The clinic serves primarily African American and Latino families from low socioeconomic backgrounds. The population and general mental health issues are described in detail by Havens, Mellins, and Ryan in chapter 5. Based on work in the Special Needs Clinic, the goals of this chapter are threefold: to discuss the impact of HIV/AIDS on family structure and family functioning, to present the family issues that have emerged for HIV-affected women and children, and to emphasize the usefulness of a family systems model in directing psychotherapeutic interventions for this population.

Using case examples, this chapter focuses on clinical techniques that have been used successfully and provides specific guidelines for incorporating family systems interventions and family therapy techniques into the mental health treatment of HIV/AIDS-affected patients. Reasons why family therapy has been an underused treatment modality with this population are also discussed.

DEFINING FAMILY

Before discussing family issues related to HIV/AIDS, it is important to define *family*. Recent studies on families in general, and more specifically on HIV-affected families, have indicated that there is not one single prototype of a family configuration, such as the traditional nuclear family (Cohen, 1994; Mellins, Ehrhardt, Newman, & Conard, 1996). Rather, today's families are characterized by more diversity and change. In this chapter, the most general and inclusive definition of family is used. A family is considered a system or subsystem that includes all significant others, adults and children, who are emotionally and psychologically connected and who may or may not be living together. In other words, the family can include HIV-infected adults and children, noninfected family members, and caregivers. In practice, the authors usually rely on the patient's own definition of family. Often, this definition includes not only traditional blood relatives and extended family members (half-siblings, second cousins), but unmarried significant others and close friends and neighbors who are considered to be like family, or *fictive kin* (Boyd-Franklin, 1989). Using the family's definition of who is family is most useful in terms of understanding how they and their support system are affected by HIV/AIDS.

HIV/AIDS IS A MULTIGENERATIONAL DISEASE

As the rate of HIV infection and AIDS steadily increases in women of child-bearing age, HIV/AIDS has become a family problem, often crossing generational boundaries and infecting many individuals within one family, including mothers, fathers, and children (Boyd-Franklin et al., 1995). Parents may be infected by their own injecting drug use or through contact with sexual partners. As women of child-bearing age become infected, the disease can also be transmitted to children prenatally or through breast feeding. By the time a child is diagnosed with HIV, one or more significant family members of the previous generation may already have died of AIDS. Because substance use often runs in families, many adult siblings may have also become HIV infected or severely impaired through their drug use. The burden of raising the children often falls to an older generation of extended family members such as grandparents and great grandparents.

Even if only one member of the extended family is infected, the effects on the rest of the family—in terms of emotional loss, child care needs, and financial burden—are staggering. Family members have to come to terms with the diagnosis of HIV in a relative and what the illness will mean for the family as a whole. The social stigma associated with HIV/AIDS and its associated risk behaviors, such as substance use and high-risk sexual behaviors, are often difficult for families to bear. The changes in family roles, concerns about the future, and instability have major effects on all family members.

In the majority of inner city families affected by HIV/AIDS, there are also preexisting psychosocial stressors (Boyd-Franklin et al., 1995; Mellins & Ehrhardt, 1994). Extreme poverty, family instability, and losses due to urban violence are common. HIV/AIDS is generally not the first stressful situation that these families have had to cope with. Many of the stressors are ongoing and coexist with the additional burden of HIV. In fact, many family members have reported, "I can't begin to think about the HIV when I'm worried about getting shot every time I go outside and I don't know how much longer I can keep a roof over my children's heads." It is important for clinicians to keep in mind the stressful situations that these families have been in for multiple generations before HIV infection and how difficult it is for them to cope with the "curve ball" of HIV when the rest of their lives feels so out of control. The following case example illustrates how HIV/AIDS can affect several generations in one family.

Patricia was a 35-year-old Dominican woman who had been diagnosed with HIV several years earlier when her 3-year-old child, Regina, developed *Pneumocystis carinii* pneumonia and tested positive for HIV. At that time, Patricia was still living with her violent and substance-using husband, Salvador, who was the father of her four children. Patricia had never used drugs and had only one sexual partner. She assumed that Salvador had been infected through his intravenous drug use. When she confirmed that he knowingly infected her, she broke off her long, conflictual relationship with him, took her four children, and moved in with her parents and her 25-year-old sister. At first, she did not disclose the diagnosis to her family. However, as Patricia's illness progressed, she was less able to keep her secret. Both she and Regina were visibly ill. She was relieved that her older three children were not infected, but was consumed with guilt for having transmitted HIV to Regina. At about this time, Salvador began to threaten Patricia's sister and father that he would take the children away from them if Patricia couldn't care for them. Learning of the diagnosis, Patricia's sister, Gloria, gave up her part-time job and college classes to take care of the children. Patricia's father, Steven, cut down his hours at work so that he would be available to take both Patricia and Regina to their increasingly frequent clinic appointments. The family struggled financially because of the loss of income. Consumed with worry about their daughter and grandchildren, Patricia's parents began to argue constantly about money and household chores.

When Patricia was hospitalized repeatedly, returning home each time looking weaker, the children began to have problems both at home and at school. Her oldest two sons (ages 9 and 11) were fighting at school and showing serious academic difficulties. Regina, whose AIDS was less advanced than that of her mother, began to worry about her own health. She became more babyish, dependent, and difficult for the adults in the family to handle. Patricia's youngest son began hitting his teacher at school and was removed from his kindergarten class. Gloria felt overwhelmed with the responsibility of caring for Patricia and her four children. Although she felt it was her family duty to care for them, she also resented having to give up her own life for her sister. The children were afraid that if something happened to their mother, they would have to return to their abusive father.

The family was referred to the Special Needs Clinic a month before Patricia's death, clearly in crisis. Every family member had been affected by Patricia's diagnosis, and each of them was struggling to cope with the multiple and sometimes competing demands that were generated by HIV. This case is not an uncommon scenario. HIV/AIDS often throws the entire family into crisis. In assessing and treating an HIV-affected patient, it is critical to examine how the entire family system is adjusting and reacting to the diagnosis.

MENTAL ILLNESS AND SUBSTANCE ABUSE ACROSS GENERATIONS

Another complicating factor in families affected by HIV/AIDS is the high incidence of substance abuse and the comorbidity of substance abuse and mental health problems. The complex interplay between substance abuse, mental illness, and history of trauma in these families cannot be overstated. Briefly, among women with AIDS in the United States, 47% have their own injecting drug use as the primary risk factor for HIV infection. Another 18% have heterosexual contact with an injecting drug–using partner as the primary risk factor (Centers for Disease Control and Prevention, 1995). It has been well documented that women with substance abuse disorders have high rates of psychiatric comorbidity, particularly depression and anxiety, as well as childhood histories of attention deficit hyperactivity disorder (ADHD; Blume, 1992; Carroll & Rounsaville, 1993; Rounsaville & Weissman, 1982). Moreover, severely traumatic life histories, especially those that include childhood sexual abuse, are associated with women's substance abuse (Fullilove, Fullilove, Kennedy, & Smith, 1991; Zierler & Feingold, 1991). Studies of women with substance abuse have indicated high rates of other kinds of trauma in their adult lives as well, including severe poverty and deprivation, physical abuse, and rape (Cottler, Compton, & Mager, 1992). Among the patients at the Special Needs Clinic, the number of HIV-positive women who report traumatic life experiences is exceedingly high.

The children of HIV-positive women are also at higher risk for numerous difficulties. Both genetic factors and extreme environmental stressors make it likely that the children will inherit substance abuse or mental health problems. Many of these children are exposed to the same kinds of traumas that their mothers were exposed to and often present with problems strikingly similar to those their mothers experienced at a young age, such as affective and anxiety disorders. In addition, these children are more vulnerable to learning disabilities, ADHD, and other developmental difficulties than are children in the general population.

In summary, before HIV, many of these women and children are at risk for mental health problems. With the additional stress of HIV in the family, there tends to be even more frequent and severe crises. Given the high comorbidity of mental illness and substance abuse in these families, it is likely that many family members, regardless of their reaction to the HIV, have a need for psychiatric and psychological interventions. At the Special Needs Clinic, there have been numerous examples of individuals whose difficulty coping with an HIV-positive family member escalates substance abuse or precipitates an affective or psychotic illness. In children, a parent's HIV diagnosis can worsen pre-existing learning disabilities, ADHD, or mood disorders. The following case example illustrates the impact that HIV/AIDS can have on long-standing substance use and mental health problems.

> Charlene was a 15-year-old African American girl referred to the Special Needs Clinic by her school. Although Charlene had never been a model student, she had attended school regularly and participated in class discussions. In the past several months, Charlene had been cutting classes, talking back to her teachers, and displaying sexually provocative behavior in the hallways. Her guidance counselor had heard a rumor that Charlene's mother was HIV infected, but did not know if the changes in her behavior were related to her mother's illness. When she tried to talk to Charlene, she was met with angry stares and silence.
>
> In her initial individual sessions, Charlene expressed a great deal of frustration and anger at her mother. She presented with pressured speech, racing thoughts, and

hypersexuality. In a tone full of rage, she told the therapist that her mother was a "drug addict who got AIDS because she deserves it," but then began to cry. She soon revealed her fear that her mother was going to die sooner because of her recently increased crack cocaine use since she had found out that she had full-blown AIDS. Charlene knew that her mother should stop using, but felt helpless to stop her. She reported that her mother had always been a "nut case, in and out of the nut house," with numerous hospitalizations and suicide attempts. Charlene also revealed that she herself had begun to experiment with drugs, mostly marijuana, and liked the way it made her feel. As the therapist assessed Charlene, she noted symptoms of mania or hypomania and began to suspect that there might be some familial mental illness, as well as a propensity for substance abuse.

With Charlene's permission, she invited Charlene's mother, Mary, to come in to discuss her daughter's recent behavior. Mary, a 38-year-old African American woman, arrived for the session looking hung over, disheveled, and depressed. She revealed a long history of polysubstance abuse, beginning when she was about 13 years old. She also reported a history of psychiatric hospitalizations and remembered being told that she was manic depressive, but never following up on any medications. It became clear that Mary had been self-medicating her mood swings for much of her life with different illegal substances, taking uppers when depressed and downers when manic. Although she had been aware of her HIV status for several years, the recent news that she had full-blown AIDS had pushed her "over the edge into an oblivion" of a severe depression, and she acknowledged that her drug use had increased substantially. When asked about Charlene's reaction to Mary's HIV, Mary admitted that she was worried about how Charlene would do without her and said that she did not want Charlene to make the same mistakes that she had.

Through psychoeducation about the comorbidity of substance abuse and bipolar disorder, Mary agreed that she and Charlene should both be evaluated by a psychiatrist at the clinic. As her history was discussed, Mary marveled at the number of people in her family (e.g., siblings, cousins, parents) who had been active substance abusers and wondered if they also had mental health problems. In addition, she agreed to attend family sessions with Charlene to work on their relationship. However, before these plans could be put into place, Charlene became more truant from school, missed her clinic appointments, and acted out with increasing frequency. At first, Mary called the therapist several times a week, worried about Charlene and her recent exploits with some older boys in the neighborhood. Her biggest fear was that Charlene would start to use heroin and end up getting pregnant at 15 as she herself had. As the weeks passed, Mary stopped coming to the clinic, was not able to sustain her will to make things better, and began to increase the frequency of her drug use. Neither she nor Charlene had ever kept their appointments to be evaluated by the psychiatrist. Mary became even more severely depressed and was eventually hospitalized after a serious suicide attempt.

At the time of her hospitalization, both Mary and Charlene were in crisis. Mary's drug use and depression had increased. Charlene's behavior had become even more flagrantly manic, and there was evidence that she was now using harder drugs herself. Fortunately, the crisis of the hospitalization provided an inroad to help this family. During the admission, Mary was finally evaluated by a psychiatrist and started on a course of antidepressant and mood stabilizer medication. Worried about her mother's hospitalization, Charlene was reengaged in treatment and also agreed to be evaluated by a psychiatrist who recommended a mood stabilizer. After Mary was discharged, she and Charlene continued their outpatient mental health treatment on a more consistent basis. Over the next several months, in family sessions, both Mary and Charlene were able to talk together about the mood disorder and substance abuse problem in their family. They continued to struggle with their old conflicts and with the impact of Mary's HIV status, but the exacerbation of mental illness and substance abuse began to lessen.

Although the details of this case may be specific to Charlene and Mary, the general themes are all too common. In fact, there are a tremendous number of cases with outcomes that are not nearly as successful as this one. Often the substance abuse and mental health problems are even more entrenched and widespread in a family system. Given the impact of HIV/AIDS on preexisting substance abuse and mental illness, it is imperative that clinicians working with this population be aware of this association and work with HIV-affected families directly around these issues. In the next section, other important family systems that have emerged in clinical work at the Special Needs Clinic are reviewed.

FAMILY ISSUES FOR HIV-AFFECTED FAMILIES

A family systems approach to treatment has resulted in the identification of numerous family issues, which in turn highlight the dire need for a family therapy approach to this work. As previously discussed, two substantial problems are that HIV/AIDS affects multiple generations of each family, and there is a high rate of comorbidity of substance abuse and mental illness in these families. In addition, families are often coping with constantly changing situations and crises that can come without warning. Opportunistic infections, dementia, and other medical complications can suddenly appear. Financial worries, child care coverage, and impending death are constant and often worsening concerns as the disease progresses. The multiple levels of problems can make it difficult for family members to identify and sort through the issues. They can feel overwhelmed by crises and paralyzed by the array of different problems confronting them at once.

A thorough review of many of the biopsychosocial issues for families affected by maternal and child HIV are presented in chapter 5 by Havens, Mellins, and Ryan. Rather than repeat them here, the ones that are most relevant to family systems interventions are highlighted. They include, but are certainly not limited to, the following: secrecy and stigma; disclosure; ostracism and alienation; confronting guilt, blame, anger, and shame; changes in family roles; concerns about the future of the family structure; permanency planning; coping with illness and death; separations and loss; and the changing configuration of the family and child placement (Havens, Mellins, & Pilowski, 1996; Mellins & Ehrhardt, 1994).

Many of these issues are addressed in the following case example. Although the initial presenting problems appeared to warrant individual treatment, family issues emerged as therapy progressed. Other family members in need of treatment were identified, and conjoint family therapy was considered. Although individual psychotherapy was maintained as the predominant mode of treatment, the therapist conceptualized the patient in family systems terms and on occasion used family systems interventions, particularly as the treatment progressed. In many of these cases, using both individual and family work in conjunction can be very effective. As stressed throughout this chapter, a flexible approach to treatment is the most practical and useful approach in work with families with numerous, complicated issues; that is, one needs to have an open mind to different treatment modalities and a willingness to use different treatment forms with the same family case as different needs and issues emerge. Further discussion of how to decide when and how to use family systems versus individual psychotherapy techniques is provided.

> Donna was a 32-year-old African American woman with AIDS referred to the clinic by her primary care physician, who was concerned about her psychological adjustment to her recent declining health. At the point at which she began individual psychotherapy, she had just been discharged from the hospital for cytomegalovirus meningitis and was concerned that she could no longer keep her diagnosis a secret from her family. She was ashamed of being HIV positive because she associated it with drug addicts and prostitutes. Unlike many of her peers, Donna had experimented only briefly with drugs and never used injection drugs. However, she had a large number of sexual partners, some of whom she knew were injecting drug users. The stigma of having AIDS was overwhelming to Donna. She was having difficulty sleeping, lost her appetite, reported a depressed mood, and had recurrent thoughts of suicide. Clearly, she met criteria for a major depression and needed psychiatric treatment. Her therapist recognized that many of her symptoms were related to her relationships with her family, not just to her AIDS diagnosis.
>
> Through individual sessions, in which she discussed the pros and cons of disclosure, Donna decided to disclose her diagnosis, both to her 58-year-old aunt who had raised her and her two sisters. However, she was not yet ready to tell her 5-year-old son, Damien, who was HIV negative. She asked for specific guidance in telling her family and actually brought them in to one of her sessions to disclose her HIV status. Soon after that, Donna had to confront her guilt about not being able to raise her son as she had planned and confront the anger and blame that some family members had expressed. In particular, she had strong reactions to her eldest sister's disapproving comments about her lifestyle and her aunt's sorrowful tears whenever she saw Donna. The roles in the family began to change as Donna's aunt took over some of the child care duties for Damien. Instead of being the "steady one" to whom her sisters turned for assistance, Donna found herself turning increasingly to them for help and support. She worried endlessly about who would take care of Damien when she was unable to and had difficulty choosing the most appropriate caregiver. Her aunt and her sisters had all indicated that they would be available to care for Damien. Many individual sessions focused on making decisions about Damien's future care, and Donna was referred to a

lawyer for legal guidance and preparation of an affidavit requesting that stand-by guardianship go to her aunt while Donna was still alive but unable to care for Damien adequately. Eventually, she selected her aunt as the future permanent care-giver of Damien.

As Donna's illness progressed, she was confined first to a wheelchair and then bedridden. The therapist made home and hospital room visits to continue the psy-chotherapy. In these visits, it became clear that Donna's family was having increas-ing trouble coping with her illness and eventual death. Much of the conversation focused on either Damien's reaction to his mother's physical condition or Donna's aunt's tendency to hover over Donna at all times. One of her sisters was hurt and disappointed that Donna had chosen their aunt to be Damien's guardian instead of her. At this point in the treatment, other family members who were in the home or visiting became regular participants in the psychotherapy. There was one very poignant meeting in which Donna was able to express her shame and regret to her aunt, who was able to reassure her that she was loved and tell her that if she could, she would change places with Donna in an instant. In another family session, Donna and her two sisters reminisced about how hard it was for them growing up without a mother and how they always had been there for each other. They prom-ised Donna that they would treat Damien as if he was their own child. Her eldest sister expressed both her sorrow that Donna was dying and her anger at Donna for "living the kind of life that got you into trouble . . . and then not letting me keep Damien." This discussion allowed Donna and her sister to talk through Donna's decision about permanency planning and resolve some of the conflicts between them. By the end of the session, Donna's sister had a clearer idea of why Donna had made the decision she did and was able to reconnect with her. In the late stages of her illness, Donna developed AIDS dementia and was unable to participate in any meaningful conversation. At this point, Damien moved out of his mother's home to live with his great aunt. The therapist was available to help the family cope with the separations and anticipatory loss of Donna. She met several times with both of Donna's sisters and the aunt to discuss how to explain to Damien what was happening, as well as to help the family begin to grieve. Using psychoeducational techniques, she helped the family members learn about what to expect from Damien in terms of changes in his behavior and emotional reactions. Immediately follow-ing Donna's death, Damien developed nightmares and considerable difficulties at school. The same therapist was able to work with Donna's aunt and Damien to help them cope with the loss of Donna and their bereavement. Damien had several individual sessions, as well as family sessions with his aunt, in which they dis-cussed his mother's death and how their new family structure would be both similar and different from his life with his mother.

Given the family issues that emerged in Donna's individual treatment, fam-ily therapy eventually became the treatment of choice. Donna's therapist, who initially worked with her individually, had a number of separate, yet related rationales for the use of a family systems approach in thinking about her case. First, HIV/AIDS was clearly affecting the entire family. At the outset of treat-ment, Donna was struggling with disclosing her HIV status to her family and coping with her own mortality. As treatment progressed, the impact of Donna's

AIDS on her entire family became more significant. Her son, her sisters, and her aunt were all having strong reactions to her illness and their impending loss. Treating Donna alone, without the context of her family, would have missed many of the important issues, both for her and for her family members. Second, a number of Donna's presenting problems had to do with the sense of secrecy and shame in this family. Her depression and anxiety were perpetuated by the lack of discussion of important issues, which in turn contributed to conflicts in the family. It is worth noting that Donna's initial depression and anxiety dissipated substantially after she disclosed her diagnosis to her family. Once the conflicts were more out in the open, there was not only symptom relief, but also an increased closeness and connection between family members that would not have been possible otherwise.

Third, the therapist realized that treating Donna for one session per week and sending her back into her family system for the other 6 days and 23 hours a week did not address some of her real, ongoing life problems. In her individual sessions, Donna focused on her relationships with her sisters and her aunt, as well as her fears about Damien's future. By working on these relationships, both in the individual work and in the family sessions, the therapist was helping Donna cope with difficult situations that she encountered every day. Near the end of her life, before she began suffering from AIDS dementia, Donna told her therapist, "You're the first person in this hospital who seems to see me as a real person with a family at home, not just an AIDS patient who is on the way out."

Fourth, family systems techniques are often more time efficient and allow the therapist to get to the heart of the matter in the limited amount of time that therapists often have with these patients. In Donna's case, she was referred to the Special Needs Clinic only 4½ months before her death. The therapist, working closely with the referring physician, recognized that Donna's life expectancy was very brief and worked quickly to help Donna with both her individual coping skills and her relationship with her family members.

Last, a strong rationale for using family system techniques is that the grief and bereavement process can be much less problematic if family members have the chance to both express and hear each other's feelings. As a result of her honest conversations with Donna about their relationship, her aunt resolved many of the ambivalent feelings about Donna's lifestyle that might have made her grieving more complicated and difficult. Damien, too, had a chance to say goodbye to his mother and to hear from her that she wasn't leaving because of anything that he had done. Unlike many children, who feel overly responsible for their parents' deaths, Damien was able to articulate, "My Mommy died because she was sick, not because of me." Within several months of his mother's death, Damien was performing at his previous level at school and beginning to reinitiate social contact with his peers. Of course, the long-term consequences of losing a parent at such a young age cannot be overlooked, but Damien's initial adjustment was much better than that of children who are not included in family mental health treatment. In summary, a family systems approach and family therapy sessions allowed the therapist to help not only the HIV-infected individual, but also to reach family members who are typically ignored by mental health systems, to address their issues, and to facilitate grief, bereavement, family reconfiguration, and overall family adjustment. In this kind of work, it is imperative that the clinician have an understanding of normative and non-normative childhood bereavement. The therapist must be available (or have another clinician available) to work with the children in the family and that person must be vigilant to the fact that these children are at risk for mental illness, from both genetic vulnerability and exposure to trauma.

GUIDELINES FOR FAMILY SYSTEM INTERVENTIONS

On the basis of the previous case examples, especially that of Donna and her family, it is evident that there is a need for both individual and family techniques in psychotherapy with this population. Yet the question of how one decides to use which technique with whom remains. In the following sections, guidelines for using both family systems interventions and actual family therapy techniques are presented. Before distinguishing between family systems interventions within individual psychotherapy and family therapy techniques, it is important to note that in this work, there is a great deal of fluidity between the two. Very often a patient will begin in individual therapy, have several family meetings that incorporate family systems interventions, and then revert to individual work. Or the converse may be true: Family therapy is begun and the therapist soon recognizes that the family conflicts are untenable and that the individual issues need to be addressed in individual psychotherapy, with some family systems interventions. In yet another scenario, the family may simultaneously be involved at the clinic in ongoing family therapy with one clinician and individual treatment with several other clinicians. Thus, the authors tend not to make such clear distinctions between family systems interventions in individual therapy and family therapy and use whatever seems to be the most appropriate and effective treatment at a given point in time.

For the purposes of clarity here, however, Boyd-Franklin et al.'s (1995) distinction between *family systems interventions* and *family therapy* is used. This distinction is somewhat arbitrary, but it is made to help readers think about how to best structure treatment. For an individual therapist interested in incorporating some family systems interventions into mostly individual work, the first set of guidelines is the most applicable. For a family therapist who would like to do more ongoing family therapy sessions, the second set of guidelines may be more useful. Boyd-Franklin et al. defined family systems interventions as direct, short-term, problem-focused interventions that involve either the patient alone or several family members at key points in the medical treatment of the HIV/AIDS patient. These interventions are based on family systems thinking and take the entire family into consideration, but may not include the whole family on a regular basis. In contrast, family therapy refers to ongoing family treatment sessions conducted on a regular, or fairly regular, basis. Such treatment relies more on the traditional family therapy techniques such as understanding the family dynamics, making a family systems diagnosis, reframing, and directive tasks.

There are times and issues that call for family work, for individual work, and for a combination of both. As a rule of thumb, family systems interventions are recommended at critical points in the HIV/AIDS patient's medical care, including initial diagnosis, hospitalizations, decisions about do-not-resuscitate orders, permanency planning, and death of a family member. More ongoing family therapy can also help with bereavement, feelings of isolation, and conflictual parent–child relationships. However, individual therapy can be very effective in helping children cope with school difficulties, confront their fears about what will happen to them if their parents die, and deal with rage at their parents for leaving. As other chapters in this book suggest, individual therapy is effective in helping the HIV-infected person cope with the diagnosis, come to terms with his or her own mortality, and adjust to other people's reactions. Individual therapy can also assist the HIV-infected person in the search for meaning in his or her life and help focus on goals for the immediate and longer term future. At the Special Needs Clinic, individual therapy has been very effective in helping a new caregiver cope with the loss of a relative, the task of raising new children, the loss of old life goals, and the creation of new life goals.

As cases tend to be complex and ever changing from week to week, there are times when a combination of individual and family work is the most effective. For example, when Mary was hospitalized after her suicide attempt, she and Charlene benefited from both family sessions that facilitated communication and collective problem solving and individual sessions that focused on Mary's coping with her depression and Charlene's coping with fears about the future, respectively.

This first set of guidelines was developed to help clinicians incorporate family systems interventions into individual therapeutic work with HIV-affected patients, to set the stage for using family therapy as the primary approach to treatment, or both. In providing these guidelines, it is assumed that the therapist is beginning individual treatment with a patient but is able to work with the entire family when and if it becomes useful. As previously stated, family systems interventions are particularly useful at critical points in the progression of HIV disease, such as coping with the initial diagnosis, making decisions about disclosure, dealing with hospitalization and deterioration of the patient, and making decisions about medical care for the patient and permanency plans for the children. At such times, it can be helpful to invite additional family members to join the identified patient's sessions or have separate sessions with one or more other subgroups of the family. Including other family members makes it possible both to help the entire family cope with the given situation and to assess the psychosocial effects of HIV on the family system.

Guideline 1: Show Genuine Interest in the Family

From the outset of treatment, it is important to convey a sincere interest in both the individual patient and his or her family. The therapist should ask about who is in the family, how the children are coping with the changes brought on by the illness, and what are any problems that the patient has noticed. A good way to join with the patient is to invite him or her to help construct a genogram of his or her family, showing that the therapist is interested in the family. This intervention also provides more useful information about the family history (McGoldrick & Gerson, 1985). In addition to asking questions about how the family is functioning and communicating, it is beneficial to let the patient know that one is open to meeting with any of the patient's significant others in any way that might help the entire family cope with this difficult situation. Expressing empathy about how HIV is affecting everyone in the entire family system is an effective way to show genuine interest in the family.

Guideline 2: Be Aware of the Family's Belief Systems

To effectively intervene in the family system, one needs to understand the patient's and family's belief systems about mental health treatment and the overall medical system. If the patient and his or her family are distrustful, reassuring them of a desire to help, without dismissing their fears or concerns, is useful. It is important to work with the family's belief system as much as possible in order to acquire their trust and help the family move forward. For example, the authors worked with a family who believed that if the HIV-infected family member went into the hospital, he would never return home. As a result, this patient was not getting adequate medical care or pain management. Through discussions with the family about how the hospital functioned and what rights the patient or family had to refuse treatments and after taking a tour of the hospital ward, the patient began to receive the medical care that he needed. This process also helped the family trust the therapist and feel that she was someone who took their concerns seriously. When other difficult issues came up, the family had an easier time turning to the therapist for support and guidance.

Guideline 3: Concrete Social Services as a Tool for Engaging and Joining

Many of these families are struggling with deprivation, poverty, and difficulty negotiating the medical and social welfare system. Concrete social services and entitlements can be an effective tool for engaging and joining with families. If patients cannot pay their rent or buy food, they cannot actively participate in psychotherapy. In the experience of staff at the Special Needs Clinic, the majority of patients need help with concrete services before they can begin to discuss their emotional and psychological needs. Help with concrete social services can range from help accessing financial entitlements and negotiating the court system to making frequent home visits when a patient or family member is homebound or has difficulty coming to the clinic. Either the therapist or a case manager, working in conjunction with the therapist, must be available to address these needs in order to engage patients in treatment. The authors have found that patients and their families are more connected to their therapists after receiving such help with concrete problems in their lives. In addition, concrete social services can help identify potential family issues and children's mental health needs. By spending time with the family discussing their needs, underlying psychopathology and dysfunctional coping mechanisms can become very clear.

Guideline 4: Keep an Open Line of Communication with Medical Providers

With the patient's or family's permission, it is useful to establish a relationship with the medical provider. Part of the crisis of an HIV/AIDS diagnosis is understanding the complicated clinical picture and potential medical treatments. Many patients appreciate having a therapist who can help them communicate directly with their physician. This guideline is very effective in individual psychotherapy, but absolutely necessary in work with families. There is often such poor communication among family members and between family members and the medical provider that improving communication between the therapist and the medical provider is an essential component of treatment. In particularly chaotic or disorganized families, a therapist who is in touch with the medical provider can help guarantee better medical care. Several studies have suggested that compliance with medical treatment is increased when patients are able to express their feelings and communicate directly with their physician (Rolland, 1987, 1994). As mental health treatment providers, therapists can facilitate that kind of relationship. Opening up the traditional individual therapist–patient relationship in this way also conveys to the patient that the therapist is willing and able to help the patient negotiate current, concrete problems. Numerous patients in individual psychotherapy finally consent to family sessions after the individual therapist has "proved" her- or himself by successfully negotiating an issue with the patient's primary care provider.

In addition, medical treatment is often enhanced when the medical providers are familiar with the patient's family situation and any potential obstacles to treatment. In many cases, families may refuse to give consent for particular procedures or may have conflicts about signing do-not-resuscitate orders. Having a therapist who can help facilitate the communication between the family and medical team is essential. In the authors' experience, part of the therapist's role is also to help the medical provider with his or her own countertransference to difficult and destructive patients, particularly when the patient is an active substance user. The family therapist can play a critical role in helping the medical provider understand the psychosocial stressors that are affecting their patients, decreasing negative countertransference, and improving the doctor–patient relationship.

Guideline 5: Use Psychoeducational Techniques

Psychoeducational techniques can be a very effective and efficient way of engaging and treating HIV-infected patients and their families. For example, psychoeducational techniques can be used to educate families about the course of HIV disease, permanency planning, and what to expect in terms of children's reactions to illness and death. Given the overwhelming nature of HIV/AIDS and the multiple stressors with which these families must cope, knowledge and understanding can be powerful tools. Psychoeducational material about learning disabilities, ADHD, and the familial transmission of mood disorders and substance abuse can be especially pertinent to these families. Whether working individually with an HIV/AIDS patient or with members of the family together, psychoeducation is recommended as part of the treatment plan.

To summarize, these guidelines were developed to help clinicians working individually with patients to incorporate family systems interventions. If one is seeing a patient in more traditional individual psychotherapy, with firm boundaries and a lack of involvement in the patient's outside life, it is much more difficult to expand the boundaries of the therapeutic relationship to include family members. However, by keeping an open and flexible stance, the therapist conveys to the patient that he or she is willing and able to help the entire family. In the following section, more specific guidelines about using family therapy with this population are presented.

GUIDELINES FOR ONGOING FAMILY THERAPY

This second set of guidelines is more specific to conducting ongoing family therapy with HIV-affected parents and children. These guidelines are based loosely on the recommendations presented by Robert Jay Green in a book titled *Family Therapy: Major Contributions* (Green & Framo, 1992). At first glance, they may look like very general tenets of family therapy. However, they have been specifically adapted to use with the HIV/AIDS-affected population at the Special Needs Clinic. They are clearly not all inclusive, but do offer some of what the authors have learned from family therapy work with this population of HIV-affected children and families.

Guideline 1: Assessment Phase
Includes a Thorough Family History

In the beginning family therapy sessions, the goal should be to learn as much as possible about the history of the family. This can be very difficult to do, particularly if the family is coming in with a current crisis that must be addressed immediately. There will certainly be times when the assessment phase has to be bypassed to help a family cope with a crisis. But as soon as possible in the treatment, the therapist should ask who is in the family, what roles they play, what changes have happened, what major life events have been experienced, how do people interact, what are alliances and boundaries between family members, what are boundaries between family members and the outside world, what are the rules and expectations in the family, and, most important, how has HIV/AIDS affected that particular family. Given the size and complexity of many of the families affected by HIV, constructing a genogram together with the family can be very helpful. It involves family members in a task with the therapist and lets them know that the therapist is interested in their story and also provides valuable information (McGoldrick & Gerson, 1985).

Guideline 2: Think About the Family System as a Whole

Any family therapist would probably follow this guideline naturally. However, it is an extremely important guideline to keep in mind, even in work with individual patients. One of the best ways to think about the family system as a whole is to try to mentally take a step back from the therapy room, look at the genogram, and think about how each person affects the other people in the family. As one listens to the family's presenting problems and conflicts, it is useful to filter what is heard through a family system model to confirm or disconfirm one's hypotheses about the system. In thinking about the family as a system, one must consider both negative and positive feedback loops. For example, how does the mother's behavior affect the daughter and how does the daughter's reaction affect the grandmother's relationship with the mother? In Donna's family, it was critical for the therapist to think about how Donna's aunt's reaction to the HIV diagnosis affected Donna's relationship with her son, Damien. Keeping the entire family system in mind allows the therapist to intervene in an effective way with every member of the family.

Guideline 3: Treatment Goals Should Be Structural in Nature

Therapists who are trained primarily in individual therapy tend to have treatment goals that include a reduction in symptoms and a lasting change in the patient's personality, attitude, or behavior. In family therapy, it is important to have structural treatment goals as well. In other words, one may or may not be able to change each person's personality, but one can help the family to make changes in how they relate to one another. Such structural change can also have a major impact on each family member's functioning. With HIV/AIDS-affected families, it can be easy to lose sight of the need for structural change. After all, the infected patient may be dying and one may, naturally, wonder what good it will do to make changes in the family structure. To the contrary, however, helping family members to alter family rules and roles can have substantial impact on how they cope with the HIV/AIDS disease progression and the griev-ing process, as well as a significant effect on the course of preexisting mental illness and substance use problems.

For example, one therapist worked with a case in which the dying mother had always been the strong and domineering matriarch of the family. When she became physically incapacitated and eventually demented, it was necessary to help her 18-year-old daughter step in and take charge of her siblings, one of whom suffered from serious depression and increasing drug use. Without that kind of structural change before the patient died, the family would have been left in complete turmoil after her death. Taking charge was very difficult for this daughter because of her mother's strong reaction to being usurped and her sib-lings' refusal to listen to her. Several family sessions were held to help the mother begin to let go of her power in the family and to help the younger children accept their sister as the adult in charge of the family. Once she took over as the caregiver, she was able to get her depressed younger brother in-volved in psychotherapy and drug treatment. If she had not been able to take charge as she did, it is likely that both his affective disorder and drug use would have worsened.

Guideline 4: Inclusion in Sessions

In traditional family therapy, the issue of who is included in sessions is very important. Many family therapists feel that all persons involved in the family should be present at every meeting. Some therapists will not work with one member of a couple or with a subsystem of one parent and a child without the other family members. In family therapy work with this population, it is crucial to be more flexible about who is included in the sessions. Given the chaotic nature of these patients' lives and their frequent medical emergencies, it is nec-essary to work with whomever in the family is available at any given moment in time. On the basis of Mellins et al.'s (1996) definition of selective kin, any family members who are considered by the family to be important are included in the family sessions. This definition of who is family and who should be in the session can change over time or even from week to week. It is recom-mended that work be done with the family members who are interested and willing to work on difficult issues, especially those who are willing to take responsibility for the problems in the family and work toward positive change. Frequently, a mother and daughter dyad is seen one week and extended family members the next week. As presented in the case examples, family therapy can range from hospital visits that include people outside of the family (e.g., the physician, clergy, and neighbors) to visits with children alone when a parent is hospitalized. Migration to and from other countries and changes in the family due to illness and death result in constant shifts in the family configuration. Taking a rigid stance about who is to be included in sessions would make it nearly impossible to work effectively with these families.

Guideline 5: Therapist as Observer and Participant

The family therapist should be both observer and participant throughout the process of therapy. He or she does not assess the family in a vacuum, but uses the way family members relate to one another and to the therapist in the context of the session. The therapist should be able to step back and observe the family system, but also be an active participant at other times. The therapist should be able to appropriately model problem solving, coping mechanisms, and social skills. In much of this work, the family therapist alternates from being the objective professional to being almost a part of the extended family. Knowing when to be close and when to be more distant requires experience and also a sense of what the family needs at that moment. For example, at a bedside session of a dying AIDS patient, the therapist may decide to back off and play the role of the observer as family members say their final goodbyes. However, when family members are struggling with a seemingly unresolvable conflict, it may be perfectly appropriate and clinically useful for the therapist to join in with suggestions and state his or her own personal position. As stressed throughout this chapter, a flexible stance should be maintained and decisions about treatment made depending on the patients' needs. In many cases, therapists attend wakes, funerals, and even dance recitals of children who have recently lost a parent, who might otherwise have been cheering for them in the audience. Yet by the same token, therapists do not become a regular part of the family system and do not take part in daily family events. Individual therapists working with HIV/AIDS patient are increasingly aware of the need to cross traditional boundaries for hospital visits and memorial services. Owing to the intense relationships that can develop with not just one patient, but with multiple members of the family, family therapists struggle with this tricky task even more so. Deciding about when to be an observer and when to be a participant is a balancing act that can vary with different cases at different times.

Guideline 6: Therapist Establishes the Structure of Treatment

Although the therapist does move back and forth from observer to participant in the treatment, it is important that, like any "good-enough" parent, he or she establish the structure of the treatment. These families are often living with a lack of any structure and need to have someone be in charge. The family therapist should determine when the sessions will be held, for how long, and what policies are about behavior during sessions (e.g., no physical violence, no intentional damage to property, or no verbal assaults that the therapist believes are abusive and not productive). If family members cannot abide by these rules, they should be asked to leave the treatment room, but they can return when they feel they can follow the rules appropriately. The notion of the therapist as the one in charge may sound patronizing and disrespectful to patients. However, it is not only necessary but also usually welcome to these families, who are struggling with a lack of limits in their lives. In setting the structure of the treatment, the therapist must, of course, be respectful and do it in a spirit of collaboration with the families.

Guideline 7: Therapist Directs the Flow of Communication

The family therapist should feel free to direct the flow and focus of communication. In sessions, the family therapist asks each person to speak for him- or herself, using the first person singular (*I*), and does not allow family members to speak for each other. Taking an active stance, the therapist should feel comfortable interrupting family members and directing others to speak. At times, the therapist may ask certain family members to speak directly to another person, while others are excluded. At other times, when the emotional reactivity is so high that it impedes communication, the therapist may ask family members to speak to (or through) the therapist rather than directly to other family members. The therapist may also "manipulate" space by changing seating and proximity of family members to one another as a means of creating and symbolizing changes in the subsystem boundaries. For example, having the caregivers sit together to negotiate a parenting conflict strengthens their alliance by temporarily excluding the children. Alternatively, moving the children to one side of the room may help them align together against their drug-abusing mother in their campaign to get her involved in substance abuse treatment.

Guideline 8: Therapist Manages the Emotional Intensity

Given the high level of conflict and real-life stressors in these families, there is bound to be considerable expressed emotion and explosiveness. It is the family therapist's responsibility to manage the emotional intensity of the session, either to decrease it when things get too heated or to increase it to bring about structural change. Of course, this guideline is much easier said than done. Many therapists have had the experience of not managing the emotional intensity well enough and ending up with what feels like a session out of control. Conversely, therapists have also felt that the family was not taking a matter seriously enough and was lacking genuine emotional reactions.

There are some simple techniques to manage the emotion in the room. First, setting firm rules about what will and will not be accepted (e.g., physical violence) from the start of treatment is helpful. Second, therapists who maintain an active stance in the treatment sessions will have an increased ability to take charge if needed, either to calm an emotional outburst or to elicit an emotional reaction. Third, one can rely on one's knowledge about the family system to control the intensity of a session. For example, a mother and grandmother may have never seen eye to eye on anything except their granddaughter's welfare. One possible intervention in a family session in which mother and grandmother are screaming at each other about past conflicts is to say, "I know you two

rarely agree on anything, but I also know that you both are committed to helping Diana with this. Can you put aside your old battles and focus instead on
helping Diana?" Last, a very effective comment to calm down a bitter fight is to
say, "Isn't this what you do at home? We are here to try to make things better.
How about if you try to do something different and not name-call here?" If, no
matter what technique is tried, the session becomes explosive and out of control,
it is entirely appropriate to tell the family members that the session cannot
continue until they can quiet down, stop yelling, or take a deep breath.

Guideline 9: Therapist Can Take Sides

Although the family therapist should avoid consistently taking sides with one
family member or subsystem against another, he or she may temporarily take
sides at one phase or point in therapy to rebalance the system or even to throw
the system off balance. In light of the crises with which these families present,
many therapists are uncomfortable taking sides, especially if a family member
might not be able to attend the next session. However, it is recommended that
the therapist always extend empathy, respect, and concern to all family members while simultaneously taking sides when and if it is appropriate. For example, in family therapy with a teenage girl who had been acting out after her
mother had died of AIDS and her grandmother, it was useful to alternately take
sides with each of them. The therapist empathized with the granddaughter about
how overly strict her grandmother was and then empathized with the grandmother about how she was desperately trying to save her granddaughter from
the same fate that befell her daughter. In this case, the taking of sides allowed
them each to feel supported, but also to begin to see the other person's point of
view. In taking sides, one caveat is to make sure that each family member feels
that there is an overall sense of equality and fairness in the treatment, if not in
any given session.

Guideline 10: Increase the Family's Awareness
of Its Interactional Patterns

The therapist should promote awareness of the family dysfunctional patterns by
pointing them out, describing the negative consequences, and suggesting possible options for change. It can be helpful to confront family members with
discrepancies between their verbal and nonverbal messages and to encourage
clear and honest communication of thoughts, feelings, and intentions. In families affected by HIV/AIDS, there is often substantial secrecy and shame. Family
members may not communicate directly. A helpful intervention is to talk about
the high level of secrecy in the family and encourage family members to think
about the effect of such secrecy. In that context, family members will often
reveal things to one another and realize that their concern about feeling ashamed
was not warranted. In some cases, it may not feel appropriate to bring up the

issue of secrets in the family directly. Therefore, one possible intervention is to have family members answer circular questions about one another (e.g., who in the family is the most afraid? the most brave? etc.) to point out how much or how little they actually know about each other. Such interventions increase family members' awareness about how their behaviors and attitudes affect those around them.

Guideline 11: Reframing

In all family therapy, but particularly in work with HIV/AIDS-affected families, it is beneficial to use positive reframing. This technique involves changing the family's frame of reference and emphasizing the positive aspects of their lives. For example, an angry attack by a child on his HIV-positive mother could be redefined as an attempt to maintain contact with and get attention from her. The positive reframing of behavior previously viewed as destructive also changes the effects of the behavior. In this case, the parent who saw her child as demanding and difficult may now view his behavior as an attempt to make contact and respond differently to him, thereby changing the pattern of their interactions. Over time, his angry attacks may lessen as the closeness with his mother increases. Given that these families are coping with multiple stressors simultaneously with few resources for coping, it is effective to build on whatever strengths they have. In one very chaotic and dysfunctional family with numerous losses and traumas, it was extremely helpful to emphasize the family members' strengths in coping with previous losses and challenge them to rise above yet another problem. Most families, regardless of how chaotic and conflictual, have some positive strengths on which to build. The use of humor and playfulness, as long as it is respectful, can also be very effective in emphasizing the positive aspects of their relationships.

Guideline 12: Collective Mourning

If a family has suffered a loss or several losses to HIV/AIDS, collective mourning is an important intervention. The secrecy and stigma of AIDS often make it impossible for family members to talk together about the deceased loved one. In family sessions, the family therapist can guide the family through a kind of shared affective experience to help them come to terms with their loss. Initially, the therapist may ask families to share memories of the deceased loved one. Although family members may initially present as shy and reluctant to talk, they can quickly revert to swapping stories, complete with laughter and tears. Another technique is to help the family develop a ritual or series of rituals to remember or let go of that person (Imber-Black, Roberts, & Whiting, 1988). In one family, they developed a ritual of watching a videotape of their deceased mother on important family holidays when they were acutely aware of her absence. Another family who was having considerable difficulty with the mourning

process because of anger at the deceased for using drugs, decided to join together to burn all of the drug paraphernalia found in her apartment. Once they
"burned" that unpleasant part of her, they were much more able to grieve the
loss. As mourning progresses, it is also important to help families develop new
rituals, without their loved one; for example, perhaps they could start a new
tradition of going to the park together on Sunday afternoons when they used to
have to stay near home to nurse the sick relative.

Guideline 13: Refrain from Using Paradoxical Family Therapy Techniques

Family therapists often have the reputation of being magicians who pull white
rabbits out of their hats. They use the interventions of paradoxical techniques
and prescribing the symptom, with marvelous effects. Although it may be possible to achieve great change through these techniques, they are not recommended for this kind of inner city HIV/AIDS-affected population. These families are struggling with so much at once that they cannot usually handle the
kind of stress that these techniques induce. Rather than stirring up the system
to effect change, the therapist should give these fragile families stable and supportive care that they can count on. "Magical" therapy techniques increase the
drop-out rate and the decompensation rate in this population. Despite the temp-
tation of a quick cure, it is far better to keep these families engaged in treatment
and work toward a slow and steady change.

Guideline 14: Countertransference and Supervision

Given the difficult issues that these families are facing, countertransferential
reactions are natural and frequent. Working closely with family systems coping
with multiple losses and serious medical illness can take a toll on even the most
seasoned clinician. It is important to be aware of countertransference in working
with these families, many of whom are active substance users despite their very
advanced AIDS. Many therapists may have strong reactions to "bad" parents
and need to be aware of their own feelings when the needs of the adults appear
to conflict with the needs of the children in the family. In addition, reaching out
and establishing relationships with patients who are dying is very difficult. This
kind of work can stir up one's own unresolved feelings about endings and loss.
At times, there may be an overlap between one's family of origin and the family
with whom one is working. It is crucial to be aware of one's attitudes toward
family members, death, and bereavement. Formal supervision for trainees, peer
supervision for staff, and even informal conversations about cases are invaluable. Having a set time to share experiences helps tremendously with the overwhelming nature of this work. In some cases at the Special Needs Clinic, family
therapists work in pairs to combat some of the family's powerful impact and
sort through the complexity of the interactional data. Another useful technique

is to use live supervision, in which another therapist or team of therapists observes the sessions from behind a one-way mirror and gives suggestions. Both cotherapy and live supervision help to keep countertransference in check and provide more objective family therapy interventions.

To summarize, these two sets of guidelines have grown out of the authors' work at the Special Needs Clinic. They have found family systems interventions and ongoing family therapy to be invaluable in work with HIV-affected families. However, it is striking that very few clinics and treatment facilities use these techniques. If, as proposed, family systems interventions have such utility with families with AIDS, why are they so underutilized? The next section addresses this important issue.

UNDERUTILIZATION OF FAMILY THERAPY

The reasons for the underutilization of family therapy with HIV-affected families are complicated and multidetermined. First, many poor and ethnic minority individuals are reluctant to seek mental health services. As a result of their own ethnic or cultural beliefs or their bad experiences with service providers, they may be reluctant to seek mental health treatment either for themselves or for their families and may feel unwilling to discuss family secrets with therapists (Boyd-Franklin et al., 1995). They may have an unspoken (or even a spoken) rule in the family that seeking psychotherapy is a sign of weakness or insanity. Even if the identified patient is willing to be involved in psychotherapy, other family members may mistrust the medical system and resist treatment. For example, a grandfather in a Dominican family forbade his grandchildren to discuss their mother's AIDS diagnosis and repeatedly undermined all attempts to engage them in psychotherapy even after their mother had died. Despite the children's pleas to come to the clinic, it went against his beliefs to have his family "air their dirty laundry" to mental health professionals.

Another major obstacle to family mental health treatment is related to the way in which medical and mental health services are generally set up, with a fragmentation of care and segregation of services by age. Most medical and mental health clinics are set up to serve either children or adults, but not both. In hospital settings, there is usually a pediatric medical clinic and an adult medical clinic, with separate psychiatry subspecialty services for each age group. Rarely do primary care staff in these settings have the time or inclination to inquire about other family members' adjustment to the HIV. They may notice that an HIV/AIDS patient seems depressed or anxious, but most AIDS medical clinics typically have limited mental health staff to treat these problems. In many cases, there are a handful of social workers who are inundated with the case management needs of hundreds of patients. In some cases, the medical provider will make a referral for an individual to be evaluated in a mental health clinic, but again the mental health services tend to be segregated by age, with little room for family systems work. Furthermore, because mental health clinics are typically in a different location with a new, unknown therapist, patients often do not follow through with referrals.

In addition, because clinics are usually set up to offer individual treatment to either adults or children, but not both, individual psychotherapy tends to be the modality of choice in hospital and mental health clinics. As a result, the clinician working with an individual child may not have the expertise to work or interest in working with the rest of the family. If the clinician does recognize mental health needs in other family members, he or she will usually refer the other family member to a separate clinic or facility for treatment. Families rarely follow through with these outside referrals. Mothers are often likely to get their children's needs met, but not their own. One of the strengths of the Special Needs Clinic is that it was set up to address the mental health needs of both parents and children simultaneously and conjointly, in the same location as medical care services, thereby reducing fragmentation of care and increasing accessibility of services for families. To the authors' knowledge, it is one of the few clinics that is structured this way.

It is important to note that even when family therapy is available to this population, the families can be very difficult to engage in treatment. If they are referred to a family therapy clinic, they may very well miss their first appointment and never comply with subsequent appointments. The multiple stressors and complications in the lives of these families may make it impossible for them to adhere to a recommendation for mental health treatment. As noted by Havens, Mellins, & Ryan in chapter 5 of this volume, outreach is a crucial strategy for engaging these families, and most clinics do not have adequate staff to do outreach and engagement work. There is often no direct liaison or ongoing communication between the mental health treatment team and the medical treatment team, which is crucial for engaging families in psychotherapy. Once again, family therapy tends to be separate from the family's ongoing medical care, making it harder for families to use this service.

Finally, in addition to the above barriers, there is often therapist resistance to family therapy work with this population. One possibility is that individually trained therapists are distrustful of family therapy techniques. They may be protective of each individual patient and believe that working with the entire family will not be fruitful and may even be dangerous for the patient. Because so many of these children and adults come from dysfunctional families, it may feel counterintuitive to individual therapists to work with the family. After all, how can they offer the identified patient a corrective experience if they are subjecting them to the difficulties of their family?

Many individual therapists express concern that discussing such difficult issues is only going to make things worse for the family members. Indeed, the kind of topics that are discussed in family therapy sessions with those who are affected by HIV/AIDS can be quite intense and emotionally laden. It has been the authors' experience, however, that family members do not shy away from these kinds of discussions. In fact, after a particularly intense family session in which three adult offspring discussed funeral plans with their dying HIV-positive mother, one of the daughters said, "Thank you for giving us the chance and space to have that conversation. We never would have done it without you and these were things that needed to be said." Very often the family members seem far less shaken after a difficult session than the therapist. They are living day to day with these extreme stressors and conflicts. In the majority of cases, they seem relieved to talk through them. Of course, the clinician must use his or her own intuition and sense of the family in deciding how much family members can tolerate talking about.

Another related possibility is that therapists have their own countertransferential fears and anxieties about having family members discuss such difficult topics as disclosure of HIV status, permanency planning, and even funeral arrangements. It may be difficult for therapists to discuss loss and death in their patients if they have not adequately grieved their own losses and disappointments. Given the often conflictual nature of these families, therapists may also worry that they will not be able to control the emotional intensity or even violent behavior of family members in session. If they think it will get out of control, therapists might avoid having family sessions. Unfortunately, the patients must go home to their families and have just these kinds of conversations without the therapist's guidance and ability to manage the emotional intensity of the discussion. Last, even family therapists, who are specially trained in family systems techniques, may resist doing family work with this population because of the complicated nature of the family dysfunction and the high degree of individual psychopathology. Given the chaotic nature of the families and the unpredictability of session times and who comes to sessions, it may seem impossible to adhere to any kind of traditional family therapy model. Yet by using a flexible approach with modifications to conventional family therapy techniques, it is possible to work effectively with this population.

CONCLUSION

In this chapter, the authors have proposed that there is strong need for family therapy for children and families affected by HIV/AIDS. As the AIDS epidemic progresses, more and more families with children are confronting difficult issues. Clinical work in an inner city mental health clinic has provided evidence that there are a myriad of complex and overlooked needs in this population. Given the multigenerational effects of HIV and the high rates of comorbidity of substance abuse and mental illness in the HIV-affected population, the family mental health issues are complicated and far reaching.

Although it may indeed be impossible to do traditional family work with this population, there is a strong need for family systems interventions, and, as noted, the authors have found ways to incorporate family work into the treatment of women and children at the Special Needs Clinic. Family systems interventions and family therapy, in combination with individual psychotherapy, are effective treatment modalities for this population. Family therapy can be effective in helping families cope with the multiple and often competing demands of living with an HIV-infected patient. This modality reduces a sense of isolation, promotes family functioning, and provides support for all family members. Family work also identifies other family members in need of treatment and addresses the issues in a time-efficient way when therapists often have limited time because of the disease progression. In addition, family therapy techniques can increase the engagement and compliance of these families in mental health treatment. Rather than separate and fragment mental health services, this population is best served by comprehensive family services, housed in one place and in liaison with the medical treatment team.

On the basis of clinical experiences at the Special Needs Clinic, two sets of guidelines have been provided to help clinicians interested in incorporating these techniques into their therapeutic work. There are modifications to traditional family therapy models that are necessary in working with this population, whether one does primarily individual work with some family systems interventions or does ongoing family therapy. For example, it is important to maintain a flexible approach to session times and who attends sessions, and it is necessary to refrain from paradoxical techniques. The various reasons why family therapy has traditionally been underutilized with this population were also discussed. Although the authors understand some of the difficulties inherent in doing this work and the resistance on the part of the individual therapist, family work can and should be undertaken.

Yet despite the authors' enthusiasm and interest in doing family therapy with this population, there are a few caveats. Although family therapy techniques have been discussed, there are many issues, populations, and particular constellations of families that are not addressed. For example, this work is based on families with children in a poverty-stricken inner city community. The recommendations do not take into account families without children, families of gay and lesbian adults, or couple relationships, although many of the same principles may apply. In addition, individual psychotherapy issues with this population have not been extensively discussed. Individual work is used quite frequently at the Special Needs Clinic, but those issues and techniques were not able to be discussed in this forum. The reader is referred to the other chapters in this book that clearly address mental health issues for other populations.

With those caveats in mind, the powerful need for a flexible and adaptable approach to family systems work is emphasized. Families are thrown into crisis when they learn of an HIV/AIDS diagnosis. For the families with whom the authors work, who are already coping with substance abuse, premorbid mental health problems, and difficult community and social issues, the crises are even more complicated and difficult to bear. Rigid and inflexible approaches to treatment are not effective and will not keep these kind of patients in treatment. Rather, it is recommended that one follow the two sets of guidelines, but above all use one's own clinical intuition and sense of the family's level of functioning to determine how to proceed.

REFERENCES

Blume, S. (1992). Alcohol and other drug problems in women. In J. H. Lowinson, P. Ruiz, R. B. Millman (Eds.), *Substance abuse: A comprehensive textbook*. Baltimore: Williams & Wilkins.

Bor, R. (1990). The family and HIV/AIDS. *AIDS Care, 2,* 409–466.

Boyd-Franklin, N. (1989). *Black families in therapy: A multisystems approach*. New York: Guilford Press.

Boyd-Franklin, N., Steiner, G. L, & Boland, M. G. (1995). *Children, families, and HIV/AIDS*. New York: Guilford Press.

Carroll, K. M., & Rounsaville, B. J. (1993). History and significance of childhood attention deficit disorder in treatment-seeking cocaine abusers. *Comprehensive Psychiatry, 34,* 75–82.

Centers for Disease Control and Prevention. (1995). *HIV/AIDS Surveillance Update, 7,* 1.

Cohen, F. (1994). Research on families and pediatric human immunodeficiency virus disease: A review and needed directions. *Journal of Developmental and Behavioral Pediatrics, 15*(Suppl.), S34–S42.

Cottler, L. B., Compton, W. M., & Mager, D. (1992). Post-traumatic stress disorder among substance users from the general population. *American Journal of Psychiatry, 149,* 664–670.

Draimin, B. (1993). Adolescents in families with AIDS: Growing up with loss. In C. Levine (Ed.), *A death in the family: Orphans of the HIV epidemic* (pp. 60–68). New York: United Hospital Funds of New York.

Fullilove, M. T., Fullilove, R. E., Kennedy, G., & Smith, M. (1991). *Trauma, crack and HIV risk* (Abstract No. POD-5477). Presented at VIIIth International Conference on AIDS, Amsterdam, The Netherlands.

Green, R. J., & Framo, J. L. (Eds.). (1992). *Family therapy: Major contributions*. Madison, CT: International Universities Press.

Havens, J. F., Mellins, C. A., & Pilowski, D. (1996). Mental health issues in HIV-affected women and children. *International Review of Psychiatry, 8,* 217–225.

Havens, J. F., Mellins, C. A., Ryan, S., & Locker, A. (1995). Mental health needs of children and families affected by HIV/AIDS. In P. G. Goldstein, H. Goodman, & G. Landsberg (Eds.), *Mental health services for HIV affected populations in New York City: A program perspective* (pp. 25–43). New York: The Coalition of Voluntary Mental Health Agencies.

Imber-Black, E., Roberts, J., & Whiting, A. (Eds.). (1988). *Rituals in families and family therapy*. New York: Norton.

McGoldrick, M., & Gerson, R. (1985). *Genograms in family assessment*. New York: Norton.

Mellins, C.A., & Ehrhardt, A. A. (1994). Families affected by pediatric acquired immunodeficiency syndrome: Sources of stress and coping. *Journal of Developmental and Behavioral Pediatrics, 15*(Suppl.), S54–S60.

Mellins, C. A., Ehrhardt, A. A., Newman, L., & Conard, M. (1996). Selective kin: Defining the caregivers and families of children with HIV disease. In L. S. Jemmott & A. O'Leary (Eds.), *Women and AIDS: Coping and care* (pp. 123–149). New York: Plenum.

Reidy, M., Taggart, M. E., & Asselin, L. (1991). Psychosocial needs expressed by the natural caregivers of HIV infected children. *AIDS Care, 3,* 331–343.

Rolland, J. S. (1987). Family systems and chronic illness: A typological model. *Journal of Psychotherapy and the Family, 3,* 143–168.

Rolland, J. S. (1994). *Families, illness, and disability: An integrative treatment model*. New York: Basic Books.

Rounsaville, B.J., & Weissman, M. M. (1982). Heterogeneity of psychiatric diagnosis in treated opiate addicts. *Archives of General Psychiatry, 39,* 161–166.

Walker, G. (1991). *In the midst of winter*. New York: Norton.

Zierler, S., & Feingold, L. (1991). Adult survivors of childhood sexual abuse and subsequent risk of HIV infection. *American Journal of Public Health, 81,* 572–575.

Chapter 7

Psychotherapy with HIV-Affected Adolescents

Sheila Ryan, Jennifer F. Havens, and Claude Ann Mellins

SCOPE OF THE PROBLEM

In the closing years of the millennium, and in poignant counterpoint to mid-century optimism about the conquest of infectious disease, the HIV epidemic is devastating families around the world. In the United States, scores of adolescents and younger children are losing their parents, and sometimes their siblings, to the disease.

In estimates published in 1992, 82,000 children and adolescents in the United States were projected to lose their mothers to AIDS by the year 2000. Of these young people, 21,000 were adolescents between 13 and 17 years of age (Michaels & Levine, 1992). In New York City, the 1992 projection was that 8,000 adolescents would be orphaned by AIDS in New York City by the end of 1995 (Michaels & Levine, 1992). More recent projections are that 15,000 adolescents in New York City will lose their mothers to HIV disease by the year 2001 (Michaels & The Orphan Project, 1996).

Although there are no current estimates of the numbers of adolescents living with mothers or fathers who have AIDS, that group is presumably considerably larger than the number orphaned, and a still larger number may be living with HIV-positive parents who do not yet meet criteria for an AIDS diagnosis.

This chapter was supported in part by Grant 5UDSSM51688-02 from the Substance Abuse and Mental Health Services Administration, HIV/AIDS Mental Health Services Demonstration Program.

With the recent advances in the treatment of HIV, in particular with the intro-duction of protease inhibitors and antiretroviral combination therapies, HIV-infected parents will be living longer, with increased capacity to care for their children. The vast majority of adolescents with HIV-infected parents will be HIV negative, yet deeply affected by their parents' HIV illness. The term *HIV-affected adolescents* is used to refer to this population.

Three salient and interrelated factors should be noted about the social dis-tribution of HIV-affected adolescents. First, owing to the close association be-tween substance abuse and HIV infection in the heterosexual population, the vast majority of these adolescents have experienced parental substance abuse. Forty-seven percent of women with AIDS in the United States have injecting drug use as their primary risk factor for HIV infection, and an additional 18% have sex with an injecting drug–using partner as their risk factor (Centers for Disease Control & Prevention, 1995). Furthermore, the majority of heterosexual men have injecting drug use as their primary risk factor for HIV infection.

Second, the adolescents with HIV-infected parents are disproportionately of ethnic minority status, reflecting the high prevalence of AIDS among African American and Latino women (Centers for Disease Control & Prevention, 1995). Third, HIV-affected adolescents are concentrated in poor neighborhoods where high rates of substance abuse and AIDS coincide with other social problems, such as poverty and violence (Levine & Stein, 1994).

This chapter focuses on psychotherapeutic issues and interventions with uninfected adolescents who live with an HIV-positive parent or caregiver or who have been bereaved by the HIV-related death of a family member. In discussing psychotherapeutic issues for HIV-affected adolescents, the authors draw on the experience of the Special Needs Clinic, a comprehensive family-based mental health clinic serving children, adolescents, and families affected by HIV/AIDS in New York City (see Havens, Mellins, & Ryan, chapter 5). Reflecting the demographics of HIV-infected women living in inner city envi-ronments, the adolescent patients of the Special Needs Clinic are predominantly African American or Latino and socioeconomically disadvantaged. The vast majority have been exposed to substance abuse in the parental generation. There-fore, the authors focus primarily on mental health issues in the population of adolescents affected by both parental HIV disease and substance abuse. Using their clinical experience and presenting case vignettes where applicable, they review biological, psychological, and social risks for mental health problems in these adolescents. Strategies for mental health assessment are presented, as are issues in the choice of treatment modalities. Psychotherapeutic issues for adoles-cents that are related to parental substance abuse, which tend to present in a consistent manner across the course of HIV illness, are reviewed. Finally, a temporal model that focuses on stages of familial HIV illness, including HIV disclosure, progression of HIV illness, late-stage illness, bereavement, and fam-ily reconfiguration is used to highlight stage-specific psychotherapeutic issues and interventions.

Clearly, there are other populations of HIV-affected teens, for example, adolescents with parents exposed to HIV through blood transfusion or heterosexual contact independent of substance abuse as well as adolescents with fathers whose HIV infection is related to sex with men. These adolescents may be from any social class or ethnicity, from urban, suburban, or rural environments. For adolescents whose parents' HIV infection is not associated with histories of substance abuse, quite different issues may emerge that are not necessarily covered in this chapter.

MENTAL HEALTH RISKS IN THE POPULATION OF HIV-AFFECTED ADOLESCENTS WITH SUBSTANCE-ABUSING PARENTS

Among HIV-affected adolescents whose parents have histories of substance abuse, there are two broad categories of risks for mental health problems: (a) increased susceptibility to psychiatric disorder on the basis of family history of mental illness and (b) exposure to disruption of attachments, neglect, and abuse due to parental substance use. As has been described in detail in chapter 5 in this book, adult substance users have increased rates of heritable psychiatric disorder, particularly affective disorders; attention deficit hyperactivity disorder (ADHD); and learning disabilities. The children of substance abusers are at increased risk for neglect, abuse, exposure to domestic violence, and disruption of attachments. Biological vulnerability for psychiatric disorder and adverse family and social environments frequently co-occur in families affected by parental substance use.

In the Special Needs Clinic, more than 400 HIV-affected children and adolescents have been evaluated and treated in the past 4 years. The most common psychiatric disorders encountered in this clinical population include affective disorders, ADHD, adjustment disorders, and learning disorders. Thirty-seven percent of the adolescents are diagnosed with affective disorders (major depression, bipolar disorder, or dysthymia), reflecting both a genetic diathesis and the extreme environmental stressors associated with parental HIV illness or death. Overall, 28% of the children and adolescents seen in the clinic are diagnosed with ADHD and 20% are diagnosed with learning disorders. High rates of exposure to physical and sexual abuse (20%), neglect (50%), and domestic violence (39%) are documented among the adolescent patients in the Special Needs Clinic; many have experienced multiple placements, repeated bereavement, and other traumas.

Onset of early substance use in adolescence is an additional grave concern for these young people; adolescent substance abuse has been significantly associated with both affective illness and ADHD (Burke, Burke, & Rae, 1994; Christie et al., 1988; DeMilio, 1989; Gittleman, Mannuzza, Shenker, & Bonagura, 1985; Greenfield, Hechtman, & Weiss, 1988; Mannuzza et al., 1991). HIV-affected adolescents are extremely vulnerable to alcohol and drug abuse, given their potential risk for psychiatric disorder, extreme experiences of stress and trauma, and social environments that provide both easy access to drugs and intra- and extrafamilial adult modeling of substance abuse.

GOALS FOR CLINICAL ASSESSMENT AND INTERVENTION

There are two overarching, closely interrelated goals in clinical work with HIV-affected adolescents: (a) optimizing normal growth and development in the face of the stressors related to parental HIV illness and (b) the ongoing recognition, diagnosis, and treatment of mental illness, where present. Inherent in both clinical goals is the aim of preventing an array of adverse outcomes, most dramatically prevention of HIV infection in adolescents, but also including exacerbation of mental illness, loss of potential academic and vocational achievement, teenage pregnancy and childbearing, and poor choice of partners in intimate relationships.

Assessment

An adolescent from an HIV-affected family referred for mental health services requires meticulous comprehensive evaluation, including differential diagnosis of psychiatric disorder and careful psychosocial assessment of the teenager and the family. Psychoeducational evaluation of those adolescents with current or historical school failure is also essential.

Adolescents' Presenting Problems and Symptoms

Adolescents affected by HIV may present with difficulties in coping with a specific event in the course of a parent's HIV illness, from diagnosis to death, or with any of the myriad emotional and behavioral problems common in the adolescent developmental stage. An adolescent who presents for treatment—or who is presented for treatment by adult caregivers—may define his or her problems quite differently from the way that parents, extended family members, school staff, or law enforcement personnel do. It is useful to note the variance in descriptions of the adolescent's problems and the attributions for the difficulties made by each of the informants.

It may be challenging to differentiate normative responses to parental illness, death, or other traumatic events from symptoms of psychiatric disorder. For adolescents who are manifesting academic or behavioral problems in school, or who have stopped attending school before high school graduation, it may be difficult to distinguish problems related to learning disabilities from those related to emerging affective disorders or acting-out responses to painful circumstances. Both psychiatric and psychoeducational evaluations can be helpful in clarifying an adolescent's diagnosis. In this process, the young person's strengths and weaknesses can be ascertained, necessity of psychiatric treatment and or academic remediation determined, and realistic recommendations can be made for the future.

Family History and Social History

A careful family history should be taken, with attention to the presence of mental illness, substance abuse, and HIV infection in the nuclear and extended family. By going back at least to the grandparental generation, the evaluator may detect patterns of multigenerational mental illness and substance abuse. It is useful to gather information on the parents' siblings, both to expand the information on family psychiatric and substance abuse problems and to generate a more complete picture of the family's social experience and environment. Unfortunately, it is common for families to have multiple members who are HIV positive or incapacitated by substance abuse or who have died of AIDS. Adolescents in such families have often been exposed to repeated loss and bereavement. Their family members have often had to carry a heavy burden of care for ill relatives, their children, and the children of family members incapacitated by substance abuse. Such preexisting responsibilities may impair the family's capacity to provide adequate support and care for the adolescent.

A detailed history of the adolescent's placement and care, as well as that of any siblings, is very useful; it is optimal to obtain the history from multiple sources to have the clearest and most comprehensive picture of the adolescent's family context. It is important to be alert for histories of broken attachments, repeated loss, disrupted placements, traumas, and periods of family chaos. Asking an adolescent to work with the therapist on a time line of personal history or an autobiography may provide a transition from evaluation to psychotherapeutic treatment of the young patient. These techniques simultaneously provide important data for assessment and material for the therapeutic process.

Social Supports and Service Needs

The various supports for the adolescent in the family and social network should be surveyed to evaluate how socially isolated or connected the young person is. In addition, the services provided to the adolescent by school and community agencies should be reviewed to ascertain whether there are service gaps that can be remedied.

The adolescent's access to health care, including reproductive health care, should also be assessed. Particularly at times when there is family disruption, interruption of benefits and health care coverage, or both, ties to primary health care providers, if they existed, may be lost. It is prudent to ensure that the adolescent has adequate access to routine care and is receiving appropriate care for any ongoing medical problems. Even adolescents who have primary care providers may be reluctant to use their services to obtain birth control or to screen for sexually transmitted diseases, issues of extreme importance as teens become sexually active.

PSYCHOTHERAPEUTIC ISSUES ASSOCIATED WITH SUBSTANCE ABUSE

Although it is common for the adolescent's presenting problems to be framed by events and circumstances associated with the parent's HIV illness, the psychotherapeutic issues in this population are typically more complex and best understood in a broader context. In addition to problems the teenager may experience in coping with HIV-related events, there are frequently psychodynamic issues, histories of psychiatric disorder, and dysfunctions in family systems and community supports that predate the parent's HIV infection. In this section, the focus is on mental health problems that emerge for the adolescent as a function of parental substance abuse. The last section of the chapter (Psychotherapeutic Issues and Interventions through the Course of Parental Illness and Loss) focuses on the specific stages of HIV illness with their associated mental health issues and interventions.

Individual Psychodynamic and Psychobiologic Issues

For many HIV-affected adolescents, mental health problems emerge from two arenas, both stemming from the strong association between HIV and substance abuse in the parental generation. The first of these arenas is psychosocial in character. The teens have often experienced difficult childhoods with substance-abusing parents, in which individual psychological development was negatively affected by a chain of misfortunes, from ruptured attachments and understimulation in infancy through multiple placements to ongoing neglect and repeated trauma throughout childhood. The second arena is psychobiological. Given the association of substance abuse and psychiatric disorder in their parents, a disproportionate number of these adolescents have a genetic predisposition for mental health problems, including learning disabilities, ADHD, and affective and anxiety disorders. Psychiatric disorders can delay and distort development and complicate coping with the stressors inherent in parental HIV disease and loss.

In adolescence there is a reprise of the psychic developmental processes of infancy and early childhood. During adolescence, the young person whose early object relations and identification with the parent were secure undergoes a process of decathexis from the early objects and develops a maturing self-identity based on a kind of synthesis of identification with and differentiation and separation from the parent (Freud, 1966, 1969). The issues associated with parental substance abuse and mental illness and suboptimal early care, including broken attachments and understimulation, may have distorted the child's early object relations. Adolescents who failed to achieve basic trust in infancy through secure attachment to a caregiver will have difficulty in confronting the developmental tasks of adolescence (Erikson, 1950), including separation from parents and development of a stable individual identity. When the parent is very ill with HIV, and perhaps dependent on a teenaged son or daughter, separation is even more challenging. When that parent has in addition a history of substance abuse, mental illness, or both that has impaired the parent's capacity for consistent caregiving, achievement of a secure identity and separation from the ill parent is extraordinarily difficult. The adolescent's own acting out or delinquency, which can be seen as related to appropriate attachment and separation from the parent (Aichorn, 1935), can itself become an obstacle to positive relationships with adult caregivers at this stage.

Ambivalence toward the parent is a normative state, particularly during adolescence. Ambivalence serves to propel the young person forward along the developmental pathway away from the dependence of childhood while simultaneously allowing him or her to maintain a positive identification with the parent, on which a positive, mature self-identity can be based. For many HIV-affected adolescents, ambivalence toward the parent is so intense and anguished that it is unmanageable or nearly so. The experiential antecedents for the negative dimension of the ambivalence may have been very closely associated in the mind of the adolescent—indeed, in the life of the parent—with parental behaviors related to risk for HIV. Perhaps the teen was neglected during the mother's crack binges or abused by a violent male partner who is reputed to have transmitted the virus to the mother. The very elements that injured the child are now seen to be causing the early loss of the parent and the abandonment of the child before he or she achieves adulthood. Yet expression of the rage that the adolescent may feel is blocked by the parent's fragility and the anxiety the adolescent feels about the impending loss.

Problems in object relations and identification and issues of highly charged ambivalence that emerge as salient psychotherapeutic issues for the HIV-affected adolescent typically originate early in life. Alternatively, failure to achieve the developmental tasks of school age (or latency) may result in other problems for the adolescent. During the school-age period, the child struggles to achieve a sense of industry (Erikson, 1950), a self-concept of competency based on grappling with school tasks and on engaging and maintaining relationships with peers. However, learning disabilities, untreated ADHD, or other factors can lead to poor school performance, perhaps compromising achievement of those crucial developmental tasks as a school-aged child. Poor impulse control associated with ADHD may have adversely affected acquisition of social skills and development of peer relationships in school and other arenas. Entering adolescence without a sense of competency in each of these areas can jeopardize a teen's developing sense of personal identity and impair his or her ability to make the transition to adulthood as an autonomous person.

For adolescents with susceptibility to affective disorder, negotiating the shoals of the terminal illness and potential loss of a parent can be very perilous.

If bereavement is a potential precipitant of affective illness, loss of a parent with whom the child had an ambivalent relationship is especially hazardous.

> Nancy was 12 years old when her mother Denise died of AIDS. Until her mother's death, Nancy was generally high functioning, a bright child with some worrisome outbursts of temper, but usually good peer relations. Although most of Nancy's care throughout childhood had been provided by her grandmother, she was deeply injured by her mother's rejection, neglect, and episodes of physical abuse.
>
> For the first several weeks after Denise's death, Nancy displayed the typical mourning signs of an early adolescent: sad mood alternating with "normal" play and socializing. She then reported seeing her mother at night. The hallucinations abated briefly with psychotherapeutic interventions designed to allow Nancy to express her intense ambivalent emotions toward her mother, including writing a letter to her expressing her sadness and rage. When the hallucinations returned, Nancy was prescribed antipsychotic medications. She did not adhere to the medication regimen, however, and within 2 months of her mother's death she had a manic episode. Over the following year, Nancy had three hospitalizations for bipolar disorder with poor control of her affective symptoms, although on medications she had no further psychotic symptoms.

As in the case of Nancy, adolescence is a common time for the onset of affective disorder. Between 20% and 30% of persons with bipolar disorder experience a first episode before age 20 (Goodwin & Jamison, 1990). Early onset of affective illness is associated with the occurrence of stressful life events (Goodwin & Jamison, 1990) and with high rates of affective disorder in family members (Weissman, Warner, Wickramaratne, & Prusoff, 1988). The elevated rates of heritable affective illness and the painful events and trauma of bereavement that are typically experienced by HIV-affected adolescents and that may precipitate episodes of affective disorders are a worrisome combination.

Family Systems Issues

As adolescents struggle with these extraordinarily charged issues, they are more or less contained within and supported by the family system. The families are often especially complex in their structures and histories: A nuclear biological family in which two parents are caring for their children is not normative in the HIV-affected population (Mellins, Ehrhardt, Newman, & Conard, 1996). Single mothering is far more typical, and often the children in the family are of different paternities. Furthermore, there may have been a history of placement of children in the care of others, and perhaps separation of the siblings, especially in families with substance-abusing parents. Other factors, including immigration, may also have led to the care of children by others within or beyond the extended family for long periods of time.

In some families, role reversal, particularly parentification of a child, is prominent. Even before the onset of HIV illness, a child, often the oldest, may have taken on the parental role when a parent's capacity to do so was impaired by substance abuse. A teen may be caring for younger children and attempting to care for the parent as well. Even in families without a history of role reversals, teenagers may assume the burden of physical care for a parent whose health is deteriorating with advancing AIDS. They may also take on responsibility for younger siblings and the overall maintenance of the household. Even when homemakers or home health aides assist with specific tasks, the mantle of responsibility for the family may fall on, or be felt to fall on, an adolescent. This is particularly the case when old conflicts within the extended family hinder relatives from assisting an HIV-positive parent and his or her children. At the Special Needs Clinic, multigenerational histories of substance abuse and mental illness are common. Parental histories of adversity in which the ill parent experienced neglect, abuse, or abandonment in childhood may result in a lack of trust in the extended family. At other times, there are conflicts in the extended family about the mother's substance abuse or choice of male partners.

Finally, the extended families are often beset by multiple and prodigious stressors. The family may be caring for or grieving the loss of several members with AIDS simultaneously, owing to the clustering of AIDS within families. Some of this clustering of AIDS cases is traceable to heterosexual transmission of the disease from one partner to the other and to vertical mother–infant transmission. Alternatively, there may be multiple family members who have histories of injecting drug use or who have injecting drug–using partners.

For individuals experiencing HIV epidemics within their own families, the emotional stress and burden of practical care may be staggering. Grandmothers and other older relatives, who may be medically fragile, may have to take on the care of another set of children after having raised their own. These children may have parents who are incapacitated by substance use or serious illness or who have died. Because the families affected by HIV illness are disproportionately economically disadvantaged, the fit between burdens and resources is egregiously poor.

Community Systems Issues

Another set of issues deeply affecting the adolescents are those related to the devastation of the communities in which they are likely to reside. Wallace (1988) and Wallace and Wallace (1990) found that in the Bronx, New York, a synergism of plagues afflicted neighborhoods, with an interaction between housing destruction, disruption of community social networks, the spread of substance abuse, and AIDS. The process of devastation in urban communities over the past few decades is hypothesized to have led to a collapse in the social ecology and public health, with epidemic substance abuse emerging as networks for social support and control of deviance are destroyed (Wallace, Fullilove, & Wallace, 1992). Of particular concern is the concentration of HIV-affected adolescents, with their intensive needs for supports and overburdened families, in communities where the larger social apparatus for support and control has been eroded.

The macroeconomic context in which this process of neighborhood destruction took place resulted in economic shifts that have decreased the demand in urban areas for low-skilled but relatively well-paid labor in manufacturing and have expanded a service sector in which good jobs require higher education or advanced technical training. This bodes particularly ill for African American and Latino young people who grow up in poor neighborhoods and are inadequately prepared for the existing job market (see Stafford, 1985). A study of HIV-affected adolescents and young adults in New York City found that only 44% of those 19 to 23 years old had graduated from high school (Cicatelli, 1996); in the general population of New Yorkers between 20 and 24 years old, more than 77% have a high school diploma (Griffin, 1995). Cicatelli also found a gap between the limited education and vocational experience of HIV-affected young people and their career aspirations. For example, many of these youth reported an interest in computer work, which tends to demand advanced education.

Certainly for young people reaching adolescence with some of the difficulties common in the population of HIV-affected teens, good progress to adulthood, already at risk, will be further threatened by the absence of appropriate controls and supports within their communities and by the dearth of prospects for persons of limited skill and technical preparation in the larger economy. With these problems, and an overabundance of proximate social models of early childbearing, substance abuse, and entanglement with police and the courts, the adolescence of these HIV-affected youngsters is a time of danger and uncertainty.

TREATMENT PLANNING: CHOOSING MODALITIES

Planning treatment for the HIV-affected adolescent involves prioritizing often complex needs and matching them with usually inadequate clinical resources. Individual, family, and group psychotherapy each have potential benefits and drawbacks; often, a combination of therapies is optimal.

Individual Psychotherapy

Issues arising from problems in object relations, and especially intense ambivalence toward an ill or deceased parent, are best addressed in individual therapy. It is usually very difficult for an adolescent to express anger or shame about a parent, particularly a frail or deceased one, in group sessions. It may be difficult, moreover, for an adolescent to express ambivalent feelings about a parent in family sessions when a strong positive or negative view of the parent dominates the family context. The individual modality allows the young patient to venture into very threatening material on his or her own agenda, and to do so with the focused support of the therapist. Individual therapy also permits the creation of a reparative relationship for the adolescent patient with the therapist, who may need to "re-parent" the patient to some degree in order to remediate lacunae in the young person's psychological development.

Family Therapy

Family therapy is often the most effective means to treat a family in the midst of a crisis related to the HIV illness of a member or a related event or challenge; it allows for provision of immediate support and screening and assessment of individual members. Certainly it is the modality to use for modifying and stabilizing the family system (see chapter 5 of this volume). When family systems are so shaken, impaired, or riven by generational and other conflicts that their capacity to care for and contain a troubled adolescent is eroded, it may be more effective for the safety and well-being of the teen to focus on strengthening the system rather than working with the youngster individually. Family therapy may also facilitate the engagement of adolescents into treatment, especially in cases in which the young person objects to being dragged into counseling by an adult caregiver who is seeking behavioral change in the teen or in cases in which the adolescent feels stigmatized by entering individual treatment, which is for "crazy people."

Group Therapy

Group treatment is the modality of choice for addressing developmental issues of social relationships and behaviors. Many HIV-affected adolescents are in acute need of support with these developmental tasks and can benefit greatly from a group modality, even when they do not explore in that context issues related to their parents' HIV or to bereavement.

Issues of parental illness and loss, negative parental behaviors with substance use and sexual relationships, and feelings of rage, shame, or self-blame may surface in groups. Especially before late adolescence or young adulthood, these issues can be too threatening to the social persona and denial defense mechanisms of group members to permit sustained attention in this context.

Other Services

In addition to one or more of these psychotherapeutic treatment modalities, adolescents in this population may require other mental health or social services. A significant fraction of the HIV-affected adolescents may require psychopharmacology for a psychiatric illness, usually for an affective, anxiety, or attention deficit hyperactivity disorder. For adolescents with learning disorders, educational remediation may be essential to keeping teens in school and allowing for the achievement of academic potential. For older adolescents who have left school, vocational assessment and help with job placement can be essential to the development of the capacity for independent living. These services are often crucial for the mental health of the adolescent and can be an important adjunct to traditional mental health treatment.

PSYCHOTHERAPEUTIC ISSUES AND INTERVENTIONS THROUGH THE COURSE OF PARENTAL ILLNESS AND LOSS

One useful model for organizing the specific issues associated with HIV illness takes into account the dynamic course of HIV illness, which moves through specific predictable stages. These stages begin with diagnosis of HIV infection and move through illness progression, late-stage illness, death, and, where relevant, family reconfiguration. Each stage presents particular challenges to the adolescent's adaption and overall family functioning. In this section, the illness-related issues that present at various points in the course of parental HIV are reviewed.

Disclosure of Parental Illness

Adolescents may initially present with problems coping with a recently disclosed diagnosis of HIV/AIDS in a parent. Alternatively, HIV-infected parents who have not yet disclosed their HIV status to their children may seek help from therapists in how to communicate this information. No matter how or when an adolescent learns of a parent's HIV diagnosis, the information is difficult to tolerate. For some teens, who may have known or suspected their parents' diagnosis, the "disclosure" by a parent brings a measure of relief; they do not have to cope with the terrifying material in isolation. For other adolescents, the communication of a parent's HIV diagnosis is a blow that they wish had been delayed until some future point.

Understanding of and Communication About HIV Illness in the Family

The therapist's communication with the adolescent about the health of an HIV-positive parent is a delicate task, especially when it is unclear what, if anything, the parent has told the teen about his or her health condition. When the HIV-positive parent is available for interviewing, it is useful to assess parent–child communication around HIV serostatus or illness. It is important to determine what exactly the parent has told the adolescent and to probe for the language the parent used, as well as for the explanation, if any, of how the parent was exposed to the virus. Clinicians should ask how the parent decided what and when to tell the adolescent and others in the family. If the parent knows or believes that someone other than he or she has given information to the child about the parent's HIV status, it is significant to ascertain if that disclosure was with parental permission, what motivated it, and to the extent possible the content of the information communicated. Rather than focusing exclusively on an isolated moment in time when the parent's HIV diagnosis was or was not "disclosed" to the teen, it is more useful to examine the quality of the ongoing communication about parental health. How often the subject is discussed and under what conditions (e.g., in response to the young person's questions or when the parent needs support from the teen) is highly relevant.

The objective for the clinician is to learn about (a) the parent's understanding of his or her health status, (b) the meaning this has for the parent, and (c) the parent's perspective on communicating this information to children and the family. The affective component of understanding is as significant here as the cognitive aspect. Shame, guilt, and blame, particularly in association with the adolescent, are not unusual and are important emotions to identify. Sometimes the ill parent will attribute the infection to the behavior of the adolescent's other parent. Alternatively, the infected parent will ascribe progression of the illness to the adolescent's behavior, for example, it stresses the parent's immune system. Either of these attributions will affect parent–teen communication about the parent's health and have an impact on the family's overall functioning.

If a parent has not informed the adolescent about his or her HIV infection, believes the son or daughter is unaware of it, and is adamant that there be no disclosure, it is still very possible to initiate treatment with the teen. It is an extraordinarily rare case in which parental health is the only significant problem in an HIV-affected adolescent's life. Obviously in treating an adolescent whose parent has told a therapist of parental HIV and does not want this disclosed to the young patient, the therapist must be very clear in communication with both parent and teen about confidentiality and its limits. Even when the therapist believes that a parent's refusal to disclose his or her HIV infection or serious illness is not in the adolescent's best interests, information must be regarded as the parent's own private information, and its confidentiality must be respected. When the parent is unavailable, the therapist will need to approach the topic with the teen in a tactful manner, respecting the confidentiality of the parent's medical information. It is best to broach the topic in a very gentle and general manner (e.g., by inquiring about whether any family member has an illness or other problem of concern to the teen), unless the parent's health status has been revealed in such a blatant manner (e.g., the parent is admitted to an intensive care unit) as to render such an approach absurd.

Shame, guilt, anger, and other feeling states may circumscribe the adolescent's willingness or ability to discuss the parent's HIV status, illness, or prognosis. The young patient may choose not to disclose to the therapist his or her awareness of parental illness until the therapist is proven to be worthy of trust with such difficult material. Adolescents, especially those in early adolescence, must often defend themselves against the painful affect associated with knowledge of parental HIV, lest it overwhelm their capacity to function and achieve normative developmental tasks. The most frequently used defense mechanisms, especially for younger adolescents, are denial and its close relative minimization.

Teens may compartmentalize knowledge of the illness, allowing it out of the box only briefly, or console themselves with the thought that the parent is "only HIV positive" and does not have AIDS.

It is not common for adolescents to attempt to cope with parental HIV illness by seeking peer social support; a study of teens with HIV-positive mothers found that not a single adolescent in the study had told a best friend about the parent's diagnosis (Draimin, Hudis, & Segura, 1992). Certainly the social stigma associated with HIV illness may be a factor in this failure to seek social support from peers. The playground taunt "Your mother's got AIDS!"— closely akin to the insult "Your mother's a crackhead!"—echoes in the minds of many HIV-affected teens.

The social stigma attached to AIDS interacts for some young people with their own painful ambivalence toward their parents (e.g., love and dependence versus pain and rage at parental substance abuse). The negative community stereotype about HIV-infected or substance-using people may coincide with the adolescent's negative feeling toward the parent, but may conflict with any positive feelings. Caught in this state of cognitive dissonance, the adolescent may opt to guard the secret from peers.

During her mother's illness, 12-year-old Beth explained,

> I could maybe tell my friend that my Mom's got AIDS. But she got AIDS because she took drugs and hung out with gross guys. I love her, and I don't want people knowing every embarrassing thing that she might have ever done. And I do not particularly choose to be known as the child of a person who did what my mother did to get AIDS. I might just as well say that I got abused and child neglected and put in foster care, since that is the truth, but I do not choose to introduce myself to people that way.

Teens may also refrain from telling friends about a parent's illness in service of denial: Telling someone else confirms the reality of the information the teen prefers to wish away. Telling someone from the peer social network brings this emotionally charged issue out of the adolescent's private realm of thought and feeling, and beyond the family context, into the area of socialization and school. The adolescent may be struggling to preserve spaces for normative functioning and development, uncontaminated by excruciating anxieties about parental health. When asked why he had not told any of his friends about his mother's advanced AIDS, 15-year-old Sam explained,

> It's bad enough to have to think about my mom being sick when I'm at home with her, or while I'm trying to go to sleep at night. I don't want to have to think about it at school or when I'm out with my friends. I don't want them asking me about it and reminding me about it.

Sometimes adolescents will give similar explanations as to why they have not discussed a parent's illness with a school counselor with whom they have a positive relationship: They are attempting to cordon off the world of school and peer relationships from the troubles of home and family.

In some cases, adolescents may learn simultaneously of a parent's HIV infection and of the parent's very advanced disease. This may occur because the parent believed it was best to defer disclosure as long as possible or because the parent was unable to bring himself or herself to tell the teen about the HIV until symptoms became very serious. In other cases, the parent is first diagnosed with HIV when already severely immunocompromised. This late-stage diagnosis may be a marker for serious problems in the functioning of the ill person as well as in the family.

Progression of Parental Illness

As the disease progresses, and the parent begins to be hospitalized with opportunistic infections, adolescents may experience increasing anxiety and distress about the parent's health status. Physical changes in the parent are very painful for the teen to observe: An emaciated mother may seem to be literally disappearing from the realm of the living. Moreover, the striking alterations in the parent's size notify the world that the parent is ill and may also raise suspicions about the parent having AIDS. Deterioration in the parent's cognitive functioning is also very painful for the adolescent to endure. In many cases, the parent is losing the ability to provide physical care and supervision to the adolescent and siblings. Even if previous caregiving was inadequate, the obvious loss of this capacity can destroy the teen's often cherished fantasy of receiving good care from the parent in the future.

The responses of teenagers to parental illness run the gamut from emotional disengagement from the ill parent and family and immersion in the peer social network to isolation from peers and confinement to home and caregiving for the parent and siblings. As noted previously, it can be difficult to ascertain which negative behaviors are actually related to adjustment to parental illness and which are related to developmental stage or underlying problems, perhaps of a long-standing nature. When a teen comes to the attention of mental health providers because of parental illness or death, there is a tendency to attribute all emotional and behavioral problems to HIV-related issues. In contrast, if the same teen were to be seen in a setting where the parent's health status was unknown, the same emotional and behavioral problems might be understood in quite a different way, and the possible impact of parental illness missed. Therapists must carefully consider both HIV-related and other causes for problems and choose appropriate interventions.

For example, the behavior of class cutting in junior high school may have very different causes. It might represent a kind of coping effort on the part of the adolescent to defend against painful thoughts about an ill or deceased parent. Young people who characteristically use defenses of distraction and denial to protect themselves against painful affect associated with such thoughts may find that these mechanisms are quite effective outside of school when they can turn on the radio or go out to shoot baskets. These defenses are often not available or effective in the classroom, so the teenager may simply stay away.

> Richard, 14 years old, was brought to treatment by his grandmother, who complained of a decline in his school performance over the previous year. Richard had until then been a very good student, with strong academic performance and a network of positive peer relations. Now Richard was doing poorly in some of his classes and cutting class to hang out in the cafeteria with other students who were performing marginally.
>
> Within a few sessions Richard began to speak about the pain he felt about his mother's illness, although he was able to focus on this issue for no more than a few minutes at a time. He explained that "it doesn't do any good to talk about this or to think about it" and readily reported on the tactics he used at home to distract himself from thoughts of this problem: He would play Nintendo or go downstairs to visit a friend. In school he was able to ward off these thoughts in some of his classes, especially the ones he enjoyed. It was difficult to distract himself in his afternoon global studies class, however, because he found it boring. Painful thoughts about his mother were most intrusive at this time. So he would frequently cut class to join other boys in the cafeteria, listening to music and socializing.

Other HIV-affected adolescents who begin to cut classes or remain truant for whole days in junior high school or high school may be responding to quite different problems. Perhaps the young person has learning deficits that make attendance at class embarrassing, discouraging, or otherwise unpleasant; in secondary schools, without some of the structures characteristic of elementary school, the student may simply opt out of classes. For example, 13-year-old David was consistently truant from junior high school for 3 months after his father's HIV disease became more serious. David was very anxious about his ill parent. The truancy, however, was not a new behavior, but an exacerbation of a problem with poor school attendance over a period of 3 years. Cutting school appeared to be more related to unaddressed learning disabilities and to household chaos then to maladaptive coping with his father's illness.

Appropriate intervention with other behaviors may require appreciation of the norms of the family and peer group. For example, Suzette initiated sexual activity shortly after her 14th birthday. The timing of this behavior was normative in her family: She herself had been born to a 15-year-old mother, and her 16-year-old aunt was pregnant with a second child. It was, moreover, consonant with the norms of her peer group, in which most of the girls become sexually active between the ages of 12 and 14. The early onset of sexual activity in this case is of concern, but of a quite different character than that of Anita, who began having sex at 14, a few months after her mother's death. In this second case, the girl's behavior was not syntonic with family and peer norms. Her grandmother and aunts were highly disapproving, and Anita shifted away from long-standing friendships with a group of girls who were generally not sexually active to a new group, whom her grandmother described as "running wild in the streets."

End-Stage Parental Illness

The last weeks, days, and hours of the parent's illness are almost invariably a time of great distress for an adolescent, whether or not he or she actually spends much time with the parent. Some adolescents vacillate between a pretense of normalcy at school and with friends and the stress of visits to the parent in a hospital. The adolescent may not know how to communicate with the parent, whose mental status may be waxing and waning. Invasive medical technology may distance the critically ill parent from the child. Some adolescents eschew contact with the parent in the final stage of illness and may express anger or fearful avoidance of the scene.

> Jamal was 14 years old when his father, home less than a year from prison, was diagnosed with AIDS. The diagnosis was a crushing blow to Jamal, who had hoped that his father's release would bring about the reunion of his parents and a cessation of their drug abuse. However, the family reunion did not long survive the prison discharge, AIDS diagnosis, and drug relapses of Jamal's father and mother.
>
> Jamal, who had severe ADHD and learning disabilities, began to have more serious behavioral problems in his special education class and moved to the home of his paternal aunt. In the year and a half between Jamal's entering psychotherapy and his father's death, Jamal was able, first haltingly and eventually with greater facility, to express his feelings about his father and his family history of neglect, trauma, and loss. He loved his father, yet feared that he himself would become like him, "a crackhead and a guy who spends most of his time upstate."
>
> Jamal was not able to bring himself to visit during his father's final hospitalization. He remained very angry with his father for his last crack binge, but he could not express this anger toward the fragile, bed-bound man whose hold on life had become so tenuous. At the same time, Jamal loved his father and was in anguish about the prospect of losing him. Jamal's therapist arranged for Jamal's father, in the final weeks of his life, to make a video message for his son, in which he expressed his love and his hope that his son would not make the mistakes he himself had made in life. His eloquence and patent sincerity were a legacy for Jamal.

Bereavement

Mourning, both in anticipation of the loss of an ill parent and after the death of a parent, is typically complicated for HIV-affected adolescents by very intense ambivalence. On the one hand, the child loves and grieves the impending or actual loss of the parent. When the history of the parent–child relationship has been one of neglect or abuse, there is still grief, including grief for the loss of the potential for a good relationship in the future. Ambivalence toward the lost parent is the most salient and difficult feature of the complicated mourning that is typical of adolescents orphaned by AIDS. Bowlby (1980) described patterns in the parent–child relationship of discontinuity and rejection that predispose children to form "anxious and ambivalent attachments" and to undergo "disordered mourning" when bereaved later in life. For HIV-affected adolescents, the parent they have lost is often the person to whom they had this anxious and ambivalent attachment.

> Beth was 12 years old when her 29-year-old drug-addicted mother died of AIDS. Beth refrained from deep explorations of her feelings about the loss of her mother during a year of intermittent group and individual therapy following her mother's death. Instead, she focused on issues related to adjusting to new care arrangements with a maternal aunt and to separation from her siblings.
>
> As the anniversary of her mother's death approached, Beth announced that she wanted to tell the therapist about a dream she had. In the dream, her mother had instructed her to do something and she had refused; with great relish, she mimed a gesture of defiance, arms crossed, and acted out her response in the dream, shouting "NO!" repeatedly. She stated that her mother had slapped her in the dream, and she had hit her mother back. She spoke about her difficult history with her mother, recalling nights when she and her siblings huddled together in bed, awaiting their mother's return home in the early morning hours, usually high and often with a man.
>
> Beth burst into tears during the next session, expressing great pain at her mother's loss, and profound loneliness that "now I have no one who can love me like a mother." Beth insisted that had she and her siblings been able to reach their mother in time during her final hours "she wouldn't have died, because her children would have been with her and she would have known that she couldn't leave us like that."
>
> As therapy progressed, she worked to identify positive aspects of her mother that were exemplified by her siblings and herself and were a kind of legacy, a kind of continuing connection. She noted that one brother had her mother's sense of adventure and a sister had her intensity; with her therapist's help, she acknowledged that she herself had her mother's special gift for verbal expression and her quick wit.

When there are strains within the family system that exacerbate the mourning process for the adolescent, resolution of grief and resumption of optimal functioning and development can be delayed. In some cases, a surviving parent or caregiving grandparent is unable to complete the mourning process; the deceased remains a dominating presence in the family, with the memory looming so large and so sacred that the adolescent cannot separate from the dead parent as he or she normatively would from a living one. In other cases, the dead parent is an anathema within the family, and the bereaved teenager is expected to sever the memory.

> Henry, a 12-year-old African American boy, lived in the care of his father, a man with advanced AIDS and an ongoing problem of alcohol abuse, with occasional relapses into crack or heroin use. Henry's mother had died 3 years before the boy's

referral for treatment. Henry's father remained extremely angry with Henry's mother, to the point of refusing to speak of her to Henry. The focus of his expressed anger was her substance abuse, which he blamed for her illness and death. Underlying his rage was grief at her abandonment of him and Henry through death.

Henry initially told his therapist that he was unable to remember very much at all about his mother, although he continued to have the occasional perception of her calling his name on the street and playground. He drew a bizarre family portrait, in which he and his father were depicted as small, very separate figures. Floating to one side was a disembodied head, which Henry said was his deceased mother, and next to that head a dark blob of virtually the same size and shape. While Henry insisted that the blob was a mistake, it lent itself to the interpretation that it was his father's negative memory of Henry's mother.

Over several sessions, Henry reconstructed his memory of his mother. He recalled favorite foods she cooked, the park where she took him as a small child, the months between his hospital visit to her at Christmas and her death at Easter. His recollection of her attire in the casket and of the minimal explanations he received from his father and other family members was detailed and very painful. He dictated these memories to the therapist, who typed them into the computer and gave Henry a printed copy of his memories so that he would have some memento of his mother. Henry illustrated this with a drawing of his mother pushing him on the swing as she had when he was a little boy.

Family Reconfiguration

As HIV disease progresses in a parent, the family anticipates the impending loss of the parent and the reconfiguration of the family. The issue of planning for the future of the adolescent and siblings becomes more prominent, whether or not it is addressed by the adolescent, the parent, or the family as a whole. When parents make formal plans for the care of the teenagers, they frequently do so without consulting the adolescents. In a survey of adolescents affected by HIV in New York City, fewer than 30% reported that they had been involved in formulating the plan for their care (Cicatelli, 1996). In New York State, a child of 14 years or older has the right to be heard in court about appointment of a guardian, and judges frequently inquire into the wishes of younger minors. As a practical matter, the state is less likely to intervene forcefully to move an adolescent from one placement to another and more likely to allow the adolescent to live where he or she wishes, as long as the placement is not entirely unreasonable and the adolescent is not involved in a serious violation of the law. Nevertheless, the issue may be hotly debated by the parent and child as illness progresses or, alternatively, may be left completely unmentioned. In either case, adolescents frequently worry about their care in the future, from the details of who will buy their clothing and what strains a move will place on maintenance of peer relations to concerns about a relationship with another adult caregiver and emotional responses to being parentless at a young age.

Working with families in which a young person in the late teens or early 20s is the potential or actual caregiver for younger siblings is a complex task.

The needs of each of the siblings must be considered, as well as those of the family itself as an entity. The difficult process of role change during the period of increasing parental incapacity when an adolescent may take on responsibility and authority in the household can provide a period of rehearsal for a future of being in charge. This time represents an opportunity for the adolescent, siblings, older family members, and service providers to assess the implications of such a plan.

> Hilda, a 17-year-old Dominican immigrant with a 16-year-old brother, Wilfredo, and a 10-year-old sister, Maria, was initially referred for mental health services for her depressive symptoms. Hilda met criteria for major depression; within a few months her mother, Dolores, who had advanced AIDS, was hospitalized briefly for depression and suicidality. Although Hilda continued to have significant symptoms, she took on increasing responsibility for her mother and siblings as Dolores's physical and mental health deteriorated.
>
> In her final months, Dolores told her children and the clinical staff that she had decided that her sister, who lived in a suburban area, should care for the youngest sibling, and the teenaged boy should choose whether to join his little sister or stay in the city with his maternal grandmother. The three children all objected to the plan. They did not feel comfortable in the homes of their maternal relatives, in part because of conflicts between the extended family and their mother and in part because those relatives had failed to intervene effectively to support them during years made difficult by their mother's alcohol abuse and choice of unstable and sometimes violent male partners.
>
> The alternative all three of the children came to espouse was that they remain in their home in the care of Hilda. Although Dolores contested this plan until the end, after her death, Hilda became de facto the guardian of her siblings. With considerable external support, she was able to carry out this responsibility and to maintain the household on a combination of public assistance and the proceeds of her poorly paid, "off-the-books" job.

Sometimes a parent will plan for an adolescent to care for younger siblings although the task is beyond the young person's capacity. This is a sensitive situation in which an already grieving and fragile young person can be racked with guilt.

> Sandra, an 18-year-old African American woman, was seen as her mother lay dying of AIDS. Her mother, Edith, a crack abuser, had been diagnosed only 4 months before her death and did not disclose that diagnosis to Sandra until a few days before her discharge from a hospital to a nursing home where she spent her final 2 weeks. Edith told Sandra that she expected her to care for two younger sisters, one 9 and the other 11.
>
> Sandra was ambivalent about how to respond to her mother's instruction that she care for her sisters. Sandra was deeply concerned about the younger girls, who had their own significant mental health problems, hardly surprising given the family's painful history of trauma and loss. She fantasized about being able to reconstitute the family to care for her siblings as she wished she had been cared for herself. She

was loathe to allow the girls to be placed in foster care, where she had experienced abuse, and had no ready resource for their care within the extended family. At the same time, she felt unable to provide care for the girls and worried that the child protection authorities would remove the children from her care. Complicating the situation even further was her reluctance to refuse her mother's deathbed request. It was difficult to converse for more than a few minutes at a time with Edith, who was emaciated, with a waxing and waning mental status, often in pain and frenzied by the incessant itching from a severe skin problem.

With support from her therapist, Sandra decided to try to locate a relative to care for the girls. An aunt in the South, Clarisse, finally emerged as a willing caregiver: Sandra had had positive experiences with her in the past and felt that she would be a better candidate for care of the younger girls than herself. On the night before Edith's transfer to the nursing home, Sandra told her mother tearfully that she had decided that she couldn't care for her sisters, but that her aunt Clarisse had agreed to take the girls. Sandra promised that she would keep in contact with the girls and would always try to help them. Edith was barely able to speak, but she nodded and squeezed Sandra's hand.

CONCLUSION

The scores of thousands of adolescents living with HIV-positive parents or surviving their deaths represent a population whose mental health is vulnerable and whose needs for treatment are complex. Because of this vulnerability, traceable to high rates of substance abuse and comorbid psychiatric illness in the parental generation, these adolescents often require access to careful mental health assessment as well as intensive interventions to support coping with a parent's HIV, to optimize the adolescent growth and development, and to diagnose and treat any mental illness.

To a great extent, their parents' HIV infection represents a failure of social and health care service systems—failure to provide treatment for substance abuse, which is the primary vector for the virus outside the gay community; failure to diagnose and treat comorbid mental illness in a timely manner; and failure to provide social and community supports necessary for health maintenance. Effective intervention with the adolescent offspring of HIV-infected parents may stop the epidemic, which has devastated the parental generation, from becoming a multigenerational plague.

REFERENCES

Aichorn, A. (1935). *Wayward youth.* New York: Viking Press.
Bowlby, J. (1980). *Loss: Sadness and depression: Vol. 3. Attachment and loss.* New York: Basic Books.
Burke, J. D., Burke, K. C., & Rae, D. S. (1994). Increased rates of drug abuse and dependence after onset of mood or anxiety disorders in adolescence. *Hospital & Community Psychiatry, 45,* 451–455.
Centers for Disease Control and Prevention. (1995). *HIV/AIDS Surveillance Report, 7*(2).

Christie, K. A., Burke, J. D., Regier, D. A., Rae, D. S., Boyd, J. H., & Locke, B. Z. (1988). Epidemiologic evidence for early onset of mental disorders and higher risk of drug abuse in young adults. *American Journal of Psychiatry, 145,* 971–975.

Cicatelli, B. (1996). *Project Independence: Needs assessment and recommendations: Final report* (Report to the New York State Department of Health AIDS Institute). New York: Cicatelli Associates.

DeMilio, L. (1989). Psychiatric syndromes in adolescent substance abusers. *American Journal of Psychiatry, 146,* 1212–1214.

Draimin, B., Hudis, J., & Segura, J. (1992). *The mental health needs of well adolescents in families with AIDS.* New York: Human Resources Administration.

Erikson, E. (1950). *Childhood and society.* New York: W. W. Norton.

Freud, A. (1966). Ego and id at puberty. In *The ego and the mechanisms of defense* (Rev. ed.; pp. 137–151). Madison, CT: International Universities Press.

Freud, A. (1969). Adolescence. In *Research at the Hempstead Child Therapy Clinic and other papers: Writings of Anna Freud* (Vol. 5, pp. 136–166). Madison, CT: International Universities Press.

Gittleman, R., Mannuzza, S., Shenker, R., & Bonagura, N. (1985). Hyperactive boys almost grown up: V. Psychiatric status. *Archives of General Psychiatry, 42,* 937–947.

Goodwin, F., & Jamison, K. (1990). *Manic depressive illness.* New York: Oxford University Press.

Greenfield, B., Hechtman, L., & Weiss, G. (1988). Two subgroups of hyperactives as adults: Correlations of outcome. *Canadian Journal of Psychiatry, 33,* 505–508.

Griffin, M. (1995). *Critical choices: Education and employment among New York City youth.* New York: Community Service Society.

Levine, C., & Stein, G. L. (1994). *Orphans of the HIV epidemic: Unmet needs in six U.S. cities.* New York: The Orphan Project.

Mannuzza, S., Klein, R. G., Bonagura, N., Malloy, P., Giampino, T. L., & Addalli, K. A. (1991). Hyperactive boys almost grown up. V. Replication of psychiatric status. *Archives of General Psychiatry, 48,* 77–83.

Mellins, C. A., Ehrhardt, A. A., Newman, L., & Conard, M. (1996). Selective kin: Defining the caregivers of HIV-infected children. In A. O'Leary & L. Sweet Jemmott (Eds.), *Women and AIDS* (Vol. 2, pp.123–149). New York: Plenum.

Michaels, D., & Levine, C. (1992). Estimates of the number of motherless youth orphaned by AIDS in the United States. *Journal of the American Medical Association, 268,* 3456–3461.

Michaels, D., & The Orphan Project. (1996, April 16). *Estimates of children and youth orphaned by maternal death from HIV/AIDS in New York State* (press release). Albany, NY.

Stafford, W. (1985). *Closed labor market: Underrepresentation of Blacks, Hispanics and women in New York City's core industries and jobs.* New York: Community Service Society.

Wallace, R. (1988). A synergism of plagues: Planned shrinkage, contagious housing destruction and AIDS in the Bronx. *Environmental Research, 47,* 1–33.

Wallace, R., Fullilove, M., & Wallace, D. (1992). Family systems and de-urbanization: Implications for substance abuse. In J. Lowinson, P. Ruiz, & R. Millman (Eds.), *Substance abuse: A comprehensive textbook.* Baltimore: Williams & Wilkins.

Wallace, R., & Wallace, D. (1990). Origins of public health collapse in New York City: The dynamics of planned shrinkage, contagious urban decay and social disintegration. *Bulletin of the New York Academy of Medicine, 66,* 5.

Weissman, M., Warner, V., Wickramaratne, P., & Prusoff, B. A. (1988). Early-onset major depression in parents and their children. *Journal of Affective Disorders, 15,* 269–277.

Chapter 8

Couples of Mixed HIV Status: Challenges and Strategies for Intervention with Couples

Robert H. Remien

The situation in which one member of a couple is HIV seropositive and the other is HIV seronegative (mixed HIV status) is a relatively new phenomenon for mental health workers to confront in their clinical work. As new HIV infections continue to occur in both the heterosexual and the homosexual populations, coupled with the phenomenon of people living longer and healthier with HIV, the likelihood of such couples presenting for treatment is increasing. It is important that therapists increase their skills to work at the dyadic level with the many challenges these couples face, in order to reduce distress and strengthen the partnership, rather than referring each to his or her separate support group or individual therapy. This chapter focuses on therapy with the couple (heterosexual, homosexual, married, and unmarried) as a unit. Therapeutic work with the larger family system, including children, is discussed in chapter 5 of this book.

PSYCHOLOGICAL DISTRESS WITHIN COUPLES

Although some studies have shown that people with HIV/AIDS have higher levels of psychological morbidity and greater sexual difficulties than both the general population and their HIV-negative counterparts (Atkinson et al., 1988; Catalan et al., 1992; Hays, Turner, & Coates, 1990), other studies have found rates of current depressive disorders among HIV-positive men and women to be more or less equal to rates found for HIV-negative men and women and general population samples (Klimes et al., 1992; Perry et al., 1990; Williams, Rabkin, Remien, Gorman, & Ehrhardt, 1991). However, HIV-positive samples compared with HIV-negative controls consistently express more symptoms of distress on both clinician-administered and self-rated scales.

Furthermore, studies of psychiatric morbidity in HIV-infected people rarely, if ever, consider the relationship status of the participants. One systematic study that assessed psychological distress in both members of male couples of mixed HIV status found significantly elevated levels of self-reported depression, anxiety, and hopelessness in both members of the couple, as compared with couples in which both members share the same HIV status (Remien et al., 1996). Other studies have shown there to be an increased vulnerability for psychological distress among heterosexual couples of mixed HIV status, particularly soon after HIV seropositive status notification. Studies have also found psychological distress to be a factor associated with risky sexual behavior (Kennedy et al., 1993). It is believed that the issues faced by individuals in mixed-status partnerships pose unique and difficult challenges to maintaining positive mental health in each member of the dyad.

CHALLENGES FOR THE COUPLE

HIV serodiscordance makes the issues that typically confront any couple particularly complex and multifaceted. Barriers to open communication that can be challenging for all couples are exacerbated as a result of the often overwhelming fear of HIV transmission, illness progression, and future loss. Avoidance of the topic is common in these couples because of the powerful emotions associated with HIV-related concerns. Major issues that typically arise include difficulties associated with future planning, fear of HIV transmission, lack of sexual spontaneity and satisfaction, decisions about pregnancy and child-rearing, fantasies of fleeing, fear of abandonment, fear of increased intimacy in the context of potential loss, caretaking concerns, and feelings of sadness, guilt, and rage.

Avoidance

It is common for mixed-status couples to avoid talking about HIV-related topics, including all of their fears and concerns about many issues. Anything that is related to the topic can feel emotionally charged. It is fairly safe to assume that every person who is aware of his or her HIV-positive serostatus and every person who is the partner of an HIV-positive person entertains, in his or her own mind, a range of fantasies about the future possibility of severe illness, physical dependence, cognitive decline, and premature death. It can be difficult to verbalize these fears to oneself and to one's partner; thus, individuals often endure these fantasies in isolation. Both members of the couple will typically express the need to "protect" the partner from these thoughts and feelings. The seronegative partner typically does not want to express his or her sadness and fear so as not to burden the partner with something else to worry about or make the partner feel bad. After all, the partner is infected and he or she is not, and so the seronegative partner thinks that his or her emotional needs are less valid. The seropositive partner likewise feels the need to protect the partner from worrying about him or her and may feel guilty for bringing HIV infection into the relationship, whether the seropositive partner already knew his or her sero-positive status before or after forming the relationship. Eventually they realize that they both share similar concerns and that, to a large degree, they are at-tempting to protect themselves from confronting the potential reality of what may lie ahead.

Sexual Risk Behavior

Because one is HIV-positive and the other is not, the fear of transmission is ever present, and difficulties associated with the need to always engage in protected sex and achievement of satisfaction with safer sex emerge. Research has shown that consistent use of condoms for heterosexual intercourse is highly effective in preventing the transmission of HIV (Vincenzi, 1994). Among couples not using condoms, the risk of HIV transmission varies widely and is influenced by several factors, including stage of HIV illness in the seropositive partner, other genital infections in the seronegative partner, bleeding as a result of inter-course, and participation in anal intercourse (Anderson et al., 1992; Seidlin, Vogler, Lee, Lee, & Dubin, 1993; Vincenzi, 1994).

Consistent maintenance of protected sex is difficult to achieve in ongoing intimate relationships (Padian, O'Brien, Chang, Glass, & Francis, 1993; Remien, Carballo-Dieguez, & Wagner, 1995). Condoms are perceived to be a barrier to intimacy. They are a constant reminder of HIV infection and therefore can interfere with the spontaneity and pleasure of sexual expression. Many couples say that using the condom is like bringing death into the bedroom because of all of the cognitive and emotional associations attached to the necessity of its use. Not using condoms, or engaging in sex behavior that may be risky, can be perceived as exciting, passionate, and a "true" expression of love and com-mitment.

Many couples do not think that unprotected oral sex is very risky for trans-mission of HIV and are willing to engage in this behavior with each other on a regular basis. Nevertheless, there is often fear and discomfort associated with the behavior that interferes with pleasure and satisfaction. Some even have con-cerns about body fluids (i.e., saliva, ejaculate, vaginal secretions) being on the uninfected partner's skin, particularly if there are cuts or sores anywhere on the body. Often these concerns are unexpressed and avoided, as are other HIV-related issues. These intrusive, and at times irrational, thoughts and fears may be felt by either the HIV-positive or the HIV-negative partner, or at times by both of them.

Caretaking Concerns

Fear of illness, loss of functioning, and dependency can be persistent, even when the infected partner is entirely asymptomatic. Distress about these concerns may be intermittent or chronic in one or both members of the couple. When illness is manifested in the HIV-positive partner, the challenge and associated distress is realized. Studies of chronically ill patients and their families have shown that the lack of control over symptoms and the debilitating effects and unpredictability of disease contribute to the stress of caregiving (Cohen & Lazarus, 1979; Jessop & Stein, 1985; Moos & Tsu, 1977; Raveis & Siegel, 1991; Zarit & Zarit, 1986). These effects can be most pronounced in spouses and partners of the person with chronic illness (Badger, 1990; Chowanec & Binik, 1989; Revenson, 1994; Rolland, 1994; Webster, 1992; Wright, 1991). Being part of a couple affected by HIV/AIDS is perceived as "a major life transition as both partners are confronted by multiple losses including the possible death of the person with AIDS, dissolution of the relationship, health, independence, intimacy, and privacy" (Powell-Cope, 1995, p. 36).

HIV presents couples with several unique challenges. Most of the literature on chronic illness and couples does not deal with communicable diseases. The transmissibility of HIV adds another major dimension of stress. Further, for gay couples or couples with a history of IV drug use, living a lifestyle seen by many as deviant, the intensity of this experience is magnified tremendously when facing another highly stigmatized condition like AIDS (Rolland, 1994). As a result of these stressors, the primary partners of people with HIV/AIDS are not always able to provide adequate support. Although support of various types is usually available for persons who are ill, the needs of their partners are less often addressed. Spouses occupy a dual role in the coping process, as primary providers of support to the ill person and as family members who need support in coping with the illness-related stresses they are experiencing (Revenson, 1994).

Future Planning

Planning for the future is an activity usually shared by two people in intimate relationships, particularly as relationships grow and solidify over time. In mixed-HIV-status relationships, this is typically fraught with mixed emotions and as a result often avoided. Coping with future uncertainty may be one of the most difficult psychological challenges for anyone living with HIV. For the mixed-status couple, it is especially difficult because of the perception that they have very different health and life expectancies. The often stated comment that "either one of us could get sick with something else . . . or hit by a bus" usually does not help because of the very present and real potential for illness and death associated with HIV infection.

The perception that the couple cannot engage in long-term future planning, like other couples not living with HIV, is experienced as a significant loss by the couple. This loss can impede development of intimacy in the relationship. Further, unexpressed and unexamined feelings of loss can hinder the couple's normal developmental tasks. When couples recognize that they are avoiding discussing the future, they may express feelings of rage and despair, feeling that it just is not fair that they must live with this overwhelming uncertainty and dread of the future. Members of couples may find that they have disparate views of optimism and hope for the future (i.e., regarding improved treatments for HIV illness), and this itself can become a significant source of conflict within the couple.

Future planning and thoughts about the future can include an array of topics, including career, savings and retirement, housing, living location, travel, vacation homes, and children. Mixed-HIV-status couples may already have children (who may or may not be infected themselves) or they may want to have children, biologically or through adoption. This can hold equally true for homosexual and heterosexual couples. Having and raising children is an extremely important life goal and activity for many people. Feeling that this possibility is either taken away from them or significantly impaired can be a difficult loss to cope with.

Isolation

Many couples of mixed HIV status feel alone and isolated. Disclosure of HIV status is a very personal matter. Generally, people with HIV are encouraged by counselors to disclose their HIV status to some people (i.e., close friends, some family members, a confidante) so that they are not so alone and can receive support. They are also, however, advised to be clear about their reasons and desire to disclose, to consider potential negative consequences of such disclosure (e.g., discrimination, rejection, hostility, etc.), and to be selective about disclosure and not disclose to others indiscriminately. Decisions about disclosure in mixed-status couples are complicated by the fact that there are two people involved. There may be significant differences within the dyad regarding desire to disclose, reasons for wanting to disclose, to whom to disclose, when to disclose, and how to disclose. Often the HIV-negative partner feels that it is up to the HIV-positive partner to make decisions about disclosure, because it is their seropositive status that is the significant information being shared. As a result they may deny their own need for others to know and to seek desired support out of deference to their partner. Often, when asked, the HIV-positive partner does not agree with this position. It is striking how often incorrect assumptions are made (by both partners) regarding their perceptions about each other's thoughts and feelings regarding disclosure.

Members of mixed-status relationships often experience the lack of support and validation of their relationship from significant other people in their lives. This can be true for either member or for both members of the couple. Seronegative partners may find that their friends and family do not think they should allow themselves to get involved or remain involved with someone who is infected because of the possibility of transmission of the virus, potential illness and caretaking, and early loss and death. Similarly, HIV-positive partners may be advised that they are placing too much burden on themselves by being involved with someone who does not share their HIV status. Mixed-status couples often do not know many, or any, other couples in the same situation. They often question the viability and validity of their relationships. Because of these many challenges there may be an ever-present fear that they or their partners will not be able to handle it and may walk out at any time.

THE THERAPEUTIC PROCESS

Working with mixed-HIV-status couples can be an extremely rewarding, as well as challenging, experience. One must believe in the couples' ability to confront the issues and the power and advantage of working with the couple as a unit rather than seeing their needs as distinct and different and only treating them individually or in separate groups. Working with the couple can facilitate the emotional and behavioral processes necessary for them to meet the challenges they face while achieving and maintaining optimal mental health and well-being.

Creating a Safe Space

It is essential that the therapist be able to create a safe environment where all of the difficult issues may be confronted. Often there is a build up of many unexpressed feelings, concerns, and conflicts by the time the couple presents for treatment. It is useful to establish a commitment to the therapy process where the couple agrees to work with the therapist for a specified period of time. This commitment may be specified as a number of sessions or as a specific length of time before evaluating the process. This helps to establish the fact that, although the work may be difficult, each member of this working alliance (both partners and the therapist) is agreeing to be there (to return to each next session) regardless of what may get expressed in the therapy room. The therapist should also consider and then discuss with the couple how they will conduct planned sessions if one of the members of the couple is not able to attend (i.e., because of illness). Although there are no definitive solutions that one could apply to all situations (e.g., meeting with one member of the couple, meeting at home, in hospital rooms, canceling), it is important that expectations be clarified before such events occur.

For a period of time, the therapy room may be a container for the tremendous fear, rage, and despair that is too frightening or overwhelming to be communicated outside of the room. In the beginning of treatment, many couples find it useful to be told by the therapist that they may want to avoid talking about some of the issues at home now that they have a place where they know these things will be discussed. This helps to establish the therapy room as the place where the couple can confront difficult feelings that do not necessarily have to spill over and interfere with their everyday functioning. By "normalizing" the emotional impact of HIV infection on the couple, therapy can also address many of the other issues encountered in relationships.

Session Content

Although couple dynamics (i.e., ways that couples communicate, express their needs, their emotions, etc.) is the important focus of most couples therapy, the content of the sessions is also important when working with mixed-HIV-status couples. The therapist may need to be the one who raises the unexpressed issues (i.e., concerns about HIV transmission, future illness, potential death). This directive approach is often necessary to facilitate discussion of otherwise avoided topics. This will involve a careful balancing of HIV-related and other issues within the relationship. Although HIV concerns are often avoided, it is also common for couples to blame HIV for all of their interpersonal and life difficulties. The therapist must pay attention and articulate this when it is observed. Although HIV cannot and should not be the sole focus of the therapy, at some time during the treatment the key HIV-related challenges must be addressed. The timing of these particular discussions will vary across couples and is up to the clinical judgment of the therapist.

Sexual Behavior

When discussing sex, it is important to speak about it frankly and directly, including frequency of sex, sexual satisfaction (what feels good and what does not), and knowledge and thoughts (rational and irrational) about HIV risk attached to specific behaviors. Each member of the couple needs to be able to express from time to time what may seem like irrational concerns about possible transmission of HIV, if it is something that enters their minds. These intrusive thoughts will interfere with sexual satisfaction and desire for sexual contact.

If the couple finds themselves engaging in nonreciprocal behaviors with each other (i.e., the HIV-positive partner performing oral sex, but the HIV-negative partner not, or the HIV-negative partner penetrating while the HIV-positive partner does not), they need to voice their feelings about this. The HIV-positive partner may feel disempowered or less worthy to voice his or her feelings of disagreement with the "default" mode of sexual behavior they have adopted. The couple may have found themselves behaving in this nonreciprocal fashion without ever discussing it, and it is important to share their feelings about it, to clear up incorrect assumptions they each may have, and to discuss any possible desired change in their sexual encounters.

Anxiety and fear (i.e., about HIV or other sexually transmitted diseases) is a hindrance to sexual satisfaction and pleasure. With time, couples can usually find ways to alleviate their fears while maintaining spontaneity and pleasure. It may, however, take time and considerable discussion and experimentation for this to happen. The therapist should not assume that both partners understand viral transmission and the levels of risk associated with specific behaviors. Either one or both of them may be reluctant to admit their lack of knowledge or may have a serious misunderstanding of basic facts. The therapist can normalize the confusion that many people have and encourage a discussion of the basic facts as well as the more ambiguous areas of risk perception. If the couple can agree on what they believe is risky and what they feel is okay for them, then they will each know what the limits are and they can relax and be creative within those bounds. When couples are successful at this negotiation, their sex with each other becomes less "cognitive" and more natural.

For heterosexual couples, pregnancy or the desire for pregnancy can be an important and challenging topic. Clearly a couple cannot become pregnant while engaging in "fully" protected sex. Nevertheless, wanting to have children and having both members of the couple be the biological parents may be a priority for some couples. Both "individual" and "couple" desires need to be fully articulated. All options regarding having children need to be considered. Some of them include sperm donation, surrogate mothers, adoption, and strategies for reducing risk of HIV transmission if sex within the couple is the chosen method of causing pregnancy. Other issues to consider are the age and current health of each member of the couple, consequences for other children or members of the family, financial resources, custody concerns, and risks to health and medical treatment options for the woman, if she is the HIV-positive partner.

Sex outside of the relationship may or may not be an accepted aspect to the relationship. Some couples may desire and strive for monogamy; others may agree to not discuss it. There may be concerns and unresolved feelings about source and time of infection of HIV in the infected partner, potential for other sexually transmitted diseases, substance use history, bisexual behavior, and so forth. If such topics are avoided, lack of mutual trust will continue to interfere with intimacy and growth within the relationship. If the HIV-positive partner is feeling less desirable, like "damaged goods," or experiencing sexual dysfunction as a result of illness or medication side effects, he or she will be seeking reassurance from the uninfected partner. The therapist can facilitate discussion of these challenging issues. It may be useful for the therapist to normalize many of these feelings and concerns by stating, "It is common in couples of mixed HIV status for one or both partners to feel . . . ." as a way of introducing some of the feelings that are difficult to express. Also, standard sex therapy techniques, such as sensate focus or paradoxical interventions (i.e., prohibiting certain sex acts), can be useful clinical interventions to help the couple overcome some of their difficulties.

Caretaking Concerns

Typically there is a strong resistance to discuss fears and concerns about illness and caretaking, whether there is already HIV illness progression or it is anticipated, because of the couple's desire to protect each other from these thoughts. When illness is actualized, it is fairly common for couples to feel some relief, realizing that they can handle it and that it is not as overwhelming and awful as they had feared. Talking about their fears can be very reassuring and can increase feelings of intimacy and caring, particularly when each member recognizes that they have both been having many of the same thoughts and fantasies, but have been hiding them from each other.

The couple needs to voice their expectations of each other and discuss limitations they may feel that they have. It is very useful and important to have the couple note and discuss ways that they currently take care of each other. The therapist may need to note that there are many ways of caring for each other and that this is bidirectional, lest the HIV-negative partner get automatically labeled the caretaker in the relationship. Couples may need help with realizing that the HIV-positive partner can help and nurture his or her partner, even in the context of illness progression. A very simple and concrete example is teaching the HIV-positive partner to inquire as to how the HIV-negative partner is coping with new physical symptoms or new health care demands being placed on him or her. This can help maintain emotional equality in the relationship, even when there is not physical equality in terms of health status.

Often there can be conflict in the relationship about the degree of involvement in each other's health care, particularly when it comes to health care for the HIV-positive partner. The negative partner may "nag" his or her partner about taking better care of him- or herself, treatment adherence, and so forth. The HIV-positive partner may feel that he or she wants a lover, not a nurse, in the relationship. Resentment can build, and it is important that partners' expectations of each other in this regard be clarified. This discussion may need to be concrete, such as discussing whether they will accompany each other on doctor visits or for HIV tests. More important, the therapist may need to facilitate a discussion of the feelings behind their behavior with, and expectations of, each other. One of the ways that the couple may need to address their caretaking concerns and behavior with each other is to involve others (i.e., family, close friends) in their plans.

Future Planning

The distress of the future's uncertainty must be acknowledged, and effective strategies to cope with this distress need to be supported. Nobody can decide the appropriateness for people living with HIV of making many long-range plans for the future. It has been shown that having meaningful goals and a sense of future is associated with psychological resilience for AIDS long-term survivors (Remien, Rabkin, Katoff, & Williams, 1992). If the couple has clearly avoided thinking about the future and having any long-range goals as a couple, the recognition of that fact can lead to a discussion of each of their perspectives regarding the future. This avoidance may be associated with a degree of hopelessness about their future as a couple or because of HIV. Although living for today or living in the moment is a useful coping strategy for people living with HIV (including couples), thinking about and discussing the future is a part of intimacy that can be important to couples. This includes discussing their dreams, hopes, and wishes and setting priorities in their lives. Simply sharing these thoughts with each other can have a very positive effect on the couple's feelings of intimacy.

It is also true that many people (and couples) may deny the potential for significant health problems in the future. This may be detrimental to the relationship if absolutely no thought is given to the possibility for HIV illness progression. The therapy room may be a good place to facilitate such a discussion. This may include planning insurance, wills, medical power of attorney, medical directives, and child custody. Getting these issues on the table for discussion can be difficult but will have a positive emotional effect in the end. To plan for such things does not mean that the couple needs to feel hopeless about the future. On the contrary, having these affairs in order allows them to go about the business of living their lives, including making plans for the future. Particularly in the wake of emerging new combination treatments for HIV disease, there is a renewed hopefulness for the potential for a closer to normal life span for people with HIV. Such hopefulness needs to be supported, provided the couple does not ignore the realities of HIV disease and the necessary medical care.

Social Supports and Disclosure

In therapy, the couple can take a look at their social support network and evaluate the extent to which it meets their needs as individuals and as a couple. They also need to explore and check out each other's assumptions about who does and who does not know about their situation, and whom they want to know. The therapist may need to legitimize both the desire to disclose and the fear of disclosure for both members of the couple. Merely framing it as a couples issue generally has a powerful therapeutic effect. At the same time, each member of the couple may have a need for a personal confidante, and this can be legitimized as well.

There may be times when one or both members of the couple may withdraw from each other, or from their social network. This is normal for all couples at different times in the relationship. It may be more pronounced at times because of HIV, such as at the time of serostatus notification, or with the onset of physical symptoms or the occurrence of an opportunistic infection. Normalizing such responses is important, as well as noting whether such emotional states are persistent, or perhaps severe (i.e., indicative of a clinical depression), necessitating referral for other psychological or psychiatric intervention.

Themes Throughout the Therapy

The therapy needs to validate the emotional concerns of both partners and help the members of the couple see that neither is more or less valid, but rather that both have legitimate emotional needs. By normalizing the emotional impact of HIV infection on the couple, the therapy can also address many of the other issues that most relationships face. Too often couples and even the therapist may blame HIV for every conflict in the relationship, as communication in general may be severely restricted. Throughout, these couples must be supported and their existence as a couple validated.

It is important to keep HIV in its place. To avoid blaming each other and to make it easier to work on a common enemy, couples are encouraged to reframe their situation, perceiving HIV as an intruder in their lives. By objectifying and extruding HIV, the couple can achieve some distance and regroup in order to mount an attack that repairs the disruptiveness of the illness. Also, there is less tendency to blame each other for the situation and dealing with the demands of the illness. One of the ways that couples can gain strength to work against the impact of HIV is by increasing their sense of identity as a couple. It is useful to facilitate a discussion of who they are as a couple and what makes them special and to make note of their strengths as a couple.

There is often a fear that talking about all of the HIV-related concerns will make those events come true or make matters worse. Couples may also fear that once they begin talking about these things, they will not be able to forget about them or focus on other things in their lives. The therapist, through both verbalization and modeling, can help the couple recognize that there is room for both direct discussion of HIV-related fears and for living their lives with some sense of normalcy, focusing on the many other aspects of their lives. HIV is just one of many identifying characteristics of their relationship, and that will probably need to be stated in many different ways in many different contexts.

Assessment of Psychopathology

The couples therapist should always be attentive to individual psychopathology, identifying its presence and understanding its impact on the couple's functioning. The most common mental disorders seen in this population are mood, anxiety, and substance use disorders. These need to be acknowledged and discussed in the couple's therapy, but should not be treated in that modality. The therapist may feel confident in his or her own assessment of the psychopathology or may need to refer for evaluation. It is probably good practice, however, to refer for treatment in most cases rather to than treat one of the members of the couple individually.

SPECIAL ROLE OF GROUPS

Multiple-couple groups can be a highly effective intervention for couples of mixed HIV status (Livingston, 1966). All of what has been outlined in this chapter can take place in a group setting. A group, however, has the potential to enhance several therapeutic processes. By bringing mixed-HIV-status couples together, isolation and the feeling that they are the only ones are quickly reduced. Couples find their worries and concerns legitimized by seeing them occur in other couples. Often the raising of particular issues by other couples will trigger within dyads discussions that have never occurred before. Couples also have the opportunity to share effective, and often creative, coping strategies with each other. Modeling of affection and intimate behaviors by some couples can greatly influence couples struggling with their own expression of these feelings and behavior. Most important, couples can offer each other support and validate each others' existence and viability as they struggle to meet all of the challenges that being a mixed-HIV-status couple entails.

SUMMARY

Working with HIV mixed status couples can be both challenging and rewarding. It is essential for the therapist to feel comfortable working with the couple as a unit rather than only treating and/or referring each to his or her separate therapy. The challenges that these couples face are many and include issues related to sex behavior, future planning, illness and caretaking, social supports, and disclosure. It is common for couples to avoid topics associated with HIV as a way of "protecting" each other from the powerful emotions associated with HIV and all of its uncertainty. This avoidance serves to impede the continued growth of intimacy necessary for positive couple functioning and mutual satisfaction.

The therapy needs to validate the emotional concerns of both partners and normalize the emotional impact of HIV infection on the couple, while helping to keep HIV in perspective. Working at the dyadic level can facilitate the emotional and behavioral processes necessary for the partners to meet the challenges they face and to reinforce their viability as a couple, in order to help them achieve and maintain optimal mental health and well-being.

REFERENCES

Anderson, D. J., O'Brien, T. R., Politch, J. A., Martinez, A., Seage, G. R., III, Padian, N., Horsburgh, C. R., Jr., & Mayer, K. H. (1992). Effects of disease stage and zidovudine therapy on the detection of human immunodeficiency virus type 1 in semen. *JAMA: Journal of the American Medical Association, 268,* 2651–2652.

Atkinson, J. H., Grant, I., Kennedy, C. J., Richman, D., Spector, S., & McCutchan, J. A. (1988). Prevalence of psychiatric disorders among men with HIV virus: A controlled study, *Archives of General Psychiatry, 45,* 859–864.

Badger, T. (1990). Men with cardiovascular disease and their spouses: Coping, health, and marital adjustment. *Archives of Psychiatric Nursing, 4,* 319–324.

Catalan, J., Klimes, I., Bond, A., Day, A., Garrod, J., & Rizza, C. (1992). The psychosocial impact of HIV infection in men with hemophilia: Controlled investigation and factors associated with psychiatric morbidity. *Journal of Psychosomatic Research, 36,* 409–416.

Catalan, J., Klimes, I., Day, A., Garrod, A., Bond, A., & Gallway, J. (1992). The psychosocial impact of HIV infection in gay men: A controlled investigation and factors associated with psychiatric morbidity. *British Journal of Psychiatry, 161,* 774–778.

Chowanec, G., & Binik, Y. M. (1989). End stage renal disease and the marital dyad: An empirical investigation. *Social Science Medicine, 28,* 971–983.

Cohen, F., & Lazarus, R. S. (1979). Coping with the stresses of illness. In G. C. Stone, F. Cohen, and N. E. Adler (Eds.), *Health psychology* (pp. 217–254). San Francisco: Jossey-Bass.

Jessop, D. J., & Stein, R. E. K. (1985). Uncertainty and its relation to the psychological and social correlates of chronic illness in children. *Social Science and Medicine, 20,* 993–999

Kennedy, C. A., Skurnick, J., Wan, J. Y., Quattrone, G., Sheffet, A., Quinones, M., Wang, W., & Louria, D. B. (1993). Psychological distress, drug and alcohol use as correlates of condom use in HIV-serodiscordant heterosexual couples. *AIDS, 7*(11), 1493–1499.

Klimes, I., Catalan, J., Garrod, A., Day, A., Bond, A., & Rizza, C. (1992). Partners of men with HIV infection and hemophilia: Controlled investigation of factors associated with psychological morbidity. *AIDS Care, 4*(2), 149–156.

Livingston, D. (1966). A systems approach to AIDS counseling for gay couples. In M. Shernoff (Ed.), *Human services for gay people: Clinical and community practice.* New York: Harrington Park Press.

Moos, R. H., & Tsu, V. D. (1977). The crisis of physical illness: An overview. In R. H. Moos (Ed.), *Coping with physical illness* (pp. 1–22). New York: Plenum.

Padian, N. S., O'Brien, T. R., Chang, Y. C., Glass, S., & Francis, D. P. (1993). Prevention of heterosexual transmission of human immunodeficiency virus through couple counseling. *Journal of AIDS, 6,* 1043–1048.

Perry, S. W., Jacobsberg, L. B., Fishman, B., Frances, A., Bobo, J., & Jacobsberg, B. K. (1990). Psychiatric diagnosis before serological testing for HIV virus. *American Journal of Psychiatry, 147,* 89–93.

Powell-Cope, G. M. (1995). The experiences of gay couples affected by HIV infection. *Qualitative Health Research, 5,* 36–62.

Raveis, V. H., & Siegel, K. (1991). The impact of care giving on informal familial care givers. *AIDS Patient Care, February,* 39–43.

Remien, R. H., Carballo-Dieguez, A., & Wagner, G. (1995). Intimacy and sexual risk behavior in serodiscordant male couples. *AIDS Care, 7,* 429–438.

Remien, R. H., Carballo-Dieguez, A., Wagner, G., & Rapkin, B. (1996). *Psychological distress in male couples of mixed HIV status.* Paper presented at the American Psychological Association Annual Meeting, August 9.

Remien, R. H., Rabkin, J. G., Katoff, L., & Williams, J. B. W. (1992). Coping strategies and health beliefs of AIDS long term survivors. *Psychology and Health, 6,* 335–345.

Revenson, T. (1994). Social support and marital coping with chronic illness. *Annals of Behavioral Medicine, 16,* 122–130.

Rolland, J. (1994). In sickness and in health: The impact of illness on couples' relationships. *Journal of Marital and Family Therapy, 20,* 327–347.

Seidlin, M., Vogler, M., Lee, E., Lee, Y. S., & Dubin, N. (1993). Heterosexual transmission of HIV in a cohort of couples in New York City. *AIDS, 7*(9), 1247–1254.

Vincenzi, I. (1994). A longitudinal study of human immunodeficiency virus transmission by heterosexual partners. *The New England Journal of Medicine, 331*(6), 341–346.

Webster, L. (1992). Working with couples in a diabetes clinic: The role of the therapist in a medical setting. *Sexual and Marital Therapy, 7,* 189–196.

Williams, J. B. W., Rabkin, J. G., Remien, R. H., Gorman, J., & Ehrhardt, A. (1991). Multidisciplinary baseline assessment of homosexual men with and without HIV infection: II. Standardized clinical assessment of current and lifetime psychopathology. *Archives of General Psychiatry, 48,* 124–130.

Wright, L. (1991). The impact of Alzheimer's disease on the marital relationship. *The Gerontologist, 31,* 224–237.

Zarit, S. H., & Zarit, J. M. (1986). Dementia and the family: A stress management approach. *Clinical Psychologist, 39,* 103–105.

Part Three

Specialized Populations and Treatment Issues

AIDS is a disease that affects communities. It is identified with particular risk groups and involves clusters of people with similar experiences or cultural expectations. Patterns of response that would be treated as abnormal in one context are valued in another. Substance abusers, the MICA patient, Latino women— these are three very different groups sharing vulnerability to AIDS. The clinician's work is to identify the patterns that exist for patients, differentiating psychological defenses from group or cultural identity, to help them establish more effective coping mechanisms. Each will require different interventions to address the stress and conflicts that they experience. In this section, each author discusses needs common to particular groups, identifying techniques that have proved useful in connecting with otherwise hard-to-reach patients.

Chapter 9

Psychotherapy with Substance-Abusing Inner City HIV-Positive Patients

Joan E. Storey

HIV disease has been known to affect both homosexual men and injection drug users since the early 1980s; however, for a long time society viewed it as a gay man's disease (Shilts, 1988). More and more, HIV is becoming a disease of substance abusers and their sexual partners. It has been estimated that 50% of all injecting drug users are infected, as compared with 20% of gay men ("AIDS and Mental Health," 1994). A recent Centers for Disease Control study (Bennett, 1996) estimated that there were 124,800 HIV-infected people in New York City, 69,000 of them injecting drug users and 11,800 of them at-risk hetero-sexuals.

Substance abusers living in the inner city are being affected disproportion-ately (Bing & Soto, 1991; Dane & Miller, 1992; Jillson-Boostrom, 1992). Inner city injecting drug users, because of economic and social conditions, are more likely to engage in high-transmission-risk drug activities. In her analysis of the impact of HIV on minority populations, Jillson-Boostrom (1992) suggested that IV drug use and minority status may "interact to create an extremely high rate of exposure" (Jillson-Boostrom, 1992, p. 239). For example, inner city residents are more apt to share and reuse needles and to get high in shooting galleries. They are also more likely to use IV cocaine than are middle- and upper class individuals (Bing et al., 1990). In 1987, the incidence of AIDS was significantly higher in minority injecting drug users than in White injecting drug users (Jillson-Boostrom, 1992). Crack (a form of cocaine chemically treated to facilitate smoking from a pipe) also contributed to the spread of HIV infection in the inner city. Both women and men felt that crack had a beneficial and stimulating effect on their sex lives (Batki, 1990). The crack epidemic caused an increase in users' indiscriminate sex and in their number of sexual partners. Because crack was inexpensive compared with heroin or high-quality cocaine, its rate of use sky-rocketed in the 1980s. Crack also appealed to many who were averse to using needles, particularly women (Bayer, 1993). Crack became the drug of choice among homeless youths and among prostitutes who exchange sex for drugs (Reulbach, 1991). In addition, men on crack maintain their erections longer; this increases vaginal dryness in their partners, leading to abrasions that allow access for the virus (Bayer, 1993).

In general, inner city substance abusers' lives are quite chaotic. Often they lack permanent housing. Typically, inner city substance abusers are disconnected from any steady social support networks. Their relationships usually revolve around acquiring and using drugs. These are relationships of convenience that dissolve when the drug needs are satisfied. Often these people have been rejected by their families because of their drug use and other questionable behaviors (e.g., stealing). As substance abusers, these individuals were disenfranchised and alienated by society even before their HIV diagnoses (Batki, 1990; Bing et al., 1990; Walker, 1991).

MENTAL HEALTH SERVICES FOR SUBSTANCE-ABUSING HIV-POSITIVE PATIENTS

HIV disease can, at times, evoke strong and often changing feelings. The intensity of these emotions and the rapidity with which they can appear and change lead many to feel overwhelmed (Hoffman, 1996). Between the years 1989 and 1995, many articles were written about individual psychotherapy with non–substance-abusing HIV-infected patients (Blechner, 1993; Borden, 1989; Markowitz, Klerman, & Perry, 1992; Sadowy, 1991; Schaffner, 1990). During the same period, there were only a few articles about individual psychotherapy with inner city substance-abusing HIV-positive patients (Dailey, 1990; Reulbach, 1991).

Most psychiatric literature on the treatment of substance abusers with HIV illness discusses the use of group therapy (Child & Getzel, 1990; Fawzy, Fawzy, & Pasnau, 1991; Zakrzewski, 1991) or family therapy (Landau-Stanton & Clements, 1993; Walker, 1991). Although group therapy is the treatment of choice for many HIV-positive patients who are not substance abusers, it is usually the only modality provided to substance abusers. The group treatments provided HIV-positive substance abusers tend to be short term, structured, and focused solely on either HIV-related issues or substance abuse issues. Often the purpose of these groups is to reduce behaviors that spread the HIV virus (e.g., unsafe sex and drug use) rather than relieve psychological stress. One of the reasons for this approach to group treatment is that much of the treatment of substance-abusing HIV-positive patients is provided in the context of substance abuse programs or medical units. Another reason is the belief that individual psychotherapy is not appropriate for patients with substance abuse. Many clinicians feel that these patients can not develop a stable therapeutic alliance. Finally, the belief that these patients are not verbal enough and are too impulse ridden to benefit from treatment prevents many clinicians from offering this option to substance-abusing HIV-positive patients.

However, there is a group of substance-abusing HIV-positive patients who need individual psychotherapy offered on an open-ended basis because (a) they are unable to tolerate the structure of a group, (b) they do not want to focus solely on substance abuse or HIV-related issues, (c) they are not connected to families, or (d) they want help with long-standing emotional and psychodynamic concerns. This view is echoed in recent literature on therapy with HIV-affected substance abusers (Hoffman, 1996; Winiarski, 1995). Increasingly, substance abusers are seeking psychological treatment in mental health settings and are being offered individual treatment. Studies of HIV-infected patients seeking mental health treatment at several New York City clinics have found that 32% to 50% of the patients treated have a substance abuse diagnosis (Bialer, Wallack, & Snyder, 1991; O'Dowd, Natali, Orr, & McKegney, 1991; Sahs & Storey, 1994).

PSYCHOLOGICAL IMPACT OF HIV DISEASE ON INNER CITY SUBSTANCE ABUSERS

Although some of the sources of distress (e.g., uncertainty, existential issues, stigma, isolation, fear and anxiety, loss of health) presented by substance-abusing HIV-infected patients are similar to those of other HIV-infected pa-tients, there are also differences. Severe ego deficits and character pathology, whether a result of or a cause of the substance abuse, often make it difficult for these patients to cope with the disease's stressors.

The HIV diagnosis places demands on substance abusers to forge relation-ships with medical providers and social service providers. However, owing to previous negative experiences with medical and social service providers, sub-stance abusers are often highly distrustful. Further, the stresses of homeless-ness and meeting day-to-day basic survival needs often take precedence over other concerns and needs. This makes it difficult for many to show up for appointments consistently or to follow through on care plans, something that can contribute to misunderstandings and, at times, problematic interactions with medical providers. In addition, these patients often did poorly in school, at-tended infrequently, and dropped out in their early teens. Inadequate education makes it difficult for them to understand the medical treatments offered to them, and this leads many inner city patients, whether substance abusers or not, to feel that the treatments offered may actually be hurting them.

As substance abusers with HIV disease, they confront the virus with little support from their families and communities. Whereas gay men created or found a community ready and available to help and support them, these patients are often shunned by their families and communities. Many people of color disassociate themselves from substance abusers with HIV disease because they fear that their communities will become identified with substance abuse (Jillson-Boostrom, 1992). This can lead to an even greater sense of isolation and shame among these patients.

For many, HIV illness and its vicissitudes change the nature of the relationship these patients have toward substance abuse. For some, the diagnosis results in renewed efforts to stop using drugs and to change their lives, whereas others are overwhelmed by their psychological reactions. Believing that they will die anyway, these patients may intensify their substance abuse. As patients learn that death is not imminent, or as they confront their first serious infection, their stance toward the substance abuse may again change. This adds to the complexity and range of feelings and challenges faced by substance-abusing HIV-positive patients.

PSYCHOLOGICALLY BASED TREATMENT APPROACH FOR SUBSTANCE-ABUSING HIV-POSITIVE PATIENTS

In the 1990s, when large numbers of substance-abusing HIV-infected people began to be seen in psychotherapy at the Columbia-Presbyterian Medical Center HIV Mental Health Clinic, it was unusual for psychiatric clinics or therapists to provide treatment to patients with active or recent substance abuse problems. The clinic was set up to meet the special needs of patients affected by HIV disease, and because substance abusers met the primary criteria for the clinic, they were considered eligible for treatment. The clinic staff recognized that like other patients with HIV disease, many substance abusers experience significant depression and overwhelming anxiety in response to the stigma of HIV/AIDS, to the devastating effects of the illness, and to dying. Further, the clinic staff found that most substance abuse programs were unable to effectively address the pressing psychological needs of these patients. Consequently, the clinic provided treatment to anyone who chose to seek out its services. The only rule was that patients could not come to their sessions high.

Over the past 6 years, it has been seen that psychotherapy can be beneficial for substance-abusing HIV-infected patients. Sometimes these patients seek treatment for only a brief period, often in the context of a particular event (e.g., the HIV diagnosis, a change in medical condition, or an attempt to reunite with family). Even in this brief period, patients can experience significant relief from psychological distress. For others, therapy can lead to involvement in long-term psychotherapy and sweeping changes. Some patients seen in the clinic are not ready or willing to enter into traditional substance abuse treatments (e.g., residential treatment, Alcoholics Anonymous [AA], Narcotics Anonymous [NA]). Insisting on a patient engaging in one of these programs can be unrealistic and counterproductive. At the same time, for therapists to ignore the substance abuse issues is to collude with patients.

The next section describes a psychotherapeutic model for HIV/AIDS patients with substance abuse disorders and severe character pathologies. The model addresses the unique difficulties that arise in engaging these patients in psycho-therapy and in helping them to benefit from it. The handling of substance-abuse–related concerns from a psychotherapeutic perspective, issues related to relapse, and issues related to working with patients in multiple counseling treatments are also discussed. Finally, three case descriptions elucidate both the treatment model and the issues that arise in treating these patients.

THE HOLDING ENVIRONMENT

The treatment model begins with the premise that substance abuse is just one of many issues and concerns HIV-positive patients bring to treatment. As a therapist, not a substance abuse counselor, the concern is with patients' overall mental health as well as their substance abuse problems. For each patient, one evaluates at what point in the illness spectrum the patient has come in, what is happening with respect to the substance abuse, and current level of psychosocial functioning and assesses what is giving the patient the most difficulty in his or her life, emotionally or otherwise. The therapist probes for what it means to the patient to be HIV positive and his or her feelings about the virus. One also examines the patient's capacity to interact with the therapist and others and his or her emotional lability and ability to tolerate and express feelings. The results of this assessment determines the therapist's stance with respect to the patient's substance abuse, the type of interventions to use, and the overall approach to the individual's treatment.

Although there are many times when the underlying psychotherapeutic process does not differ from work with other HIV-infected patients, there are times, particularly in the initial phases of treatment or when there has been a resurgence in substance abuse, when modifications to the therapeutic approach are necessary. In working with these patients, much attention needs to be paid to engaging the patient in the treatment and establishing a therapeutic alliance. It is only in the face of a strong alliance that the patient can begin to tolerate interpretations or pressures for change.

The overall goal in the therapeutic relationship is to create a "holding environment" where patients can come regularly to talk about the strong feelings evoked by the disease and by their often chaotic lives. In that context, patients learn to engage in a dialogue about their lives and experiences and the therapist helps them to reflect on their lives, feelings, and behaviors. This allows patients to make more active choices, to be more in control of their feelings, and to improve the quality (as defined by the patient) of their lives.

When substance abuse is addressed in the therapy, abstinence is not the goal. Rather, the therapist continually focuses on increasing patients' motivation and ability to decrease drug use in order to (a) increase longevity; (b) improve or prevent the exacerbation of psychiatric problems; (c) improve relationships with family, friends, and medical and social service providers; or (d) to change their living situations.

As part of the therapeutic dialogue, the therapist helps patients to connect their drug use to present feelings or problems. The therapist works with patients to change the way they characteristically cope with adversity (e.g., denial, confrontation, avoidance) so that patients are better able to engage in or tolerate substance abuse treatments.

HELPING PATIENTS TO UNDERSTAND
THE NATURE AND GOALS OF PSYCHOTHERAPY

Were it not for the virus, most of these patients would not seek out psychotherapy. For many of these patients, previous contacts with people in the psychiatric professions were negative (some were forced to go as children or were evaluated by psychiatrists while in prison). Some come to treatment simply because they were told to by a doctor, nurse, or caseworker, but they are not really clear why they are there. Some feel that if they do not follow through on the referral, medical care or social benefits will be denied. Others come knowing they are suffering from considerable pain and anxiety and seek out help on their own, but often they too do not really know what therapy can do for them.

Thus, inner city HIV-positive patients with substance abuse problems may enter treatment with hesitancy, fears, and great shame. They may also expect to receive something concrete from the therapist and may feel disappointed when only talking is offered. Consequently much of the initial work in the treatment is on developing a therapeutic relationship, educating patients about the therapeutic process and the way it works, and developing their ability to talk about and reflect on their lives. For some patients, it is necessary as a precursor to the more insight-oriented work to help them with the more concrete aspects of their lives.

HANDLING PATIENTS WITH CHAOTIC LIVES
IN THE FORMAT OF THERAPY

The pace of treatment, attendance at sessions, and the way the therapist responds to missed appointments may be different for patients with substance abuse problems. Some patients attempt to engage in treatment several times over a long period before they come regularly, whereas others will come regularly for a period of time, then disappear from treatment only to reappear several months later. Disappearances may be related to medical issues, family pressures, substance abuse, impulsivity, or dynamic issues in the treatment.

It is common for these patients to make several tries before being able to engage fully in treatment. Although the therapist may perceive the treatment to be discontinuous, the patients do not. When they come in, they often proceed as if there has been little time between visits. Patients who have only seen a therapist once every 6 months will tell other health care providers that they are in treatment, that the therapy has really helped them, and that they come regularly to treatment. The therapist appears to become part of their psychic lives. For some patients, this more internal fantasy relationship is enough. Other patients use these brief treatment episodes as a precursor to becoming more intensively involved in the treatment.

In the initial phases of treatment, the therapist almost always calls or contacts a patient who does not show up for a session. Interpretations about the absence are not offered. Although missed sessions may indicate resistance to treatment or may signify other treatment-related issues, like avoidance of strong emotions, there are a number of other reasons these patients miss their appointments. Many inner city substance-abusing patients have had very little experience with consistency in life or with developing relationships. They live life in a crisis mode where one reacts to the most immediate events with little attention to other concerns. These patients are also often too overwhelmed by their immediate feelings to remember their appointments. In addition, they attend medical clinics where appointments times have little relevance to the actual time the patient is seen. They are used to dropping in to see social service providers when they have a specific need and then waiting several hours to be seen. The concept of a regular no-specific-need appointment time that is held for patients whether they are there or not is new.

Calling to reschedule appointments in the initial phase of treatment reinforces the concept of regularity and wards off possible dangers to the treatment alliance. It is only after being engaged in the treatment for several months that the patients are able to "protect" their appointment times. In addition, many of these patients experience lack of outreach on the part of their therapists as a lack of caring. In doing the outreach, one must be careful to make sure the patient does not experience the therapist as a scolding schoolteacher or as mistrusting the patient. Over time, some patients respond to this outreach. They may still miss appointments, but will call afterward to reschedule. However, some are unable to respond. In those situations, after having made several attempts, the therapist tells a patient that she or he is always welcome in treatment, but that the therapist will no longer attempt an extensive outreach. The responsibility for treatment is in the patient's hands.

CONTAINING AFFECT: THE THERAPIST
AS SELF-OBJECT AND ORGANIZER

Many substance-abusing patients are used to acting out their feelings as well as blunting them or changing them through the use of drugs and alcohol. Consequently, when affects emerge they often do not know what they are feeling or are unable to regulate and tolerate their feelings. The therapist, by acting as a self-object, can help patients to become more aware of feeling states and the impact of these states on behavior. This is particularly effective with patients who answer every inquiry by saying "I don't know" or with silence. During this phase, the therapist focuses on labeling for the patients the myriad of emotions presented. The goals are to help them to know what they are experiencing and to develop their ability to reflect on and discuss their feelings.

More volatile, angry, substance-abusing patients may need to use their sessions as a place to unload, to discuss everything that has gone wrong with their lives and their week. They neither expect nor want the therapist to respond to them. Questions about what the patient was experiencing or that are aimed at helping the patient reflect on the situation are perceived as not being understanding, and the therapist is seen as being on the other person's side. The therapist, by listening empathically and calmly, serves as a respository for the patient's strong affects. Some patients may need to proceed like this for many months before they can engage in a dialogue or begin to see the more reality-based issues involved.

Once patients perceive the therapist as stable and empathic, the therapist can begin to help them to organize their experiences. The therapist provides patients with an explanation and understanding of their reactions. This is achieved through listening to the affect(s) underlying the patients' descriptions of their lives and by understanding them in the context of their previous life experiences. By helping to organize patients' reactions and by helping patients to understand the myriad of emotions that underlie them, patients' feelings become less alien and frightening. Patients then no longer need to act out or control their feelings through drug use.

When confronted with a volatile patient, the therapist must find a way to respond empathically while at the same time representing reality for the patient. After allowing the volatile patient to vent, the greatest therapeutic benefit comes from engaging the patient in a dialogue about what led to the anger and how the patient perceived the experience. The therapist tries to help the patient by reflecting on how she or he must have felt during the event. For example, if a patient rages about having to wait for 3 hours to see the doctor, the therapist might comment that the patient felt like the doctor did not care about him or her, or if the patient said something during the tirade about seeing other sick people, the therapist might comment on how it really is very difficult to have to sit with other people who seem so ill knowing that it might happen to you. Often the patient's sense of having been heard allows the anger to dissipate, freeing the patient to focus on other things. Patients like this have difficulty recognizing that the doctor may have had an emergency or that it was not a personal slight.

SUBSTANCE ABUSE: THE ROLE OF THE THERAPIST

The therapist works with the patient as a whole, not just with his or her substance abuse. Unlike substance abuse counselors, therapists are not responsible solely for the elimination of drug use. This raises the dilemma for therapists regarding how much to focus on patients' substance abuse problems. A rigid approach is not useful with this population. During a patient's initial evaluation, a patient is rarely told that she or he must engage in substance abuse treatment in order to begin therapy. Many patients are only able to engage in a substance abuse treatment program after they have used therapy to be able to contain their emotional responses, to feel more in control of their lives, and to improve their interpersonal skills. Moreover, most patients have been told by numerous people to enter substance abuse treatment, and they have not.

In determining one's initial position regarding substance abuse, the therapist considers the patient's presenting problem(s), present medical and emotional state, and previous lifestyle; the patient's stance with respect to the substance abuse and the function substance abuse serves for the patient; the patient's treatment goals, previous substance abuse treatments, and the impact of substance abuse on his or her emotional and physical health; the patient's psychodynamics; and the nature of the therapeutic alliance. If a patient has many failed substance abuse treatments, it may not be helpful to address the substance abuse (unless this is the patient's manifest presenting problem) until a strong alliance has been developed and many of the patient's other issues (e.g., depression, anxiety, and narcissistic vulnerabilities) have been addressed. As the treatment evolves and as the patient's own relationship to the drugs and the therapist changes, so will the degree of focus on substance abuse issues.

There are times when a therapist needs to have a stronger stance with respect to the patient's substance abuse, for example, when substance abuse results in homelessness, continually involves the patient in violent episodes, results in the patient becoming suicidal, or severely affects his or her relationship with significant others or children. During these times, the therapist needs to keep a firm and consistent focus on the substance abuse, yet at the same time she or he needs to take care not to be so ardent that the treatment relationship is destroyed (Storey, 1996).

REFERRALS TO ANCILLARY SUBSTANCE ABUSE TREATMENTS

One of the roles of the therapist is to increase a patient's readiness to enter or stay in substance abuse treatments. This can be done in a variety of ways. One is to discuss the substance abuse in the context of patients' psychiatric problems. For example, one can point out to a patient that whenever he or she goes on a binge, he or she becomes more depressed. Then as the patient becomes depressed, he or she is less able to comply with medical treatment, which impairs the patient's health status. Or one can talk about how when the patient drinks, he or she is more apt to get into fights with his or her spouse, and when the spouse goes to stay elsewhere the patient becomes panicked that the spouse will never come back.

In working with substance abusers, the therapist can actively refer patients to substance abuse programs such as AA, NA, outpatient substance abuse programs, 28-day inpatient programs, and long-term residential treatment. It is important to help the patient see that the substance abuse treatment does not replace the psychotherapy but rather complements it. In making referrals, one needs to find a program that meets the patient's psychological and medical needs. For example, schizoid patients, patients who are not able to listen empathically to others or who are highly disorganized do not do well in AA and NA. Similarly, medically ill patients or patients who are asymptomatic but who believe they are dying may be resistant to entering long-term residential treatment (Storey, 1996).

The referral may have to be made many times before the patient successfully follows through. It is natural to feel somewhat disappointed and angry when patients do not follow through with referrals. However, such an event allows the therapist to engage the patient in a discussion of what gets in his or her way of following through. Is she or he afraid of being controlled by someone else? Does she or he really want to stop using? Does she or he become overwhelmed by sitting in a group? Is there a fear that the therapist will abandon him or her if she or he is successful? Would she or he find life too boring without substance abuse? Often no one else will have bothered to be interested in these issues. Exploring and understanding the patient's subjective experience of substance abuse treatment also allows one to intervene therapeutically in a way that will decrease the patient's resistance to or inability to tolerate the substance abuse treatment.

Once the patient has engaged in a treatment, the same tactic can be used when the patient wants to leave the program or feels dissatisfied with it. Most patients in substance abuse treatments are simply told that they need to "get with the program." Although this may be true, the patient's immediate reactions or feelings often prevent him or her from succeeding. When these reactions are explored and processed in the psychotherapy, however, the patient is better able to participate in substance abuse treatment programs.

It is natural that as patients become involved in substance abuse treatment programs, they will bring into psychotherapy material related to their substance abuse treatment. This can be a tricky time in the therapy. Some patients will engage in splitting, seeing the therapist as the good person and the substance abuse counselor as withholding and bad, or vice versa. Some substance abuse treatment programs have antitherapy stances. Patients may also be getting two different messages from the treatments. In response to this, it is helpful to explore patients' reactions and feelings to their treatment and counselors, to help them to be able to see why substance abuse counseling may be different from therapy, and to help them to understand why both treatments are needed.

The substance abuse counselor may pressure the therapist to be more forceful and active with respect to the patient's drug use. The author has had some substance abuse counselors tell her that because she continues to see a patient who is active, she is an enabler. In the face of this, it helps to remember that the interventions and treatment goals of substance abuse treatment differ from those of therapy. The substance abuse counselor's goal is to change the person's behaviors and to stop all drug use through whatever means possible, whereas the therapist is addressing a wide array of problems that affect the patient's mental health, one of which is substance abuse.

RELAPSE

Relapse is an ongoing issue in treating HIV-positive substance-abusing patients. Patients in the early stages of recovery often find it too difficult to admit the possibility of relapse. If the therapist tries to address it, the patient may cut the therapist off. Nonetheless, there are reasons and ways to address it actively. With a new patient or one with whom there is a weak alliance, it helps for the therapist to discuss relapse issues in the third person. This may prevent the patient from feeling that the therapist is making a prediction about his or her behavior or that she or he is distrusting. By addressing the issue and preparing the patient for the possibility, when relapse does occur she or he will feel less ashamed, dejected, and helpless. In addition, the patient will be less afraid that the therapist will abandon him or her or throw him or her out for using.

Some patients stop using drug or alcohol in the context of the medical or social crisis that brought them into treatment. However, as time passes or the crisis resolves, maintaining abstinence is difficult. The work in this case is to prepare patients for the possibility of relapse both so that patients will feel they can come back to treatment and tell the therapist about the drug use and to ensure that the patient does not overreact to the slip. This can be done through interventions like saying, "Let's talk about what it will be like when you get your first social security check and you pass the dealer on your corner" or "I know you don't plan on using again, but when you have a bad day and someone comes by with some stuff it might be hard not to join in." Some patients feel that comments like this indicate that the therapist does not trust them or does not have any faith in them. The therapist can tell the patient in response that she or he is not saying that the patient is going to use, but that it is important that they talk about it, so that in the highly unlikely event that it does occur, the patient will know it is something that can be talked about, without fear of punishment or being thrown out of treatment.

Relapse is often accompanied by significant guilt and depression. When it occurs, the patient needs psychoeducation about the difficulty of recovery. Normalizing the relapse by helping the patient understand the difference between a slip and a relapse can help patients feel less upset by the crisis. If a patient has not become involved in AA, NA, or a substance abuse program, the therapist needs to gently and empathically stress the need to get additional help and support.

Some patients will hide their relapses from the therapist for many months. The first few times this occurs, the therapist can react the same way she or he does to anything else the patient brings up in treatment: They explore it. What made the patient feel she or he could not tell the therapist about the slip? What did she or he think the therapist would say or do, and why is the patient telling the therapist now? When patients finally reveal their slip or relapse, the therapist can feel taken in or disappointed. It is helpful to remember that slips are common and expected. However, if the patient continues to hide relapses, one needs to focus on the impact of hiding things on the therapeutic relationship and to discuss ways in which the therapist can help the patient be more open.

CASE EXAMPLES AND DISCUSSION

Several cases are presented to explicate the different ways practitioners can work in psychotherapy with substance-abusing patients with the HIV virus. In the first case, a year-long treatment with a man in the terminal phase of the illness is described. This case shows the way the therapist moves among addressing illness-related concerns, substance abuse issues, and issues related to death and dying based on an assessment of the patient's most pressing psychological need and the state of the therapeutic alliance with the patient.

> Luis, a 36-year-old Latino man, was referred because he had become severely depressed and suicidal while hospitalized for *Pneumocystis carinii* pneumonia. When I met him in the hospital, he made little attempt to be likable. He told me that he had become suicidal because everyone in his family was angry at him because, for the third time, he had gone on a crack binge and sold the TV they had given him. He was guilty and ashamed about this. At the same time, he was furious that his family would turn their back on a dying man. Although seemingly disinterested, he accepted an appointment for therapy.
>
> In our initial sessions, Luis spewed out his anger about his life circumstances, described the many horrific things he had done in the past, including setting animals on fire and killing someone in a knife fight over drug territory. He alternated between being furious at his family and feeling depressed and dejected about having screwed up his renewed relationship with them. Although he ignored most of my attempts to get him to reflect on his experiences, he appeared to experience relief from using me as a repository for his feelings.
>
> I learned that his mother had left the family to live with another man when Luis was 5. Luis's father was physically and emotionally abusive. Luis vacillated between blaming his family for his problems and feeling that he had just been born a bad person. I validated his feelings of anger and abandonment. I tried to help Luis recognize his sadness about his behavior and temper his sense of himself as a terrible person. In the context of these talks, Luis began to let me ask more questions and to listen to me.
>
> Luis had a 12-year-old son. Although he often did not see his son for years, his identity as a father was quite important to him. He was angered that his son only came to see him when he wanted money. Often his son's mother would refuse or delay the son's ability to see Luis. Luis always tried to save money to buy his son things. But if there were a few days' delay in seeing him, Luis would spend the money on drugs, disappointing his son yet again. Luis blamed his ex-wife for the situation.

I continually affirmed Luis's identity as a father. I discussed how sad, hurt, and helpless he felt when his son did not show up, especially because Luis did not know how much longer he would live. As we developed more of a working relationship, I was able to engage Luis in a dialogue about his previous history as a father, the periods in which he was unavailable to his child, and his present inability to protect his money for his son. This allowed him to feel less angry at his son and to feel more connected to him.

Luis had a complex relationship to his substance abuse. He freely admitted that if not for the HIV disease, he would still use drugs. However, he knew his substance abuse interfered with family relationships that, because of his illness, were more important to him. During the first few sessions, I gently mentioned that he might have trouble sticking to not using drugs. I did not actively address substance-abuse-related issues. However, whenever Luis received his social security check, he ended up using crack and would feel extremely ashamed. He would insist these were just slips and they would not reoccur. Luis was connected with a community-based substance abuse program for HIV-positive people, but rarely attended. He felt that the counselors and other participants were phony and had nothing to offer him.

I did not challenge his perception, but began to focus more on his substance abuse. I tried to help him understand his triggers (e.g., having money, letting a drug-using friend into his apartment) for using so that he could avoid feeling so awful in the future. Despite this, his substance abuse escalated. During the first 4 months of treatment, he periodically went on crack binges. These episodes always resulted in Luis's becoming suicidal and calling 911 with requests that he be taken to an emergency room. The staff of the emergency room on these occasions always suggested that he enter residential treatment, but he would refuse. I let him know that I thought this would be beneficial, but I did not make it a condition for his staying in therapy. Given Luis's belief about the importance of autonomy to his quality of life and his limited life span, I recognized that residential treatment might never be an option for him.

After several episodes of this, I stressed the connection between his substance abuse and his suicidality. He needed to address his substance abuse not because drugs were a horrible thing, but because after he used drugs he tended to become suicidal. Eventually, he chose to enter a 28-day program for mentally ill chemical abusers. During the last 5 months of his life, Luis stopped using crack and cocaine. Two issues related to HIV/AIDS were salient for Luis. One was his fears and concerns about suffering, death, and dying. He said he did not mind dying, yet he did not want to suffer. The second had to do with the fact that as he became sicker, he was losing his autonomy and independence. He felt a life in which one had to be taken care of by others was not worth living. During his more angry, hostile periods, he would talk about reading books about how to kill oneself. Luis always answered my questions about having a specific intent or plan to kill himself in the negative.

Initially the treatment solely focused on reflecting and validating his feelings. Later I engaged him in a dialogue about how humiliating it was for him to have to rely on others and for him to no longer feel like he had any autonomy. At the same time, Luis was terrified about death. He frequently asked what it felt like to die. He feared that he would become panicked as he died or would suffer in some way.

Whenever Luis got angry or depressed he would stop taking his medications. Sometimes he would flush them down the toilet in anger. When he was in the hospital, he was often inconsistent in his medical compliance. When the anger resolved, he would demand new prescriptions. During one of his hospital admissions, Luis refused to allow any further diagnostic tests, so the hospital wanted to discharge him. This infuriated him. He felt the doctors did not care about him. As usual, Luis needed me to listen to him and absorb his anger before he could discuss the situation. Six months into the therapy, he was more open to my probing and more receptive to my responses. I found out that he was petrified of the pain that would accompany his tests, but that if a particular medical provider stayed with him he would acquiesce. I also helped him to understand the hospital's dilemma. They wanted to try to help him, but if he said he did not want their help they had no option but to send him home. I also let him know that going home and not having the tests, if that was what he wanted, was a reasonable option. The choice was his. He chose to have the test.

In his last 2 months, he deepened his relationship with his family and had fewer conflicts with medical providers. He became less panicked about dying and more focused on dying in a way that he left him feeling more in control. He spent his last week at home, heavily sedated. He died in his bed surrounded by his family.

It was clear from his behavior in sessions that Luis's most pressing need, from a mental health perspective, was to have a safe, consistent, and empathic place where he could review his life and organize his experience of it in a way that would allow him to die feeling better about himself and his relationships. Two factors influenced the initial decision to listen to Luis's life story and to absorb his strong feelings of hatred. First, psychodynamically speaking, independence, autonomy, and control were core concerns for Luis. If the therapist had been more active, Luis would have felt less in control. When he felt less in control, he responded with defensive acting out and angry behavior.

Although the aforementioned psychodynamic factors contributed to the decision not to address the substance abuse in the initial phase of treatment, there were other reasons for this. Medically, it was likely that he had less than a year to live. Furthermore, he insisted that drug use was no longer an issue. Any attempt to strongly focus on the substance abuse might have triggered hostile defensive behaviors and the likelihood of his fleeing from treatment. Finally, addressing Luis's substance abuse early on would have been dangerous to his precarious psychic balance. It might have had a negative effect, increasing his already significant feelings of shame and guilt about these behaviors and possibly leading to further depression and panic.

Waiting for substance abuse to become more germane to the therapy allowed the therapist to address the drug abuse in a personal context (Luis's suicidality) rather than from a global and seemingly, at least from the patient's perspective, moral response. When Luis's substance abuse escalated, the therapist still did not insist that he enter residential treatment. The therapist knew that it would be difficult for him to commit to living in such a constrained environment given his medical condition and his personal need for freedom. Instead, the therapist told him that his approach to his substance abuse was not working and that he needed to do something differently. The therapist purposely did not specify what it was that he had to do; she left that part of it up to him.

The next case describes a more crisis-oriented treatment with a man who had just been diagnosed HIV positive. In this case, the therapist only indirectly addressed the patient's substance abuse problems, and focused more on issues related to his emotional response to the HIV diagnosis, his desire to reconnect with his family before what he perceived as his imminent death, and his interactions with social service and health care providers.

> Alvin, an African American in his early 30s, was diagnosed HIV positive while in the hospital with tuberculosis. He was a crack abuser and had been homeless for several years. He came to his first two sessions eager to talk about virus-related concerns. Alvin viewed his diagnosis as a death sentence. He feared being stigmatized by others and expressed a desire to become reunited with his family, from whom he was estranged. Our work revolved around validating his experience of loss and depression while at the same time helping him to recognize that he had a future. He said he was done with drugs; he just wanted to stay healthy. I supported Alvin in this desire, while at the same time reflecting that as he felt better it must be difficult for him to fight the urge to use drugs. He denied that it would be a problem.
>
> Alvin missed our next three appointments; however, he always responded to my outreach efforts by calling and scheduling another appointment. When he finally showed up, he told me he only came because he had been crying all day, and his counselor told him he should come. He had visited his mother and told her that he was HIV positive, but she would not let him into her apartment. He had also received his first welfare check and used it on a 3-day crack run. He was full of self-recriminations. I commented that he must have felt that all would be forgiven when he told his mother about the diagnosis. Her reaction must have shocked him and made him feel really awful and rejected. He acknowledged my comments with lots of head shaking and by calming down. He admitted that on many occasions he had approached his family, telling them he had reformed, only to relapse to drug use and petty crimes. I supported his desire to reconnect with his family, suggesting that he might have to move more slowly. We discussed how he might have to communicate with them via the phone or through letters before they could be more available to him.
>
> Alvin experienced his drug relapse as having come out of the blue. I pointed out the relationship of the relapse to his disappointment with his family. This allowed him to feel less self-punitive. In the context of his relapse, I educated him about how substance abuse recovery involved many slips and instructed him about the differences between a slip and a relapse. I also suggested that there might be other times when his feelings would get in the way of his desire to not use.
>
> Alvin missed his next appointment and did not respond to several outreach calls. I then received a call from a program, Directly Observed Treatment (DOT), that ensures that patients take their tuberculosis medications. The DOT staff go to patients' homes and watch them take their medications to ensure that they don't

stop taking the medications and become infectious again. If patients do not comply, public health laws require them to be quarantined. The counselor there said that Alvin had not been seen in a week and was at risk of quarantine. When he returned to treatment several weeks later, he was belligerent and angry. He had been forced by his housing facility to go to a substance abuse program that he hated and felt was a waste of time. He had gained weight and no longer felt ill.

About halfway through the session, I brought up DOT. He explained that the DOT counselors did not come to his house on his schedule, so he saw no reason to wait around for them. I asked Alvin what he understood about what would happen if he was not there when they came. He understood. He was angry: "I take my medications, I don't have all day to wait for them. I told them I take them!" I calmly explained that the rules of the program were that he had to take them in front of people and if he did not, it was the same as if he had not taken them. I tried to increase his desire to comply by pointing out that quarantine could be worse than the substance abuse program.

As we discussed the situation, Alvin told about how he had once gone to jail for petty crimes (e.g., fare beating), even though the judge had gone out of his way to help him, because he repeatedly failed to show up for his community service sentence. I now understood Alvin differently. It seemed likely that Alvin was headed for quarantine and that in some way it was what he wanted. In a nonaccusatory fashion, I engaged Alvin in a discussion of the benefits of being "contained." I pointed out that the only times Alvin had been drug free was when incarcerated and suggested that quarantine would help with his desire not to use. We discussed the other benefits such as having regular food prepared and not having to cope with being rejected by his family. Alvin acknowledged that quarantine did not seem so awful to him. He began to see his decision to be noncompliant as perhaps a rational choice and was considerably less angry at the world. He then missed the next three sessions and did not respond to my outreach.

Given Alvin's depressed and panicked response to his HIV diagnosis, his most urgent need in the first sessions was for the therapist to listen calmly and attentively to his fears and to reeducate him about the virus and its sequelae. He also needed help in considering living life infected with HIV.

When Alvin's mother rejected him, he did not have the capacity to engage in a dialogue about it. Here, Alvin needed the therapist to articulate and reflect back to him the feelings that underlay his reactions. As the therapist conveyed the meaning of his experience to him, he began to understand himself better and so felt more internally organized. With this accomplished, Alvin calmed down enough to engage in problem solving.

A stronger focus on Alvin's drug use would have been met with an extremely negative reaction and would have been detrimental to the potential therapeutic alliance. The therapist did not refer him to a substance abuse program (but she knew others had). The therapist felt that given his level of impassivity, his emotional reactivity, his difficulty with interpersonal relationships, and his belief that he would die imminently, he did not have the capacity to succeed in a substance abuse program. A failure in a substance abuse program would likely exacerbate his depression and sense of hopelessness and may have hindered his willingness to try again later.

Alvin's case demonstrates the way some substance abusers briefly engage in or are amenable to treatment as a result of a specific stressor or event. It also shows the discontinuity that can exist in these treatments. The treatment may only consist of five or six sessions that occur over several months. The patient's demeanor, emotional state, and concerns may change over this period. The therapy nevertheless serves an important function. This patient was not able to make any major changes in his life, but did end up feeling less anxious, fearful, and depressed about his HIV diagnosis, and perhaps he had more compassion for himself.

This final case presents the focused use of psychotherapeutic interventions to help decrease the patient's resistance to substance abuse treatment. It also demonstrates how to work with patients who are engaged in substance abuse treatment separately from their psychotherapy. In this case, unlike the first two cases, HIV-related concerns were secondary to substance abuse–related issues.

Regina, a 46-year-old African American crack abuser with a high T-cell count and no medical complications, had been trying to engage in treatment for over 2 years. She had recently completed her first 28-day residential drug treatment program. When she returned, she was glowing about her accomplishment and was totally committed to her recovery. She was involved in a 3-day-a-week aftercare program. Yet within a week her attitude changed.

She felt if her social problems (she wanted to move to a different apartment) were not solved she would relapse. Because the aftercare program could not help her with her social problems, she no longer found it helpful. In addition, she did not like sitting and listening to others talk about their problems. She also was furious at her substance abuse case manager. Initially, I remained neutral, listening and reflecting what I heard from Regina. Toward the end of the session, I told Regina that I had worked with a lot of substance abusers and that in my experience, when patients did not follow through with aftercare, they tended to relapse (Storey, 1996).

Regina responded by saying that she felt that until her social problems were solved, substance abuse treatment would not be helpful. I let her know that I appreciated what she was saying and that I knew how much she wanted to move to a different apartment. I then gently challenged her belief that leaving the program would help her get her apartment. I pointed out that given all the cutbacks in social services it might take a long time to solve her social problems and that if she were "active" it might be hard for her to follow through on the social issues. Regina seemed to listen to this (Storey, 1996).

I then explored her anger at the substance abuse counselor. Regina had told the counselor she missed her groups because their meeting times interfered with the times she needed to see her welfare workers. The counselor offered to refer her to another group. Regina felt rejected and felt that the counselor had given up on her. I helped Regina to see that the counselor's focus was on helping her to stay clean and that she was willing to do anything to further that effort, even refer her elsewhere. Regina was calmer (Storey, 1996).

It was only at this point that I addressed Regina's belief that the groups could not be helpful to her. I brought up Regina's previous session and how helpful she found her residential program, with its focus on substance abuse issues. I asked her what was different. She acknowledged that they had been helpful, but said she no longer found it helpful to hang around with other addicts. Because Regina felt differently about an HIV support group she attended, I asked her what was helpful to her about it. She said that by listening to the women talk about their HIV issues, she learned what might happen to her and that it helped her feel less alone. She then started to smile. I commented on this and she said she had realized that the substance abuse group might do the same thing for her (Storey, 1996).

I discussed how different groups and different treatment settings have different focuses, and they each complemented the other. She then revealed that she had not disclosed her HIV status in the substance abuse group and that she had some strong feelings about this. I discussed how her fears about disclosure might be contributing to her negative reaction to the group, and she became quite tearful. I let her know that it was her choice whether to reveal her HIV status to the group (Storey, 1996).

As our session came to a close, she again brought up the issue about how the time the substance abuse group met really interfered with her pursuing her social service needs. Having already focused on her denial and emotionally laden issues, I validated the reality issues involved and provided her with a phone number of another substance abuse group that met at a different time. When she came in for the following meeting, she had already had her intake appointment for this group (Storey, 1996).

This case illustrates how to intensively focus on substance abuse within a psychotherapeutic context. The decision to actively intervene with Regina's substance abuse problems was based on several factors. First, unlike with Luis and Alvin, Regina's medical status was stable, and she had no overriding situational crisis dominating her life. Her greatest difficulties derived from her ongoing crack use. In addition, as the therapist had previously had several periods of brief interventions with Regina, a strong alliance had been developed. Finally, Regina's decision to enter a residential treatment program signaled her readiness to more actively address her substance abuse.

In her first session back, rather than jumping into relapse prevention, the therapist affirmed Regina's sense of accomplishment and offered admiration for her having finally decided to address her substance abuse problem. The therapist hoped that by building up Regina's reservoir of self-esteem and self-efficacy, Regina would be better able to cope with her substance-abuse–related problems when they reemerged. Any attempt to focus more directly and actively on relapse prevention, in this situation, might have lead Regina to feel that the therapist was nonsupportive. Further, relapse prevention is usually extensively addressed in substance abuse treatment programs; for the therapist to address it in the absence of a specific event would be superfluous.

Throughout the sessions, knowing that ultimatums or demands made Regina more oppositional, the therapist carefully avoided engaging Regina in a power struggle over her substance abuse. When Regina came to her session wanting to drop out of aftercare, the therapist did not tell her she had to stay in the program. Rather, she listened empathically, absorbing her anger. However, the therapist also did not agree with her assessment of the situation. Knowing Regina valued her opinion, she spoke to Regina about her work with other substance abusers and helped her reality test her beliefs. In working with Regina's negative reaction to her substance abuse counselor and group, the therapist focused on exploring her experience of the events. Intervening in this manner prevented Regina from seeing the therapist as either an ally or an enemy of the substance abuse counselor.

One of the advantages of treating Regina in long-term psychotherapy is that when Regina said she did not like her substance abuse group, the therapist could draw on her reservoir of information to point out that there were other groups Regina had liked. This provided an avenue to soften Regina's response. It also freed Regina to discuss how being in a group with people who were not HIV positive was somewhat painful for her. Had the therapist not had such a strong and long-term relationship with Regina, this intervention would not have been possible.

CONCLUSION

The cases presented are representative of the spectrum of HIV-infected patients with substance abuse problems who seek psychological services. Substance abuse treatment alone would have been ineffective with each of these patients because (a) the psychological need (e.g., life review and coping with death and dying) was not usually addressed by substance abuse treatments, (b) the patient could not yet tolerate or conform to traditional substance abuse treatment because of his or her current psychological situation or lifestyle, or (c) because the patient did not view his or her substance abuse as a problem.

As the cases illustrate, when inner city patients with HIV disease and substance abuse problems seek out psychological services, they present a challenge. In the early stages of treatment, problems can arise when these patients do not conform to therapists' traditional expectations of patients with respect to attendance at sessions and their behavior in the session. Doing psychotherapy with this population requires flexibility and an open-door policy, patience, wit and humor, a high tolerance for deviant behaviors, an acceptance of people's limitations, and the ability to tolerate failure and rejection.

The psychotherapeutic approach to working with substance abusers differs from that of the substance abuse counselor. The psychotherapist addresses substance abuse in the context of the patient's total psychological situation rather than as a discrete problem that takes precedence over all others. The decision of when and how to intervene with the substance abuse is based on the psychotherapist's assessment of patients' immediate psychological needs, their explicit presenting problem, their medical situation, and their readiness for substance abuse treatment. In addition, there is a recognition that patients' shifting medical status may influence both the patients' and the therapists' stance toward the substance abuse. Psychotherapists continually move between exploring and understanding patients' inner experiences of their life situations and applying gentle pressure on patients to address the substance abuse problems. When patients relapse or continue to use substances, it is addressed in the context of helping patients improve their relationships with family and medical providers, their health, and the way the substance abuse contributes to patients' current psychological status. This is in contrast to the approach used in substance abuse programs, where counselors police the client's substance abuse behaviors, often refusing to continue treatment unless the patient agrees to a period of residential treatment. Such an approach is not inherently bad or wrong. Indeed, the treatment offered by substance abuse programs often facilitates the therapist's ability to work with the patient in psychotherapy.

In summary, this chapter has presented a model that facilitates the therapist's ability to work successfully with this group of patients. The key elements are as follows:

• The development of an individualized treatment plan based on a complete psychosocial evaluation of the patient. This includes an assessment of (a) the patient's most pressing psychological need, (b) the patient's readiness for substance abuse treatment, and (c) the patient's beliefs and feelings about being HIV positive and the patient's medical status.

• Active outreach, flexibility, and a willingness to initially engage patients on their terms.

• The creation of a holding environment and the use of therapeutic techniques where the therapist acts as a container for the patient's intense affects and the continual engagement of the patient in an ongoing dialogue about the patient's experiences in order to help the patient become more aware of the emotional responses evoked. The goals are to help the patient feel less overwhelmed by these events and feelings and to enable him or her to act out less.

• Substance abuse is addressed in the context of the patient's overall problems and not as a discrete problem. There is a recognition that for some patients referral to substance abuse programs should only be made when their immediate psychological problems have been resolved or when there is already a strong alliance with a patient. Referral to substance abuse programs are made over and over again, with a focus on understanding and working with the issues that prevent patients from successfully following through on them.

REFERENCES

AIDS and mental health. (1994). *Harvard Mental Health Letter, 10*(8), 1–4.

Batki, S. L. (1990). Substance abuse and AIDS: The need for mental health services. *New Directions for Mental Health Services, 48*, 55–67.

Bayer, R. (1993). The HIV/AIDS epidemic in New York. In A. R. Jonson & J. Stryker (Eds.),

The social impact of AIDS in the United States (pp. 243–299). Washington, DC: National Academy Press.

Bennett, A. (1996, May 5). Study pinpoints where AIDS virus is spreading. *Wall Street Journal*, p. B2

Bialer, P. A., Wallack, J. J., & Snyder, S. L. (1991). Psychiatric diagnosis in HIV-spectrum disorders. *Psychiatric Medicine, 9*(3), 361–375.

Bing, E., Nichols, S. E., Goldfinger, S. M. , Fernandez, F., Cabaj, F., Dudley, R. G., Krener, P., Prager, M., & Ruiz, P. (1990). The many faces of AIDS: Opportunities for intervention. *New Directions for Mental Health Services, 48*, 69–82.

Bing, E. G., & Soto, T. A. (1991). Treatment issues for African-Americans and Hispanics with AIDS. *Psychiatric Medicine, 9*(3), 455–467.

Blechner, M. J. (1993). Psychoanalysis and HIV disease. *Contemporary Psychoanalysis, 29*(1), 61–80.

Borden, W. (1989). Life review as a therapeutic frame in the treatment of young adults with AIDS. *Health and Social Work, 14*(4), 253–258.

Child, R., & Getzel, G. (1990). Group work with inner city persons with AIDS. *Social Work With Groups, 12*, 65–80.

Dailey, L., Jr. (1990). Therapy with inner-city AIDS clients. *New Directions for Mental Health Services, 46*, 65–74.

Dane, B. O., & Miller. S. O. (1992). *AIDS: Intervening with hidden grievers.* Westport, CT: Auburn House.

Fawzy, I., Fawzy, N., & Pasnau, R. O. (1991). A model of psychiatric intervention for AIDS patients. *Psychiatric Medicine, 9*(3), 409–422.

Hoffman, M. A. (1996). *Counseling clients with HIV disease: Assessment, intervention, and prevention.* New York: Guilford Press.

Jillson-Boostrom, I. (1992). The impact of HIV on minority populations. In P. I. Ahmed (Ed.), *Living and dying with AIDS* (pp. 236–254). New York: Plenum Press.

Landau-Stanton, J., & Clements, C. D. (1993). *AIDS, health and mental health: A primary source-book.* New York: Brunner/Mazel.

Markowitz, J. C., Klerman, G. L., & Perry, S. W. (1992). Interpersonal psychotherapy of de-pressed HIV-positive outpatients. *Hospital and Community Psychiatry, 43*(9), 885–890.

O'Dowd, M., Natali, C., Orr, D., & McKegney, F. P. (1991). Characteristics of patients attending an HIV-related psychiatric clinic. *Hospital and Community Psychiatry, 42*, 615–619.

Reulbach, W. (1991). Counseling chemically dependent HIV positive adolescents. In M. Shernoff (Ed.), *Counseling chemically dependent people with HIV illness* (pp. 31–43). New York: Haworth Press.

Sadowy, D. (1991). Is there a role for the psychoanalytic psychotherapist with a patient dying of AIDS? *Psychoanalytic Review, 78*(2), 199–207.

Sahs, J., & Storey, J. E. (1994, November). *An HIV mental health clinic.* Poster presented at Arden House Annual Scientific Conference, Department of Psychiatry, College of Physi-cians & Surgeons of Columbia University, New York.

Schaffner, B. (1990). Psychotherapy with HIV-infected persons. *New Directions for Mental Health Services, 48*, 5–20.

Shilts, R. (1988). *And the band played on.* New York: Penguin Books.

Storey, J. E. (1996). Substance abusing HIV+ patients in psychiatric residency training. *HIV/ AIDS curriculum.* Washington, DC: American Psychiatric Association.

Walker, M. (1991). *In the midst of winter: Systemic therapy with families, couples, and individu-als with AIDS infection.* New York: W. W. Norton.

Winiarski, M. G. (1995). HIV and AIDS. In Arnold M. Washton (Ed.), *Psychotherapy and sub-stance abuse: A practitioner's handbook* (pp. 428–450). New York: Guilford Press.

Zakrzewski, P. A. (1991). Short term group work with intravenous drug using people with AIDS in a hospital setting. In M. Shernoff (Ed.), *Counseling chemically dependent people with HIV illness* (pp. 55–65). New York: Haworth Press.

Chapter 10

Group Psychotherapy for Mentally Ill Chemically Abusing Patients with HIV/AIDS

Linda Jaffe Caplan

Recent literature has shown a high prevalence of HIV/AIDS infection among individuals with psychiatric and substance abuse histories who are living in urban centers (Empfield et al., 1993; Silberstein et al., 1994; Susser et al., 1993). Factors contributing to HIV risk and infection include inaccurate information about AIDS transmission, unsafe sex practices, impaired interpersonal skills, poor judgment, and patterns of substance abuse (Cournos, McKinnon, Meyer-Bahlburg, Guido, & Meyers, 1993; Kalichman, Kelly, Johnson, & Bulto, 1994; Tynes, Suatter, McDermott, & Winstead, 1993). Premorbid histories of depression, suicidal ideation and behavior, and substance abuse before HIV infection are common among HIV/AIDS psychiatric patients (Markowitz, Rabkin, & Perry, 1994; Silberstein et al., 1994; Wiener, Schwartz, & O'Connell, 1994).

Although studies have documented the need for specialized services (Tynes et al., 1993; Wiener et al., 1994), few treatment programs have been developed for people with significant psychiatric and substance abuse histories. Whereas community-based HIV/AIDS groups are available to mentally ill chemically abusing (MICA) patients, they often are experienced by such patients as too stimulating, threatening, or otherwise inaccessible (Millan & Ivory, 1994). Limited by their impaired social skills, their sense of personal fragility, their difficulty in tolerating painful affect, and the inadequacy of their defenses, MICA patients are frequently unable to participate meaningfully in such groups. Unable to trust wholeheartedly, to share freely, or to attend regularly, they hover on the periphery. MICA patients may be disruptive to the group process, and at times they may become too frightened even to attend (Daniolos, 1994; Mayers & Spiegel, 1992).

This chapter describes a therapy group for MICA patients with HIV/AIDS conducted over a 2-year period at Columbia-Presbyterian Medical Center's HIV Mental Health Clinic, an urban clinic serving the diverse needs of a multiethnic, multiracial inner city population. The structure and format of the group were modified to address the special psychological needs of this population.

MICA patients often have difficulties attending regularly, establishing basic trust, and affiliating and sharing with the group. In general, these patients lack the social and psychological skills necessary to engage freely, spontaneously, and nondefensively with one another. Within HIV/AIDS MICA groups, it is imperative for the therapist to promote the development of a group identity, to enhance patients' communications, and to facilitate the giving and receiving of support.

This chapter discusses the structure and development of an HIV/AIDS group for MICA patients. Case material is provided throughout the chapter to highlight issues related to group formation and group functioning. Topics include (a) the need for a long-term, open-ended group format; (b) the unique role of the therapist as the emotional glue, conduit, and container; (c) interpretation as a means of balancing individual and group needs; and (e) the concept of support as a developmental milestone rather than as a defining group characteristic. Topics related to patients' substance abuse and countertransferential concerns are also discussed.

AN HIV/AIDS MICA GROUP: A CASE STUDY

Membership

All members of the group had HIV/AIDS and histories of significant psychiatric impairment. Their diagnoses included the major affective disorders, severe character pathology, and schizophrenia. Most had histories of multiple psychiatric hospitalizations. Suicidal ideation and behavior were common and usually predated their HIV/AIDS diagnoses. Patients had difficulties coping with everyday stressors. They were isolated; their relationships with family and friends were strained. Many had had no contact with parents or siblings for many years.

In addition, all patients reported significant substance abuse histories, including alcohol, cocaine, crack, and heroin. Several had been substance free for years; some attended methadone maintenance programs, Alcoholics Anonymous (AA), or other community-based substance abuse programs. Others remained active, drinking, using crack, cocaine, heroin, or marijuana. Criteria for group membership, however, included neither abstinence nor participation in any 12-step program. For many MICA patients, patterns of alcohol and drug use are multiply determined and complex. Their alcohol and drug use is intimately intertwined with their concepts of self, value systems, lifestyles and personal identifications, characteristic styles of coping, and defensive structures. Issues related to abstinence or participation in substance abuse programs such as AA, therefore, were considered on a personal basis and were thought of as potential therapy goals rather than as treatment prerequisites.

In addition to group psychotherapy, most of these patients also participated in individual therapy. Several were prescribed psychotropic medications, including antidepressants and antipsychotics. A treatment team approach was maintained whenever possible.

Although membership criteria were uniform, the members themselves were quite diverse. Ed, for instance, was a highly provocative gay man who had only a fleeting relationship with truth and honesty. On intake, for example, he claimed to be a hair stylist. Several sessions later, he said he was a psychologist. He plucked the hair from his head and dressed in a flamboyant manner, as if he were cruising. He presented himself as sensitive, caring, and insightful, yet he often stunned the group with his crazy, bizarre, masochistic, and impulsive behaviors. On one occasion, he flew to Texas with a man he did not know and engaged in unprotected sex and indiscriminate IV drug use. On another occasion, he nonchalantly spoke about how just that weekend he had awakened his father in the middle of the night to drive him to the George Washington Bridge. Feeling suicidal, he got out of the car, stood by the bridge railing, and contemplated jumping. Instead, he urinated, got back in the car, and drove home, attributing no significance whatsoever to his suicidal behavior.

In contrast, Carol, an African American bisexual woman in her late 20s, was a breath of fresh air. She was blunt, direct, and, at times, painfully honest. She had a lovely sense of humor and could be quite warm and caring. She often spoke derisively about herself, using her wit and intelligence to cover up her profound sense of sadness, loneliness, and despair. Carol also had an explosive temper. She had been physically and sexually abused as a child and had fits of rage during which she could be quite destructive. As a child, she had tried to kill her foster mother. As an adult, she had trashed her apartment and had threatened her boyfriend with a knife.

Philip was a middle-aged African American, bisexual, but very closeted. He felt that it was no one's business what he did. He was well spoken and well educated. As a young man, he had been a dancer on Broadway. He had also worked as a tailor and as a dog groomer. For many years, his life had been stable. He traveled frequently, used drugs recreationally, and drifted in and out of relationships with lovers, friends, and family. In later years, things had begun to unravel. He lost his job, began using crack, and developed *Pneumocystis carinii* pneumonia. At the time he joined the group, his health was failing. He supplemented his income by collecting bottles and dreamed of returning to full-time employment.

Other members of the group included Chuck, a young gay man on death's door who spoke poignantly about his continuing compulsion to use cocaine;

Hank, an illiterate, homeless man who successfully passed himself off as a hospital employee; Hal, a professional musician who struggled with a lifelong heroin addiction; Larry, a drug counselor, doing drugs; and Cesar, who repeatedly sought out medical professionals who were incompetent and dangerous.

Although members differed with regards to age, gender, sexual orientation, level of education, psychiatric diagnosis, and progression of illness, they nevertheless perceived themselves as like-minded. Uniformly, they had sought group therapy to help them deal with being HIV positive.

Group members felt scared, angry, and depressed. They experienced themselves as stigmatized, alone, and unloved. They were afraid of the illness. They were afraid of relationships. Many had never previously told anyone, including their friends, families, and partners, that they were HIV positive. Too schizoid, mistrustful, or self-occupied, they experienced profound difficulties engaging in the group process.

Course of Treatment

Initially, group attendance was erratic. Although several members attended regularly, others came sporadically; they seemed to view the group as if it were a drop-in center. The group itself often functioned as a discontinuous series of one- and two-session workshops.

Numerous therapist outreach efforts were provided. The therapist periodically called patients who had missed sessions to remind them of group therapy. She encouraged individuals to attend when they were able, and she underscored their contributions to the group process. In addition, she conveyed members' concerns about their absences. Throughout the conversation, the therapist's tone was welcoming and accepting, conveying to patients an open-door policy.

Over the course of time, however, the group became more stable. A core membership developed. Attendance became regular, and participants began to identify themselves as part of an ongoing group.

An increased sense of affiliation and belonging developed. Members began to trust one another and to let down their guard. There was a decrease in their sense of marginalization. They spoke openly about their psychiatric hospitalizations, current symptomatology, and drug behaviors. They began to value themselves and to perceive each other as capable individuals. A schizophrenic man, for example, was able to act as the voice of reason and sanity in an otherwise outrageous session. In this particular group, Ed was considering whether he should return to his masseuse. At his previous appointment, his masseuse had massaged his penis using various unknown substances while sticking things up his penis. Several days later, Ed's penis was still hurting. Bill, the schizophrenic, looked directly at Ed and unequivocally said, "I don't know about you, but I'd see a doctor." The other members concurred, adding that the masseuse's behavior was abusive.

Group members began to develop a capacity to relate to one another, to give and receive support. They exchanged telephone numbers, talked to each other throughout the week, shared information, helped each other arrange doctors' appointments, and visited each other in the hospital. They began to worry about each other and to miss each other when they were absent. Philip, who never socialized with anyone, invited Hal for coffee. He worried when Hal went into the hospital and subsequently called him on several occasions, just to check up on him.

In other words, the group began to function as a group. Members discussed their hopes, fears, and relationships. They talked about sex, about safer sex, and about the difficulties telling a partner they were HIV positive. They gently prodded Larry to tell his common-law wife he was positive. They discussed AA and the lure of drugs. They spoke of suicide, of their fears of loss of control, and of their feelings of hopelessness and despair. Carol shared how, on breaking up with her boyfriend, she had hidden in the woods for weeks, too fearful and despondent to make contact with anyone. They began to explore their own behaviors. Philip, for example, came to realize that his drug use was not random and that, in fact, he went on a drug run every time his T-cell count dropped. As he began to articulate his fears of dying, of being physically dependent and emotionally alone, he was able to engage more realistically in his medical care, to go to doctors when needed, and on several occasions to insist on hospitalization when necessary. He also became more able to help Cesar, who suffered from chronic leg pain, to evaluate his doctor's competence.

NEED FOR A SPECIALIZED GROUP

Throughout the past 10 years, group psychotherapy has become the treatment of choice for many persons infected with the HIV virus (Beckett & Rutan, 1990; Tunnell, 1991). For patients who are able to participate meaningfully, group psychotherapy helps to diminish feelings of isolation and stigmatization. It provides opportunities for individuals to explore issues related to illness, physical deterioration, multiple losses, and death (Beckett & Rutan, 1990; Tunnell, 1991). Members offer each other support and understanding. Basic trust, a capacity for self-reflection, object constancy, an ability to tolerate painful affects, and adequate social skills are presumed.

HIV/AIDS patients with multiple psychiatric and substance abuse issues also experience the stresses and strains of being HIV positive. They too feel isolated, confused, and fearful. They require support, an outlet to express their feelings, and a source for information regarding treatment options, possible side effects, and clinical trials. Lacking the psychological skills necessary to participate meaningfully in traditional psychotherapy groups, MICA patients require specialized groups that address their unique psychological needs. Difficulties trusting, sharing, and empathizing are common among MICA patients. Most pointedly, they lack the skills necessary to attend regularly, to interact freely, and to give and receive support wholeheartedly.

COMPONENTS OF THE GROUP MODEL

Throughout this section, a group model for HIV/AIDS MICA patients is discussed that addresses their special needs. Generally, these patients have difficulties affiliating, engaging freely and openly with one another, and relating empathically. They are skittish, impulsive, and mistrustful. Self-concepts are often poorly defined, and self–other differentiation is frequently inadequate. Specifically, attention is given to (a) group structure and format, (b) the unique role of the therapist, (c) the importance of interpretation as a means of simultaneously fostering individual and group development, and (d) the relationship between support and self–other differentiation. Concerns related to patients' substance abuse and countertransferential issues are also discussed.

The Group Format

First, the HIV/AIDS MICA group was, by design, open ended. It is not simply a lack of commitment, deteriorating health, or familial pressures that prevents MICA patients from attending group regularly. Often, members' internal worlds are as chaotic as their external worlds. Never having obtained the capacity for object permanence, patients' relationships with reality are fragmented and discontinuous.

Regular attendance presupposes the capacity to perceive objects in the world as permanent and stable. For many, "out of sight, out of mind" means out of sight, out of existence. These patients have difficulty conceiving that others actually exist as separate and real when they are not in their direct line of experience. For these patients, the open-endedness of the group is a necessary precondition to group commitment and regular attendance. Psychologically, these patients need to come and go, to test the waters repeatedly ("Oh, so they're still here") as they attempt to incorporate a greater sense of object permanence within themselves. If the group was time limited or attendance was mandatory, many HIV/AIDS MICA patients would fail to become members.

Cesar, for example, missed the first several group sessions before he attended his initial meeting. After each missed appointment, I spoke with him. He apologized profusely, always promising to attend next week's therapy group. On one occasion, Cesar forgot about the group. On other occasions, he got drunk, became confused, or simply did not feel up to it. Soon after Cesar attended his first session, he became a regular, only missing when his health precluded his traveling.

Unique and Central Role of the Therapist

Initially, the therapist served as the glue that kept the group together. She was the constant in an otherwise unstable group. Her actual presence served as an anchor. She acted as the group memory, providing patients with a sense of continuity and permanence that would otherwise have been absent.

As the group progressed, the centrality of the therapist continued. She served as the emotional conduit through which members began to communicate effectively with one another. She provided the links between members that enabled them to reach out to one another safely and comfortably. Her presence offered patients a sense of comfort and security as they began to take risks within themselves and with each other. She served as a container and as a buffer, modulating patients' affects and communications, within themselves and with each other.

In a very poignant, highly charged group session, Chuck spoke of his intention to go on a drug run immediately after leaving the group meeting. The other members became quite anxious and disturbed. His talk stimulated multiple feelings, of helplessness, anger, fear, and so forth. The therapist's tone and demeanor—which were calm, matter of fact, and seemingly unflappable—helped the group members tolerate their anxieties as they began to problem solve with Chuck. (On this particular occasion, Carol escorted Chuck home and stayed with him until his lover returned from work.)

On a different occasion, George, a new member, spoke vehemently and evangelically about AA, intimidating several members in the process. Having assessed that the group was unable to withstand his veiled aggression, the therapist intervened by saying, "AA really seems to be working for you, George, but not everyone's the same, you know," followed by "George, I can see how important AA is to you, but I think some of the other members may be feeling uncomfortable with your forcefulness."

BALANCING GROUP AND INDIVIDUAL NEEDS

As members began to experience themselves as part of a group, a new phase of treatment emerged. For many, an emergent sense of belonging was a new and heady experience. Many patients had felt isolated, alone, and stigmatized throughout much of their lives. They identified with each other, reveling in their perception of sameness and uniformity. As wonderful as these feelings were, they also were experienced as potentially overstimulating and overwhelming. Possibilities for friendship and increased closeness underscored patients' sense of personal fragility. It taxed their poorly developed self-identities and weakly defined ego boundaries. To help patients tolerate feelings of intimacy while preserving their shaky senses of autonomy, it was imperative for the therapist to maintain a balance between the individual and the group. This was done primarily through interpretation, with the therapist's comments focusing almost exclusively on the group's emerging sense of identity while simultaneously underscoring the diversity and individuality of its membership (i.e., "There are a number of ways in which everyone is the same. However, each of you is unique"). In this manner, a sense of group identity was fostered. Simultaneously, the therapist enhanced individuals' development. As Philip's health deteriorated, for example, such comments as these were common:

There are a number of ways in which people here are the same. Everyone, for example, is HIV positive. But there are also are a number of differences. Ed was only recently diagnosed HIV positive and his health is excellent. Carol, on the other hand, has been living with this disease for quite a while. I wonder how we can all help Philip as he prepares for his doctor's appointment.

This interpretation allowed patients to feel close to Philip while maintaining appropriate psychological distance.

SUPPORT AS A DEVELOPMENTAL MILESTONE

Essential to the capacity to give and receive support are a number of psychological abilities, including the ability to trust, a willingness to engage with others, and a capacity to empathize. These capacities, while presumed within conventional HIV/AIDS groups, are glaringly absent for many individuals with psychiatric and substance abuse histories. Carol, for example, was initially too suspicious to give out her phone number, let alone go out for coffee. Philip felt too independent to let anyone know he needed help. Ed and Cesar were too self-absorbed to notice anything beyond themselves.

Also, the ability to differentiate oneself from others must be sufficiently secure in order to give and receive support. Without such differentiation, an individual is unable to accurately perceive a genuine need in another. For example, Philip, in deteriorated health, began to discuss his thoughts about dying. He felt that if he were to lose his capacity to live alone, life would no longer be worth living. Initially, other members were appalled. They identified with Philip and experienced his wishes to let go—which he experienced as hard-won accomplishments—as individual death sentences. They experienced his desire to die on his own terms, in relation to their own lives, as a sign of weakness and despair. As they were able to better differentiate themselves from others, to see the ways in which they, in fact, were different from Philip, they began to provide real support. They offered suggestions that addressed Philip's real needs, for example, Meals on Wheels. They became more able to tolerate the expression of painful affects. They listened as Philip lamented lost his capacities, like his ability to work or to cook for himself. It was only as the group progressed—as they developed a capacity for trust, an ability to empathize, and an ability to differentiate themselves from one another—that they were able to give and receive support.

SUBSTANCE ABUSE

Patterns of alcohol and drug use are multiply determined and complex. They are intimately related to patients' value systems, identifications, coping styles, and defensive structures. The psychological meaning of patients' drug use varies from individual to individual. No two persons use alcohol and drugs in exactly the same way for precisely the same reasons.

Throughout the group, patients' alcohol and drug use were raised as topics for discussion, as issues to be explored and understood. Patients discussed Ed's drug use openly and directly. The therapist said to the group, "Ed, now, feels he doesn't have a drug problem since he only uses drugs when someone offers him some. What does everyone think of Ed's drug use?" This comment allowed patients to question Ed's impulsivity, his judgment, and the numerous ways in which he imperiled his life through drugs and other high-risk behaviors. Carol spoke of the physical dangers inherent in ingesting unknown substances from strangers. Hank questioned Ed's motivations, and Cesar wondered about the moral implications of Ed's behavior.

As patients talked about Ed's drug use, they also reflected on their own alcohol and drug behaviors. Patients put their own substance use in perspective. They began to establish goals for themselves and to develop their own substance abuse treatment plans. Issues related to abstinence and relapse were explored in the same manner.

COUNTERTRANSFERENCE

Working with patients with HIV/AIDS often evokes intense feelings and countertransferential reactions in the therapist (Bernstein & Klein, 1995; Tunnell, 1991). The cumulative effects of listening and caring for deteriorating and dying patients can be quite profound (Gabriel, 1993). Feelings of anger, loss, guilt, and helplessness are common. Incidence of staff burnout and traumatic stress reactions are reported in the literature (Gabriel, 1993).

Treatment with HIV/AIDS MICA patients can be all the more challenging. These are patients who are prone to action. Their judgment and impulse control are frequently impaired. They engage in risky behaviors like unprotected sex and indiscriminate drug use. Suicidal ideation and behavior are common. MICA patients often disappear from psychiatric care for indeterminate periods of time before returning to treatment.

Ed, for example, frequently shared with the group his most recent sexual conquest, which routinely included the practice of unsafe, unprotected sex. Raul suddenly disappeared from the group and from the clinic to go on a drug run. Months later, he died of drug-related illnesses. His health in relation to HIV had remained stable. Philip learned to control his crack use; however, his weight continued to decline. He became weaker, his health deteriorated, and he was hospitalized repeatedly for *Pneumocystis carinii* pneumonia.

A sense of outrage and moral indignation are common when working with MICA patients with HIV/AIDS. Feelings of worry, fear, uncertainty, and helplessness can be overwhelming. The effects of caring for dying patients can be cumulative.

A team approach in which patient information is shared often is helpful when working with HIV/AIDS MICA patients. In this manner, feelings of uncertainty and powerlessness can be assuaged. Regular supervision and ongoing staff support can mitigate against feelings of helplessness, powerlessness, and moral outrage.

CONCLUSION

This chapter described a therapy group that was designed to address the special needs of HIV/AIDS-infected MICA patients. Specifically, attention was given to the need for a long-term, open-ended group model. The unique role of the therapist as the emotional glue and container was discussed. The importance of interpretation as a means of simultaneously fostering individual and group development was explored, as was the relationship between support and self–other differentiation. Topics related to patients' substance abuse and countertransferential issues were also discussed.

REFERENCES

Beckett, A., & Rutan, J. S. (1990). Treating persons with ARC & AIDS in group psychotherapy. *International Journal of Group Psychotherapy, 40,* 19–29.

Bernstein, G., & Klein, R. (1995). Countertransference issues in group psychotherapy with HIV-positive and AIDS patients. *International Journal of Group Psychotherapy, 45,* 91–100.

Cournos, F., McKinnon, K., Meyer-Bahlburg, H., Guido, J., & Meyers, I. (1993). HIV risk activity among persons with severe mental illness: Preliminary findings. *Hospital & Community Psychiatry, 44,* 1104–1106.

Daniolos, P. T. (1994). House calls: A support group for individuals with AIDS in a community residential setting. *International Journal of Group Psychotherapy, 44,* 133–152.

Empfield, M., Cournos, F., Meyer, I., McKinnon, K., Horwath, E., Silver, M., Schrage, H., & Herman, R. (1993). HIV seroprevalence among homeless patients admitted to a psychiatric inpatient unit. *American Journal of Psychiatry, 150,* 47–52.

Gabriel, M. (1993). Group therapists and AIDS groups: An exploration of traumatic stress reactions. *Group, 18*(3), 167–176.

Kalichman, S., Kelly, J., Johnson, J., & Bulto, M. (1994). Factors associated with risk for HIV infection among chronic mentally ill adults. *American Journal of Psychiatry, 151,* 221–227.

Markowitz, J., Rabkin, J., & Perry, S. (1994). Treating depression in HIV-positive patients. *AIDS, 8,* 403–412.

Mayers, A., & Spiegel, L. (1992). A parental support group in a pediatric AIDS clinic: Its usefulness and limitations. *Health and Social Work, 17,* 183–191.

Millan, F., & Ivory, L. I. (1994). Group therapy with the multiply oppressed: Treating Latino, HIV-infected injecting drug users. *Group, 18*(3), 154–166.

Silberstein, C., Galanter, M., Marmor, M., Lifshutz, H., Krasinski, K., & Franco, H. (1994). HIV-1 among inner city dually diagnosed inpatients. *American Journal of Drug & Alcohol Abuse, 20,* 101–113.

Susser, E., Valencia, E., & Conover, S. (1993). Prevalence of HIV infection among psychiatric patients in a New York City men's shelter. *American Journal of Public Health, 83,* 568–570.

Tunnell, G. (1991). Complications in group psychotherapy with AIDS patients. *International Journal of Group Psychotherapy, 41,* 481–498.

Tynes, L, Suatter, F., McDermott, D., & Winstead, D. (1993). Risk of HIV infection in the homeless and chronically mentally ill. *Southern Medical Journal, 86,* 276–281.

Wiener, P, Schwartz, M., & O'Connell, R. (1994). Characteristics of HIV-infected patients in an inpatient psychiatric setting. *Psychosomatics, 35,* 59–65.

Chapter 11

HIV and the Traditional Latino Woman

Ivan C. Balan

The Latino community in the United States has been disproportionately affected by the AIDS epidemic (Fernandez, 1995). Latinos account for approximately 18% of the AIDS cases in the United States, although they account for only 8% of the general population (Centers for Disease Control and Prevention, 1995). Latino women account for 21% of those AIDS cases (Centers for Disease Control and Prevention, 1989). Diaz, Buehler, Castro, and Ward (1993) reported that heterosexual contact has become the most prevalent route of exposure for foreign-born Latino women: For Central American women, 46.9% were exposed through heterosexual contact; for Cuban women, 39%; Dominican women, 47.6%; Mexican women, 35.8%; and South American women, 60%. For U.S.-born Latinas, intravenous drug use remains the most frequent mode of transmission (55.8%; Diaz et al, 1993). Most cases of heterosexual infection of women have been attributed to unprotected sexual relations with a partner who is either bisexual or is an intravenous drug user. However, there are a number of cultural factors that place Latino women at significant risk for HIV infection even when their partners are neither bisexual or IV drug users.

This chapter presents three case studies of women who were seen at the HIV Mental Health Clinic at the Columbia-Presbyterian Medical Center. They were brought together in a support group designed for Spanish-speaking women to share their experiences and feelings regarding becoming HIV positive. Before being diagnosed, they believed their risk of becoming infected with HIV was minimal. None of the women in this population was sexually promiscuous or had history of IV drug use. They shared the same risk factor: A husband with no history of IV drug use, but who was sexually promiscuous with women. This risk factor was minimized by all the women because they believed sexual promiscuity in their husbands, albeit unwanted, was to be expected and tolerated based on Latino gender norms. These gender norms and sex role expectations place Latino women at risk and have to be understood in order to institute effective HIV risk reduction programs.

HIV AND LATINO GENDER ROLES

The basic structure of Latino gender roles is defined by *marianismo* and *machismo*. Marianismo, derived from the adoration of the Virgin Mary in the Catholic church, is the belief that women are superior to men spiritually and thus able to tolerate the suffering they experience (Stevens, 1973, as cited in Ramos-McKay, Comas-Diaz, & Rivera, 1988). Latino women are expected to be obedient, submissive, and homebound (Ramos-McKay et al., 1988). Machismo is the belief that men are intellectual, rational, authoritarian, physically dominant, and always sexually available, regardless of marital status (Sluzki, 1982). Although the rigidity of these roles varies on the basis of acculturation, level of education, and socioeconomic status, they remain a core part of the Latino culture. There are both positive and negative aspects to these roles, affecting many aspects of life; however, a detailed discussion of these aspects is beyond the scope of this chapter. As such, the focus is on how these gender roles create a risk of HIV infection, even within relationships that appear to be of minimal risk.

Although the more traditional gender roles are associated with hypersexuality in men, the opposite holds true for women. It is actually the responsibility of the male (fathers and brothers) to protect the chastity of the unwed daughters and sisters. This is done mostly by keeping them at home, thus establishing their identity of being *una mujer de la casa* (a woman of the home), which clearly demarcates a difference from being *una mujer cualquiera* (any woman) or *una mujer de la calle* (a woman of the streets). Women are supposed to be virginal at the time of marriage and to engage in sex not for their own pleasure but for procreation and the pleasure of their husbands. Sex is also not a proper subject for a woman of the home to speak about, not even with her husband. Hence, when one of the women discussed here would buy her husband condoms to use with the other women with whom he had sexual relations, she was reprimanded for speaking about sex, something that a "proper" woman would not do. This places the Latino woman at a significant disadvantage by not only limiting sexually related conversations between husband and wife, but by also limiting the information that Latino women can receive or seek out in regards to sexual matters. Results can be overwhelming: When women are aware of their husbands' extramarital affairs, they feel obliged to tolerate it because of cultural norms. They lack the power to confront their husbands, even when they are put in danger by remaining quiet. In a study of condom use in a sample of Latino clinic patients with sexually transmitted diseases, it was reported that whereas 70% of the male respondents agreed that it is okay to have sex without a condom if you trust your partner (even within the context of a primary relationship), only 33.7% of the women agreed (San Doval, Duran, O'Donnell, & O'Donnell, 1995). One reason for this discrepancy may be that the men may feel more assured that their primary partners are monogamous, whereas the women are not as secure in this belief.

Machismo assumes and encourages hypersexuality and continuous sexual availability (Sluzki, 1982). Furthermore, it is generally accepted that the male sexual urge is uncontrollable, thus the constant need for chaperons when men and women are together, for men cannot be trusted to control their impulses (Leiner, 1994). This promiscuity can be particularly dangerous in relation to HIV infection. It has been suggested that machismo could lead more traditional Latino men to engage in more frequent and riskier sexual activity (Amaro, 1988, and Magna et al., under review, as cited in Fernandez, 1995). The activity could be riskier in numerous ways. It has been reported that Latino men are more likely to engage in intercourse than in other sexual acts. Exacerbating this risk is the perception of condom use in relation to machismo. Condoms are often perceived as not macho. They are contrary to standards of machismo, such as sexual readiness, aggressiveness, and the devaluing of the woman of the streets. If condoms interfere with sexual functioning, there is also the risk that the man's reputation will be tarnished by his not functioning adequately during sex.

Although it would appear as though the cultural construct of machismo would have to be done away with to decrease the risk of HIV infection within the Latino population, there are several aspects of machismo that have been suggested as strengths in reducing risky behavior. It has been suggested that reinforcing the machismo aspects of family protection and protection of the wife's virtue may play vital roles in encouraging these men to use condoms when engaging in extramarital relations.

ISSUES IN THE TREATMENT
OF THE HIV-POSITIVE LATINO WOMAN

Psychiatry and the Latino Culture

When discussing issues pertaining to HIV-related psychiatric treatment with this population, it is crucial to discuss the general issue of psychological or psychiatric treatment within the context of the Latino culture. Within this culture, psychiatric problems are presented through the concept of *nervios*, defined as "a rich idiom for expressing emotional upset, somatic distress, and social dislocation" (Guernaccia, Parra, Deschamps, Milstein, & Arguiles, 1992, p. 193). This term encompasses not only psychotic disorders, but also depression and anxiety (Jenkins, 1988). Thus, a common chief complaint is often "my nerves have been bothering me" or "I am suffering from nerves." It has been suggested that for effective treatment of ethnic populations, an understanding and framing of treatment within the patient's cultural context is necessary (Swerdlow, 1992). At the very least, the clinician must maintain respect for cultural conceptions of illness and folk medicine, even if, as often happens, they are vastly different from the conceptions of Western medicine.

Another basic issue of treatment that has to be addressed, explored, and normalized is patients' decisions to seek psychiatric treatment. Often, patients come to treatment thinking they are "going crazy." They have noted and accurately classify certain symptoms (i.e., sadness, tearfulness), but easily misperceive other symptoms (i.e., memory loss) as being signs of "craziness." The referral to see a mental health professional often validates these fears because psychology and, more so, psychiatry are still perceived as treatments for persons who are "crazy." Within this context, psychoeducation becomes an important component of the treatment.

> Mrs. R is a 50-year-old Dominican woman, diagnosed HIV positive in November 1993 when, as part of a full physical, she flippantly agreed to be tested for HIV, never expecting to receive a positive result. She was referred to the HIV Mental Health Clinic by her nurse practitioner at the Infectious Disease Clinic because of her depression. When contacted to arrange the initial visit, she asked if I was Dominican, for she feared that I might know her or someone in her family. At the initial visit, she complained of depression, insomnia, poor appetite, social withdrawal, and problems with her memory and concentration. She was also preoccupied and ruminating about her death and about being rejected by friends and family.
>
> A few sessions into her treatment, Mrs. R. painfully admitted that she believed that she was beginning to experience symptoms of schizophrenia, a disorder present in two family members. An exploration into this revealed that Mrs. R. was experiencing memory problems, which she related to schizophrenia. On being informed that memory difficulties could be attributed to depression, she was visibly relieved. Because of the severity of her symptoms, the possibility of psychopharmacological treatment was raised. Mrs. R. steadfastly refused, relaying the experience of one of her sisters when she was treated with psychotropic medication. This discussion also elicited fears that if she had to see a psychiatrist, it would mean she was crazy.
>
> It was only after 6 months of individual treatment that, through the exploration of her fears about antidepressants, psychoeducation, and support, Mrs. R. agreed to a psychopharmacology consult after noting that her psychiatric condition was not improving. Mrs. R. had a quick, favorable response to an antidepressant. She noted improved sleep and appetite. She was also pleased to note that her memory and concentration improved over time, further relieving her concerns that her "schizophrenia" might still manifest itself. Currently, she maintains a cooperative relationship with her psychiatrist and looks back at her fears of antidepressants with humor.

The patient–doctor relationship must also be considered within a cultural context. Traditional cultures tend to view the medical profession with great respect. Often, mental health professionals are looked on to provide answers to problems and to counsel people on what they should or should not do. Hence some education as to the purpose of therapy may be helpful for the patient. The doctor–patient relationship within the setting of the medical treatment often becomes an issue in psychotherapy. Often, patients will come to the psychotherapy session and disclose that they are not following the treatment plan prescribed by their physician. This usually relates to fears about the medication or, if they tried the medication, to side effects they experienced. Because within the Latino culture doctors are viewed as authority figures who are not to be questioned but obeyed, patients avoid raising their concerns and asking questions of their physicians because they fear being disrespectful. Thus, patients may reject the prescribed treatment without ever informing their physicians that their recommendations are not being followed. As such, encouraging patients to ask questions of their health care provider and working with them on this becomes an important aspect of the treatment. The benefits to this work are twofold: First, it establishes an open treatment relationship between patient and doctor, allowing for an accurate assessment of the efficacy of the treatment. Second, it places patients in a collaborative role with the physician, increasing their involvement in the treatment and offering them an opportunity to exert control over their treatment and lives. One patient recently expressed the feelings of empowerment that she experienced after refusing an increase in her antidepressant medication to help her combat a situational stressor. She spoke of telling her psychiatrist that even if her dosage were increased, her concern about her current financial situation would persist and that it was the resolution of those problems, not the medication, that would decrease her depression.

Knowledge of HIV and AIDS

Within this population, HIV-related knowledge is significantly limited. Education must be done in the most basic areas of HIV and AIDS, including modes of transmission, disease progression, and availability of medications to combat opportunistic infections. Because these women had perceived the virus as something that would not affect them, they did not pay close attention to advances in the field. Once diagnosed, increasing knowledge comes with emotional turmoil. This group is usually uncomfortable receiving AIDS-related publications at home, thus their information on the latest development is delayed. The experience of watching news programs on television is now emotionally laden as they see people with AIDS in deteriorated physical states, bringing about increased anxiety and decreasing the concentration that they can maintain on the informative aspects of the program. If there are members of the household who are not aware of the patient's HIV status, watching such programs becomes increasingly difficult because of the content as well as the fear that by watching such programs others will realize that they are infected. Thus, the hospital setting usually becomes the principal means of information gathering, whether from physicians, mental health professionals, social workers, or other patients. Helping a patient to sort through the information received, which is often conflicting and confusing, is enormously anxiety-reducing for the patient.

Shame

In considering the feelings elicited by an HIV-positive diagnosis, shame constitutes one of the most intense feelings this group of women experiences. Until their diagnosis, their experiences with AIDS were severely limited and something considered too foreign to their lifestyle to be of personal importance. To many Latinas, AIDS affects only gay people and drug users (Fernandez, 1995). This is a strongly held belief within this traditional group of women. It is also the basis for the shame they are experiencing. Of greatest concern to them is that others will view them as *mujeres de la calle* as opposed to their self-identity, which is based on being *mujeres de la casa*.

> Mrs. H. is a 60-year-old Latino woman diagnosed HIV positive in April 1995. She believes she was infected by her husband of 33 years, from whom she has been separated for the last 8 years due to his increasing use of cocaine. Mrs. H. was referred to the clinic by her infectious disease clinician because of her depression. She came to the first session accompanied by her youngest daughter, the only person she had told of her diagnosis. During the first part of the initial session, when her daughter was in the office, Mrs. H. barely spoke; either she allowed her daughter to respond for her or she responded to questions with one- or two-word responses. Halfway through the session, after her daughter had left the office, she began to speak more freely. She expressed that although her daughter knew of the diagnosis, she still felt uncomfortable discussing her feelings and reactions to this situation in front of her daughter.
>
> Initial sessions focused on her disbelief that she could be HIV positive, owing to her lifestyle. She reported that of her 13 brothers and sisters, she was the most conservative and serious. She spoke of herself as *una mujer de la casa* whose sexual experiences were very limited and who had not had other sexual partners since meeting her husband. Mrs. H. had known her husband was having extramarital affairs since approximately 5 years into their marriage, but considered this the norm for Latin men. However, since discovering her diagnosis, she had been expressing much anger toward her husband for doing this to her. She stated that if she would have known she was at risk for contracting the virus she would have insisted on using condoms or would have separated from her husband sooner. She states that in the late 1980s, "They weren't talking about this [AIDS] like they do now. How was I supposed to know I was in danger?"
>
> Mrs. H.'s greatest concern was and continues to be the fear that "this will manifest itself and everyone will know what I have." In August 1995, Mrs. H. was hospitalized because of swelling of her hands and legs, believed to have been brought about by a combination of prescription and nonprescription medication that Mrs. H. began to take when she experienced an exacerbation of her allergies. She was placed in the AIDS unit of the hospital and, out of fear of others discovering her diagnosis, prohibited visitors except her youngest daughter. This daughter was

away at the time of the hospitalization and had to be contacted to return to New York, as Mrs. H. had not informed her other children of her diagnosis. She has yet to tell her two other children or her husband out of fear that they will tell others. She has very few friends and none that she considers truly close enough to discuss this issue. An exploration of her fear of disclosure revealed that Mrs. H. believes that people will think she was promiscuous or *una mujer de la calle*. Her greatest concern is that her family and friends in the Dominican Republic will learn of her diagnosis. Intellectually, she realizes that her family would be supportive. However, the shame she experiences from being HIV positive keeps her from disclosing her status to them because of what they will think about her. Unfortunately, it also keeps her isolated and withdrawn. She spoke of her concerns, fears, and feelings regarding HIV only once a week, during her therapy sessions.

Aside from individual psychotherapy, Mrs. H. was referred for a psycho-pharmacology consult because of the severity of her depressive symptoms, which included auditory hallucinations. She responded well to an antidepressant and a small dose of antipsychotic medication. The individual treatment has focused on HIV-related education, support, and more recently an exploration of Mrs. H.'s patterns of coping and how they relate to her current situation. Progress here has been uneven. Mrs. H.'s knowledge of HIV has improved and her expectations of her illness and its progression are now more accurate. At the time of admission, she expected to live a few months, although she had not been diagnosed with AIDS and has a T4-cell count near 500. She has now made plans to return to the Dominican Republic to do repairs on her house for future use and speaks of seeing her grand-children grow.

The area of least improvement, and possibly the most crucial to this patient, has been in working toward building a support system. After 15 months of treat-ment, Mrs. H. has not disclosed her diagnosis to anyone but her daughter. Further-more, her fear of meeting someone she knows in the Latino Women's group has prohibited her from joining the group, something which is recommended periodi-cally during treatment. Currently, she is in conflict about joining the group; it is something she is interested in doing and believes she would benefit from; however, her fear of being recognized by someone in the group remains too intense.

Familialism

Familialism, the strong family ties that form a basic tenet of the Latino culture, is usually viewed as an important source of support for the individual. Unfortu-nately, the HIV-positive Latino woman is often unable to access this source of support. Most of these women feel that because of their love and concern for their family, they cannot inform them of their diagnosis because of the pain it would inflict on them. Furthermore, because of the strong ties between indi-viduals and their families, there is concern that community knowledge of an HIV status can lead to shame and rejection for the entire family. A most diffi-cult realization for some of these women is that the support they had expected to receive from the family is not there at this time of need. At times, the family may react with unrealistic fears, telling patients to separate their eating utensils, to use different bathrooms, or not to carry or kiss grandchildren. Because of the unstated expectation that familial support will always be present, such experiences are devastating to the patients who experience them. These types of familial reactions are also destructive in that they validate patients' sense of shame about their illness. This can result in patients' isolation and social withdrawal, further exacerbating the emerging symptoms of depression.

Mrs. M. is a 59-year-old Dominican woman diagnosed HIV positive in April 1995. She decided to be tested for the virus after being told that her husband of 7 years had recently had sexual relations with a woman in the Dominican Republic who was rumored to have AIDS. Mrs. M. was aware that her husband had frequent sexual experiences outside of their marriage. Being informed about AIDS, she had bought and given her husband condoms to use when having sex with other women, telling him that she did not want to get sick. This would usually result in an argument, where he would insult her for suggesting that he was having sex outside the marriage, for speaking about sex in this manner, and for buying condoms, something he did not consider appropriate for her to do. On being confronted with her diagnosis, Mrs. M.'s husband denied that she could have been infected by him.

Mrs. M. lives with three of her six adult male children, with whom she reports having a troubled and emotionally aloof relationship for numerous years. She informed these three sons about the diagnosis because she has felt closer to them than to the others. They responded to her with anger and rejection and with threats toward her husband, whom they forbade to enter the apartment. This reaction was devastating for the patient to deal with because, even in his denial, her husband had expressed the greatest amount of support toward her situation. Currently, she considers telling her children of her diagnosis to have been a grave mistake, owing to the rejection she is experiencing from them. Although she tends to all household responsibilities, they reprimand her for not keeping separate plates, glasses, and eating utensils for herself as well as not separating her laundry from theirs. Much of Mrs. M.'s discussions in therapy deal with her anger toward her sons, who were not supporting her emotionally even after the sacrifices she had made for them while raising them as an only parent. With the sons' refusal to allow her husband into the apartment, Mrs. M. began to feel completely alone in dealing with this situation. Contrary to cultural norms, she was forced to seek support outside of her family.

Mrs. M. had known two other people who had died of AIDS through her work at the church she attends. Thus, she had been able to identify her pastor and a few other church members as sources of support because they had not rejected the other church members who had died. Because she had discussed her illness with her pastor and friends from church, Mrs. M. came to treatment with a lesser degree of shame and isolation than was seen in the other women in her situation. As such, she quickly expressed interest in joining a support group with other Latino women. It is apparent that she has formed supportive connections with the other women in the group. However, her attendance is inconsistent because of her extended visits to the Dominican Republic and problems with her Medicaid coverage. As such, her improvement has been marginal.

For these women, the isolation can be extreme, as they feel there is nowhere to turn. The communities most affected by AIDS, such as the gay community and the substance abuse community, have developed significant support networks for their members throughout the past years. AIDS has also been a part of living within those communities. A significant number of persons who are HIV positive have lost close friends or relatives to AIDS (Martin, 1988; Perry, Fishman, Jacobsberg, & Frances, 1992). Unfortunately, these women are in a situation where the supports present for those communities are not in place for them. Furthermore, they often do not know anyone else who is infected or has died. In the few instances where one of these women has known someone who died of AIDS, the cause of death was kept vague or secret, adding to the sense of shame and the community perception that this is a taboo subject. As a result, they experience their situation as unique.

TREATMENT CONSIDERATIONS

Individual Psychotherapy

Individual psychotherapy treatment often provides the first opportunity for the patients to discuss their feelings and reactions to their diagnosis. Their expectation is that within the clinic context, they will not be rejected. The first few sessions offer an opportunity to normalize patients' experiences of the situation, as well as to confront the many myths and preconceptions that they have regarding their illness. Because of their lack of knowledge about HIV progression, many believe that they have 1 to 2 years of life remaining, which is usually a gross understatement on the basis of their current health. Once patients establish a more accurate impression of their actual health, anxiety is often reduced and work toward other treatment goals can begin. In the initial stages of treatment, goals usually focus on stabilizing patients' emotional state, learning about HIV, and developing a support network. Afterward, work can continue in terms of exploring life-long coping mechanisms and issues that continue to affect patients' lives—the work of any psychotherapy. Thus, although patients' illness and physical concerns permeate the treatment, the degree to which it becomes the direct focus of the psychological treatment varies. Individual psychotherapy allows patients an opportunity to discuss HIV-related concerns and fears in a setting that affords the greatest degree of confidentiality. Therefore, the issues presented by patients tend to be the most personal they experience, and as a result, personal growth can be most pronounced. However, for the population discussed in this chapter, who functioned well in society before being diagnosed, a priority of treatment may be to involve them in a support group to decrease their shame and sense of isolation.

Group Psychotherapy

Group treatment for these patients is not an easy process, although it is often tremendously beneficial. One of the cultural values within the Latino community is that family problems remain in the family and are not discussed with anyone else. Added to this is the fear these women have of meeting someone in the group they know. These two issues are enough to dissuade many in this population from agreeing to enter group treatment. However, for those women who do, the rewards can be significant. After fearing entering group treatment, one patient spoke of the comfort in being able to walk to the bus stop with one of the other members and, although the conversation did not relate to AIDS, knowing that the other person understood her current problems in the context of her health and her fears. For many, the group provides their only opportunity to discuss feelings and reactions to their illness with others who face a similar situation. It is also an opportunity to exchange information about new treatments, folk remedies, and entitlements.

One technique used to encourage the women to enter the group was to begin forming a connection between them before their meeting. By normalizing the experiences that these patients reported in the individual sessions as also occurring to other women in the same situation, these patients began to feel less isolated. One patient, while only in individual treatment, came to ask whether the other women were experiencing what she had been reporting, thus exhibiting the degree to which she had already joined with these women. Nonetheless, the pivotal aspect of these women's decision to join the group was the relationship that had been established with the individual therapist and the knowledge that the same therapist would be leading the group.

Decisions about the purpose of the group must be explored by the clinician before beginning the group. Because of issues regarding discussing family problems outside of the family, the traditional group psychotherapy approach may be less effective with this population than in a more middle-class population. Often, the most important thing offered in these groups is the ability to talk with others in a similar situation, a typical goal of the support group. As such, members will often exchange telephone numbers and contact each other outside of group. This is a decision discussed in group and accorded by the members. For some, family and personal issues may be significant enough to warrant a joint treatment of individual and support group, which is ideal but demands greater commitment from the participants and may pose a challenge in this time of managed mental health care.

CONCLUSION

The issues that arise in the psychotherapeutic treatment of HIV-positive Latino women need to be conceptualized and addressed within a culturally sensitive context. The therapist needs to develop an appreciation for the fear, shame, and isolation that is faced by this group, who have perceived themselves as being at no risk for HIV infection and lack the supports that are needed to cope with this situation. Psychotherapy can help these women to learn about HIV in a safe environment, accurately assess their capabilities, work through issues of shame, and begin to build a support system for themselves, all in the hope of allowing them to continue enjoying the fulfilling aspects of their life and developing the ability to cope with the more difficult times.

REFERENCES

Centers for Disease Control and Prevention. (1995). *HIV/AIDS surveillance report, 7*(2), 16.

Diaz, T., Buehler, J. W., Castro, K. G., & Ward, J. W. (1993). AIDS trends among Hispanics in the United States. *American Journal of Public Health, 83*, 504–509.

Fernandez, M. I. (1995). Latinas and AIDS: Challenges to HIV prevention efforts. In A. O'Leary & L. Jemmott (Eds.), *Women at risk: Issues in the primary prevention of AIDS*. New York: Plenum Press.

Guernaccia, P. J., Parra, P., Deschamps, A., Milstein, G., & Arguiles, N. (1992). Si Dios quiere: Hispanic families' experiences of caring for a mentally ill family member. *Culture, Medicine, and Psychiatry, 16*, 187–215.

Jenkins, J. H. (1988). Ethnopsychiatric interpretations of schizophrenic illness: The problem of "nervios" within Mexican-American families. *Culture, Medicine, and Psychiatry, 12*, 301–329.

Leiner, M. (1994). *Sexual politics in Cuba: Machismo, homosexuality, and AIDS*. Boulder, CO: Westview Press.

Martin, J. L. (1988). Psychological consequences of AIDS-related bereavement among gay men. *Journal of Consulting and Clinical Psychology, 56*, 856–862.

Perry, S., Fishman, B., Jacobsberg, L., & Frances, A. (1992). Relationships over 1 year between lymphocyte subsets and psychosocial variables among adults with infection by human immunodeficiency virus. *Archives of General Psychiatry, 49*, 396–401.

Ramos-McKay, J. M., Comas-Diaz, L., & Rivera, L. A. (1988). In L. Comas-Diaz & E. E. H. Griffith (Eds.), *Clinical guidelines in cross-cultural mental health*. New York: Wiley.

San Doval, A., Duran, R., O'Donnell, L., & O'Donnell, C. R. (1995). Barriers to condom use in primary and nonprimary relationships among Hispanic STD clinic patients. *Hispanic Journal of Behavioral Sciences, 17*, 385–397.

Sluzki, C. E. (1982). The Latin lover revisited. In M. McGoldrick, J. K. Pearce, & J. Giordano (Eds.), *Ethnicity and family therapy* (pp. 492–498). New York: Guilford Press.

Swerdlow, M. (1992). "Chronicity," "nervios," and community care: A case study of Puerto Rican psychiatric patients in New York City. *Culture, Medicine, and Psychiatry, 16*, 217–235.

Chapter 12

Stranger in a Strange Land: The Psychologist on the AIDS Unit

Maria R. Derevenco

"Shh," said Mr. J., one of the nurses, seemingly jokingly to Dr. B. "Don't you say any more, the psychologist will analyze you." Both dissolved into giggles as I approached them in the hallway. I had been on the unit for about 3 weeks.

Dr. L., a new psychology fellow, asked in multidisciplinary rounds for his assessment of Ms. A., explained that the patient's punitive introjects of her parents were the reason for her lack of cooperation with the staff. To his astonishment, the team moved on to the next case, as if he hadn't spoken.

INTRODUCTION AND BACKGROUND

The exchanges above are a clear message that the psychologists have left the (relative) comforts of the psychology clinic and the psychiatric ward and have become the "other" to the inhabitants of the medical world.

Words such as *multidisciplinary team* are misleading to the psychologist entering a medical setting: There are multidisciplinary teams in the outpatient clinic and on the psychiatric unit, but they are composed of clinicians with similar orientations, be they psychiatrists, psychiatric nurses, or social workers. Psychologists may feel like "junior citizens" in these settings, but they are citizens nonetheless, and can speak the language. This is not so on the medical ward. *PET scan* and *t.i.d.* have meaning to a psychologist who has rotated through an inpatient psychiatric service, but *crypt antigen* and *hematocrit* are in a foreign language.

Although there is a developing literature on psychologists' practice in hospitals (Dorken, 1993; Enright, Resnick, DeLeon, Sciara, & Tanney, 1990; Ludwigsen & Enright, 1988; to cite but a few), it is concerned with psychologists' roles and functions within mental health settings. So far, little has been written about psychologists on medical units. Miller and Swartz (1990) presented a frank and stimulating discussion of power issues in interprofessional relationships on medical wards; Orr and Wallack (1990) specifically addressed the role of the consultation–liaison psychologist on an AIDS team, in a model of care quite similar to the one described in this chapter; and Cummings (1992) highlighted general issues related to psychology on a medical service, some of which are also addressed in this chapter.

This chapter focuses on the psychologist's integration and functioning on the AIDS service rather than on work with patients. It is based on my experience of the past 8 years as the (now) senior psychologist for an AIDS program at a large academic medical center, and it also incorporates what I have learned through my psychiatrist teammates and by supervising six generations of postdoctoral psychology fellows.

The AIDS program at St. Luke's/Roosevelt Hospital Center in New York City was designated in 1987 by New York State to provide comprehensive care to AIDS patients and to train physicians in the treatment of HIV-related disease. The program began in fall 1987 with specialized inpatient units at each of the hospital's two sites. The program's outpatient service, staffed by the same clinicians, offers continuity of care to patients after the resolution of the acute medical crisis requiring hospitalization. All core staff members work on this service by choice; the medical house staff rotate monthly through the inpatient unit. There are weekly multidisciplinary rounds in which each patient's progress, needs, discharge plan, and follow-up care are discussed.

Although the state originally mandated a "vague 'case management' component to address the social and emotional needs of patients" (M. Grieco, personal communication, 1996), the hospital's Task Force on AIDS, co-led by the chairman of the Department of Medicine and director of the new program, decided from the beginning to include a position for a psychiatrist. A few months into the program's existence, when it became apparent that the patients presented a vast array of neuropsychological disturbances, a position for a psychologist with neuropsychological expertise was added.

The program planners intended the mental health component to be fully integrated into the service and independent of the funding vagaries of another department. Thus, a relatively uncommon organizational feature is that the psychiatrist and the psychologist are an integral part of the clinical–teaching staff of the program, funded by the Medicine Department, and are not on loan from the Psychiatry Department. The resulting structure is akin to Strain and Grossman's (1975) hybrid model of consultation–liaison, to Greenhill's (1977) critical care model of consultation–liaison, or, in the psychological literature, to Cummings's (1992) on-site model.

The actual role of the program's psychologist (beyond providing neuro-psychological assessments and traditional psychotherapeutic services to individual patients) was relatively undefined when the program began. Over several months of discussions with the associate medical director of our site and with my counterpart at the program's other site, it became clear that, in addition to neuropsychological and differential diagnosis and individual and group treatment, there were many needs for staff education, support, and team building. Thus, the psychologist's role came to encompass clinical work with patients as well as staff consultation.

Conceptual Framework: The Biopsychosocial Model and Mental Health Consultation

I approached the AIDS unit with great anticipation and enthusiasm, but also with anxiety. I had been trained in Caplan's (1970) model of mental health consultation, and I welcomed the opportunity to broaden my role beyond traditional work with individual patients. One of the first and most helpful readings on HIV/AIDS at the time was M. A. A. Cohen (1987), which opened the way for further explorations of the biopsychosocial model of understanding and treating illness. AIDS was recognized to require a biopsychosocial treatment approach because of its unique combination of devastating effects on all major organ systems, including the central nervous system, as well as on patients' psychological and social adaptation, owing to the fatal nature of the illness and to the stigmatization and prejudice associated with it (M. A. A. Cohen, 1987; Fullilove, 1989; Kelly & St. Lawrence, 1988; Lyons, Larson, Anderson, & Bilheimer, 1989; Tross & Hirsch, 1988). In addition, research in psychoneuroimmunology (Antoni, Schneiderman, Fletcher, & Goldstein, 1990; Gorman & Kertzner, 1990; Kiecolt-Glaser & Glaser, 1986, 1987) has demonstrated a link between stress, dysphoric affects, and immune dysfunction.

The biopsychosocial model, as articulated by Lipowsky (1967, 1975), Strain and Grossman (1975), Engel (1977), and Kimball (1979), among others, attempts to avoid the mind–body dualism of traditional medical practice and has contributed to the expansion of consultation–liaison psychiatry. Lipowsky (1967) and Levy (1989) provided in-depth historical reviews of the evolution of psychosomatic medicine (the theories about the connection between psychosocial factors and physical illness) and consultation–liaison psychiatry (the clinical application of these theories in medical settings). Such reviews are beyond the scope of this chapter but were instrumental in the conceptualization of the psychologist's functioning on the AIDS unit.

The psychologist's role on the AIDS team was modeled in the terms defined by Caplan (1970) and Strain and Grossman (1975). The *consult model* in psychiatry (Strain & Grossman, 1975) is similar to Caplan's (1970) *client–patient-centered consultation*. It is defined as an interaction between two professionals in which one, the consultant, is assisting the other, the consultee, with a particular problem related to work with a patient; crucial features are the consultee's continued responsibility for care and the freedom to accept or reject the assistance without penalty, similar to the traditional medical consultation. The advantages of functioning as a consultant are a degree of autonomy, independence, and status as an "expert"; however, this is counterbalanced by not being a full member of the team and by a loss of control over the implementation of one's recommendations.

The *liaison model* in psychiatry, as described by Strain and Grossman (1975), emphasizes formal teaching of medical personnel on psychosocial issues in addition to case consultation. In the liaison model, the psychiatrist is part of the unit and thus has broader license to define the scope and boundaries of a consult request and greater control over implementation of recommendations, partly because of continuous involvement with the team (see also Lipowsky, 1967; Miller & Swartz, 1990).

Consultee-centered consultation, as defined by Caplan (1970), is akin to, but somewhat broader than the liaison role described above. The need for this type of consultation results especially from lack of self-confidence or loss of professional objectivity in the consultee (Caplan, 1970). Because in this type of consultation the consultee is engaged in a very personal manner, it is particularly important to keep clear sight of her or his autonomy and of the boundaries between consultation and psychotherapy. Although consultee-centered consultation may be overtly sanctioned, or even requested and initiated by the staff, it is also likely to arouse the most resistance, as it evokes narcissistic vulnerabilities and defenses, such as devaluation and splitting (discussed in greater detail below).

In *program-centered consultation* (Caplan, 1970), the psychologist draws on expertise in systems theory, organizational issues, group dynamics, and research design to assist the program as a whole in efforts such as team building, program self-evaluation, or research development. The consultee is usually the program director or the program's leadership group (steering committee, quality assurance team, etc.). At times, my role has encompassed program-centered consultation as well as collaborative research projects (on house staff knowledge and attitudes about AIDS, the treatment of AIDS delirium, treatment adherence of AIDS patients with tuberculosis).

My functioning on the unit has been mostly based on the liaison model: Although I perform many patient-centered consultations, I am also part of the formal and informal policy-making committees of the unit and the program, and I participate in teaching the house officers and nursing staff.

The Limits of the Biopsychosocial Model:
On Avoiding Psychological Reductionism

A vast majority of the psychosomatic literature has been an attempt to counterbalance the bias of the medical model by emphasizing the influence of the psyche over the soma. Biological reductionism deemphasizes the patient's psychological makeup and needs. However, a great deal of psychological reductionism was evident in many classic psychosomatic models (Alexander, 1950; Deutsch, 1959; Dunbar, 1935; Schur, 1955; Sperling, 1967), which posited clear causative connections between personality traits and psychological states on the one hand and illness on the other. Although clearly an oversimplification of the psyche–soma relationship, psychological reductionism is promoted by various popular self-help and New Age writers and lecturers, some of whom are influential in the HIV/AIDS community.

An important issue, also discussed by Cummings (1992), became obvious after a short time on the AIDS unit, namely, the relevance of the somatopsychic as opposed to the psychosomatic direction of the mind–body relationship. Misperception of the directionality of this relationship by the staff, a quite common occurrence, leads to underdiagnosis of AIDS-related medical problems.

> A psychology intern came to supervision with the test protocol of a 32-year-old Haitian woman admitted with first-onset psychotic symptoms, including confusion, disorientation, delusions, and hallucinations, and provisionally diagnosed with schizophrenia. I was immediately suspicious, as the onset of psychotic symptoms at the patient's age is highly unusual. As we reviewed the materials, it became obvious that the patient had focal neuropsychological deficits not congruent with psychosis. There was no available sexual history, other than that she had a 6-year-old son, and no assessment of HIV risk behaviors. On further inquiry by the intern, it was discovered that the patient had had several episodes of pneumonia (of unknown etiology), that both she and her son had been sick fairly often in the past year or so. The patient agreed to HIV testing for herself and her son; both were diagnosed with HIV infection. The patient was transferred to the AIDS unit and diagnosed with delirium; her workup revealed an AIDS-related brain infection.

As Sontag (1983) eloquently pointed out, finding psychological meaning is an attempt to gain (illusory) control over a terminal illness. This seems particularly true with regard to AIDS. Because the pressure of the soma on an AIDS service is more intense than on a regular medical–surgical unit as a result of the patients' fatal prognosis, there may be a tendency to counterbalance it by attributing illness manifestations to psychological factors. Many requests for consults, from physicians as well as nurses, refer to supposedly highly anxious or manipulative or unmotivated patients who are in fact either floridly delirious as a result of yet-undiagnosed underlying medical conditions or suffering from HIV-related dementia. Similarly and predictably, every July the new psychology fellows misinterpret the findings of mental status exams as evidence of psychological distress, when in fact the patients are profoundly demented or in a stuporous stage of delirium.

Notwithstanding the somatic pressure, the psychologist has to strive to maintain a balanced focus on the patient as a whole person, on his or her illness and immediate medical needs, on psychological needs and issues, and on the patient within the context of the ward at a particular time, and to balance a systemic view with an individualized one.

INTEGRATION ON AN INPATIENT AIDS UNIT

This section addresses, in practical terms, the psychologist's integration on an inpatient AIDS unit. The presentation is approached from a systemic perspective, as an interaction of the consultant with the environment, and is organized around the three domains of the biopsychosocial model.

THE BIOLOGICAL DOMAIN

At the risk of restating the obvious, it should be emphasized that it is essential for the psychologist to be as knowledgeable as possible about HIV/AIDS and associated opportunistic infections, about the various medications used in their treatment, and about their multiple side effects (including many psychological and psychiatric side effects), as well as about drug interactions. This is necessary not only to gain credibility with patients and colleagues, but also to avoid misdiagnosis and possible harm to the patient. During my first year on the unit, I mistakenly attributed a patient's requests for higher doses of methadone to drug-seeking behavior when the patient was in fact approaching withdrawal because one of his tuberculosis medications accelerated the metabolization of methadone. Fortunately, the drug liaison nurse caught my error and taught the entire staff about this drug interaction, which was unknown even to the physicians.

The psychologist may be the clinician who spends most private time with a patient, and thus may be told of complaints or symptoms that have not been reported to the medical staff. On several occasions during mental status interviews, patients questioned about hallucinations have reported visual phenomena such as seeing strings or bits of things, which are in fact "floaters" associated with *Cytomegalovirus* retinitis; they had not complained about these symptoms out of fear of being thought "crazy" by the nurses or physicians.

THE SOCIAL DOMAIN

Understanding the Environment

The psychologist entering a non–mental health setting such as an AIDS unit has to keep in mind the process nature of this undertaking. Lipowsky's (1967) and Caplan's (1970) reflections on this matter, written from a psychiatrist's point of view, remain germane for psychologists today, particularly with regard to the entry stage.

The psychologist on a medical unit has to spend time and energy observing the new environment and learning about its formal and informal organizational, authority, and communication structures. It is desirable to form a relationship with a "native" of the culture, who can become a valuable guide on its mores and customs. It is also important to discover which individuals wield social influence in the environment, to understand the attributes that lead to this position, and to form an alliance with such individuals in order to gain credibility with the team.

On our staff, there are two or three nurses, veterans of the team, liked and respected by most people, who wield uncanny power of acceptance or rejection. Woe to the medical intern, junior attending physician, or any other new staff member who displeases them by being arrogant, not hard-working enough, lacking in humor, and so forth (I have yet to figure out all their criteria), because that person will never make it on the team.

As a novice in the medical territory, the psychologist must learn the language of the land in order to survive and to gain credibility in the eyes of teammates and patients alike (many AIDS patients are extremely knowledgeable medically). A good medical dictionary such as *Stedman's* (1990) is a must, as is a basic text such as the *Merck Manual* (Berkov, 1992) or Isselbacher et al.'s (1994) *Harrison's Principles of Internal Medicine.* Basic knowledge of human anatomy and physiology is assumed; if this is lacking, one must go back either to undergraduate texts or, failing that, to the reference library. Even faint memories of Latin can help one decipher the etymology of most medical terms.

Our fellows are requested to keep running lists of words, abbreviations, and concepts they do not know and to review them with the dictionary or in supervision; in my experience, it takes only a few months to achieve basic mastery.

A related issue is the ability to read chart notes as well as laboratory reports and other diagnostic tests. The fellows are carefully taught these skills, as there have been many instances in which a behavioral disturbance was in fact attributable to a yet-undiagnosed medical condition.

The unit staff is organized in a hierarchical structure focused on quick solutions to critical situations: The purpose of the acute care setting is to get patients better and ready for discharge as soon as possible. The psychologist must be able to tolerate the hierarchy and the fact that it is the physicians who have ultimate responsibility for the patients. There is also a need to recognize and deal with the tendency to marginalize those who are not "real" doctors. As Lipowsky (1967) observed early on, and Miller and Swartz (1990) and Belar and Deardorff (1987) have noted, when physicians' attitudes about psychological issues vary from ambivalent to hostile, even benevolent skepticism is welcome.

A more egalitarian and collaborative relationship with physician colleagues is facilitated by a strong sense of one's expertise, internal locus of control, awareness of and tolerance of competitiveness and conflict, availability and flexibility in dealing with consult requests, and a nondefensive, nonaggressive approach on the psychologist's part. Stressing commonality of goals while acknowledging different areas of expertise has seemed to be a productive stance.

As a corollary to the above, the consultant's presentations and notes have to be brief, relevant, and to the point, answering the referral question in concrete terms. Recommendations, in particular, must be clear, detailed, and directed at the appropriate target, be it the physician, the nurse, or other personnel. One must unlearn some of the psychological jargon that is likely to be devalued as "psychobabble" by the medical or nursing staff.

It has been helpful to communicate recommendations directly (in person or by phone) to the staff members involved, as notes can be read cursorily or not at all, and to document the communication in chart notes. This has been an effective way to consolidate relationships with staff and to counteract the possible marginalization of the psychologist's findings and recommendations.

Last but not least, the consultant should be sensitive to multicultural issues. Particularly in New York City, staff members and patients come from many different countries; their world views, values, and customs may be quite distinct from the current U.S. norms.

Some of the more salient issues encountered on our unit have included attitudes about illness and death, the role of the family in caring for the sick; privacy or secrecy of family matters, the patient–doctor relationship and patient autonomy, confidentiality, hierarchical relationships and responses to authority, and prejudice against the groups at highest risk for HIV infection, homosexuals and drug users.

Cultural differences pose problems in staff–patient relationships and also in the interactions among staff members. For example, male physicians-in-training and patients from cultures where women are not treated as equals respond defensively or contemptuously to women in authority positions, whereas their female counterparts tend to be overly submissive and lacking in assertiveness.

Difficult as it may be, the psychologist should attempt to not respond countertransferentially, but to maintain an empathic stance and get involved in efforts to educate the staff and reduce prejudice (such as mentorship, teaching experientially, etc., now undertaken by many medical institutions).

BECOMING PART OF THE UNIT

To function effectively on an AIDS unit, the psychologist as stranger to the medical world must acquire what has been termed *referent power*, in addition to *expert power* (French & Raven, 1959). Simply put, the consultant must become someone the consultees can relate to and identify with, a member of the group used as a standard for attitudes and behaviors (the referent group); this is based on perceived similarities of motivations, beliefs, and behaviors between consultant and consultee.

The consultant should actively seek to get to know the rest of the team and allow them to become familiar with her or him. This is achieved by spending as much time as possible with team members and seeking out informal venues for contact, such as hanging out at the nursing station, engaging in every kind of small or big talk, going to lunch at the cafeteria, and asking about teammates' work at opportune moments.

The most crucial factor in establishing credibility and acceptance by the staff is being of practical help (Lipowsky, 1967). However, early on in the entry stage, attempts to do so may be frustrated by unconscious processes involved in what I've termed the "test case" (discussed below).

Some difficulties of the entry stage of consultation can be traced to what Caplan (1970, p. 54) termed "distortions of perceptions and expectations," illustrated by the first vignette at the beginning of this chapter. The consultant, a stranger entering the system, appears to set off powerful anxieties in the consultees, particularly around issues of narcissistic vulnerability. The psychologist may be perceived as a mind reader or analyst, a theme I encountered numerous times during my first year on the AIDS unit. Latent, covert communications of these distorted perceptions tend to be numerous and at times difficult to detect; the consultant must be especially vigilant about them and must counteract them overtly and vigorously. An example of such covert communications are staff "jokes" about my being a "shrink" or "analyzing" people; I respond in similarly humorous but clear ways by saying that I'm busy enough with the patients and don't need additional work; that I get to do all the "shrinking" I want at my private office; or some other such remark.

Overt communications of such distorted perceptions involve open requests for advice or psychotherapy for a staff member or relative of a staff member. However seductive such requests may be, appearing to indicate trust and respect, they should be refused in a polite but clear manner by indicating that the nature of the relationship is collegial, not therapeutic, and that issues of privacy and confidentiality would be compromised in a dual relationship and by offering an appropriate referral. In a crisis situation, the psychologist should offer common human comfort and encourage the staff member to seek immediate relief by informing the responsible supervisor of the crisis.

A first-year medical intern with whom I had a good working relationship during his rotation on the AIDS unit approached me on the intensive care floor where I was following up on one of my patients. He was highly distressed, having just found out that his very young sister was pregnant. He was terrified about his parents' reaction, as he was from a very traditional and religious family; he was also enraged at his sister and her boyfriend. He felt he was too upset to work and wanted to set up an appointment with me at my private office for that evening. I sat with him in a conference room for about 15 minutes, offering an empathic ear and trying to reassure him that his worst fears might not come to pass; I also suggested that he inform the attending physician of his inability to focus on work and that he request the rest of the shift off, and I offered to refer him to a colleague. All this was done. For the next year and a half, whenever we ran into each other in the hallway, he was clearly eager to avoid me. At the beginning of his rotation as a third-year resident, he approached me in a warm manner and told me the relatively happy ending of the story, acknowledging that things had worked out well by following my suggestions.

Another issue of particular relevance at the entry stage is that of "turf." Staff members whose area of expertise and activity are closest to that of the psychologist seem to fear being undermined or made redundant by the new consultant's presence. Thus, although I have not been able to find any references to this in the literature, I have experienced (and heard about it many times from other psychologists on multidisciplinary teams) overt or covert conflicts between social workers already in the system and the newly introduced psychologist. Such turf issues emerge periodically on our unit, too, and the most successful mode of handling them has been to disengage as early and as politely as possible, avoiding one-upmanship at all costs; "processing" these issues is most often counterproductive. Usually, such conflicts arise around patients or professional activities perceived as too valuable to share. For example, a social worker who has been seeing a patient in individual psychotherapy may be threatened when the physician requests a psychological or psychiatric consult, feeling the patient and the much-prized therapy case may be taken away. Turf issues seem to recede as the psychologist becomes more established on the unit, only to reemerge as a response to systemic stress.

On our unit there has been little if any turf conflict between psychologists and psychiatrists, in spite of many anecdotal references to this issue. Mutual respect, at the very least, has been the rule, as the psychologists and psychiatrists have almost always formed strong bonds as teammates who support and complement each other.

THE PSYCHOLOGICAL DOMAIN

Goodness of Fit: Consultant Characteristics and System Demands

The importance of professional identity, of preferred modes of interaction and communication, and of personal needs and style became especially apparent through the struggles of several supervisees who experienced their time on the AIDS unit as ultimately disappointing.

A psychologist with a high need for external validation, for example, will not do well on an AIDS unit: As a consultant, she or he is unlikely to be a focus of attention. Furthermore, because of the high level of stress, the staff may not be available to give much praise for one's good work. Similarly, someone who works best under structured conditions is ill suited for consultation work, which is erratic by nature and requires a high level of frustration tolerance (see also Belar & Deardorff, 1987, regarding these issues).

Psychologists, particularly recent graduates, who tend to be overinvested in long-term, insight-oriented treatment, are likely to be disappointed on an AIDS unit. The pace of the service is too rapid, and the patients often too ill to engage in long-term treatment; regular appointments are a rarity as patients are whisked off the unit at any moment for tests and procedures. There is little, if any privacy, and boundaries are often hard to maintain (e.g., when two of the psychologist's patients share the same room). This is not to say one cannot do psychodynamic psychotherapy in the hospital, only that it cannot be expected to be the major part of the psychologist's work and that one needs to be prepared to also use other treatment modalities more congruent with the AIDS unit setting.

The psychologist needs to be aware of personal limits of tolerance for gruesome multimodal stimulation, as the AIDS unit often provides a veritable assault on all the senses, with sights, smells, and sounds not encountered in traditional settings of psychologists' work. If one has particular sensitivities or phobias, it is best to try to limit exposure.

> A few years ago, I was urgently called to the unit because the psychology fellow was in a dead faint in the middle of the hallway; the fellow, with a known sensitivity to the sight of blood, had wanted to comfort a patient while the nurse was reinserting an IV. Medical attention was promptly and sympathetically rendered, but the incident is still remembered years later.

The psychologist's self-presentation is an important element in becoming a successful member of the AIDS team. My observations coincide with those of Belar and Deardorff (1987) and Schenkenberg, Peterson, Wood, and DaBell (1981), in that a "shrinklike" manner is a deterrent to the psychologist's integration on the unit. Staff psychologists and fellows who were overly identified with a psychoanalytic stance and presented themselves in a remote, reserved, underactive manner and who spent their time in the office with the door closed were never truly accepted and given credibility by the staff.

An open, active, and engaging approach will increase acceptance by medical personnel. It is important not to wait to be called in emergencies, but to be as present as possible on the unit and to reach out to help.

NARCISSISTIC VULNERABILITY AND THE CONSULTATION PROCESS

"I'm Not Crazy and I Won't Talk to You": Patients' Narcissistic Vulnerability

This is often the first response from many patients the psychologist is asked to evaluate. Unlike at the clinic or in the private office, the AIDS patients on the ward seldom initiate a request for psychological help; most times, the medical intern, or even the private attending physician, has mentioned only in passing, if at all, the intent to seek a psychological consult; the patient's formal consent is not required for such a consult, as it would be for physical tests or procedures. The patients are always medically acutely ill, debilitated, often confused, and almost always focused on their most pressing somatic complaints. Under these circumstances, the psychologist must be aware that, together with the patient, she or he has to generate a mandate for assessment and intervention; otherwise, the patient may have problems, but may not experience needs for intervention (Erskine, 1995, p. 45). Unless patient and psychologist can construct a joint understanding of the (medical) presenting problem that calls for psychological intervention, any further contact is perceived by the patient at best as irrelevant and surely as intrusive.

There are particular problems of respecting personal autonomy and dignity when the patients require acute care but may be in no position to make informed decisions about their condition or needs.

> Mr. Z., a 38-year-old man who had known of his HIV infection for a few years, was admitted to the hospital for the first time with chills and a fever of a few days' duration. During his first night on the unit he spiked a fever of 105 °F and became confused, agitated, and uncooperative with staff's attempts to alleviate his discomfort, such as providing him with a cooling blanket. In the morning, when the psychologist was called to consult, she found Mr. Z. very agitated; his roommate was dying, gasping for air and moaning, a most frightening companion. (On inquiring, she was told by the head nurse that it was night and there were no other beds; the roommate was not to be resuscitated; the patient would be moved as soon as a bed became available.) As the psychologist introduced herself, Mr. Z. immediately dismissed her, stating that he was a sick man, in the hospital for the first time, subject to abysmal treatment; he could not sleep because of the gasps of his dying roommate; he did not need a psychologist, he needed a change of room. The psychologist reassured him that the staff did not think him crazy, but that they were concerned about the effects of this first hospitalization on him and because when people run a fever as high as he had, there are effects on the brain that need to be monitored. The psychologist also assured him that his reaction to his dying roommate was totally understandable, that he had every reason to be upset, and that the staff was already trying to change his room. At that point, Mr. Z. acknowledged how scared he was and admitted to confusion, disorientation, and hallucinations indicative of delirium. He responded well to an explanation of what delirium is, to recommendations for a central nervous system workup, and for neuroleptics. As the tests established his delirium was caused by a brain infection, he was treated and improved markedly over a few days. After discharge, he came to the clinic for psychotherapy based on the alliance that had been formed during his hospitalization.

This patient was right, in a way: He did not need a psychologist as much as he needed a change of room. However, he very much needed to have his delirium diagnosed and the underlying cause treated as soon as possible. This example illustrates the extreme vulnerability of the medically ill patient faced with the hospital system, the need for the psychologist to be aware of and sensitive to the realities of patient concerns, and the importance of forging an alliance based on the basic needs expressed by the patient. This case also highlights the common practice of patients' concealing or denying problems, psychological or medical, because of intense fear about their implications or meanings. As a therapeutical alliance develops, there is an opportunity to offer support as well as to explore the psychological aspects and meaning of the illness.

THE AIDS UNIT AS A NARCISSISTICALLY VULNERABLE SYSTEM

Although psychologists are used to understanding individuals in terms of narcissistic pathology, this conceptualization has also been used to describe system dynamics in organizations, notably by Harris and Bergman (1986). Several factors appear to contribute to narcissistic vulnerability of the AIDS service.

First, the AIDS unit and its staff are confronted daily with the "incurability paradox" (Stern & Minskoff, 1979): Terminally ill patients are by definition not curable, yet medical personnel are trained to cure, and feel effective only by restoring the patient to health. The failure to achieve a sense of mastery over the disease is a constant source of narcissistic injury. This was especially true in the earlier stages of the epidemic, when fewer weapons against the disease were available, but it remains a highly charged issue even now, especially with regard to terminally ill patients.

Another source of vulnerability is the staff's identification with their patients. The social stigmatization and rejection of AIDS patients has been well documented (see Blendon & Donelan, 1988; Gerber et al., 1989; among others); it also seems to extend to those institutions and individuals caring for people deemed fearful and contemptible (Blumenfield et al., 1987).

The staff of the AIDS unit deals with patients suffering not only the effects of an acute trauma (the illness requiring hospitalization), but also of chronic stress trauma (Sandler, 1967) of a terminal illness. In a parallel process, the staff is multiply and repeatedly traumatized in caring for these very ill people. AIDS has been aptly defined as "an attack on the self" (Cohen & Abramowitz, 1990); this reverberates powerfully from patients to staff by means of projective identification.

The AIDS unit staff receives powerful, primitive projections from the terminally ill patients, who unconsciously perceive the staff as the omnipotent parent who can make everything right and whose power is envied and feared. These projective identifications, while warding off intolerable feelings in the patient, evoke them in the staff. As they are difficult to contain and process, these feelings are likely to be further projected onto the consultant (see also Moylan & Jureidini, 1995, regarding this issue).

One of the most powerful fears in patients and staff (and in consultants) is that of being evaluated and appraised (Erskine, 1995), *looked at* as opposed to *looked after* (Winnicott, 1974). This seems to be the source of Caplan's (1970) "distortions of perceptions and expectations" (p. 54). Instead of the empathic "mirror," the "other" becomes a threat, akin to the mythical Gorgon whose powers are feared (Erskine, 1995, p. 50).

EFFECTS OF SYSTEMIC NARCISSISTIC
VULNERABILITY ON THE CONSULTATION PROCESS

Conceptualizing the AIDS unit as a narcissistically vulnerable system allows the consultant to understand such puzzling phenomena as the "test case" mentioned earlier and other failures of seemingly welcomed, well-intended consultation efforts.

The Test Case

This is ostensibly a request for a consult on a patient perceived by the staff, at that moment, as very difficult, if not the most difficult, in spite of the fact that such patients have been managed successfully before the consultant's arrival. The definition of the patient as beyond the staff's capacity, and the denial of the staff's ability to deal with the situation, is an expression of fantasies, wishes, and fears of the consultant's omnipotence. The unwary consultant, finally feeling useful and accepted as a helper, may welcome the overt request, as well as the unconscious attribution of omnipotence. As proven by my own experience as well as that of the fellows, this is a grave mistake, doomed as a means of proving oneself. By assuming sole responsibility for the problem, the consultant accepts the omnipotence fantasized and at the same time feared by the staff. However, the psychologist most likely cannot produce significant changes in the patient "bequeathed" to her or him by the staff. This failure sets the stage for staff's projection of powerlessness onto the consultant, and for subsequent devaluation. After I played my part a few times in this scenario, it became apparent that the only viable approach to the test case is to involve the whole team in whatever solution one devises.

> In my first month on the unit, I was called to consult on a young man admitted for treatment of Herpes Zoster (requiring contact isolation) and *Pneumocystis carinii* pneumonia. The reason for the consult request was the patient's unwillingness to respect the isolation precautions and his lack of cooperation with the intravenous medication; he was also abusive to staff members and made excessive demands for anxiolytics. In spite of my prior knowledge and experience of consultation, my first attempts to resolve the problem were directed solely at working with the patient. I did manage to establish good rapport with him, saw him daily, and taught him progressive relaxation to help him deal with anxiety. He reported some relief, but this did not influence his behavior on the unit. However, he became "my patient" in the eyes of the staff. After about 10 days, the head nurse complained publicly, in rounds, that whatever I was doing wasn't working, and asked the psychiatrist to order restraints or sedation for the patient. Under the sting of humiliation, I seemed to instantly regain my consultation skills. I proposed that before restraining him, we should, as a team, agree on a set of acceptable and unacceptable behaviors for this patient, develop a behavioral plan including rewards and consequences, and contract with him for a few days. The attending physician, the head nurse, and myself went to the patient and clearly defined acceptable and unacceptable behaviors and

what rewards and penalties he could expect. The patient agreed to the contract only reluctantly and angrily, but his behavior changed dramatically in the next few days. Months later, I was told by one of the nurses that the idea of using the team to set limits had been praised by the head nurse in the nursing meeting the following week, during which she expressed for the first time her satisfaction at having a psychologist on staff.

Splitting

Defensive splitting and us-versus-them attitudes are another consequence of narcissistic vulnerability in the system, occurring at times when the staff feels particularly powerless (when most patients on the unit are critically ill, when there are multiple deaths on the unit in a short period, or under threats of budget cuts or layoffs). Splits can occur between staff and patients, or between staff groups (nurses versus social workers, nonphysicians versus physicians, nurses and social workers versus psychologists). The psychologist has to be wary of engaging either part of the split, as well as of interpreting it from an outsider's perspective.

> Early on in my tenure on the unit, during rounds about a dying patient who was ambivalent about further treatment, to the frustration of the resident, but seemingly abetted by several of the nurses, I made what I thought was an astute interpretation regarding the intrapsychic origins of the split within the patient. Both nurses and resident dismissed my statement in derisive and hostile terms, as it was not relevant to their understanding of the situation and ignored their own plight in trying to deal with this patient.

Devaluation

Yet another narcissistic systemic defense is the devaluation of the consultant. The status of stranger on the AIDS unit facilitates the devaluation of the psychologist's contributions when these threaten the system's defensive balance. Just as the narcissistic patient cannot tolerate the analyst's separate subjectivity as manifested in interpretations, nor the state of needing and envying the powerful analyst, the narcissistically vulnerable system will either ignore the consultant's direct interpretations (or interventions perceived as interpretations) or will respond with hostility and rejection. This seems to explain many consultation failures described in the literature (see also Lipowsky, 1967; Gandlin, 1985). Moylan and Jureidini (1995) described two failed consultation efforts taking place simultaneously in England and Australia, eerily similar to the experience described below.

> The head nurse of a medical ward that functioned for a time as a satellite unit for the AIDS program requested that I run a support group for her nurses, who were finding it difficult to work with AIDS patients and had expressed an interest in a forum to discuss their feelings. After much effort, a time was set for weekly meet-

ings, but for a good number of weeks, when I went to that unit at the appointed time, the staff was too busy, there was a crisis, or some other event precluded the group meeting. After a few more weeks, the head nurse started designating participants to go to group, amid much grumbling from the very people supposedly in need of support. The staff complained that the group itself was becoming a stressor. When I decided to put a formal end to the meetings, the nurses expressed much regret and wanted to continue.

IMPLICATIONS FOR THE CONSULTATION PROCESS

The psychologist's awareness of and sensitivity to the issues discussed above dictates a consultative stance based on respect for the consultees' strengths as well as for their vulnerability and an appreciation of the shared nature of the experience of caring for fatally ill patients.

The staff deserves what Taylor (1987) described as the introspective–empathic approach, with the goal of assisting them in achieving increased self-regulation and decreasing the sense of loneliness and powerlessness in the face of illness. Several issues seem relevant in this regard.

First, just as in working with medical patients, the consultant must take into account the staff's self-defined needs and priorities and jointly construct a mandate for any intervention, so that the consultant's actions and statements are not experienced as unwanted and intrusive. It is particularly important to keep in mind that the consultant, especially if functioning as a member of the team, has not been chosen as team therapist, and it is therefore advisable to refrain from interventions that may be perceived as psychoanalyzing the staff.

I have found that inclusive "we" statements, in which I place myself explicitly alongside the staff, can be easily heard. Switching the focus from causal inquiries about the problem (which can be experienced as finger pointing and assigning blame) to defining the effects of the problem on all concerned has proven to be an effective intervention strategy. In a similar situation to that described above, in which the staff was split around a patient's ambivalence about further treatment, instead of interpreting the split, I chose to address the effects of the patient's indecision on all of us: Namely that the patient was handling his own agonized feelings by seemingly delegating to us the decision-making task. Such interventions also take into account the fact that the staff is part of a broader system, which includes the patient and a superordinate entity, the hospital, each with their own particular demands.

Without feeling omnipotent or patronizing, the consultant should aspire to fulfill the holding role of the good-enough parent (Winnicott, 1974), who reflects back to the child its sense of uniqueness and aliveness and who can function as a protective filter (Judd, 1995) of otherwise unendurable experiences.

Besides always offering an empathic and calm response to staff anguish, one way to fulfill this function is to reframe the tasks faced by consultees.

Decreasing the distance between the demands of the ego ideal and the individual's actual capacity to achieve a desired result minimizes the risk of narcissistic injury and of further traumatization.

In a rather typical situation on the AIDS unit, the staff is faced with the patient who is ambivalently facing death, on the one hand refusing further tests and procedures and on the other unable to make a decision about going to a skilled nursing facility. The staff vacillates between suggesting aggressive measures, such as a brain biopsy (or insertion of a feeding tube, or some such invasive procedure), and pressuring the patient to agree to not being resuscitated. A reframing of the team's goal from providing a cure to providing care usually results in a decrease in tension in the staff, and in some reasonable compromise solution, such as sending the patient home with hospice care.

COUNTERTRANSFERENCE ISSUES

A literature too rich to even cite here discusses countertransferential reactions in psychotherapy. It should be emphasized that I use the term countertransference in the totalist sense (Kernberg, 1975), as a phenomenon emerging within an interpersonal field, with both conscious and unconscious aspects, and that can be put to use to deepen the understanding of the interaction between patient and therapist.

The Choice to Work on an AIDS Unit

An obvious first issue is one's choice of doing this type of work. Not only have I been asked this question countless times by friends, colleagues, and strangers, but I ask it of myself every year as I probe the fellowship applicants' motivations. Regardless of the reasons given as an answer, it seems that working with AIDS patients always fulfills some deeply personal, only partly conscious (if at all conscious) need of the consultant. It can be an unconsciously counterphobic reaction, a desire to go right up against fears of death or loss; an attempt at rescue and reparation; a wish to bargain with fate through engagement with the most frightening plague; or a fantasy of omnipotence. Or it could be all of the above, and maybe more.

Fears of Contagion

In spite of any rational understanding of HIV transmission risks, most trainees appear to experience fear of HIV infection within a short time of starting work on the unit. The unconscious origins of this terror appear to be multidetermined and related to complex, highly personal issues of identity and to dread of identification with feared aspects of one's self. Usually this fear is kept private and fosters a sense of shame about one's own irrationality and vulnerability (Frederick, 1996). It may become public only through the expression of other, less charged somatic complaints: When in September the fellows begin to take days off for illness and report frequent visits to the employee health service with seemingly trivial complaints, we now know it's time to bring up fears about HIV and to encourage them to explore these issues in supervision or in their own therapy.

Omnipotence

Medical personnel directly at risk for HIV infection often appear to express fear of contagion in counterphobic ways, by neglecting or ignoring universal precautions, such as handling specimens or sharp instruments without using gloves. Psychologists' reactions of omnipotence manifest predominantly as unreasonable expectations of successful work with difficult patients. For example, in a scenario often repeated, a fellow will misjudge the severe character pathology of a patient with a long-term drug addiction and will attempt to advocate for some special privilege for the patient, such as going on a pass, arguing that through their joint work the patient is ready to give up drug use; invariably, whenever such pleas are heeded, the patient's toxicology screen on return to the unit is found to be positive for illegal drugs.

Difficulties in Dealing with Death

The AIDS unit as a whole seems involved in the uneasy handling of death typical of this time and place (Nuland, 1994; Ruitenbeek, 1969). As a result, patients' deaths are rarely acknowledged in a public manner, even when they happen within minutes of our team rounds; exceptions are patients who have been particularly dear to the staff for various reasons (such as long-time survival or appealing personal characteristics). It took several years of gentle prodding by the then-chaplain and a few other staff members to find a solution to this problem. We now have a Death Book in which every patient's passing is recorded; the book disappears periodically and unaccountably from its usual place, only to reemerge just as mysteriously, hardly having missed a death. The amazing accuracy of this book seems to embody the highly efficient grapevine that communicates the news of patients' deaths no matter where and when they occur; one just has to be in the loop to find out.

Dealing with Grief

The socially constructed structures of grief do not define or prescribe a role for nonfamily caregivers in the mourning process. Thus, the psychologist working with AIDS patients is often at a loss as to the professionally and socially appropriate response to a patient's death. Going to the funeral, the writing of condolence notes, and ongoing contact with the former patient's significant others are issues not addressed in our professional training and etiquette. These are wrenching questions, particularly for the psychodynamically oriented psychologist, imbued with concepts of abstinence and neutrality.

A former fellow recently asked me if I considered it odd that several of his now-dead patients are still vivid presences in his mind, several years after he completed his training. While assuring him that I personally found this absolutely normal, as I still think in this way about patients who have been dead for nearly a decade, I also had to tell him that some colleagues, not involved with AIDS work, have responded to me as odd when I mentioned this.

Fragmented Perceptions of the Patient

The psychologist on the AIDS unit, like the rest of the staff sitting in multidisciplinary rounds every week, is often familiar with a patient's most intimate physiological functions before ever encountering the patient, who may not be referred for consultation for some time. Although it may be vital to attend to the soma, this may prevent the psychologist from fully entering the patient's psychic world. An example of this phenomenon is the difficulty faced by the fellows in obtaining a full history and in generating a diagnostic formulation of their AIDS patients. It is as if the patient can only exist in the present and can only be perceived as fragmentary images. This countertransferential response seems to reflect, in a parallel process, the patient's own sense of self-fragmentation and disconnection in response to the massive somatic attack of the HIV infection (Cohen & Abramowitz, 1990). It requires sustained, conscious effort to maintain a focus on the internal world of the patient as a whole.

Psychic Numbing

Lifton (1976) discussed an inability to feel and an incongruence of knowledge and feeling in response to trauma, which is distinct from denial. Numbing is an ongoing countertransference danger on the AIDS unit, one that threatens to turn patients into cases and humane caregivers into rote reporters of grievous physiological damage. The shielding function of numbing extracts a heavy cost in lost opportunities for connection, no matter how painful these may be.

CONCLUSION

The medical wards, and the AIDS unit in particular, are challenging environments for psychologists. At the same time, these settings provide unique opportunities for broadening psychological practice and for bridging the gaps in the biopsychosocial model. A firm grounding in both behavioral neuropsychology and a psychodynamic understanding of behavior, though rarely offered together during doctoral training, allows psychologists to bring relevant contributions to patient care and to participate more productively as partners in the medical system.

As patterns of practice in psychology are changing, with fewer opportunities in long-term psychotherapeutic work, and as the medical system emphasizes primary care, psychologists can develop new and expanded roles in health care. This would require changes in the training and socialization of psychologists to allow them to function effectively in nontraditional settings.

REFERENCES

Alexander, F. (1950). *Psychosomatic medicine*. New York: Norton.

Antoni, M. H., Schneiderman, N., Fletcher, M. A., & Goldstein, D. A. (1990). Psychoneuroimmunology and HIV-1. *Journal of Consulting and Clinical Psychology, 58*, 38–49.

Belar, C. D., & Deardorff, W. W. (1987). *The practice of clinical health psychology*. Oxford, UK: Pergamon Press.

Berkov, R. (Ed.). (1992). *Merck manual of diagnosis and treatment* (16th ed.). Rahway, NJ: Merck Research Laboratories.

Blendon, R. J., & Donelan, K. (1988). Discrimination against people with AIDS: The public's perspective. *New England Journal of Medicine, 319*(5), 1022–1026.

Blumenfield, M., Smith, P., Milazzo, J., & Seropian, S. (1987). Survey of attitudes of nurses working with AIDS patients. *General Hospital Psychiatry, 9*(1), 58–63.

Caplan, G. (1970). *The theory and practice of mental health consultation*. New York: Basic Books.

Cohen, J., & Abramowitz, S. (1990). AIDS attacks the self: A self-psychological exploration of the psychodynamic consequences of AIDS. In A. Goldberg (Ed.), *Progress in self psychology* (pp. 157–172). Hillsdale, NJ: Analytic Press.

Cohen, M. A. A. (1987). Psychiatric aspects of AIDS: A biopsychosocial perspective. In G. P. Wormser, R. H. Stahl, & E. J. Bottone (Eds.), *AIDS and other manifestations of HIV infection* (pp. 579–621). Park Ridge, NJ: Noyes.

Cummings, J. W. (1992). Psychologists in the medical-surgical setting: Some reflections. *American Psychologist, 23*, 76–79.

Deutsch, F. (1959). *On the mysterious leap from the mind to the body*. New York: International Universities Press.

Dorken, H. (1993). The hospital practice of psychology: CHAMPUS 1981-1991. *American Psychologist, 48*, 409–417.

Dunbar, H. F. (1935). *Emotions and bodily changes*. New York: Columbia University Press.

Engel, G. L. (1977, April 8). The need for a new medical model: A challenge for biomedicine. *Science, 196*(4286), 129–136.

Enright, M., Resnick, R., DeLeon, P., Sciara, A. D., & Tanney, F. (1990). The practice of psychology in hospital settings. *American Psychologist, 45*(9), 1059–1065.

Erskine, A. (1995). The initial contact. In A. Erskine & D. Judd (Eds.), *The imaginative body: Psychodynamic therapy in health care* (pp. 43–59). Northvale, NJ: Jason Aronson.

Frederick, R. (1996, August). *Internalized homophobia: Theoretical and clinical implications*. Paper presented at the Annual Convention of the American Psychological Association, Toronto, Ontario, Canada.

French, J. R. P., Jr., & Raven, B. (1959). The bases of social power. In D. Cartwright (Ed.), *Studies in social power*. Ann Arbor: University of Michigan Institute of Social Research.

Fullilove, M. T. (1989). Anxiety and stigmatizing aspects of HIV infection. *Journal of Clinical Psychiatry, 50*(Suppl. 11), 5–8.

Gandlin, W. (1985). Psychiatric consultation to the medical ward: A group analytic and general systems point of view. *International Journal of Group Psychotherapy, 35*(2), 263–278.

Gerber, B., Maguire, B., Badner, V., & Altman, D. (1989). Fear of AIDS: Issues for health professional education. *AIDS Education and Prevention, 1*(1), 39–52.

Gorman, J. M., & Kertzner, R. (1990). Psychoneuroimmunology and HIV infection. *Journal of Neuropsychiatry & Clinical Neurosciences, 2*(3), 241–252.

Greenhill, M. H. (1977).The development of liaison programs. In G. Usdin (Ed.), *Psychiatric medicine*. New York: Brunner/Mazel.

Harris, M., & Bergman, H. C. (1986). The narcissistically vulnerable system: A case study of the public mental hospital. *Psychiatric Quarterly, 58*(3), 202–212.

Isselbacher, K. J., Braunwald, E., Wilson, D., Martin, J. B., Fauci, A. S., & Kasper, D. L. (Eds.). (1994). *Harrison's principles of internal medicine* (13th ed.). New York: McGraw-Hill.

Judd, D. (1995). Life-threatening illness as psychic trauma: Psychotherapy with adolescent patients. In A. Erskine & D. Judd (Eds.), *The imaginative body: Psychodynamic therapy in health care*. Northvale, NJ: Jason Aronson.

Kelly, J., & St. Lawrence, J. (1988). *The AIDS health crisis: Psychological and social interventions*. New York: Plenum Press.

Kernberg, O. (1975). *Borderline conditions and pathological narcissism*. New York: Jason Aronson.

Kiecolt-Glaser, J. K., & Glaser, R. (1986). Psychological influences on immunity. *Psychosomatics, 27*, 621–624.

Kiecolt-Glaser, J. K., & Glaser, R. (1987). Psychological moderators of immune function. *Annals of Behavioral Medicine, 9,*16–20.

Kimball, C. P. (1979). Liaison psychiatry: Of approaches and ways of thinking about behavior. *Psychiatric Clinics of North America, 2*(2), 201–210.

Levy, N. B. (1989). Psychosomatic medicine and consultation-liaison psychiatry: Past, present and future. *Hospital and Community Psychiatry, 40*(10), 1049–1056.

Lifton, R. J. (1976). *The life of the self.* New York: Basic Books.

Lipowsky, Z. J. (1967). Review of consultation psychiatry and psychosomatic medicine. I. General principles. *Psychosomatic Medicine, 29*(2), 153–171.

Lipowsky, Z. J. (1975). Physical illness, the patient and his environment: Psychosocial foundations of medicine. In M. Reiser (Ed.), *American handbook of psychiatry*. New York: Basic Books.

Ludwigsen, K., & Enright, M. (1988). The health care revolution: Implications for psychology and hospital practice. *Psychotherapy: Theory, Research, Practice and Training, 25,* 424–428.

Lyons, J. S., Larson, D. B., Anderson, R. L., & Bilheimer, L. (1989). Psychosocial services for AIDS patients in the general hospital. *International Journal of Psychiatry in Medicine, 19*(4), 385–392.

Miller, T., & Swartz, L. (1990). Clinical psychology in general hospital settings: Issues in interprofessional relationships. *Professional Psychology: Research and Practice, 21,* 48–53.

Moylan, D., & Jureidini, J. (1995). Pain tolerable and intolerable: Consultation to two staff groups who work in the face of potentially fatal illness. In A. Erskine & D. Judd (Eds.), *The imaginative body: Psychodynamic therapy in health care*. Northvale, NJ: Jason Aronson.

Nuland, S. B. (1994). *How we die*. New York: Alfred A. Knopf.

Orr, D. A., & Wallack, J. J. (1990). Multidisciplinary approaches to consultation-liaison psychiatry: The C-L psychologist on an AIDS treatment team. *Psychosomatics, 31,* 441–447.

Ruitenbeek, H. M. (1969). Reflections on death and mourning. In H. M. Ruitenbeek (Ed.), *The interpretation of death* (pp. 1–11). New York: Jason Aronson.

Sandler, J. (1967). Trauma, strain and development. In S. S. Furst (Ed.), *Psychic trauma*. New York: Basic Books.

Schenkenberg, T., Peterson, L., Wood, D., & DaBell, R. (1981). Psychological consultation/liaison in a medical and neurological setting: Physicians' appraisal. *Professional Psychology, 12*, 309–317.

Schur, M. (1955). Comments on the metapsychology of somatization. *Psychoanalytic Study of the Child, 10,* 119–164.

Sontag, S. (1983). *Illness as a metaphor*. London: Penguin.

Sperling, M. (1967). Transference neurosis in patients with psychosomatic disorders. *Psychoanalytic Quarterly, 36*, 342–355.

Stedman's medical dictionary (25th ed.). (1990). Baltimore: Williams & Wilkins.

Stern, R., & Minskoff, K. (1979). Paradoxes in programming for chronic patients in a community clinic. *Hospital & Community Psychiatry, 30*, 613–617.

Strain, J. J., & Grossman, S. (1975*). Psychological care of the medically ill: A primer in liaison psychiatry.* New York: Appleton-Century-Crofts.

Taylor, G. J. (1987). *Psychosomatic medicine and contemporary psychoanalysis* (Stress and Health Series, Monograph 3). Madison, CT: International Universities Press.

Tross, S., & Hirsch, D. A. (1988). Psychological distress and neuropsychological complications of HIV infection and AIDS. *American Psychologist, 43*(11), 929–934.

Winnicott, D. W. (1974). *Playing and reality.* Harmondsworth, England: Penguin.

Chapter 13

Beyond Science: Miracles, Miracle Cures, and AIDS— The Role of the Psychotherapist

George V. Gushue

One of the paradoxes that haunt those who work in the shadow of AIDS is that so much is known, yet can so little can be done. Indeed, there have been numerous "breakthroughs" in the nearly 15 years since the first reports of the illness now known as AIDS began to circulate. Some of these have led to further advances in scientific knowledge or medical treatment, and others have proved to be dead ends. Over the years there has been a cacophony of plausible theories, well-designed studies, inconclusive results, conflicting conclusions, new treatments, false starts, and dashed hopes. Yet, for all this effort, the possibility of a definitive cure still seems remote. The seemingly fragmentary and inconclusive state of medical knowledge about AIDS presents particular challenges for those diagnosed with HIV. First, in spite of all the exceptions and qualifications that may be cited, many HIV-positive individuals experience their diagnosis as catastrophic, as quite literally a death sentence. Although the course of the illness can be slowed with proper treatment, patients understand all too well that, to date, most people diagnosed with HIV die of AIDS-related causes. Thus, many patients see the primary function of medical treatment as not to help them get well but rather as an attempt to buy time while fending off the inevitable. Although research on both the virus itself and treatments for it continues at an unprecedented pace, uncertainty abounds. Medicines that raised great hopes both within and outside of the scientific community several years ago are now deemed of limited value. Within this context, each patient must find his or her own way to cope with the radical ambiguity occasioned by the limited efficacy of current treatments and the uncertain and constantly changing knowledge base about AIDS.

Over the past decade, popular culture in the United States has shown a growing interest in healing methods that fall outside mainstream medical practice. Whole sections in bookstores—indeed, whole bookstores—are devoted to such topics as holistic medicine and alternative treatments. One set of alternative approaches advocates the application of various kinds of interventions that cover a broad spectrum. Some of these treatments give greater emphasis or greater nuance to the advice one would expect from a physician (e.g., regarding diet and exercise). Others favor "natural" (vs. pharmacological) remedies that proponents suggest are less toxic to the human body (see Castleman, 1996; Giller & Mathews, 1994; Murray, 1994). Still others have reported the use of natural or pharmacological agents that are not currently approved for medical treatment in this country (see Abrams, 1992). A second set of alternative approaches to healing has a more spiritual or holistic focus. Such perspectives highlight the connection between the mind or spirit and the body. Here, too, a wide range of positions is adopted. Some authors inform their readers that stress reduction can influence the body's natural healing process (see Benson, 1975). Other writers take a more metaphysical tack, suggesting, for instance, that restoring balance to the human energy field can promote healing (see Barnett & Chambers, 1996; Brennan, 1987). Still others suggest that faith, spirituality (Benson, 1996; Harpur, 1994), or various forms of prayer (e.g., Dossey, 1996) may effect healing.

Such "extrascientific" means pose a dilemma for the psychotherapist, especially one working within the context of a medical setting. This may be especially so for those trained in the scientist–practitioner model who are thus accustomed to seeking empirical validation to support claims. Confronted by patients' reports of regimens not prescribed by medical providers, psychotherapists find themselves attempting to assess whether or not such efforts promote psychological health. For instance, do such strategies represent healthy attempts by patients to achieve a sense of personal agency in an area in which the current state of scientific knowledge and treatment leaves them feeling hopeless and overwhelmed? Do such strategies enable some patients to maintain their psychological equilibrium when ordinary medical knowledge seems to fail them? Or, to the contrary, to what extent do the coping strategies mentioned above represent a flight into fantasy? Does such denial deprive the patient of the opportunity to work through and resolve the issues that arise in this life-threatening situation? Should dubious treatments be considered a form of suicide if chosen as replacements for the current medical standard of care?

The literature on illness, spirituality, and alternative treatments is vast; a full consideration of these topics is beyond the scope of this chapter. Instead, the foci of this chapter are two particular extrascientific coping strategies frequently used in the author's experience at an urban HIV/AIDS mental health clinic:

patients' belief in miracles and miracle cures and issues that these beliefs may pose for the psychotherapist. In this chapter, it is argued that a patient's belief in miracles or alternative treatments is neither desirable nor undesirable. Rather, in each case, it is the therapist's responsibility to assess whether a particular patient's adherence to a particular belief system facilitates or inhibits the patient's availability for the work of psychotherapy. It is further suggested that one criterion that may be used in making such an assessment is a consideration of whether a patient's beliefs enable him or her to work effectively toward two therapeutic goals in psychotherapy with people with AIDS, namely (a) the ability to tolerate uncertainty and (b) the ability to integrate hope and despair. Thus, the following paragraphs begin with a discussion of these two therapeutic tasks. Two later sections are devoted to a discussion of potential issues for the therapist who is presented with patients' beliefs in miracles or miracle cures. Each of these strategies is considered from the perspective of the two tasks, noted and illustrated with case material. Countertransferential issues regarding religion and nontraditional treatments are also discussed. A final section briefly alludes to parallel process issues, as therapists themselves must manage the two tasks in response to their patients.

TWO TASKS

Psychotherapy goals with persons with HIV/AIDS are as varied as the persons themselves. This is not only due to the fact that different people had different psychological concerns before their HIV diagnosis, but also, depending on the individual, because the work often emphasizes differing themes related to infection with the virus itself. For instance, for some, the central issue in therapy may be coping with the actual or anticipated losses occasioned by becoming infected with the virus. Some people may grieve decisions made in the past that they now believe led to their HIV-positive status. Others may grieve the loss of a future that now appears to be cut short. For some, an HIV diagnosis may signal the need to revisit issues with their immediate or extended families that have been left unresolved. Others may struggle primarily with feelings of guilt amplified by the social stigma attached to the virus. Still others may need assistance coping with overwhelming feelings of anger at the person who most likely infected them, as well as loss and abandonment if that person has left them or is sick or dying. Many times, patients achieve a level of adjustment that allows them to function adequately until a new crisis (e.g., a dramatic drop in one's CD4 count; a first, or new, opportunistic infection or hospitalization; the realization that one is no longer able to work) causes them to revisit the issues just mentioned or brings up still others. These examples offer a sense of the wide range of AIDS-related issues that may become salient during the course of psychotherapy (for a more extensive discussion, see Rabkin, Remien, & Wilson, 1994; Tunnell, 1991; and Winiarski, 1991).

Finally, there may well come a time, especially in the end stages of the illness, when the patient indicates to the therapist (directly or indirectly) that he or she is no longer interested in psychotherapy per se, but rather solely in receiving support. At this point, some patients terminate treatment and others enlist the therapist's help in sealing over painful feelings. The following paragraphs address the context of a patient who is still seeking and engaged in psychotherapy.

As noted above, the focus of this chapter is limited to two central tasks of therapy with people who are HIV positive. This is not to suggest that these are the only, or the most important, therapy goals, but simply that they are crucial for the psychological well-being of persons living with AIDS. The first task is fostering the client's ability to cope effectively with uncertainty. Uncertainty is central to the psychological experience of being HIV positive, and it occurs on a number of different levels. For instance, the act of disclosing one's HIV status to a partner, coworker, date, or one's family is charged with uncertainty. Even the most carefully thought-out and elaborate calculations about how someone will respond to the news are frequently mistaken, sometimes for better and sometimes for worse.

Current medical knowledge about AIDS is another area in which uncertainty seems to predominate. Although much is known, much more seems unclear. For instance, as this chapter is being written, three protease inhibitors have just recently gone on the market. The initial test results have showed more promise than any other pharmacological intervention in recent memory. Although not a cure, these drugs have slowed the progression of the virus in clinical trials and even dramatically lowered the amount of the virus detectable in the bloodstream (see Kaplan, 1996; Loftus & Gold, 1995). Researchers have also cautioned, however, that as yet the long-term efficacy and effects of these new medicines are unknown (see Kaplan, 1996; Smart, 1995). Consequently, scientists and medical providers alike warn against too much optimism. This caveat is not lost on those who remember the euphoria that greeted the development of AZT almost a decade ago (see Monette, 1988). Like so many other potential treatments before it, AZT carried significant side effects and ultimately proved to be of limited utility in combating the virus. Its characterization for many years as the best medication "yet available" fell far short of the overly high hopes it had raised. Even at the level of basic science, although much more is known today about the microbiology of the virus than even a few years ago, much remains shrouded in mystery. Thus, whereas for many illnesses the appropriate medical treatments indicated are clear and effective, this is not the case with AIDS.

A final area in which a person who is HIV positive or living with AIDS experiences radical uncertainty is with respect to his or her own health. Although recent improvements in earlier diagnosis and treatment have made AIDS somewhat more like a chronic illness than an imminent death sentence, many patients live anticipating the day that their health will begin a marked and irreversible decline. AIDS has not yet become an illness that can be controlled indefinitely. Most patients know that sooner or later their health will probably begin to deteriorate; the big uncertainty is not if, but rather when and how.

Many patients can cite stories of friends who were seemingly healthy and died almost overnight. There are also counterexamples of individuals whose indicators are bad (i.e., CD4 count, viral load) but who are able to work, socialize, do household chores, exercise, and care for partners and families. Many patients report that each time they enter the hospital, they wonder, "Will this be the time I don't come out?" Those who have never been hospitalized wonder when the first opportunistic infection will occur. Some report the horror of finding a new mark on their skin, unsure at first glance if it is a bruise or a Kaposi's sarcoma lesion. Many patients report butterflies in their stomachs as they wait for the latest seemingly unpredictable results of their blood work. Many state that they experience their lives as fragile, vulnerable, and constantly at risk. Thus, one key task of psychotherapy with a person who is HIV positive is promoting the patient's ability to tolerate multiple levels of uncertainty and the stress of living in a universe in which there is little he or she can know for sure.

The second central task considered in this chapter grows out of the first: helping the patient integrate feelings of hope and despair. The terms *hope* and *despair* are used in a very general sense in this chapter to refer to a broad range of feelings of optimism or pessimism that patients experience regarding their serostatus. A patient's response to the extreme uncertainty of being HIV positive often alternates between intense feelings of hope—as in a rush of euphoria following a good result on some test—and deep despair—such as the overwhelming sense that the same good news is merely postponing the inevitable. Until a cure is found, any other good news somehow falls short of the news one had been hoping to hear. After diagnosis, to function adaptively, an individual must achieve a degree of psychological flexibility that allows him or her not to be overwhelmed completely by the consequences of that diagnosis, but at the same time not to deny them.

The preceding sentence may strike some readers as strange. Should therapists ever encourage their HIV-positive patients to feel despair? What about the need for a positive outlook, finding the will to live, keeping someone's spirits up, healthy denial, and so forth? What is being suggested here is not that therapists should encourage patients to feel things they are not feeling, but rather that therapists may need to assist patients in articulating feelings that are already present. The goal is to help patients stay in touch with all facets of their reality, which for most includes both hope and despair. Many patients need no help in expressing their despair, and may even count on the therapist's being able to tolerate feelings that are unbearable or unacceptable to families or partners. Some patients may need assistance in exploring the more hopeful aspects of their experience that go unacknowledged. Other patients, however, focus exclusively on the positive, continually stating that everything is "fine" and minimizing the impact that their diagnosis is having on their lives. Here again a crucial aspect of the patient's emotional life is being dismissed. For instance, sadness and anger are among the expected responses to an HIV diagnosis. As long as they are denied, they remain unavailable for treatment and, over time, some resolution. A key factor in psychological health is that an individual be able to acknowledge and integrate the disparate dimensions of his or her affective experience. It is precisely those aspects that are denied or disavowed that are likely to impair a person's ability to function. The difference between healthy denial and denial is that in the former case the person is aware of the feelings he or she is choosing not to dwell on at the moment, whereas in the latter the person is simply not aware of those feelings.

The task for therapists, then, is to assist patients in meeting the challenge of allowing feelings of hope and despair to coexist. Living with such conflicting feelings is not easy, and frequently patients try to resolve the tension by favoring one to the exclusion of the other. Thus, for some feelings of despair (excluding all hope) may give way to depression, and for others feelings of hope (excluding all despair) may result in denial, thus excluding vital areas of the patient's psychological experience from treatment.

In summary, to achieve an adaptive level of functioning in their day-to-day activities as well as to be available for the ongoing work of psychotherapy, patients may need assistance with two tasks. First, patients will need to achieve some ability to tolerate the radical uncertainty regarding both the overall state of scientific and medical knowledge about HIV/AIDS and the ultimately unpredictable course the virus takes in their own lives. Second, they may need help in achieving the psychological flexibility required to incorporate the intensely felt, but not mutually exclusive, feelings of both hope and despair that patients experience in response to their serostatus, medical treatment, and variations in health and the impact that all of these have on their lives.

The following sections consider two strategies used by some patients to cope with the radical uncertainty occasioned by their diagnosis as well as to integrate opposing feelings of hope and despair. The first is religious faith, more specifically belief in miraculous healing. The second is alternative medicine, especially belief in a miracle cure. It is important to note that these two strategies are considered from the psychotherapist's point of view. It is not the function of the therapist to evaluate whether an individual's faith in God, miraculous powers, or alternative forms of healing are well founded or not. Rather, the discussion below suggests that these strategies (as well as others) be assessed according to the degree to which they facilitate or inhibit the two treatment goals previously discussed. First, does an individual's faith in a miraculous cure or an alternative treatment enable him or her to tolerate (yet preserve) the radical uncertainty that attends an HIV/AIDS diagnosis? Second, does a person's belief in miracles or nontraditional medicine enable him or her to incorporate feelings of both hope and despair without denying one or the other?

MIRACLES

Physical healing and faith have been associated across the centuries and across cultures. In many traditional cultures, the role of the priest or shaman combines both religious and medicinal functions. In the Pali canon of Buddhism, the Sakyamuni Buddha is portrayed as a healer (Birnbaum, 1979). Miraculous heal-ings were one of the signs that the authors of the Hebrew Bible used to illustrate the authenticity of prophets (e.g., Elijah & Elisha), associating them with God's mercy and dominion over creation. Similarly, early Christian writers referred to numerous accounts of healings by Jesus as testimonials both to his divine nature and to what they perceived to be the transformative power of individual faith. In the United States, faith healings have long been a staple of fundamentalist preachers, whereas mainstream religious communities have tended to found hos-pitals. Prayers for those who are ill occupy a place in many religious services.

Even though Hippocrates may have sworn by Apollo, since the Enlighten-ment, at least, men and women of science have traditionally taken a more skep-tical position regarding divine assistance in physical healing. The classical psy-choanalytic stance has viewed religion with deep suspicion (e.g., Freud, 1927/1961). Some change has been noted over the past decade as more and more authors from within the scientific community have begun to call attention to the connection between mind and body (e.g., Benson, 1996; Chopra, 1989; Segal, 1986). These writers have asserted that beliefs and attitudes do play an impor-tant role in physical healing.

Perhaps the place to start when encountering a patient's religious beliefs is with the feelings those beliefs spark in the therapist. The area is sensitive both for atheists and believers alike. Most therapists will have either positive or nega-tive associations to the topic of religion. Personal history and conviction aside, psychology is a science, and its attempts to understand human behavior and to design effective treatments are ultimately based on reason, not on faith. Reli-gious belief is a topic that receives scant attention in most training programs. Thus, even after years of clinical training, therapists must frequently find their own way in deciding how to work therapeutically with issues of faith, partic-ularly when the therapist's own feelings diverge sharply from those of the patient. It is important to note that this divergence can exist (and perhaps be felt even more keenly) when therapist and patient share the same religious tradition, but belong to differing currents within that tradition (e.g., liberal vs. conserva-tive). Similar beliefs may be equally problematic, leading the therapist to accept some aspects of the patient's experience that deserve further inquiry.

Although issues regarding religion or spirituality may be present in work with any patient, they may be especially salient in therapy with patients who are HIV positive. For instance, it is not unusual for people in life-threatening circumstances to turn to spirituality in their attempts to come to terms with their situation. In addition, some of the shrillest and most stigmatizing voices during the AIDS epidemic have been raised in the name of religion. Thera-pists may be much more comfortable working with a patient who expresses justifiable anger than with one who embraces the very religion that seems to condemn him or her. As this brief overview suggests, the therapist's own effort to be as aware as possible of his or her sympathetic or antagonistic countertransference is imperative for working around religious issues with HIV-positive patients.

It is a commonplace that religious faith has been a source of comfort for many facing serious illness, and even death. The key issue for the psychotherapist attempting to engage a person with HIV/AIDS who has come for treatment is, however, the extent to which that person's religious beliefs facilitate his or her ability to (a) tolerate uncertainty and (b) integrate hope and despair. The following paragraphs briefly look at two cases in which patients expressed a belief in miracles as a part of their strategy for coping with their HIV/AIDS status. All identifying information has been changed to protect the patients' anonymity.

> Ana was a 57-year-old Honduran woman who had been diagnosed with AIDS some 2 years before she was referred for treatment by her medical provider because of depression and suicidal ideation. When she presented for psychotherapy, she had already had two opportunistic infections, and during the 2 years she was in psychotherapy, gradually began to lose her sight as a result of *Mycobacterium avium* complex (MAC). A recovering alcoholic with a history of numerous sexual partners, Ana had survived a sexually and physically abusive relationship with her ex-husband and had worked in a cooperative movement in Honduras before moving to the United States with her children, all of whom were now grown.
>
> Shortly before she began treatment, Ana, a nonpracticing Catholic, had begun to attend a Pentecostal church. Ana had told the pastor (who had himself lost a family member to AIDS) of her diagnosis. Until her death, she disclosed her HIV status to only one other member of the church (who was herself HIV positive) because she feared the harsh judgments of her fellow church members, who frequently expressed strict opinions. At the same time, Ana herself was remarkably accepting of the exploits of other women in a therapy group whose mores were very different from the ones she had now adopted.
>
> Ana frequently quoted from the Bible during individual and group sessions. She found that it gave her a sense of forgiveness for her "wicked" past as well as for the increasing irritability she experienced as her illness progressed. She found that reading the Bible eased the isolation and the periods of acute sadness and "black thoughts" she experienced in her illness. As her eyesight began to falter and her hospitalizations became more frequent, she began to pray that God would cure her. She was supported in this prayer by the brothers and sisters at the church to which she belonged. Unbeknownst to her brothers and sisters in the church, she also at times expressed her anger at God for not coming through for her and continued to laugh along with her fellow HIV support-group members at their more worldly adventures.

Ana's case represents an adaptive use of belief in miracles as a coping strategy in dealing with late-stage consequences of AIDS. Ana firmly believed in miracles and struggled to come to some understanding of a God who could cure her but did not. Her belief in a God who cared for her and could cure her helped her to keep (or regain) her psychological balance during the numerous medical ups and downs of her final year and a half of life. The possibility of a cure helped her to maintain enough hope to remain engaged in life and connected to friends and family. On the other hand, the particular form of spirituality that Ana embraced also made room for her "black thoughts" and for an awareness of the reality of her medical decline. Ana's hope in a miracle permitted her to be more realistic about her failing health; bolstered by the possibility that God might cure her, Ana found the courage to contemplate candidly the seriousness of her deterioration. It is suggested that this particular coping strategy was adaptive precisely because it allowed the patient room for both hope and despair, allowing her to stay engaged with life and to make the full range of her experience available in her psychotherapy sessions. The next case illustrates a different approach.

> Teodora was a 48-year-old woman from the Dominican Republic who was infected with the HIV virus through sexual relations with her husband, whom she stated was a womanizer throughout most of their married life. Teodora was a member of a Pentecostal church, although a different one from Ana. She was especially proud of the fact that her husband had accepted Jesus as his savior during the final year of his life. He apologized profusely to her for his past behavior and for infecting her with the virus. They were reconciled, and Teodora cared for him until he died. It was clear that his dying "in the Lord" was a source of great solace for her.
>
> Teodora also believed in the possibility that God would cure her, something she actively prayed for if "it were God's will." When members of her therapy group explored feelings about death, Teodora alternately reminded them that if one were to ask with enough faith he or she would be cured, and that in any event death was going to be with God in God's kingdom and should not be feared. Teodora denied any feelings of anger toward her deceased husband, stating that these were wiped away in their reconciliation and his acceptance of the Lord. In any event, she would remind the others, Christians forgive those who wrong them. When members of the group expressed anxiety, she would earnestly urge them to try what she had found helpful: prayer and trust in the Lord. She would bring Bible tracts and invite others to join her for worship.
>
> Members of the group were somewhat more circumspect when Teodora was present, but nodded vigorously in agreement with her. When Teodora was asked what she hoped to get from the group, she stated that she wanted to help support others and would rebuff any challenge to her stated equanimity. Teodora left the group after roughly 3 months, citing the need to care for her granddaughter.

Needless to say, Teodora's particular style of belief in miracles and general approach to her religion represented a less-than-optimal strategy for coping with her HIV status. Her tenaciously held faith did not assist her in tolerating uncertainty; rather, she attempted to eliminate uncertainty through the sheer and imposing clarity of her beliefs. Although her faith and her belief in the possibility of miracles enabled her to maintain hope, they did so by banishing feelings of despair. Thus, using the criteria of the two tasks mentioned above, insofar as Teodora's belief in miracles permitted her to integrate neither uncertainty nor feelings of despair, it impeded her work in therapy as well as a healthy psychological adaptation to her HIV status. These split-off feelings of despair then remained unavailable to both patient and therapist and ultimately, therefore, to any kind of resolution.

The cases of Ana and Teodora offer contrasting examples of the psychological benefit of belief in miracles. Again, the issue of concern to the psychotherapist is not the content of a patient's beliefs, or whether or not the therapist agrees with them, but rather the function they serve for the patient. This section has briefly noted two patients who invoked seemingly similar religious beliefs to help them manage their feelings about AIDS, but did so in ways that had very different psychological consequences. In the first case, the patient's belief in the possibility of a miraculous cure enabled her to maintain a sense of hope as her health began to deteriorate. From this position of relative strength, she was also able to acknowledge her fears, her anger, and some realistic awareness of her declining health. This patient's beliefs helped her lead a more integrated life and supported her psychotherapy. In the second case presented, the patient's religiously based optimism left no room for any other type of feeling. Consequently, the patient's feelings of rage or despair were never articulated, ultimately to the patient's detriment inasmuch as the patient never had the opportunity to work through them. Because this set of beliefs failed to help the patient manage the two tasks outlined above, from a psychotherapeutic vantage point it was a form of resistance that the therapist was not able to resolve successfully and that ultimately led to the patient's premature termination of treatment.

MIRACLE CURES

The term *miracle cures* is used in this chapter to refer to a broad range of alternative treatments and holistic medicine practiced in addition to or instead of the treatment prescribed by one's physician, sometimes with his or her knowledge and approval, sometimes without. As noted above, the lack of a cure for AIDS and the limited efficacy of current treatments has been the cause of tremendous frustration for patients and physicians alike for whom the daily consequences literally entail life or death. This vacuum has spawned a multitude of possible cures or experimental treatments, some with origins in the halls of science, others in the basements of apartment buildings, and still others in the forests of Central and South America and Africa. For example, the tabloids and TV news magazine programs followed by the author's patients are filled weekly with reports of someone or other who discovered a plant growing on the patio of his home in a remote village in the Caribbean that has cured him of AIDS. One patient was seeking money to travel to Italy where he had learned that medical doctors were experimenting with a treatment that involved heating the blood to levels where the virus was destroyed. Although such efforts may seem like pure fantasy to some, almost anyone affected by the AIDS epidemic over the past decade can cite his or her personal litany of rumors of possible cures and disappointments. The pressure to find something, anything, that might avert death, or at least stave it off, is tremendous.

As with issues about religion discussed in the previous section, a clinician must begin by exploring his or her own attitudes toward alternative treatments. Many people, if not all, have been exposed to some sort of either curative or preventative home remedy that they consider normative, for instance, chicken soup when ill, extra vitamin C during the winter months, or attempts to eat or abstain from certain foods in service of a healthier diet. There is tremendous variation, however, regarding the point at which one may seek the assistance of a medical professional. How high does the fever have to be or how long must it persist? How sharp the pain? There is also variance in the degree to which individuals follow the regimen set out by their doctor to the letter, especially if they find it cumbersome.

More recently, a growing body of literature takes issue with mainstream medical practice advocating natural or holistic cures (e.g., Castleman, 1996; Weil, 1995). Does the therapist find merit in these claims or regard them as the contemporary equivalent of the snake oil sold by charlatans in previous generations? In addition, there are tremendous cultural variations in attitudes toward homemade medicine. For instance, whereas the primary physical healer in the lives of White European Americans may be a licensed medical professional, in other cultures traditional healers who use remedies made from roots, bark, and plants are considered normative. In New York, for example, numerous *botánicas* —shops that sell herbal remedies for the body and the soul—are vestiges of that tradition. Thus, a therapist must struggle to be aware of his or her culturally conditioned responses to patient practices that may be completely acceptable within the patient's world view. Such an examination leaves a therapist with a better chance of obtaining a reliable answer to the question: Is this pathology, or simply a different perspective?

As with the issue of a patient's presentation of beliefs in religious miracles, the position taken here is that a patient's interest in or pursuit of a miracle cure is neither desirable nor undesirable (except for cases where the patient's life may be put at risk, as is discussed below). As with anything else, what is of crucial importance is what this quest for an alternative treatment means to the patient and whether the patient is willing to work with the therapist in exploring that meaning. It would seem adaptive if it (a) facilitates the patient's efforts to tolerate uncertainty and (b) enables him or her to integrate hope and despair.

Luisa is a 50-year-old Puerto Rican woman who is participating in a women's AIDS therapy group. Her estranged husband, who she believes infected her, died about a year ago. Luisa was originally admitted to the clinic for depression and discontinued her psychotropic medications in consultation with her psychiatrist shortly after joining the group.

It is not unusual for group members to report to each other the results from the latest visit to their medical providers, together with CD4 counts and medications that have been prescribed. Exploring the feelings that are provoked by the varying treatment regimens followed by different members is often a focus of group sessions. Particularly common are concerns that arise when one is not getting a medication that someone else is taking. Fears that someone else's doctor may be providing better treatment than one's own are made explicit and discussed.

With similar frequency, members compare with each other the various home remedies they are trying. Someone's aunt or cousin will have made a special concoction that tastes awful but is worth a try. One member states that the only thing she takes is *uña de gato* tea (named for a plant), and that she had told that to her doctor, who replied, "Whatever you're doing, keep doing it." Today, Luisa is beaming. She has just returned from a visit to Puerto Rico; there is a plastic bag under her chair. When the session ends she begins to hand out leaves from the *trés estrellas* plant (also thought to be helpful for people with AIDS) that she gathered from behind her father's house in the countryside. The other members enthusiastically take them home.

Clearly, the discussions about leaves, teas, and other home remedies is one way in which the members of this group manage their uncertainty about effectiveness of their medical treatments and anxiety regarding the unpredictable course of their illness. Preparing a tea helps to bind anxiety insofar as it imparts a sense of agency. The patient experiences him- or herself as at least doing something in her or his own behalf, not merely being the passive recipient of outside interventions. For the patient, this represents an increase in control. Although it is certainly true that these home remedies allow patients to maintain a sense of hope, what about the integration of despair? Are these simply exercises in denial, and consequently counterindicated?

Certainly, a potential danger with patients' explorations of alternative treatments is that they could degenerate into mere flights from reality—enabling the patient to maintain a false sense of hope at the expense of despair. This did not seem to be true for the women in the therapy group. In this case, the various teas were seen by the patients primarily as a means to symptom relief, not as cures in and of themselves. It is crucial, however, that the therapist in this situation help patients to identify and articulate their despair. For example, when the subject of teas or leaves came up in group, the therapist would intervene around the patients' sense of frustration, how hard it was to be taking fistfuls of prescribed medications and still not be getting better. A second theme of interventions addressed the patients' feelings of impotence, how perhaps attempts to do something were intended to relieve the feeling that one could do nothing. Yet another set of interventions addressed the magical wish for a cure that perhaps suggested feelings of hopelessness among the members. In the case cited above, group members were able to work with these sorts of interventions and to acknowledge that at least some of the interest in and energy around the various teas had to do with attempts to manage feelings of despair. In this case, it was up to the therapist to make this particular coping strategy more adaptive by making explicit a range of feelings that the patients were seeking to ignore. Yet once these feelings were made available to the group, the patients were able to acknowledge and incorporate them.

At times a tension arises between the therapist's efforts to work with the psychological dimensions of issues like alternative treatments and concern for the patient's physical well-being. This is exacerbated in cases where the patient is not informing his or her medical provider of alternative treatments he or she may be pursuing. The most extreme case occurs when a patient is refusing treatments deemed medically necessary in favor of some unproven cure. The danger here is that a patient may forego interventions that could have helped until it is too late for them to be of any real benefit.

On the one hand, how can a mental health provider who is not medically trained make any judgments in this arena? On the other hand, at what point does a therapist conclude that a person's life is at risk and therefore disclose confidential information? Such a disclosure signals the inevitable end of the treatment relationship. Even if a patient elects to continue to see the therapist, he or she will be far more reticent. When a doubt exists, it is the author's preference to encourage patients to talk to their medical providers, or to explore in psychotherapy the reasons that they are reluctant to do so. Talking about options available to patients, should their medical providers disagree with what they are doing, is often helpful.

There are other times when the therapist feels compelled to intervene more directly, for instance, when the patient is engaging in a home treatment that is likely to harm him or her. Different therapists will come to differing conclusions about exactly when such a direct intervention is necessary to prevent physical harm. In one case, a patient whom I shall call Altagracia (35 years old) told me that she was drinking water mixed with bleach. When I asked why, she answered that if bleach can kill the AIDS virus on a hypodermic needle, it must be able to kill the virus inside a person as well. I told her to stop. I did my best to explain why her reasoning was faulty and recommended that she speak with her physician. She did stop, and although my direct intervention was met with compliance regarding water and bleach, the patient's underlying anxiety had not been addressed, as is seen in the following paragraphs.

Shortly after the incident with bleach and water, Altagracia joined an HIV therapy group, as did Rosario (42 years old), who was also born in the Dominican Republic. Both were estranged from their former husbands, were raising young children, and had become friends through the therapy group. Occasionally, they would visit each other's homes and take their children on joint outings. When they had been attending the group for about a year, they began traveling to another borough on certain days to receive shots in the buttocks from a "doctor" (a woman who stated that she had graduated from a medical school in her country of origin) who claimed to have discovered an experimental formula that seemed to have cured AIDS in at least one case. The patients met this "cured" person and were impressed by his experience. They were sure he was being truthful as he was said to be a former priest. First, the patients had to pass through several levels of treatment. There was a charge for each shot, though after a time the doctor was willing to extend them credit. Each appealed to her family and friends for money. Altagracia worked overtime cleaning homes to raise more funds for treatment. A couple of months into their experimental treatment, the issue surfaced in group.

> When, after a year, Altagracia and Rosario missed two sessions in quick succession for "doctors' appointments," the group pressed them for an explanation. In response they revealed that they had begun to pursue an experimental treatment and told the group about the procedure, the supposed cure, and the payments. Both Rosario and Altagracia glowed with joy, stating that they felt better, convinced that they were on the cutting edge of a medical breakthrough. When asked why they had not brought this up in previous sessions, they stated that they had been afraid that the therapist would tell their medical providers (who worked in the same hospital) what they were doing.
>
> The other members of the group reacted strongly to Rosario's and Altagracia's announcement. Over the months that followed, these members challenged them strongly, stating that they were wasting their money, that they should be talking to their "real doctors," and that a real cure would have been reported in the newspapers. Some in the group stated they themselves would never do such a thing. These kinds of comments only hardened Rosario and Altagracia's position. They insisted that they were feeling much better and that the other members of the group were being overly cautious.
>
> The therapist repeatedly suggested that both sides in this dispute represented aspects of the group experience that all the members could find within themselves. He suggested that the emotion both sides experienced around this issue might be related to how difficult it was to cope with the uncertainty of the situation. When two members attempted to deny uncertainty by taking dramatic steps about which they became strident, they threatened the equilibrium provided for others by absolute faith in one's physician. What if there were a better way? Similarly, while Rosario and Altagracia held all the optimism (hope for a cure) for the group, the others held all of the realism (if not pessimism). The challenge, the therapist suggested, was for each member to find both sides within herself.

This continued debate was put on hold when Rosario and Altagracia discontinued their treatment after finding out the person who had allegedly been cured of AIDS had had a relapse. It heated up again when they began a new alternative treatment, now with a licensed physician in private practice who had them making monthly purchases of a medication made in Central America. This time, however, there was a difference.

> After learning of the new alternative treatment, one of the those opposed to their experimentation stated in a session, "I understand what Altagracia is doing; she is fighting for her life. So am I." In a later session, Rosario admitted her grave doubts about the treatment, and admitted being sick was just too frightening not to have

"something" to cling to, even if in her heart she knew it wasn't a cure. Several weeks later, when routine blood work showed an elevated liver enzyme, and after talking to the group, Rosario "outed" herself to her medical provider. Altagracia did the same a couple of months later.

Thus, although Altagracia may have been willing to give up drinking water mixed with bleach to mollify her therapist, this original intervention did little to help her to manage the overwhelming anxiety she experienced when confronted with the radical uncertainty occasioned by her diagnosis. The case example just presented illustrates one therapist's efforts to facilitate patients' ability to tolerate uncertainty and to integrate hope and despair on a group level. Not only may there have been little medical evidence to recommend the two patients' choice of alternative treatments, but neither did they appear to have been adaptive psychologically. From a psychological perspective, it was not bad science per se, but rather the attempt to make the uncertain certain against all odds and to deny feelings of despair that needed to be challenged. The task for the therapist in this group was to attempt to hold on to the competing factions and the elements of hope and despair they represented. Resolution became possible when members of one faction were able to find and reintegrate some split-off part of themselves in members of the other faction. When the group became capable of better tolerating uncertainty and integrating feelings of hope and despair, it appears that this particular coping strategy (i.e., the alternative treatments described above) was no longer necessary.

THERAPISTS AND THE TWO TASKS

Finally, it should be observed that although the focus of this chapter has been on patients, therapists themselves need to engage in their own parallels to the two tasks outlined above. Therapists too, must be able to tolerate new uncertainties in the treatment. For instance, work with some HIV-positive patients will mean that the therapist will never know in advance if a particular person will be well enough to come in on a given day. Often it will be medical necessity, not mutual agreement, that determines when and how termination takes place. Rabkin, Remien, and Wilson (1994) and Winiarski (1991) have written about therapists' attempts to adapt flexibly to these altered circumstances.

In addition, the therapist must also struggle to integrate his or her own feelings of hope and despair. It is seductive to believe that one's own patients will not become ill. Some therapists have reported feeling prematurely ready to disengage from a patient who is becoming ill, finding it easier to deal with the patient's death than his or her diminished life. Others have spoken of feelings of anger at patients who die. Was there perhaps too much hope?

As was noted above, at this writing protease inhibitors have been on the market for about 2 months. I hear stories from colleagues about dramatic improvements in some patients. Someone who looked gaunt and hollow only a few months ago now appears robust. Patients are beginning to talk about "what if" there is a long-term future and the implications of that changed scenario for love lives or careers. One colleague reported his own amazement and joy at this "tectonic shift." I am discomforted by the fact that I am utterly unable to allow myself to fully connect emotionally with my colleague's enthusiasm. I feel myself holding back. It would seem that at this moment I am having difficulty integrating hope, no doubt fearing renewed disappointment. Attempting to discern whether this is realism or resistance is my task at present.

CONCLUSION

This chapter briefly examined two coping strategies used by some HIV-positive patients: belief in miracles and miracle cures. It has been suggested that from the psychotherapist's perspective the crucial question when presented with these strategies (or others) is whether they facilitate the patient's availability for psychotherapy. It was further suggested that two treatment goals be used as criteria in making such an assessment. First, does a particular patient's belief system enable him or her both to acknowledge and to tolerate the overwhelming uncertainty that an HIV diagnosis brings to the patient's life? Second, does the patient's belief in miracles or the pursuit of alternative treatments assist him or her in integrating feelings of hope and despair without needing to disavow one or the other? To the extent that these strategies facilitate these two tasks, they make the full range of the patient's emotions available to the therapist and further the work of psychotherapy. To the extent that either strategy represents an attempt by the patient to close off one part of his or her experience, they suggest denial, indicating an important area that the therapist will need to address.

REFERENCES

Abrams, D. (1992). Dealing with alternative therapies for HIV. In M. Sande & P. Volberding (Eds.), *The medical management of AIDS* (3rd ed., pp. 111–128). Philadelphia: Saunders.

Barnett, L., & Chambers, M. (1996). *Reiki: Energy medicine.* Rochester, VT: Healing Arts Press.

Benson, H. (1975). *The relaxation response.* New York: Avon Books.

Benson, H. (1996). *Timeless healing: The power and biology of belief.* New York: Scribner's.

Birnbaum, R. (1979). *The healing Buddha.* Boulder, CO: Shambhala.

Brennan, B. A. (1987). *Hands of light: A guide to healing through the human energy field.* New York: Bantam Books.

Castleman, M. (1996). *Nature's cures.* Emmaus, PA: Rodale Press.

Chopra, D. (1989). *Quantum healing: Exploring the frontiers of mind/body medicine.* New York: Bantam Books.

Dossey, L. (1996). *Prayer is good medicine.* New York: HarperCollins.

Freud, S. (1961). *The future of an illusion* (J. Strachey, Trans.). New York: W. W. Norton. (Original published 1927)

Giller, R. M., & Mathews, K. (1994). *Natural prescriptions.* New York: Ballantine Books.

Harpur, T. (1994). *The uncommon touch: An investigation of spiritual healing.* Toronto, Ontario, Canada: McClelland & Stewart.

Kaplan, A. H. (1996). Perspective: Research highlights at the UCLA Center for AIDS research. *AIDS research and human retroviruses, 12(10),* 849–852.

Loftus, R., & Gold, D. (1995). Protease inhibitors: Where are they now? *GMHC Treatment Issues, 9(1),* 1–6.

Monette, P. (1988). *Borrowed time: An AIDS memoir.* New York: Avon Books.

Murray, M. T. (1994). *Natural alternatives to over-the-counter and prescription drugs.* New York: William Morrow.

Rabkin, J., Remien, R., & Wilson C. (1994). The role of the counselor. In *Good doctors, good patients: Partners in HIV treatment* (pp. 158–171). New York: NCM.

Segal, B. S. (1986). *Love, medicine, and miracles.* New York: Harper & Row.

Smart, T. (1995). Viral resistance to protease inhibitors. *GMHC Treatment Issues, 9(6),* 1–5.

Tunnell, G. (1991). Complications in group psychotherapy with AIDS patients. *International Journal of Group Psychotherapy, 41,* 481–498.

Weil, A. (1995). *Spontaneous healing.* New York: Alfred A Knopf.

Winiarski, M. (1991). *AIDS-related psychotherapy.* New York: Pergamon Press.

This chapter is dedicated to the memory of Theodor Dimitriu, MD, my father, and Adam Munz, PhD, my mentor. Together with my AIDS patients, many of whom are no longer, they taught me most of what I know about the meanings of death, life, and of the work I do.

My former and current colleagues and supervisees in the HIV/AIDS Center Programs also deserve recognition and gratitude for enriching my understanding and experience by contributing theirs.

Chapter 14

Conclusion

Lucy A. Wicks

As medical science continues to move forward, working toward a containment of HIV/AIDS, hopes are stirred as a cure seems to be possible. With the development and marketing of a new family of drugs, the protease inhibitors, this hope has grown strong. The media, along with AIDS professionals, openly talk of the possibility of a cure; of the hope that AIDS might now be considered a chronic disease like diabetes; of the hope that AIDS will soon be under control. Would that it be so. In reality, we do not yet know what will happen. Will the new drugs work over the long term or, like AZT, provide only a respite? Will they prove too toxic to be used as a maintenance dose? Will they be too expensive or too difficult to reasonably offer a cure to all people with AIDS? There is no doubt that the issues presented by AIDS treatment will continue to challenge medical practitioners, ethicists, politicians, and economists for years to come. Therapists will have to continue to help their patients adjust to the changing landscape of AIDS treatment.

Clinicians working with patients affected by AIDS are already being presented with difficult issues raised by medical advances. Not all patients respond to the treatment, nor can all patients tolerate the medication. Protease inhibitors provide hope for some, but not all, patients. Issues also exist for those patients who do respond well. Patients will have to address the issues of long-term compliance with an extremely expensive and difficult medical protocol, as well as facing life as a long-term survivor, coping with losses of loved ones, and addressing the problems of living seen in all psychotherapy treatments. Further, these patients will continue to face societal stigma and pressure relating to the disease, further affecting patients' ability to deal with this process. It is the work of clinicians to support their patients and to nurture their hope; however, this work must also ground hope within a framework of individual assessment and the development of personal awareness and understanding.

The stigma associated with AIDS continues to be overwhelming for many, leading to psychological distress, avoidance and denial of both information and treatment, and continued high-risk behaviors. In response to misinformation about medical advances, a wave of newly infected patients is being seen who believe that they no longer need to worry about safer sex or clean needles. Clinical support will continue to be needed to help people deal with the uncertainty, fear, guilt, and distress about their disease and the experiences they have concerning their health and medical care.

Although all the contributors to this book work in specialized AIDS treatment clinics, the material they discuss will be of use to the solo practitioner or clinician working in a general practice. Patients present in treatment for non–AIDS-related concerns who are in fact infected with the virus. At other times, patients become aware of their HIV status only later in treatment. In these cases, AIDS may emerge at a later point as a central concern. In other situations, specialized AIDS treatment may not be available to patients, and they will seek out support from clinicians to whom they are referred. These cases may appear to require little specialized understanding; however, clinicians should educate themselves to identify latent material and be prepared to deal with these issues more directly. Because medical issues and psychological reactions can be difficult to tease apart, developing a network of specialists for consultation and referral resources can greatly facilitate the treatment in any setting.

Throughout this book, the authors have presented material concerning the psychological treatment of these patients. Although each chapter addresses different topics, several themes run throughout the text. First, each author has highlighted the need to treat psychological concerns expressed by AIDS patients. Second, each has addressed the need to understand and differentiate the dual role of medical issues, clarifying what might be called the physical and symbolic meanings of the disease for patients' lives. Third, each has acknowledged the need to address countertransferential needs within the treatment of AIDS patients. I would like to summarize these points, as I believe they form a foundation to understand the treatment of AIDS-infected patients.

First, AIDS patients are in need of and deserving of psychological assistance that goes far beyond social supports. The therapeutic process can be a powerful and dynamic one when working with AIDS patients. Although this may seem an obvious point, often health care practitioners become overwhelmed at the prospect of treating AIDS patients, feeling that their medical and social needs far outweigh their psychological needs. Often I hear "This patient comes from such a chaotic family we need to focus on permanency planning, housing, and economic supports" or "These patients are too sick to be concerned about understanding themselves." Although these patients require psychosocial supports, I believe that it is an error to avoid addressing their underlying concerns. My experience is that meeting patients' psychological needs enhances their ability to participate in medical treatment, improves the quality of their lives, and increases their ability to function effectively in their lives. By not addressing these needs, patients can remain in a childlike dependency on the professionals who need to take care of them.

AIDS is a disease that affects individuals within the context of their previous psychological experiences and relationships; patients' reactions to being diagnosed with AIDS or becoming ill will be profoundly affected by who they are as individuals and where they come from culturally, socioeconomically, and medically. Work with patients to unravel the multiple determinants of their reactions to illness will permit them to make decisions within a choice framework rather than an emotionally reactive framework.

As seen in many of the case studies presented, direct confrontation with mortality can challenge patients to finally face their demons, or it can drive them into despair and meaninglessness. Therapy can provide patients with an understanding and nurturing environment to confront their fears, resolve life-long self-destructive patterns, and support the evolution of their goals and relationships. In helping patients deal more effectively with multiple forms of loss (e.g., loss of health, loss of friends and loved ones), the clinician helps patients develop new tools and understanding with which to face their lives. In the evolving world of health care and psychological services, clinicians must continually work to help patients cope with cycles of hope and hopelessness, uncertainty, and fantasies about what the future will bring.

A second theme contained in these chapters is that there must be awareness of the dual role of medical concerns for these patients. On the one hand, patients must address real physical challenges, maintain good relationships with their physicians, participate in unpleasant medical procedures, and follow difficult medical regimes. On the other hand, these events in their lives often trigger reactions and fantasies that can become their focus and interfere with or support their involvement in their medical treatment. Helping patients understand AIDS as a metaphor in their lives often helps patients deal with the physical reality of AIDS more effectively and creatively.

Clinicians working with patients within a psychological setting seek to understand the medical concerns as psychological stressors to help patients work through unproductive or self-destructive reactions. Psychotherapists are challenged to focus on the psychological meaning of events while simultaneously identifying and clarifying patients' choices and decisions within the medical framework. Clinicians work to support coping mechanisms and processes of self-reflection, separating the effects of physical disease and psychological reaction and acknowledging the very real effects of the disease. This process includes understanding and working with the debilitating nature of pain and medical illness. There must be consideration and understanding about how a person's medical treatment affects his or her compliance within a psychotherapeutic process. To achieve this, psychological assessment should include consultation with physicians to ensure differential diagnosis between possible psychological and medical etiology for psychological symptoms.

Finally, we have seen the need for each therapist to understand how his or her work with these patients is affected by his or her experiences, expectations, and biases. Although this is the case for all therapeutic relationships, it becomes central in dealing with this population because of the nature of the disease and the fact that the groups predominantly affected are culturally and socially disenfranchised. If a clinician feels hopeless in the face of illness, disgusted by medical issues, or fearful of contagion, this will be communicated to patients. The same is true of racial and sexual prejudice. Without ongoing self-examination, clinicians working with this population are prone to a variety of countertransferential traps; prejudice relating to a patient's identified risk group, risk-taking behavior, the death and dying process, and racial and ethnic conflicts can complicate the host of issues raised in any intense treatment relationship. Clinicians must address their own fears of disability and experiences of loss. They must confront their grief and understand how it is possible to continue to seek to be involved with others knowing that they may die. It is only when we, the clinicians, can make the grief work meaningful to ourselves that we can support our patients' journeys to understanding their own experiences.

Index